IN·R.

AI Tools and Techniques

AI Tools and Techniques

Edited by

Mark H. Richer

Mountain Lake Software, Inc.

 ABLEX PUBLISHING CORPORATION
NORWOOD, NEW JERSEY

Library of Congress Cataloging-in-Publication Data

AI tools and techniques/[edited] by Mark H. Richer.
    p. cm.
    Bibliography: p.
    Includes index.
    ISBN 0-89391-494-0
    1. Artificial intelligence—Data processing. I. Richer,
Mark H. II. Title: Artificial intelligence tools and techniques.
Q336.A17 1988
006.3—dc19
                                 88-21983
                                     CIP

Ablex Publishing Corporation
355 Chestnut Street
Norwood, New Jersey 07648

To my family and friends. Without love, work and knowledge would not be gratifying.

Contents

List of Contributors

Robert M. Abarbanel
Apple Computer, Inc.
20525 Mariani Avenue, MS-22C
Cupertino, CA 95014

Raymond L. Bates
USC Information Sciences Institute
4676 Admiralty Way, Suite 1001
Marina del Rey, CA 90292-6695

Daniel G. Bobrow
Intelligent Systems Laboratory
Xerox Palo Alto Research Center
3333 Coyote Hill Road
Palo Alto, CA 94304

John H. Boose
Knowledge Systems Laboratory
Boeing Adv. Tech. Center, 7L-64
Boeing Comp. Serv., P.O. Box 24346
Seattle, WA 98124

Jeffrey M. Bradshaw
Knowledge Systems Laboratory
Boeing Adv. Tech. Center, 7L-64
Boeing Comp. Serv., P.O. Box 24346
Seattle, WA 98124

James Davidson
Teknowledge, Inc.
1850 Embarcadero Road
P.O. Box 10119
Palo Alto, CA 94303

Lee D. Erman
Teknowledge, Inc.
1850 Embarcadero Road
P.O. Box 10119
Palo Alto, CA 94303

Brian Drummond
IntelliCorp, Inc.
1975 El Camino Real West
Mountain View, CA 94040-2216

Robert E. Filman
IntelliCorp, Inc.
1975 El Camino Real West
Mountain View, CA 94040-2216

Scott Fouse
Teknowledge Federal Systems, Inc.
501 Marin Street, Suite 214
Thousand Oaks, CA 91360

Frederick Hayes-Roth
Teknowledge, Inc.
1850 Embarcadero Road
P.O. Box 10119
Palo Alto, CA 94303

Victoria P. Gilbert
IntelliCorp, Inc.
1975 El Camino Real West
Mountain View, CA 94040-2216

Kenneth M. Kahn
Intelligent Systems Laboratory
Xerox Palo Alto Research Center
3333 Coyote Hill Road
Palo Alto, CA 94304

Jay S. Lark
Teknowledge, Inc.
1850 Embarcadero Road
P.O. Box 10119
Palo Alto, CA 94303

Theodore A. Linden
Advanced Decision Systems
1500 Plymouth Street
Mountain View, CA 94043-1245

Robert Mac Gregor
USC Information Sciences Insitute
4676 Admiralty Way, Suite 1001
Marina del Rey, CA 90292-6695

Lawrence Z. Marcosian
Reasoning Systems, Inc.
1801 Page Mill Road
Palo Alto, CA 94304

Mark H. Richer
Mountain Lake Software, Inc.
1041 Lake Street
San Francisco, CA 94118

Alfred D. Round
Knowledge Systems Laboratory
Stanford University
701 Welch Road, Building C
Palo Alto, CA 94304

Stephen W. Smoliar
USC Information Sciences Institute
4676 Admiralty Way
Suite 1001
Marina del Rey, CA 90292-6695

Mark J. Stefik
Intelligent Systems Laboratory
Xerox Palo Alto Research Center
3333 Coyote Hill Road
Palo Alto, CA 94304

Marilyn Stelzner
IntelliCorp, Inc.
1975 El Camino Real West
Mountain View, CA 94040-2216

William R. Swartout
USC Information Sciences Institute
4676 Admiralty Way, Suite 1001
Marina del Rey, CA 90292-6695

Frederich N. Tou
Sun Microsystems, Inc.
2550 Garcia Avenue
Mountain View, CA 94043

About the Editor

Mark Richer is a founder and the president of Mountain Lake Software, Inc., located in San Francisco. Mountain Lake Software, Inc. specializes in object-oriented user interface and application programming tools for the Macintosh and other computers. Mr. Richer was formerly a scientific programmer on the Guidon Project at Knowledge Systems Laboratory in the computer science department at Stanford University. He was the co-designer and principal implementor of Guidon-Watch, a multiwindow graphic interface to the NEOMYCIN knowledge-based diagnostic system. He earned an M.S. in computer science and artificial intelligence from Stanford University, as well as an M.A. in educational technology from Stanford University.

Preface

AI Tools and Techniques is an in-depth study of advanced techniques, current commercial tools, and evolving research tools used to build knowledge-based systems. The book is intended primarily for practitioners and students who use artificial intelligence software tools and techniques to build commercial or research systems. All these individuals have in common a need to select, understand, and use various AI tools and techniques. Consequently the book can be used both as a professional reference and as a text in a graduate seminar. We assume the reader has an understanding of fundamental AI concepts and terms and is interested in examining a range of tools and techniques in depth.

A bird's eye view of the terrain covered in this book reveals the general structure and organization: in general, chapters appearing earlier in the text describe enabling technology for subsequent chapters. For example, the knowledge-based development tools described in Part II of the book depend upon the object-oriented and access-oriented programming techniques described in Part I. Specialized tools such as SimKit™, discussed in Part III, are built using knowledge-based development tools such as KEE®, described in Part II. Finally, Part IV provides two examples of how AI vendors and researchers are building bridges from knowledge-based systems, including KEE, to conventional systems.

Object-Oriented and Access-Oriented Programming

The book starts with a discussion of advanced AI programming methods that can augment the basic functional programming features provided in LISP. These methods include variations of the object-oriented, access-oriented, and rule-based programming paradigms that have evolved within the AI community. The flexibility of the LISP language has lent itself well to experimentation with these ideas. In Chapter 1, Stefik and Bobrow present a survey of object-oriented programming tools and techniques with an emphasis on describing fundamental principles and exploring variations of the methodology that have been used in different languages and tools. The primitive element in object-oriented programming is the *object*. Objects store both state (*instance variables*) and behavioral descriptions (procedures or *methods*) in a single data structure, and provide an excellent basis for supporting data abstraction in computer programs. Object-

SimKit is a trademark of IntelliCorp, Inc.
KEE is a registered trademark of IntelliCorp, Inc.

oriented programming facilities are often provided in AI tools as an extension to the LISP language.

In Chapter 2, Stefik, Bobrow, and Kahn describe access-oriented programming and how it can be integrated into a multiparadigm programming environment that includes functional, object-oriented, and rule-based programming facilities. In access-oriented programming, fetching or storing data can cause procedures or other actions to be executed. Access-oriented programming is often implemented using object-oriented programming features. Thus, LISP often acts as an enabling technology for implementing object-oriented programming, and in turn, object-oriented programming can be the enabling technology for implementing access-oriented programming. The authors use the Loops knowledge programming system as an example of a multiparadigm programming environment.

Tools and Techniques for Acquiring, Representing, and Explaining Knowledge

In Part II of the book, several knowledge engineering tools and methodologies that are useful for building a range of knowledge-based systems are described. These tools provide methods for acquiring, representing, and explaining knowledge. General purpose tools provide an entire environment for building complex systems, often providing several techniques and methodologies for solving complex problems.

In Chapter 3, I present criteria for evaluating general-purpose expert system development tools along with a description of four important commercial tools: ART®, KEE, Knowledge Craft®, and S.1. The criteria used to evaluate expert system tools in this chapter are: basic features for representing, acquiring, and explaining knowledge, the development environment, functionality, support, and cost. Each criterion is discussed in detail, and then applied to each of the four tools described in the chapter.

In Chapter 4, Filman describes KEEworlds™, an augmentation of KEE's frame-based structures which allows reasoning with worlds and truth maintenance in the KEE system. With this extension, a KEE program can create multiple *worlds,* each with its own set of assumptions. A *truth-maintenance system* keeps track of which assumptions a derived fact depends on, and withdraws conclusions that are later found to be false. KEEworlds is based on de Kleer's work on the Assumption-based Truth Maintenance System (ATMS). The integration of the ATMS with a frame representation system is a novel

---

ART is a registered trademark of Inference Corporation.
Knowledge Craft is a registered trademark of Carnegie Group Inc.
KEEworlds is a trademark of IntelliCorp, Inc.

combination requiring some fundamental changes to KEE's internal data structures. A hypothetical trucking company forms the basis of many examples that illustrate the use of KEEworlds.

The following three chapters in Part II contain descriptions of tools and methodologies currently in use at several important artificial intelligence research centers. These tools are somewhat more specialized, but they have been used in a range of knowledge-based applications.

In Chapter 5, Boose and Bradshaw present a detailed description of Aquinas, a knowledge-acquisition workbench. Most knowledge engineering environments include some tools for acquiring knowledge from experts, but for the most part an expert system developer must depend on his or her own methodologies and software tools to build a knowledge base. Aquinas addresses this problem by offering a workbench with a variety of tools that support multiple methodologies for knowledge acquisition. Aquinas is designed to be a front-end tool for other knowledge engineering environments such as KEE.

In Chapter 6, Bates and Mac Gregor describe NIKL (New Implementation of KL-One) and related systems, which have evolved from a long line of knowledge representation languages of which KL-One is probably the most well known. These systems combine a formal and practical approach to knowledge representation and reasoning, which the authors believe is generally missing from the current generation of commercial artificial intelligence tools.

In Chapter 7, Swartout and Smoliar discuss the current results of the Explainable Expert Systems project. As the name indicates, this project focuses on capturing the knowledge that an expert uses to explain the skills and knowledge he or she possesses. An expert's ability to explain and articulate what he or she is doing, and why, is a critical aspect of being an expert. Experts are often asked to justify their actions and conclusions, and we certainly have even more reason to want an expert system to provide such explanations and justifications, particularly for critical decision-making tasks such as medical diagnosis and treatment.

Specialized Tools and Techniques

Various artificial intelligence tools that are used for specialized applications are discussed in Part III. In Chapter 8, Round describes several artificial intelligence simulation tools and how they evolved from conventional simulation tools and object-oriented programming languages. He demonstrates how the object-oriented and access-oriented programming techniques described in Part I make it easier to build and understand simulation models.

Drummond and Stelzner present a detailed description of SimKit, a model-building simulation toolkit, in Chapter 9. SimKit is developed in KEE, but interesting simulation models can be built using a *direct manipulation* interface, often without the need for KEE and LISP programming. Using KEE and LISP, programmers develop domain-specific toolkits or SimKit *libraries* that end-users (e.g., domain experts) use to build specific models (e.g., a particular factory configuration).

In Chapter 10, Linden and Markosian discuss *transformational synthesis*—a data-directed programming technique that is used in automatic programming, planning, and other AI applications. Transformational synthesis is a technique for constructing programs, plans, or other complex conceptual objects by evolving them through small, independent changes. It is one of the techniques supported by REFINE™—a knowledge based development environment that is built around a high-level program specification language. Transformational synthesis is used by the REFINE compiler to synthesize programs automatically from their specifications. This chapter describes how transformational synthesis is also used to synthesize plans for a multiple robotic vehicle application, resulting in planning software that is unusually flexible and extensible.

Building Bridges from Knowledge-Based to Conventional Systems

In Part IV of the book, two systems that are building bridges from knowledge-based systems to conventional systems are examined. Abarbanel, Tou and Gilbert describe KEEconnection, a bridge between KEE and SQL (Structured Query Language) relational databases in Chapter 11. The authors explain how to map database tables in an SQL database into units (or frames) in KEE, and vice versa, and how to map queries on a KEE knowledge base into SQL statements. A simple example is used to describe how a mapping from a database to KEE is created and modified, how data from a SQL database can be loaded into KEE units for knowledge-based processing, and how subsequent updates to the KEE units can be mapped back into updates to the SQL database.

In Chapter 12, Hayes-Roth, Erman, Fouse, Lark, and Davidson describe ABE™, an environment that is designed to allow programs written in different languages on different machines and operating systems to solve problems cooperatively. The authors call ABE a *cooperative operating system*, in the sense that operating systems principally provide a computational metaphor and composition methodology rather than act simply as low-level resource managers. ABE provides solutions to some of the more difficult and frustrating problems that face programmers and users alike as they struggle to find ways to integrate and combine the different technologies that they have available to them.

REFINE is a trademark of Reasoning Systems, Inc.
ABE is a trademark of Teknowledge, Inc.

Acknowledgements

As editor I must take final responsibility for the organization and content of the book, but the book would not have been possible if not for the generous help of many individuals. Of course without the contributions of the many fine authors there would be no book at all.

I am also very grateful to those individuals who helped review parts of the manuscript and provided other valuable suggestions and advice: Robert Abarbanel, John Boose, Brian Drummond, Robert Filman, Peter Karp, Jonathan King, David Leserman, Mark Musen, Julie Richer, Alfred Round, William Swartout, and Masoud Yazdani. Barbara Bernstein and Carol Davidson of Ablex Publishing Corporation were very supportive throughout the project, providing invaluable help with the editing and production of the manuscript. This book would not have been possible without the training and inspiration I received from former teachers and colleagues at Stanford University and elsewhere. Finally, I am grateful to my wife, Julie, for all her help and patience.

Mark H. Richer
San Francisco, California
December 14, 1988

Part I

Object-Oriented and Access-Oriented Programming

Chapter 1

Object-Oriented Programming: Themes and Variations*

Mark J. Stefik
Daniel G. Bobrow
Intelligent Systems Laboratory, Xerox Palo Alto Research Center

Many of the ideas behind object-oriented programming have roots going back to SIMULA (Dahl and Nygaard, 1966). The first substantial, interactive, display-based implementation was the Smalltalk language (Goldberg and Robson, 1983). The object-oriented style has often been advocated for simulation programs, systems programming, graphics, and AI programming. The history of ideas has some additional threads including work on message passing as in Actors (Lieberman, 1981), and multiple inheritance as in Flavors (Weinreb and Moon, 1981). It is also related to a line of work in AI on the theory of frames (Minsky, 1975) and their implementation in knowledge representation languages such as KRL (Bobrow and Winograd, 1977), KEE (Fikes and Kehler, 1985), FRL (Goldstein and Roberts, 1977), and Units (Stefik, 1979).

*Thanks to Ken Kahn and Mark Miller who were especially generous with their time and ideas as we prepared this article for publication. Thanks also to Sanjay Mittal and Stanley Lanning who read earlier drafts and who contributed to the design and implementation of Loops. Ken Kahn, Gregor Kiczales, Larry Masinter, and Frank Zdybel helped broaden our understanding of the variations in object-oriented languages as we worked together on the design of CommonLoops. Much of the discussion in this paper was inspired by the electronic dialog of the members of the Common LISP Object-Oriented Programming Subcommittee.

Special thanks to John Seely Brown and Lynn Conway, who encouraged our work on Loops, and helped us to develop larger visions while we slogged through the bits. Thanks also to Bill Spencer and George Pake for maintaining the kind of intellectual environment at PARC that has allowed many different projects in language design to flourish.

This paper was previously published in *AI Magazine, 6(4)*, 40–62, Winter 1986. It is reprinted here with the kind permission of the editors and the publisher.

One might expect from this long history that by now there would be agreement on the fundamental principles of object-oriented programming. As it turns out, the programming language community is still actively experimenting. Extreme languages can be found which share the description *object-oriented* but very little else. For example, there are object-oriented operating systems that use a much more general notion of message sending than in most of the languages described here.

This article is an introduction to the basic ideas of programming with objects. A map of the field is naturally drawn from where one stands. Most of the examples will be from the authors' own system, Loops (Bobrow and Stefik, 1981), and we will describe other object languages from that vantage point. We have not tried to be complete in our survey; there are probably fifty or more object-oriented programming languages now in use, mostly with very limited distribution. We have selected ones we know that are widely used for applications in artificial intelligence or have a particularly interesting variation of an issue under discussion. For pedagogical purposes we begin with a white lie. We introduce *message sending* and *specialization* as the most fundamental concepts of object-oriented programming. Then, we will return to fundamentals and see why some object languages don't have message sending, and others don't have specialization.

Basic Concepts of Object-Oriented Programming

The term object-oriented programming has been used to mean different things, but one thing these languages have in common is *objects*. Objects are entities that combine the properties of procedures and data since they perform computations and save local state. Uniform use of objects contrasts with the use of separate procedures and data in conventional programming.

All of the action in object-oriented programming comes from sending *messages* between objects. *Message sending* is a form of indirect procedure call. Instead of naming a procedure to perform an operation on an object, one sends the object a message. A *selector* in the message specifies the kind of operation. Objects respond to messages using their own procedures (called *methods*) for performing operations.

Message sending supports an important principle in programming: *data abstraction*. The principle is that calling programs should not make assumptions about the implementation and internal representations of *data types* that they use. Its purpose is to make it possible to change underlying implementations without changing the calling programs. A data type is implemented by choosing a representation for values and writing a procedure for each operation. A language supports data abstraction when it has a mechanism for bundling together all of the procedures for a data type. In object-oriented programming the *class* represents the data type and the values are its *instance variables*; the operations are methods the class responds to.

Messages are usually designed in sets to define a uniform interface to objects that provide a facility. Such a set of related messages is called a *protocol*. For example, a protocol for manipulating icons on a display screen could include messages for creating images of icons, moving them, expanding them, shrinking them, and deleting them. When a message protocol is designed for a class, it should be made general enough to allow alternative implementations.

There is additional leverage for building systems when the protocols are *standardized*. This leverage comes from *polymorphism*. In general the term polymorphism means "having or assuming different forms," but in the context of object-oriented programming, it refers to the capability for different classes of objects to respond to exactly the same protocols. Protocols enable a program to treat uniformly objects that arise from different classes. Protocols extend the notion of *modularity* (reusable and modifiable pieces as enabled by data-abstracted subroutines) to polymorphism (interchangeable pieces as enabled by message sending).

After message sending, the second major idea in object-oriented programming is *specialization*. Specialization is a technique that uses class *inheritance* to elide information. Inheritance enables the easy creation of objects that are almost like other objects with a few incremental changes. Inheritance reduces the need to specify redundant information and simplifies updating and modification, since the information can be entered and changed in one place.

We have observed in our applications of Loops that changes to the inheritance network are very common in program reorganization. Programmers often create new classes and reorganize their classes as they understand the opportunities for factoring parts of their programs. The Loops programming environment facilitates such changes with an interactive graphics browser for adding and deleting classes, renaming classes, splitting classes, and rerouting inheritance paths in the lattice.

Specialization and message sending synergize to support program extensions that preserve important variants. Polymorphism extends downwards in the inheritance network because subclasses inherit protocols. Instances of a new subclass follow exactly the same protocols as the parent class, until local specialized methods are defined. Splitting a class, renaming a class, or adding a new class along an inheritance path does not affect simple message sending unless a new method is introduced. Similarly, deleting a class does not affect message sending if the deleted class does not have a local method involved in the protocol. Together, message sending and specialization provide a robust framework for extending and modifying programs.

Fundamentals Revisited

Object languages differ, even in the fundamentals. We next consider object languages that do not have message sending, and one language that does not have specialization.

Variations on Message Sending. When object languages are embedded in LISP, the simplest approach to providing message sending is to define a form for message sending such as:

(send object selector arg1 arg2...)

However, some language designers find the use of two distinct forms of procedure call to be unaesthetic and a violation of data abstraction: a programmer is forced to be aware of whether the subsystem is implemented in terms of objects, that is, whether one should invoke methods or functions.

An alternative is to unify procedure call with message sending. Various approaches to this have been proposed. The T (Rees, Adams, and Meehan, 1984) programming language unifies message sending and procedure calling by using the standard LISP syntax for invoking either methods or functions. For example, (display obj x y) could be used either to invoke the display method associated with obj, or to invoke the display LISP function. A name conflict resulting in ambiguity is an error.

CommonLoops (Bobrow, Kahn, Kiczales, Masinter, Stefik, and Zdybel, 1985) takes this unification another step. LISP function call syntax is the only procedure calling mechanism, but ordinary LISP functions can be extended by methods to be applied when the arguments satisfy certain restrictions. In LISP, functions are applied to arguments. The code that is run is determined by the name of the function. The LISP form (foo a b) can be viewed as:

(funcall (function-specified-by 'foo) a b)

Sending a message (send a foo b) in object-oriented programming can be viewed as equivalent to the invocation of:

(funcall (method-specified-by 'foo (type-of a)) a b)

The code that is run is determined by both the name of the message, foo, and the type of the object, a. A method is invoked only if its arguments match the specifications. In this scheme a method with no type specifications in its arguments is applied if no other method matches. These methods are equivalent to ordinary functions, when there are no other methods for that selector. From the point of view of the caller, there is no difference between calling a function and invoking a method.

CommonLoops extends the notion of method by introducing the notion of *multi-methods* to Common LISP. It interprets the form (foo a b...) as:

(funcall (method-specified-by 'foo (type-of a) (type-of b)...) a b...)

The familiar methods of *classical* object-oriented programming are a special case where the type (class) of only the first argument is used. Thus there is a continuum of definition from simple functions to those whose arguments are fully specified, and the user need not be aware of whether there are multiple implementations that depend on the types of the arguments. For any set of arguments to be a selector, there can be several methods whose type specifications match. The most specific applicable method is invoked.

A variation among object oriented languages is whether the method lookup procedure is *built-in*. In the languages we have described here, there is a standard mechanism for interpreting messages—with the selector always used as a key to the method. In Actors, the message is itself an object that the receiver processes however it wishes. This allows other possibilities such as pattern matching on the message form. It also allows *message plumbing* where the receiver forwards the entire message to one or more other objects. Splitting streams to allow one output to go to two sources is a simple example of the use of this feature.

Variations on Specialization. Specialization as we have introduced it so far is a way to arrange classes so that they can inherit methods and protocols from other classes. This is a special case of a more general concept: the concept is that objects need to handle some messages themselves, and to pass along to other objects those messages that they don't handle.

In actor languages (Lieberman, 1981) this notion is called *delegation* and it is used for those programming situations where inheritance would be used in most other object languages. Delegation is more general than specialization, because an *actor* can delegate a message to an arbitrary other object rather than being confined to the paths of a hierarchy or class lattice.

If delegation was used in its full generality for most situations in actor programming, the specifications of delegation could become quite verbose and the advantages of abstraction hierarchies would be lost. Actor programs would be quite difficult to debug. In practice, there are programming clichés in these languages that emulate the usual forms of inheritance from more conventional object languages, and macros for language support. However, since there is no standardization on the type of inheritance, it makes it more difficult for a reader of the code to understand what will happen.

GLOSSARY FOR OBJECT-ORIENTED PROGRAMMING

class. A class is a description of one or more similar objects. For example, the class apple, is a description of the structure and behavior of instances, such as apple-1 and apple-2. Loops and Smalltalk classes describe the instance variables, class variables, and methods of their instances as well as the position of the class in the inheritance lattice.

class inheritance. When a class is placed in the class lattice, it inherits variables and methods from its superclasses. This means that any variable that is defined higher in the class lattice will also appear in instances of this class. If a variable is defined in more than one place, the overriding value is determined by the inheritance order. The inheritance order is depth-first up to joins, and left-to-right in the list of superclasses.

class variable. A class variable is a variable stored in the class whose value is shared by all instances of the class. Compare with *instance variable*.

composite object. A group of interconnected objects that are instantiated together, a recursive extension of the notion of object. A composite is defined by a template that describes the subobjects and their connections.

data abstraction. The principle that programs should not make assumptions about implementations and internal representations. A *data type* is characterized by operations on its values. In object-oriented programming the operations are methods of a class. The class represents the data type and the values are its instances.

default value. A value for an instance variable that has not been set explicitly in the instance. The default value is found in the class, and tracks that value until it is changed in the instance. This contrasts with initial values.

delegation. A technique for forwarding a message off to be handled by another object.

initial value. A value for an instance variable that is computed and installed in the instance at object creation. Different systems provide initial values and/or default values.

instance. The term *instance* is used in two ways. The phrase *instance of* describes the relation between an object and its class. The methods and structure of an instance are determined by its class. All objects in Loops (including classes) are instances of some class. The noun *instance* refers to objects that are not classes.

instantiate. To make a new instance of a class.

instance variable. Instance variables (sometimes called slots) are variables for which local storage is available in instances. This contrasts with class variables, which have storage only in the class. In some languages instance variables can have optional properties.

lattice. In this document we are using *lattice* as a directed graph without cycles. In Loops, the inheritance network is arranged in a lattice. A lattice is more general than a tree because it admits more than one parent. Like a tree, a lattice rules out the possibility that a class can (even indirectly) have itself as a superclass.

metaclass. This term is used in two ways: as a relationship applied to an instance, it refers to the class of the instance's class; as a noun it refers to a class all of whose instances are classes.

message. The specification of an operation to be performed on an object. Similar to a procedure call, except that the operation to be performed is named indirectly through a *selector* whose interpretation is determined by the class of the object, rather than a procedure name with a single interpretation.

method. The function that implements the response when a message is sent to an object. In Loops, a class associates *selectors* with methods.

mixin. A class designed to augment the description of its subclasses in a multiple inheritance lattice. For example, the mixin NamedObject allocates an instance variable for holding an object's name, and connects the value of that variable to the object symbol table.

object. The primitive element of object-oriented programming. Objects combine the attributes of procedures and data. Objects store data in variables, and respond to messages by carrying out procedures (methods).

perspective. A form of composite object interpreted as different views on the same conceptual entity. For example, one might represent the concept for "Joe" in terms of JoeAsAMan, JoeAsAGolfer, JoeAsAWelder, JoeAsAFather. One can access any of these by view from each of the others.

polymorphism. The capability for different classes of objects to respond to exactly the same protocols. Protocols enable a program to treat uniformly objects that arise from different classes. A critical feature is that even when the same message is sent from the same place in code, it can invoke different methods.

protocol. A standardized set of messages for implementing something. Two classes which implement the same set of messages are said to follow the same protocol.

selector. The selector in a message specifies the kind of operation the receiver of a message should perform. Also see *message*.

slot. See instance variable.

specialization. The process of modifying a generic thing for a specific use.

subclass. A class that is lower in the inheritance lattice than a given class.

superclass. A class that is higher in the inheritance lattice than a given class.

Classes and Instances

In most object languages objects are divided into two major categories: *classes* and *instances*. A class is a description of one or more similar objects. In comparison with procedural programming languages, classes correspond to types. For example, if number is a type (class), then 4 is an instance. In an object language, apple would be a class, and apple-1 and apple-2 would be instances of that class. Classes participate in the inheritance lattice directly; instances participate indirectly through their classes. Classes and instances have a declarative structure that is defined in terms of object variables for storing state, and methods for responding to messages.

Even in these fundamentals, object languages differ. Some object languages do not distinguish between classes and instances. At least one object language does not provide a declarative structure for objects at all. Some languages do not distinguish methods from variable structure. Languages also differ in the extent to which variables can be annotated.

Themes

We begin by describing classes and instances as they are conceived in Loops. We will then consider some variations.

What's in a Class? A class in Loops is a description of one or more similar objects. For example, the class Apple provides a description for making instances, such as apple-1 and apple-2. Although we usually reserve the term instance to refer to objects that are not classes, even classes are instances of a class (usually the one named Class). Every object in Loops is an instance of exactly one class.

Figure 1 shows an example of a class in Loops. A class definition is organized in several parts—a class name, a metaclass, superclasses, variables, and methods. The metaclass part names the metaclass (Class in this case) and uses a property list for storing documentation. A *metaclass* describes operations on this class viewed as a Loops object. The *superclass* part (*supers*) locates a class in the inheritance network. The other parts of a class definition describe the places for specifying data storage and procedures.

Variables in objects are used for storing state. Loops supports two kinds of variables; *class variables* and *instance variables*. Class variables are used to hold information shared by all instances of the class. Instance variables contain the information specific to a particular instance. Both kinds of variables have names, values, and other properties. We call the instance variable part of a class definition the *instance variable description,* because it specifies the names and

Truck

MetaClass Class

EditedBy *(* dgb "29-Feb-85 4:32")*

doc *(** This sample class illustrates the syntax of classes in Loops.*

Commentary is inserted in a standard property in the class.

—e.g. Trucks are ...)

Supers (Vehicle CargoCarrier)

Class Variables

tankCapacity 79 *doc (* Gallons of diesel.)*

Instance Variables

owner PIE *doc (* Owner of truck.)*

highway 66 *doc (* Route number of the highway.)*

milePost 0 *doc (* Location on the highway.)*

direction East *doc (* One of North, East, South, or West.)*

cargoList NL *doc (* List of cargo descriptions.)*

totalWeight 0 *doc (* Current weight of cargo in tons.)*

Methods

Drive Truck.Drive *doc (* Moves the vehicle in the simulation.)*

Park Truck.Park *doc (* Parks the truck in a double space.)*

Display Truck.Display *doc (* Draws the truck in the display.)*

The class, called Truck, inherits variables and methods from both of its superclasses (Vehicle and CargoCarrier). The form of the definition here shows the additions and substitutions to inherited information. In this example a value for the class variable tankCapacity is introduced, and six instance variables (owner, highway, milePost, direction, cargoList, and totalWeight) are defined, along with their default values. The Methods declaration names the procedures (Interlisp functions) that implement the methods. For example, Truck.Drive is the name of a function that implements the Drive method for instances of Truck.

Figure 1. Example of a Class Definition in Loops

default values of variables to be created in instances of the class. It acts as a template to guide the creation of instances. For example, the class Point might specify two instance variables, x and y with default values of 0, and a class variable associated with all points, lastSelectedPoint. Each instance of Point would have its own x and y instance variables, but all of the instances would use the same lastSelectedPoint class variable; any changes made to the value of lastSelectedPoint would be seen by all of the instances. Default values are the values that would be fetched from the instance variables if the variables have not been assigned values particular to the instance. As motivated by Smalltalk, Loops also has *indexed* instance variables, thus allowing some instances to behave like dynamically allocable arrays.

A *class* specifies the behavior of its instances in terms of their response to messages. A *message* is made of arguments and a *selector*. The class associates a selector (e.g., the selector Drive in Figure 1) with a *method*, a procedure to respond to the message. When a message is sent to an instance, its response is determined by using the selector to find the method in a symbol table in the class. The method is located in the symbol table and then executed. Since all instances of a class share the same methods, any difference in response by two instances is determined by a difference in the values of their instance variables.

What's in an Instance? Most objects in a Loops program are instances (that is, not classes). For example, in a traffic simulation program there may be one class named Truck and hundreds of instances of it representing trucks on the highways of a simulation world. All of these truck instances respond to the same messages, and share the class variables defined in the class Truck. What each instance holds privately are the values and properties of its instance variables, and perhaps an object name. The variables of an instance are initialized with a special token indicating to the Loops access functions that the variables have not been locally set yet. Figure 2 shows an example of an instance object.

Instantiation and Metaclasses. The term "metaclass" is used in two ways: as a relationship applied to an instance, it refers to the class of the instance's class; as a noun it refers to a class all of whose instances are classes. The internal implementation of an instance is determined by its metaclass.

For example, to create a new instance of the class MacTruck a New message is sent to MacTruck. This creates a data structure representing the truck with space for all of the instance variables. The method for creating the data structure is found in MacTruck's metaclass—Class. To create a new class (e.g., the class PickUpTruck, an instance of the class Class), a New message is sent to Class. The method for creating and installing the data structure is found in the metaclass of Class called MetaClass. The New method creates a data structure for the new class, with space for class variables, instance variable description, and

Automobile-1

Class Automobile

Instance Variables
   highway 66
   milePost 38
   direction East
   driver Sanjay
   fuel ?
   ...

Instances have local storage for their instance variables. If no local value has been set yet, default values for instance variables are obtained from the class. In this example, the "?" in the value place for the instance variable fuel indicates that the actual value is to be obtained by lookup from the class Automobile. Methods and class variables are not shown since they are accessed through the class.

Figure 2. Instance of an Automobile in a Traffic Simulation Model

a method lookup table. The new class is also installed in the inheritance network. Figure 3 illustrates this process of instantiation.

AbstractClass is an example of a useful metaclass in Loops. It is used for classes that are placeholders in the inheritance network that it would not make sense to instantiate. For example, its response to a New message is to cause an error. Other metaclasses can be created for representing some classes of objects as specialized LISP records and data structures.

Classes and Instances, Revisited

The distinction between classes and instances is usual in object languages. In applications where instances greatly outnumber classes, a different internal representation allows economies of storage in representation. It also provides a natural boundary for display of inheritance, and hence helps to limit the visual clutter in presentations of the inheritance network.

The object language of KEE (Fikes and Kehler, 1985) does not provide distinct representations for classes and instances. All objects, or *units*, as they are called in KEE, have the same status. Any object can be given *member* slots which will be inherited by instances of this object. Proponents of this more uniform approach have argued that for many applications, the distinction does little work and that it just adds unnecessary complications. Similarly there is no such distinction in actor languages (Lieberman, 1981). Inheritance of variables in these languages is generally replaced by a copying operation. ThingLab (Borning, 1979), a constraint-driven object language, used prototypes rather

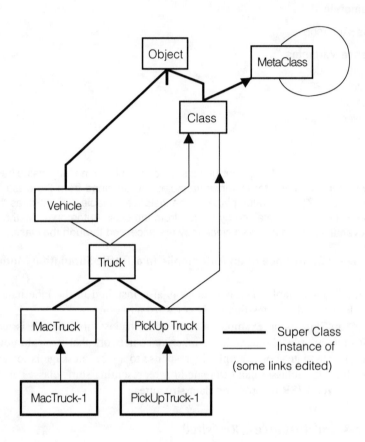

━━━━━	Super Class
─────	Instance of

(some links edited)

Instantiation is the process of making a new object. In Loops, this process begins when a New message is sent to a class. In this figure, the instance MacTruck-1 is created by sending a New message to MacTruck. The line between MacTruck-1 and MacTruck indicates the instance-of relationship between the instance and its class. Similarly, a class like PickUpTruck is created by sending a New message to Class. The line between PickUpTruck and Class indicates the instance-of relationship between the class PickUpTruck and its metaclass Class. Every object has an instance-of relationship with exactly one class. Class and MetaClass are called metaclasses, since all of their instances are classes. Another important metaclass is AbstractClass (not shown). AbstractClass is the metaclass for classes not meant to be instantiated (e.g., like Vehicle).

Figure 3. Instantiation

than classes to drive object creation, and specialization was simply instantiation followed by editing.

In Object LISP (Drescher, 1985), the declarative structures conventionally associated with classes are dispensed with. Objects are simply binding environments, that is, *closures.* An operation is provided for creating and nesting these environments. Object variables are LISP variables bound within an object environment; methods are function names bound within such an environment. To get the effect of message sending, one ASKS for a given form to be evaluated in the dynamic scope of a given object. Nested environments are used to achieve the layered inheritance effect of specialization. Use of an ASKS form, however, precludes the unification of message-sending and procedure call that is now appearing in other object languages.

Not all object languages have metaclasses. Since Flavors are not objects, instances of Flavors have no metaclasses. All Flavor instances are implemented the same way: as vectors. Loops uses metaclasses to allow variations in implementation for different classes. For example; some objects provide a level of indirection to their variable storage, allowing updating of the object if there are changes in its class definition. Smalltalk-80 has metaclasses, and uses them primarily to allow differential initialization at object creation time. Common-Loops (Bobrow et al., 1985) makes more extensive use of metaclasses than Loops, using them as a type of "escape mechanism" for bringing flexibility to representation and notations of objects.

Another difference in systems is whether instance variables of an object can be accessed from other than a method of the object. Proponents of this strict *encapsulation,* as in Smalltalk, base their argument on limiting knowledge of the internal representation of an object, making the locus of responsibility for any problems with the object state well-bounded. A counter argument is that encapsulation can be done by convention. Loops allows direct access to object variables to support a knowledge representation style of programming. This is particularly useful, for example, in writing programs that compare two objects.

Not all object languages provide property annotations for variables. In Smalltalk, Flavors, and Object LISP, variables have values and nothing more. However, languages intended primarily for knowledge engineering applications tend to support annotations. For example, KEE, STROBE (Smith, 1983), and Loops, which are all direct descendants of the Units Package, have this. Annotations are useful for storing auxiliary information such as dependency records, documentation, histories of past values, constraints, and certainty information.

In Loops, the approach to annotating variables has evolved over time. In its most recent incarnation, property annotations have been unified with a means for triggering procedure call on variable access (*active values*) (Stefik, Bobrow, and Kahn, 1989). These annotations are contained in objects and it is possible to annotate annotations recursively.

The distinction between class variables and instance variables varies across object languages. Smalltalk makes the same distinction as Loops (and was the source of the idea for the Loops developers). Flavors does not have class variables. KEE provides *own* and *member* declarations for slots, serving essentially the same purposes as the distinction between class and instance variables. CommonLoops provides primitives for describing when, how, and where storage is allocated for variables. From these primitives, the important notions of class variables can be defined, except that they share the same name space as other object variables.

Most object languages treat variables and methods as distinct kinds of things. Variables are for storage and methods are for procedures. This distinction is blurred somewhat by active values in Loops, which make it possible to annotate the value of a variable in any object so that access will trigger a procedure. The distinction is blurred also in languages like KEE, STROBE, and the Units Package in which methods are procedure names stored in instance variables (which they call *slots*). In these languages there is an additional kind of message sending: sending a message to a slot. For specified kinds of messages, the value returned can be just the value of the slot.

Another important extension in the Units Package, KEE, and STROBE is that slots are annotated by datatypes. The datatype distinguishes the kind of data being kept in the slot, be it an integer, a list, a procedure, or something defined for an application. An object representing the datatype provides specialized methods for such operations as printing, editing, displaying, and matching. These datatype methods are activated when a slot message is not handled by a procedure attached to the slot itself. The form of message forwarding and representation of datatypes as objects provides another opportunity for factoring and sharing information. Thus, what all slots of a given type share, independent of where they occur, is characterized by methods in the corresponding datatype object.

Inheritance

Inheritance is the concept in object languages that is used to define objects that are almost like other objects. Mechanisms like this are important because they make it possible to declare that certain specifications are shared by multiple parts of a program. Inheritance helps to keep programs shorter and more tightly organized. The concepts of inheritance arise in all object languages, whether they are based on specialization or delegation and copying.

We began with the simplest model of inheritance, hierarchical inheritance. We will then consider multiple inheritance, as it is in Loops and other languages.

Hierarchical Inheritance

In a hierarchy, a class is defined in terms of a single superclass. A specialized class modifies its superclass with addition and substitution. *Addition* allows the introduction of new variables, properties, or methods in a class, which do not appear in one of its superclasses in the hierarchy. *Substitution* (or *overriding*) is the specification of a new value of a variable or property, or a new method for a selector that already appears in some superclass. Both kinds of changes are covered by the rule, "All descriptions in a class (variables, properties, and methods) are inherited by a subclass unless overridden in the subclass" (see Figure 4).

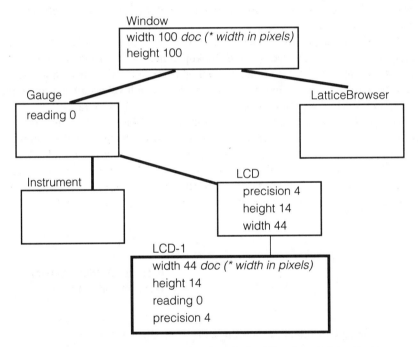

In hierarchical inheritance in Loops, the description of a class is inherited by every subclass, unless it is overridden in the subclass. The instances of the class LCD have a class precedence list for getting their description—LCD, Gauge, Window, Object. The default value for the instance variable width is 44 (rather than 100), because LCD is closer in the search path than Window. In this example, the *doc* property of the instance variable width is still inherited by instances of LCD—passing along documentation about the use of the variable.

Figure 4. Hierarchical Inheritance of Instance Variables

The values to be inherited can be characterized in terms of a *class precedence list* of superclasses of the class determined by going up the hierarchy one step at a time. Default values of instances are determined by the closest class in the superclass hierarchy, that is from the first one in the class precedence list. Figure 5 illustrates essentially the same lookup process for methods.

There is always an issue about the *granularity of inheritance*. By this we mean the division of a description into independent parts, that can be changed without affecting other parts. In Loops, any named structural element can be changed independently—methods, variables, and their properties. For example, substituting a new default value for one instance variable does not affect the inheritance of the properties of that variable, or the inheritance of other instance variables. Figure 4 shows this for the independent inheritance of documentation when a default value is changed.

Several approaches for implementing inheritance are possible, offering different tradeoffs in required storage, lookup time, work during updating, and work for compilers. For example, the lookup of default values need not involve a run-time search of the hierarchy. In Loops, the default values are cached in the class, and updated any time there is a change in the class hierarchy.

The position of a variable is determined by lookup in the class, but the position of this variable is cached at first lookup. Changes in the hierarchy affecting position of instance variables simply require clearing the cache.

In Flavors, the position of an instance variable is stored in a table associated with a method, and is accessed directly by the code. This gives faster access, but requires updating many method tables for some changes in the hierarchy.

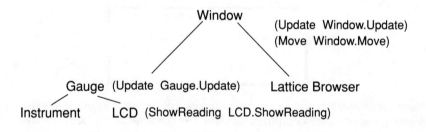

In hierarchical inheritance in Loops, the description of a class is inherited by every subclass, unless it is overridden in the subclass. This inheritance can be characterized as a *first-found* search through superclasses. In this figure, the Move method for the class LCD is inherited from Window.

Figure 5. Hierarchical Inheritance of Methods

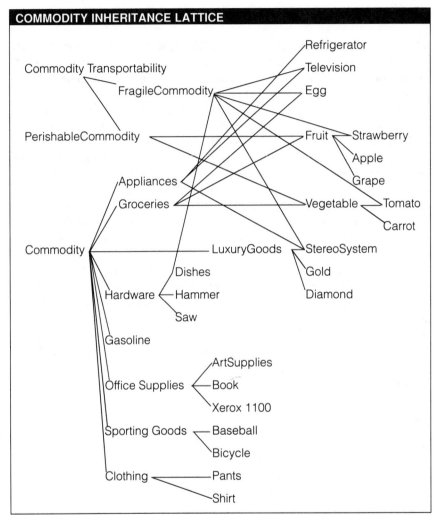

COMMODITY INHERITANCE LATTICE

This lattice illustrates the use of multiple superclasses to factor inherited information in a network of classes. Multiple inheritance allows increased brevity in specifications by increasing the ability to share descriptions. For example, the class StereoSystem in this lattice inherits information from LuxuryGoods, Appliances, and Fragile-Commodity. In a strictly hierarchical system, it would be necessary to duplicate information in the hierarchy—for example by creating classes for FragileAppliances or FragileLuxuryAppliances. In a hierarchical scheme, the methods and variables associated with fragility would need to be replicated for each different use.

Figure 6. Multiple Inheritance in a Lattice

19

Multiple Inheritance in a Lattice

Inheritance is a mechanism for elision. The power of inheritance is in the economy of expression that results when a class shares description with its superclass. *Multiple* inheritance increases sharing by making it possible to combine descriptions from several classes.

Using multiple inheritance we can factor information in a way that is not possible in hierarchical inheritance. Figure 6 illustrates this in a lattice of commodities. The class StereoSystem inherits descriptions from LuxuryGoods, Appliances, and FragileCommodity. The methods and variables describing FragileCommodity are also used for Egg, StereoSystem, and other classes. It would be necessary to duplicate the information about fragility in several classes such as FragileAppliances, FragileGroceries, FragileFruit, and FragileLuxuryGoodsAppliances in a strictly hierarchical system. In contrast, multiple inheritance lets us package together the methods and variables for FragileCommodity for use at any class in the network.

A class inherits the union of variables and methods from all its superclasses. If there is a conflict, then we use a class precedence list to determine precedence for the variable description or method. The class precedence list is computed by starting with the first (leftmost) superclass in the supers specification and proceeding depth-first *up to joins*. For example, the precedence order for DigiMeter in Figure 7 first visits the classes in the left branch (DigiMeter, Meter, Instrument), and then the right branch (LCD), and then the join (Gauge), and up from there.

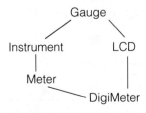

Local supers of DigiMeter: (Meter LCD)

Order of Inheritance:

(DigiMeter Meter Instrument LCD Gauge...)

In multiple inheritance it is possible to inherit things from several superclasses. The precedence of different inherited values is determined by a search as shown.

Figure 7. Order of Inheritance in a Lattice

The left-to-right provision of the precedence ordering makes it possible to indicate which classes take precedence in the name space. The up-to-joins provision can be understood by looking at examples of *mixins*. Mixins often stand for classes that it would not make sense to instantiate by themselves. Mixins are special classes that bundle up descriptions and are "mixed in" to the supers lists of other classes in order to systematically modify their behavior. For example, PerishableCommodity and FragileCommodity are mixins in Figure 6 that add to other classes the protocols for being perishable or fragile. Another example of a mixin is the class NamedInstance, which adds the instance variable name to its subclasses, and overrides methods from Object so that appropriate actions in the Loop symbol tables take place whenever the value of a *name* instance variable is changed. DatedObject is another mixin which adds instance variables that reflect the date and creator of an object. Mixins usually precede other classes in the list of supers, and are often used to add independent kinds of behavior.

When mixins are independent, the order of their inclusion in a supers list should not matter. Like all classes in Loops, mixins are subclasses of Object. If the up-to-joins provision was eliminated from the precedence ordering, then the depth-first search starting from the first mixin would cause all the other default behaviors for Object to be inherited—interfering with other mixins later in the supers list that may need to override some other part of Object. Changing the order of mixins would not eliminate such interference, since most mixins need to override the behavior of Object in some way. The up-to-joins provision fixes this problem by insuring that Object will be the last place from which things are inherited. Although this effect could also be achieved by treating Object specially, we have found that analogous requirements arise whenever several subclasses of a common class are used as mixins. The up-to-joins provision is a general approach for meeting this requirement.

Multiple Inheritance, Revisited

A major source of variation in object languages that provide multiple inheritance is their stand towards precedence relations. In Smalltalk-80, multiple inheritance is provided, but not used much or institutionalized. Smalltalk-80 takes the position that no simple precedence relationship for multiple inheritance will work for all the cases, so none should be assumed at all. Whenever a method is provided by more than one superclass, the user must explicitly indicate which one dominates. This approach diminishes the value of mixins to override default behavior.

Flavors and Loops both use a fixed precedence relationship, but differ in the details. The two approaches can be seen as variations on an algorithm that first linearizes the list of superclasses (using depth-first traversal) and then eliminates duplicates to create a class precedence list. In Flavors, all but the first appearance of a duplicate are eliminated. In Loops, all but the last appearance of a duplicate are eliminated.

CommonLoops takes the position that experimentation with precedence relationships is an open issue in object-oriented programming. In CommonLoops, the precedence relation for any given class is determined by its metaclass, which provides message protocols for computing the class precedence list.

Method Specialization and Combination

One way to specialize a class is to define a local method. This is useful for adding a method or for substituting for an inherited one. In either case a message sent to an instance of the class will invoke the local method. The grain size of change in this approach is the entire method.

A powerful extension to this is the *incremental specialization* of methods, that is, the ability to make incremental additions to inherited methods. This is important in object-oriented programming because it enables fine-grained modification of message protocols. In the following we consider two mechanisms for mixing of inherited behavior. The first mechanism ←Super (pronounced "send super") allows procedural combination of new and inherited behavior. It derives initially from Smalltalk and is used heavily in the Loops language. Then we will consider an interesting and complementary approach pioneered by the Flavors system in which there is a declarative language for combining methods.

Procedural Specialization of Methods

Incremental modification requires language features beyond method definition and message sending. In Loops, ←Super in a method for selector M1 invokes the method for M1 that would have been inherited. Regular message sending (←) in a local method cannot work for this, because the message would just invoke the local method again, recursively.

An example of its use is shown in Figure 8. In this example, Gauge is a subclass of Window. The method for updating a Gauge needs to do whatever the method for Window does, plus some initial setting of parameters and some other calculations after the update. The idiom for doing this is to create an Update method in Gauge that includes a ←Super construct to invoke Window's method. This is better than duplicating the code from Window (which might need to be changed), or invoking Window's method by procedure name (since other classes might later be inserted between Window and Gauge).

Window
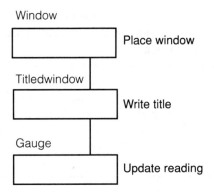
Place window

Titledwindow

Write title

Gauge

Update reading

[Gauge.Update (self)

  (* First update the gauge parameters.)

(← self SetParameters)

  (* Now update using the method from a superclass.)

(← Super self Update)

  (* Now do other things.)

  …]

In this example, Gauge is a subclass of other classes (say Window), which have their own methods of updating. The Update method for Gauge needs to do whatever the method for Window does, except that some parameters need to be set first and then some other computations need to be done afterwards. This effect is achieved by using the ←Super construct, which allows embedding an invocation for Window's method inside new method code for Gauge.

Figure 8. Example of Using ←Super

←Super provides a way of specializing a method without knowing exactly what is done in the higher method, or how it is implemented. ←Super uses the class precedence list to choose when a method appears in more than one superclass. The precedence ordering is the same as that used for object variables.

←Super uses the class precedence list in order to preserve the correctness of protocols under changes to the inheritance lattice. The most obvious definition of ←Super would be to search for the supermethod from the beginning of the class precedence list. This fails for nested versions of ←Super, and even for a ←Super in a method which is not defined locally, but is inherited. A second incorrect implementation would use the class precedence list of the class in which the method was found. This gives incorrect results for classes with multiple superclasses. To insure that protocols work the right way in subclasses, ←Super starts the search in the objects class precedence list at the class from which the current method is inherited. Because ←Super is defined this way, inherited methods using ←Super consistently locate their supermethods, and common changes to the lattice yield invariant operation of the message protocols.

Combination of several inherited methods is also important. A simple version combines all of the most-local methods for a given selector, that is, all of the methods that have not themselves been specialized. These methods are called the *fringe* methods, and the construct for invoking them all is called ←SuperFringe. For example, in Figure 9 the class DigiMeter combines the updating processes for LCD and Meter by using ←SuperFringe to invoke the ShowReading methods of its superclasses.

For selective combination of methods from different classes Loops provides a construction called DoMethod. DoMethod allows the invocation of any method from any class on any object. It can be viewed as an escape mechanism, allowing one to get around the constraints imposed by message sending. It also steps outside the paradigm of object-oriented programming and opens the door to a wide variety of programming errors. When programs are written using standard message invocations, then protocols keep working even when common changes are made to the inheritance lattice. This happy situation is not the case when programs use DoMethod. Since DoMethod allows specification of the class in which the message will be found, it encourages the writing of methods that make strong assumptions about the names of other classes and the current configuration of the inheritance lattice. Programs that use DoMethod are likely to stop working under changes to the inheritance lattice.

Declarative Method Combination

Flavors supports a declarative language for combining methods at compile time. An important new distinction made in Flavors is that there can be three named parts to a method—a *before* part, an *after* part, and a *main* method, each of which is optional. By default, the main method overrides any inherited main method, but the before and after parts are all done in a nested order determined by the class precedence list. Thus a supplier of a method in a mixin can ensure that whatever the main method, its before method will be executed.

A declarative language used in a newly defined method can specify other than the default behavior for combination of inherited method parts. For example, *and* combination of before methods allows the execution of the entire method to stop if one of the before methods returns nil. The defwhopper combinator allows a compile time construction of the equivalent of ←Super.

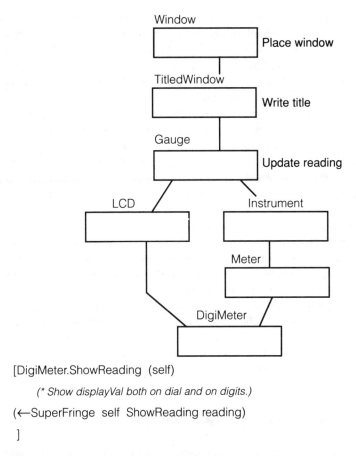

[DigiMeter.ShowReading (self)

  (* Show displayVal both on dial and on digits.)

(←SuperFringe self ShowReading reading)

  ]

In this example, DigiMeter combines the classes of LCD and Meter. To show a reading, a DigiMeter must carry out the ShowReading methods in both its LCD portion and its Meter portion. This combination of protocols can be done by using the ←SuperFringe construct to invoke the ShowReading methods for all of the superclasses. The method above invokes the original ShowReading methods of both Meter and LCD.

Figure 9. Example of Using ←SuperFringe

The concept of organizing methods and variables into classes that can be mixed together for use in combination admits at least two distinct philosophies for assigning responsibility for the viability of the combination. In Flavors responsibility is assigned, at least in part, to the suppliers, that is, to the classes that are being combined. Combinator specifications include things like do this method before the main method, or do it after the main method, or do parts of it at both times. The intention is to get the specification right once in the supplier so that consumers need not know about it. When this kind of specification is successful, it reduces the total amount of code in the system since consumers need only specify the order of superclasses.

In Loops, responsibility for method combination is assigned to the consumer; that is, the local method uses the procedural language and the special form ←Super to combine the new behavior with behavior inherited.

It is important to consider the effects on program change when evaluating alternatives like this. How often are suppliers changed? Consumers? To what extent are suppliers independent? Do mixins need notations for indicating what kinds of classes they are compatible with? What kinds of changes in the suppliers require changes in the consumer classes?

CommonLoops takes the position that both philosophies are worth exploring, and that continued experimentation in the refinement of method combinators is called for. It provides a primitive RunSuper (analogous to the Loops ← Super) in the kernel. Methods are represented as objects in CommonLoops; this means that a system can have different kinds of methods with different techniques for installing them or displaying their sources. Flavor-style methods would be a special kind of object with extra specifications for combinators. These specifications would be interpreted at appropriate installation and reading times by Flavors-style discriminator objects for those methods.

Composite Objects

A *composite object* is a group of interconnected objects that are instantiated together, a recursive extension of the notion of object. A composite is defined by a template that describes the subobjects and their connections. Facilities for creating composite objects are not common in the object languages we know, although they are common in application languages such as those for describing circuits and layout of computer hardware. The current Loops facility is based on ideas in Trillium (Henderson, 1986), which is a language for describing how user interfaces for copiers are put together.

Principles for Composite Objects

Composite objects in Loops have been designed with the following features:

- Composite objects are specified by a class containing a description indicating the classes of the parts and the interconnections among the parts.

The use of a class makes instantiation uniform so that composite objects are *first class* objects.

• Instantiation creates instances corresponding to all the parts in the description.

The instantiation process keeps track of the correspondence between the parts of the description and the parts in the instantiated object. It fills in all of the connections between objects. It permits multiple distinct uses of identical parts.

• The instantiation process is recursive, so that composite objects can be used as parts.

For programming convenience, the instantiation process detects as an error the situation where a description specifies using another new instance of itself as a part, even indirectly. Instantiation of such a description would result in trying to build an object of unbounded size. An alternative is to instantiate subparts only on demand. This allows the use of a potentially unbounded object as far as needed.

• It is possible to specialize a description by adding new parts or substituting for existing parts.

This reflects the central role of specialization as a mechanism for elision in object-oriented programming. The language of description allows specialization of composite objects with a granularity of changes at the level of parts.

An Example of a Composite Object

Composite objects are objects that contain other objects as parts. For example, a car may be described structurally as consisting of a body, a power system, and an electrical system. The body has two doors, a hood, a chassis, and other things. Parts can themselves contain other parts: a door has various panels, a window, and a locking system. Objects can also be parts of more than one container: the fan belt can be viewed as a component of the cooling system or of the electrical charging system.

Figure 10 shows the Loops class definition of Mercedes240D defined as a composite object. Mercedes240D is a subclass of the mixin CompositeObject that supports protocols for instantiation that will interpret descriptions of parts. The value of the instance variable engineSystem will be filled by an instance of the class DieselEngine. In that instance of DieselEngine, the value of the instance variable numCylinders is initialized to 4 and transmission to 4Speed.

The body instance of the Mercedes240D will be initialized to an instance of Body300. Its instance variable style is set to the value of the style from the Mercedes240D, that is, traditional. In addition, the color property of the style instance variable will be set to ivory. These exemplify the propagation of values from the containing instance to those parts contained in it.

The class variable StandardCarStuff indicates a number of variables for the body part that will inherit values from the car. For example, the color of the body is the color of the car. Finally, the instance variable parts will be set to a list of all the immediate parts of the Mercedes240D. If any of the parts are themselves CompositeObjects, their parts will be instantiated too.

Mercedes 240D

MetaClass Class
EditedBy *(* dgb "15-Feb-82 14:32")*
doc *(* This class is a CompositeObject representing a car and its parts.)*

Supers (CompositeObject Automobile)

ClassVariables
Manufacturer DaimlerBenz
StandardCarStuff ((color (@color))(owner(@owner)))...)

InstanceVariables
yearManufactured NIL
owner NIL
style traditional
color ivory
engineSystem NIL
        part (DieselEngine (numCylinders 4)
                (transmission (QUOTE 4Speed))...)

body NIL
        part (Body 300
                (style (@style))
                (color (@color))
                StandardCarStuff)

Figure 10. Mercedes 240D

Perspectives

Perspectives are a form of composite object interpreted as different views on the same conceptual entity. For example, one might represent the concept for "Joe" in terms of views for JoeAsAMan, JoeAsAGolfer, JoeAsAWelder, JoeAsAFather.

We will first describe perspectives as they are used in Loops, and then contrast this with other languages.

Perspectives in Loops

Perspectives in Loops are implemented by independent linked objects representing each of the views. One can access any of these by view name from each of the others. Because the linked objects are independent, the same instance variable name in more than one of the objects can mean different things, and can be changed independently. For example, Figure 11 illustrates an object Inverter-1 which has the perspective DisplayObject as well as the perspective Layout-Description. Both perspectives may have instance variables named xCoordinate

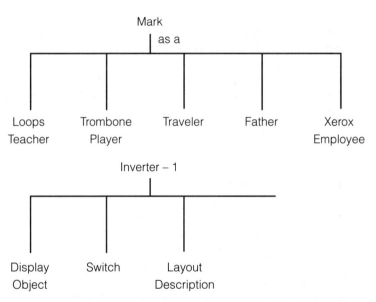

For some applications, it is important to have different perspectives or views of an entity, with independent name spaces. In the upper portion of this figure, the entity Mark is shown with perspectives for LoopsTeacher, TrombonePlayer, Traveler, and so on. Each perspective offers a different view of Mark in a distinct object with its own variables and methods. For example, the TrombonePlayer perspective would contain information relevant to Mark's ability to make music. In the example of an inverter, shown in the lower part of the figure, variables with the same name, such as xCoordinate and yCoordinate, may have one meaning in the perspective DisplayObject and another meaning in the perspective LayoutDescription.

Figure 11. Perspectives

and yCoordinate, but with different interpretations. For a DisplayObject, the variables could refer to the coordinates in pixels on a workstation display. For a LayoutDescription perspective, the variables could refer to coordinates in the silicon chip on which the inverter is fabricated.

Perspectives were designed in Loops to have the following properties:

• Perspectives are accessed by perspective names.

Given an object, one can ask for its Traveler perspective using the name "Traveler." A given perspective name has at most one perspective of an object. Perspectives form a kind of equivalence class.

• Perspectives are instantiated on demand.

This contrasts with usual composite objects in which all the parts are created at instantiation time. Additional views can be added as needed to any object.

Perspectives can be compared with class inheritance. In inheritance only one variable is created when there is a coincidence in the names of variables inherited from different superclasses. Thus inheritance assumes that the same name is always intended to refer to the same variable. For perspectives, variables of the same name from different classes are used for different views and are distinct. When classes are combined by inheritance, all of the instances of the combined class have the same structure (that is, variables and methods) and all of the structure is created at once. For perspectives, the situation is different. Instances have varying substructure.

Variations on Perspectives

The term perspective was first used for different views of the same conceptual object in KRL, and later in PIE (Goldstein and Bobrow, 1980). Each view had an independent name space for its slots. However, in neither PIE nor KRL was a perspective a full-fledged object; access to the view could only be obtained through the containing object.

Although the terminology of perspectives is not widespread, some other object languages (e.g., Snyder, 1985) have a similar capability to combine the structure of multiple classes in this way. Snyder suggests that name coincidence in multiple inheritance ought not imply identity. He believes that this violates an important encapsulation principle of object-oriented programming—that users of objects ought not to have privileged access to the internals of those objects. He extends that notion to classes which inherit from previously defined classes. For his language, inheritance from a superclass means the embedding of an instance of the superclass in the subclass. Messages of the superclass are to be inherited explicitly, and implemented by passing the message on to the embedded instance.

Examples of Object-Oriented Programming

Examples of programming can be presented at several levels. This section considers three examples of object-oriented programming that illustrate important idioms of programming practice. The first illustrates the use of message sending and specialization. The second example illustrates choices among techniques of object combination. The third example illustrates common techniques for redistributing information among classes as programs evolve.

Programming the Box and the BorderedBox

Object-oriented programming has been used for many programs in interactive graphics. The following example was motivated by these applications. We will consider variations on a program for displaying rectangular boxes on a display screen. This example explores the use of message sending and specialization in a program that is being extended and debugged.

Figure 12 gives our initial class definition for the class Box. Instances of this class represent vertically aligned rectangular regions on a display screen. The four instance variables store the coordinate and size information of a box. The origin of a box in the coordinate system is determined by the variables xOrigin and yOrigin and the default origin is at (100, 200). The size of a box is determined by variables xLength and yLength and the default size is 10 x 30. Operations on a box include moving it to a new origin, changing its size, and changing the shading inside the box. In the following we will specialize the Box class and also uncover a bug in it.

Message protocols define an interface for interacting with boxes. Instances of Box are created by sending it a New message. Size and position of an instance are established by sending it a Reshape message. Shade is established by sending it a Shade message. These messages provide a structured discipline for interaction with boxes, that is, a data abstraction. Outside agents need only know the relevant messages. They need not know the implementation of a box in terms of its instance variables.

Suppose that we wanted to create another kind of box with a visible border that frames it in the display. This BorderedBox would be essentially a Box with a border. This suggests that we employ inheritance and specialize the class definition of Box.

In programming BorderedBox several choices about the interpretation and representation of the border need to be made. The foremost question is about the treatment of coordinates of the border, that is, whether the border frames the outside of the box or is included as part of the box. For example, is the border included in the length measurements? If the border is on the outside, is the origin on the inside or the outside of the border? The answers to these questions do not come from principles of object-oriented programming, but rather from our intentions about the meaning of the BorderedBox program. The answer affects the meaning of the instance variables xOrigin, yOrigin, xLength, and yLength inherited from Box. For this example, we will assume that the borders are

Box

MetaClass Class

> EditedBy *(* dgb "31-September-84 11:23")*
>
> *doc (* Rectilinear box that can be displayed.)*

Supers (DisplayObject)

Instance Variables

> xLength 10 *doc (* length of the horizontal side.)*
>
> yLength 30 *doc (* length of the vertical side.)*
>
> xOrigin 100 *doc (* x coordinate of origin—lower left corner.)*
>
> yOrigin 200 *doc (* y coordinate of origin—lower left corner.)*

Methods

Move Box.Move	*doc (* Moves box (change origin) in the display.)*
	args (newXOrigin newYOrigin)
Reshape Box.Reshape	*doc (* Changes the location and axes of the box.)*
	args (newXOrigin newYOrigin NewXlength
	newYLength)
Shade Box.Shade	*doc (* Fills the inside of the box with a new shade.)*
	args (newShade)
Draw Box.Draw	*doc (* Displays the box.)*

Instances of this class represent vertically aligned rectangular regions on a display screen. The four instance variables store the coordinate and size information for a box. For example, the origin in the coordinate system is determined by the variables xOrigin and yOrigin and the default origin is at (100, 200). Operations on the box are defined by messages to the box. They include moving it to a new origin, changing the size of the box, and changing the shading inside the box.

Figure 12. Class Definition for the Box

intended only to make the boxes easier to visualize in the display and that for this purpose they will be treated as part of the box.

The next step is to decide whether any of the methods of Box need to be specialized in BorderedBox. Since a border needs to be redrawn when a box is increased in size, it is clear that at least the Reshape method needs some revision. Figure 14 shows a specialized Reshape method that uses ←Super to invoke the Reshape method from Box. The specialized Reshape also invokes local methods to Draw and Erase the boundary. These methods plus one for setting the size of the boundary must be added to BorderedBox. The Draw and Erase methods are for internal use, but the SetBorder method will become part of the external protocol. Figure 13 shows these methods together with a new instance variable for recording the size of the border.

The use of a variable for borderSize brings up a question of how the methods of the original Box class work for shading. In fact, they cannot work if the shade is not saved as part of the state of an instance (or is otherwise computable).

BorderedBox

MetaClass Class

    EditedBy *(* mjs "1-Oct-84 01:67")*
    doc *(* Like a Box except displays a black border. The origin is the
        outside of the border.)*

Supers (Box)

InstanceVariables

    borderSize 2 *doc (* width of the border.)*

Methods

    Reshape BorderedBox.Reshape
    SetBorder BorderedBox.SetBorder *doc (* Set a new border size.)*

                    args (newBorderSize)

    EraseBorder BorderedBox.EraseBorder
    DrawBorder BorderedBox.DrawBorder

A BorderedBox is like a box except that it is drawn with a variable-sized border in the display. BorderedBox is implemented by specializing Box. A new instance variable borderSize is added to record the size of border. The width of the border is included as part of the dimensions of the box.

Figure 13. Class Definition for the BorderedBox

(BorderedBox.Reshape (self newXOrigin newYOrigin newXLength newYLength)

   (←self EraseBorder) *(* Erase old border.)*

   (* Now Reshape box as before)

   (←Super self Reshape newXOrigin newYOrigin newXLength

   newYLength)

   (←self DrawBorder) *(* Draw new border.)*

   ]

The specialized Reshape method needs to redisplay a revised border when the shape of the box changes. ←Super is used to invoke the Reshape method from Box. The specialized Reshape also invokes methods to Draw and Erase the boundary. These methods plus one for setting the size of the boundary must be added to BorderedBox. The Draw and Erase methods are for internal use and the SetBorder method is part of the external protocol.

Figure 14. Reshape Method for BorderedBox

Box's Reshape method should use the current shade in order to fill new areas when a box is expanded. To fix this deficiency, we can now go back to the definition of Box to add a shade instance variable that will be saved by the Shade method. We can also modify Box's Reshape method to use this new variable.

   After the shade bug is fixed, we should ask whether the specialized class BorderedBox must also be changed. BorderedBox will inherit the shade instance variable and the revised Shade method. Furthermore, the specialized Reshape method in BorderedBox, which uses ←Super, will effectively inherit the shade changes from Box's Reshape method. In this example, the inheritance mechanisms of the language work for us in just the right way. This illustrates how language features can provide leverage for accommodating change.

Programming the DigiMeter

Gauges are favorite pedagogical examples in Loops because they use features of both object-oriented and access-oriented programming. They are defined as Loops classes and are driven by active values.

   Figure 15 illustrates a collection of gauges in Loops. Gauges are displayed in a *window*, an active rectangular region in the bitmap display. They have a black title bar for labels and a rectangular center region in which they display values. Instances of LCD (for "little character display") show their values

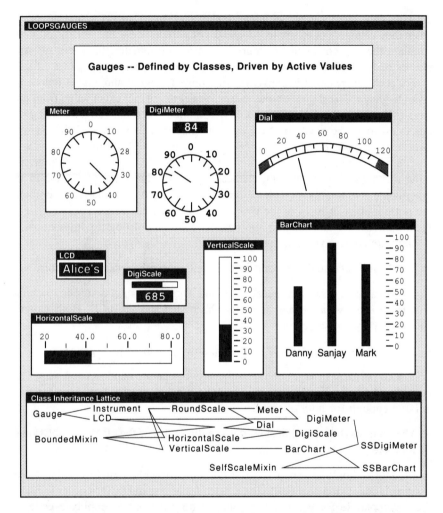

Gauges are tools used to monitor the values of object variables. They can be thought of as having probes that can be inserted on to the variables of an arbitrary Loops program. Gauges are defined in Loops as classes and driven by active values—the computational mechanism behind access-oriented programming in Loops. A browser at the bottom of the figure illustrates the relationships between the classes of gauges. From this figure, we can see that the DigiMeter is a combination of a Meter and an LCD. Other kinds of gauges, mimicking oscilloscope traces or chart recorders, would also be useful.

Figure 15. Gauges in Loops

digitally, but most gauges simulate analog motion to attract visual attention when they change. For example, subclasses of VerticalScale and HorizontalScale simulate the movement of "mercury" as in a thermometer. Instances of sub-classes of RoundScale move a "needle" in a round face.

For some purposes it is convenient to combine digital and analog output in a single gauge. The digital output makes it easy to read an exact value from the gauge. The analog output makes it easy to notice when the gauge is changing and to estimate the position of the current value in a fixed range. With gauges like this it is easy to tell at a glance that something is "half full."

The programming of combination gauges gives rise to a choice of program-ming techniques for combining classes. Figure 15 shows the DigiMeter as an inheritance combination of a Meter and an LCD. Such a gauge needs to combine the programmed features of the two classes. In the following we will consider the arguments for choosing an appropriate technique of object combination.

Here are some goals bearing on the design of a DigiMeter:

• The DigiMeter should respond in the standard way to gauge protocols.

For example, a single request to Set the DigiMeter should suffice, without having to send separate messages for the meter and the LCD. Both gauges should display the same correct value.

• The DigiMeter should use a single window to display both gauges.

The combination gauge should not have two separate windows and bars. The component gauges should appear in a single window on the display screen that is large enough for both of them.

• The combined description should make direct use of the classes for LCD and for Meter.

DigiMeter should use some method for combining Meter and LCD. This does not preclude making changes to the classes for Meter and LCD in order to make them compatible for combination, but we do not want to duplicate code or descriptions in DigiMeter. The class descriptions should continue to work whether the classes are used alone or in combination.

The three techniques of object combination supported in Loops are perspec-tives, composite objects, and multiple inheritance.

Using perspectives for combination, we would create a DigiMeter with one perspective for the Meter and one for the LCD. Unfortunately, the direct ap-proach to this would result in the creation of separate windows for each gauge. We could fix this for all of the gauges in the lattice, for example, by making a window be a perspective of a gauge. The main utility of perspectives is that they support switching among multiple views and instantiating these views on demand. In this application, we always need to create all of the views, and the views are very closely associated. Hence, the main features of perspectives don't do much work for us.

Using composite objects as the method combination, we would create a Digi-Meter with a Meter as one part and an LCD as another part. Again, the straight-forward combination would yield a separate window for each gauge. As before, we could revise all of the gauges in the lattice, perhaps treating a window as a part of a gauge. In addition, the DigiMeter description would need to identify the window parts of the Meter and LCD as referring to the same window. The main benefit of composite objects is to describe for instantiation a richly connected set of objects and to differentiate between objects and their parts. In this appli-cation, the connections between the parts are relatively sparse and the part/whole distinction doesn't do much work for us.

Using multiple inheritance for combination, we would create a DigiMeter as a class combining an LCD and a Meter. Since the LCD and Meter classes inherit their window descriptions from the same place, multiple inheritance yields exactly one window. As in the other cases, we may need to tune parts of the window description to make sure that it is large enough for both gauges, but this is a straightforward use of the inheritance notion. In multiple inheritance it is important to ask whether same-named variables in the combined class refer to the same thing. For this application, we need to be on the alert for the use of variables in Meter and LCD that have the same name but different meanings, but there are no such conflicts in this case.

The preceding arguments suggest that multiple inheritance is the most appro-priate technique of object combination for this application. The next step in designing a DigiMeter is to understand and design the interactions between the constituents. The main interactions are:

- The window should be large enough to accommodate both gauges.

- The methods for displaying both gauges should be invoked together.

The first interaction can be handled by specializing the method (UpdatePar-ameters) that establishes the window parameters. The major window sizing constraints come from the Meter, which must provide room for the calibrated circle and its interior needle. In the Loops implementation the DigiMeter method uses ←Super to invoke the parameter-setting code for the Meter and then revises them to allow extra room at the top of the window for the LCD.

The second interaction can be handled by specializing the Show Reading method for showing a reading. As shown earlier in Figure 9, this method consists of a simple application of ←SuperFringe which invokes the original ShowReading methods of both Meter and LCD. In Flavors this would have involved the application of a progn method combinator.

The Evolution of Classes—Gauge Examples

Most of our applications of Loops take place in a research environment in which new goals and ideas are always surfacing. In such an environment frequent revisions and extensions are a constant part of programming. To cover the kinds of reorganizations that we carry out in our work we have developed some idioms for systematic program change. This section considers three cycles of revision in the design of Loops gauges. Each cycle of revision has these steps:

- A new goal or requirement is introduced for the design.

- A conflict in the current organization is recognized between sharing of code and flexibility.

- A new factoring of information is chosen to ease the conflict.

Cycle 1. In our first example we will consider the addition of a DigiScale to the class inheritance lattice. A DigiScale will be a combination of a HorizontalScale and an LCD as in Figure 16.   A major design constraint for this example is that

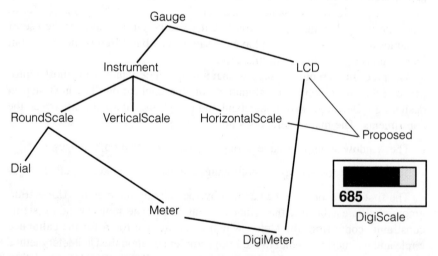

The proposed DigiScale will be a combination of a HorizontalScale and an LCD. An unusual programming constraint in this case is that we want to omit the tick marks from the horizontal scale portion. At issue is the fact that the code inherited from Instrument bundles in one chunk the drawing of the gauge and the drawing and labeling of the tick marks.

Figure 16. Programming the DigiScale

the DigiScale must be visually compact. To make it small we want to omit the tick marks and labels from the horizontal scale portion. Such a gauge would present both an exact digital value and an analog indication of the value within its range.

However, the plan of omitting the tick marks also interacts with the inheritance of existing code from HorizontalScale and Instrument. In particular, the display of instruments is governed by the ShowInstrument method of Instrument, which carries out the following sequence of steps:

- Draw the instrument structure (circular dials, and so forth).

- Draw and label the tick marks.

- Print the scale factor.

For the DigiScale this organization is too coarse. This illustrates a common situation where inheritance in a subclass requires finer granularity of description than was provided in the superclass. The situation arises often enough in our programming that we have a name for it—a *grainsize conflict*. In Loops, pieces of description which are intended to be independently inherited must be independently named—e.g., methods have their own selectors and instance variables have their own variable names. A specific fix in this case is to decompose the ShowInstrument method into several smaller methods that we can independently specialize, reorder, or omit.

Cycle 2. Sometimes a grainsize conflict is the first state in recognizing new possibilities in a design. In the previous example, we considered the creation of a special kind of horizontal scale that has no tick marks. We could generalize that idea to have vertical scales or even round scales without tick marks. Another observation in the same vein is that the round scale gauges differ from the others in the way that they indicate their values. Round scale gauges use a needle. Vertical and horizontal scale gauges use space filling—like the sliding of a column of mercury. Several other kinds of gauges are possible—such as a PieScale gauge—a round scale gauge that uses an expanding "slice of pie" to indicate its value.

This suggests that there are some independent properties of gauges that we could recognize:

- *Calibration*—gauges can have tick marks and scale factors or not.

- *Indicator style*—gauges can use needles or space filling to present values.

The recognition that a particular distinction arising in a subclass can be generalized is a common occurrence in object-oriented programming. Often there is a motivation to move structure up in the lattice to increase the amount of sharing.

We call this *promotion* of structure. Figure 17 illustrates a simple case of this where a method M1 and an instance variable IV1 are initially duplicated in two sibling classes.

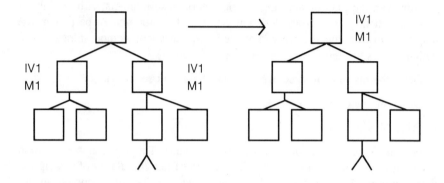

Often there is a motivation to move structure up in the class lattice in order to increase sharing. We call this *promotion* of structure. In this case a method M1 and an instance variable IV1 are initially in two sibling classes. Promotion would move them to their common superclass.

Figure 17. Promoting Methods and Variables

Promotion would move them to their common superclass. The Loops environment encourages and facilitates such activities by making them easy to do with interactive browsers that show the inheritance structure, and allowing menu-driven operations to make changes.

Figure 18 shows a first attempt to organize a class lattice for these distinctions. In this attempt, instruments are partitioned into CalibratedInstrument and UncalibratedInstrument. This partitioning tries to exploit the observation that the best-looking uncalibrated instruments are also the space-filling ones. The classes VerticalGraph, HorizontalGraph, and PieGraph are created as uncalibrated space-filling gauges. The main problem with this approach is the duplication of code. For example, code is duplicated between HorizontalScale and HoritzontalGraph, and between VerticalScale and VerticalGraph. This leads to a different proposal for a lattice as shown in Figure 19.

In the second proposal, a mixin is created for the code that generates tick marks and labels. The gauge lattice appears essentially the same as before the reorganization except that the classes are now uncalibrated. Classes like Vertical-Graph have calibrated subclasses like VerticalScale that use the CalibratedScale mixin. The mixin establishes the procedural connection between instrument

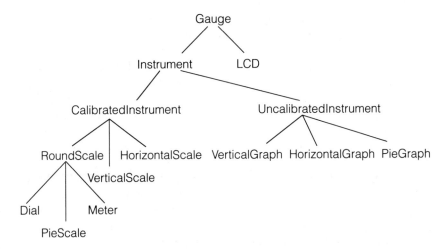

This lattice shows gauges partitioned into CalibratedInstrument and UncalibratedIn-strument which exploits the observation that the best-looking uncalibrated instru-ments are also the space-filling ones. However, code is duplicated, for example, between HorizontalScale and HorizontalGraph.

Figure 18. Rearranging the Lattice of Gauges

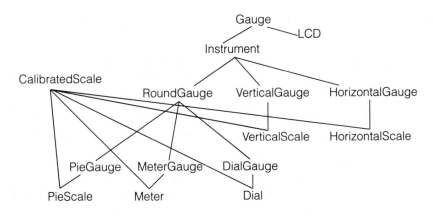

In this arrangement, a CalibratedScale mixin is created for tick marks and labels. In this reorganization there is a CalibratedScale mixin which is added to uncalibrated classes to create tick marks. For example, VerticalScale is a subclass of Vertical-Graph and uses the CalibratedScale mixin.

Figure 19. Rearranging the Lattice of Gauges, Again

drawing and tick mark drawing. Each subclass also supplies specialized local methods for arranging the tick marks and labels.

Cycle 3. Gauges have upper and lower bounds for the values that they display. When data go out of range, the standard behavior is to light up an "out of range" indicator and to "pin" the gauge to the maximum or minimum value. This highlights a nuisance with analog gauges. Their readings become useless when data go out of range. One idea is to have gauges automatically recompute their extreme points and scaling factors as needed. For example, if a gauge goes out of bounds, it could automatically increase the maximum reading by about 25 percent of the new high value subject to some constraints of display aesthetics.

The rescaling requirement is independent of the style of display, that is, it is independent of whether we are spinning a needle or driving mercury up and down. This suggests using a uniform technique for revising the scale for all the gauges. The natural choice for additive behavior is a mixin.

Unfortunately there is a difficulty in doing this for the BarChart. The BarChart is unique among the gauges in Figure 15 in that it displays several values at once. A SelfSealingMixin could be easily defined that would work for all of the gauges except the BarChart. This mixin would just use the value of the gauge in computing a new maximum. For a BarChart, it is necessary to look at all of the bars to determine the maximum. This seems to lead to the following design choices for using mixins:

• We could design two mixins. One for the BarChart and one for all the other gauges. (Equivalently we could just mandate that the gauge mixin should not be used with BarChart.)

• We could design one mixin that worked differently for the BarChart and the other gauges. The method for computing the maximum would need to check whether it was being used in a class with BarChart as a superclass.

• We could modify the definition of the single-value gauges by adding a method to simply return the value when asked for the maximum value.

The first two choices do not extend well if we later add additional multi-value gauges. In our Loops implementation, we chose the third option.

Usually we think of mixins as classes that we can mix in with any class whatsoever. For example, when the DatedObject mixin is added to a class it causes instances to have a date instance variable initalized with their date of creation. Some kinds of mixins are designed to be used with a more limited set of classes. This example illustrates a case where the *mixees* can fruitfully be modified slightly to accommodate the mixin. The modification broadens the set of classes with which the mixin is compatible.

Conclusion and Summary

Objects are a uniform programming element for computing and saving state. This makes them ideal for simulation problems where it is necessary to represent collections of things that interact. They have also been advocated for applications in systems programming since many things with state must be represented, such as processes, directories, and files. Augmented by mechanisms for annotation, they have also become important in the current tools for knowledge engineering.

As object languages have become widespread, considerable interest has been expressed in developing standards so that objects could be used as a portable base for programs and knowledge bases. Towards this end, the Common LISP Object-Oriented Programming Subcommittee is now considering several proposals to extend Common LISP with objects.

The diversity of language concepts discussed here suggests that research is very active in this area. Standards will need to provide the kind of open-endedness and flexibility that enables languages to endure.

As object-oriented programming has taken hold in the mainstream of AI languages, they have reinforced a more general principle. There are multiple paradigms for programming. Procedure-oriented programming and object-oriented programming are but two of a larger set of possibilities that includes: rule-based programming, access-oriented programming, logic-based programming, and constraint-based programming. Different paradigms are for different purposes and fill different representational niches.

In this chapter, we have not tried to describe all of the ways in which features of object-oriented programming have been achieved in the context of other systems. For example, logic programming has inspired some interesting mergers. In Concurrent Prolog (Shapiro and Takeuchi, 1983), objects are represented by processes, and messages are passed to the process along a stream. Delegation is used to achieve the effect of inheritance. In Uranus (Nakashima, 1982), objects are bundles of axioms in a database. Inheritance is done by following links in the databases, using a logic-based language to express the methods.

In Uniform (Kahn, 1981), objects are represented by expressions, and methods as operations on objects that would unify with the *head* of the method. Inheritance is implemented by viewing one expression as another (through an axiom that states, for example, that (SQUARE X) is equivalent to (RECTANGLE XX)). This has the nice property that "inheritance" can go in both directions—from specialization to super, and from super with the right parameters to specialization.

Languages that combine multiple paradigms gracefully are known as hybrid or integrated languages. Languages that succeed less well might be called "smorgasbord" languages. In any case, language paradigms are no longer going their separate ways and attempting to do all things. Separate paradigms now co-exist and are beginning to co-evolve.

References

Bobrow, D. G., Kahn, K., Kiczales, G., Masinter, L., Stefik, M. J., & Zdybel, F. (1985). *CommonLoops: Merging Common LISP and object-oriented programming* (Technical Report ISL–85–8). Palo Alto, CA: Xerox Palo Alto Research Center.

Bobrow, D. G., & Stefik, M. J. (1981). *The Loops manual* (Technical Report KB–VLSI–81–13). Palo Alto, CA: Xerox Palo Alto Research Center.

Bobrow, D. G., & Winograd, T. (1977). An overview of KRL, a knowledge representative language. *Cognitive Science, 1(1)*, 3–46.

Borning, A. (1979). *A constraint-oriented simulation laboratory* (Stanford Computer Science Department Report STAN–CS–79–746). Stanford, CA: Stanford University.

Dahl, O. J., & Nygaard, K. (1966). SIMULA—an Algol-based simulation language. *Communications of the ACM, 9*, 671–678.

Drescher, G. L. (1985). *The Object LISP user manual (preliminary)*. Cambridge, MA: LMI Corporation.

Fikes, R., & Kehler, T. (1985). The role of frame-based representation in reasoning. *Communications of the ACM, 28(9)*, 904–920.

Goldberg, A., & Robson, D. (1983). *Smalltalk-80: The language and its implementation*. Reading, MA: Addison-Wesley.

Goldstein, I., & Bobrow, D. G. (1980). Descriptions for a programming environment. *Proceedings of the National Conference on Artificial Intelligence* (pp. 187–189). AAAI-80. Stanford, CA.

Goldstein, I. P., & Roberts, R. B. (1977). NUDGE, a knowledge-based scheduling program. *Proceedings of the International Joint Conference on Artificial Intelligence* (pp. 257–263). IJCAI-77. Cambridge, MA.

Henderson, D. A. (1986). The Trillium user interface design environment. *Proceedings of the ACM Conference on Computer Human Interaction* (pp. 221–227). Boston, MA.

Kahn, K. (1981). Uniform—A language based upon unification which unifies (much of) LISP, PROLOG, and Act 1. *Proceedings of the International Joint Conference on Artificial Intelligence* (pp. 933–939). IJCAI-81. Vancouver, B.C.

Lieberman, H. (1981). *A Preview of Act 1* (Artificial Intelligence Laboratory Memo No. 625). Cambridge, MA: Massachusetts Institute of Technology.

Minsky, M. A. (1975). A framework for representing knowledge. In P. Winston (Ed.), *The psychology of computer vision*. New York: McGraw-Hill.

Nakashima, H. (1982). PROLOG/KR—Language features. *Proceedings of the First International Logic Programming Conference*. Marseille, France: ADDP-GIA.

Rees, J. A., Adams, N. I., & Meehan, J. R. (1984). *The T manual* (4th ed.). New Haven, CT: Yale University.

Shapiro, E., & Takeuchi, A. (1983). Object oriented programming in concurrent PROLOG. *New Generation Computing 1*, 25–48.

Smith, R. G. (1983). *Structured object programming in STROBE* (AI Memo No. 18). Ridgefield, CT: Schlumberger-Doll.

Snyder, A. (1985) *Object-oriented proposal for Common LISP* (ATC–85–1). Palo Alto, CA: Hewlett Packard Laboratories.

Stefik, M. J. (1979). An examination of a frame-structure representation system. *Proceedings of the International Joint Conference on Artificial Intelligence* (pp. 845–852). IJCAI-79. Tokyo, Japan.

Stefik, M. J., Bobrow, D. G., & Kahn, K. (1989). Integrating access-oriented programming into a multi-paradigm environment. In M. Richer (Ed.), *AI tools and techniques*. Norwood, NJ: Ablex Publishing Corporation.

Weinreb, D., & Moon, D. (1981). *Lisp Machine Manual*. Cambridge, MA: Symbolics, Inc.

Chapter 2

Integrating Access-Oriented Programming Into a Multiparadigm Environment*

Mark J. Stefik
Daniel G. Bobrow
Kenneth M. Kahn
Intelligent Systems Laboratory, Xerox Palo Alto Research Center

The Loops knowledge programming system (Bobrow and Stefik, 1983) contains a number of integrated paradigms of programming. It builds on the function-oriented programming of Interlisp-D (Sanella, 1983) and adds the familiar paradigms of rule-oriented and object-oriented programming. Its most unusual contribution is the addition of an access-oriented programming paradigm not found in most systems.

In *access-oriented* programming, fetching or storing data can cause procedures to be invoked. In terms of actions and side effects, this is dual to object-oriented programming. In object-oriented programming, when one object sends a message to another, the receiving object may change its data as a side effect. In access-oriented programming, when one object changes its data, a message may be sent as a side effect.

Access-oriented programming is based on an entity called an *annotated value* that associates *annotations* with data. These annotations can be installed on object variables and can be nested recursively. In Loops there are two kinds of annotated values: *property annotations* and *active values*.

Property annotations associate arbitrary extendible property lists with data. Active values associate procedures with data so that methods are invoked when

---

*This paper was previously published in *IEEE Software, 3(1)*, 10–18, January, 1986. It is reprinted here with the kind permission of the editors and the publisher. A shorter version of this article appears in *Conf. Record HICSS-19*, Hawaii International Conference on System Sciences, January 8–10, Honolulu.

data are fetched and stored. Active values are the basic computational mechanisms of access-oriented programming.[1]

In the access-oriented paradigm, programs are factored into two kinds of parts: parts that *compute* and parts that *monitor* the computations. Figure 1 shows this kind of factoring for a traffic simulation program. The traffic simulation program has two modules, called the simulator and the display controller. (This example was inspired by related work in Smalltalk-80 [Goldberg and Robson, 1983] on the partitioning of various programs into models, views, and controllers.)

The simulator represents the dynamics of traffic. It has objects for such things as automobiles, trucks, roads, and traffic lights. These objects exchange messages to simulate traffic interactions. For example, when a traffic light object turns green, it sends messages to start traffic moving.

The display controller has objects representing images of the traffic and provides an interactive user interface for scaling and shifting the views. It has methods for presenting graphics information. The simulator and the display controller can be developed separately, provided there is agreement on the structure of the simulation objects.

Access-oriented programming provides the glue for connecting them at runtime. The process of gluing is *dynamic* and *reversible*. When a user tells the display controller to change the views, the controller can make and break connections to the simulator as needed for its monitoring.

To illustrate this example, suppose that the simulator is running and the next event is a traffic light turning green. The traffic light object could then send a go

---

[1]Access-oriented programming in Loops went through several stages of development. From the beginning, Loops provided one level of property values for annotating object variables. Active values were added shortly thereafter. The unification of these two ideas and their representation as objects was proposed after several years of experience and was under development at the time this article was written.

Access-oriented programming has historical roots in languages like SIMULA and Interlisp-D, which provide ways of converting record accesses into a computation for all records of a given type. It is also related to the virtual data idea in some computer architectures. For example, in the Burroughs B5000, a tag bit associated with data caused data access to be converted into a procedure invocation.

More immediate predecessors are the ideas of procedural attachment from frame languages like KRL (Bobrow and Winograd, 1977), FRL (Roberts and Goldstein, 1977), and KL-One (Brachman, 1979). Attached procedures are programs that are associated with object variables and that are triggered under specific conditions.

Access-oriented programming in Loops is intended to satisfy a somewhat different set of purposes than attached procedures. This has led to a synthesis of ideas with some important differences. Although a thorough historical review is beyond the scope of this article, we occasionally return to attached procedures to show how language features in Loops diverge from that work.

Simulation model   Interface   Display controller

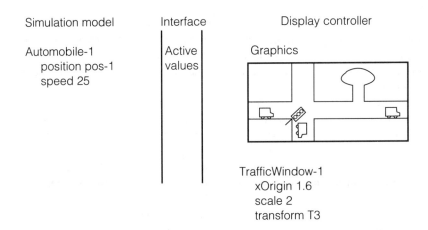

This traffic simulation shows an interactive graphical simulation system for city traffic. The traffic simulator's objects include automobiles, city blocks, emergency vehicles, and traffic lights that exchange messages to simulate traffic interactions. The display controller has objects for traffic icons, viewing transformations, and windows that display different parts of the city connected to the simulation objects by active values.

Figure 1. Traffic Simulation

message to each of the stopped vehicles. One of the vehicles, say Car37, receives the message and computes its initial velocity and position.

When the method in Car37 updates its position instance variable, it triggers an active value that then sends an update message to the display object StreetScene13. StreetScene13 may then make a change to the computer display screen so that an image representing Car37 appears to move.

This sequence of events shows how the updating of the computer display is a side effect of running the simulator.

Basic Concepts of Access-Oriented Programming

In Loops there are two kinds of annotated values: *property annotations* and *active values*. Property annotations associate extendible sets of arbitrary properties with data. Active values associate procedures with data so that methods are invoked when data are fetched and stored.

Annotated values have several important characteristics:

Annotations are invisible to programs that are not looking for them. This is the first invariant of access-oriented programming. Adding and removing annotations are common changes to programs in this paradigm. Making these changes to programs does not cause the programs to stop working, unless the programs use the annotations. New annotations do not interfere with old programs that do not refer to them. For active values, this claim ultimately depends on the condition that the user-defined procedures have noninterfering side effects.

Annotations have a low computational overhead when there are no annotations and also when there are annotations that programs do not reference (such as unreferenced properties). This characteristic takes noninterference a step further. Not only are annotations invisible to programs that ignore them, but they also do not slow things down much. Accesses can either be a function call or compiled open, and the Loops implementation reduces the overhead to a single type check which has microcode support.

Annotations are recursive; they too can be annotated. This extends the main invariant above to cover multiple annotations (that is, adding annotations to data that are already annotated). This characteristic allows the creation of descriptions of descriptions in the case of nested properties and of multiple, independent side effects in the case of nested active values.

Annotations can be efficiently accessed starting from the annotated object. This constraint demands that annotations can be accessed quickly and in a standard way. This characteristic is important for programs that reference annotations explicitly (for example, using the value of a particular property). It is also important for programs that test annotations implicitly (for example, automatic testing for and triggering of active values).

It distinguishes annotated values from ad hoc data structures for annotations that point to their data. Such annotations would have the other characteristics, but would require that programs either search for pointers to data or else provide idiosyncratic arrangements for storing and indexing the annotations.

Annotations are objects that can be specialized and used with standard protocols. This characteristic comes from the features of object-oriented programming to simplify the creation of new kinds of annotations.

Active values have their own variables for saving state. This characteristic comes for free, because active values are objects. As will be shown later, this feature removes a potential path of interaction between active values that are intended to be independent.

Active Values

Active values convert a variable reference to a method invocation. They can be installed on the value of any object variable or property. When an active value has been installed, any part of the program that accesses the variable will trigger the commutation. This is the major lever for elision in the access-oriented programming paradigm.

Elision is the ability to state concisely and without redundancy what is intended. This is a hallmark of appropriate language support for a paradigm. By eliminating excess verbiage, the programmer can focus on the essentials, having both less opportunity for mistakes and more easily understood programs.

An alternative approach would be to provide a functional interface for changing each variable that needs to be monitored. Active values eliminate the need for functional interfaces since they can be installed on each variable as needed.

Active values appear in variables of objects. Each active value contains a localState to hold the value that should appear in that variable. Since an active value is an object, it can also contain additional information in other variables of the active value object. So users can easily view the contents of an active value, an active value is shown as

#[< *activeValueClass* > *localState otherSlot1*$_1$ Value $_1$...]

The class of the active value <activeValueClass > determines the behavior of the active value on access. Below is an example of an active value installed in a Loops object. In this example, an active value is the interface between objects in a simulator and a display controller. The object Automobile-1 represents an automobile in a traffic simulation model. The xPosition instance variable represents the position of the car in the simulation world. The value of xPosition has been made into an active value to connect Automobile-1 with objects in the display controller.

```
Automobile-1
    speed 25
    xPosition
        #[InformDisplayController 50
           viewObjects (<DispObj1> <DispObj2>)]
```

When the simulation stores (that is, puts) a value into xPosition, the Loops access functions will recognize the active value and will send it a Put-WrappedValue message. The protocol for the PutWrappedValue message is defined by the InformDisplayController class for the active value.

In this case, update messages will be sent to appropriate objects, DispObj1 and DispObj2, in the display controller. These objects respond by updating the views in windows of the display.

InformDisplayController is an active value class that updates objects in the display controller. Its special method for storing informs all elements contained in its instance variable viewObjects.

Like other classes in Loops, classes for active values are organized in the inheritance lattice. The class ActiveValue defines a standard protocol for *putting* and *getting* values. This protocol is specialized in each kind of active value to describe the particular side effects of getting or putting a value. Most subclasses of ActiveValue either specialize the GetWrappedValue protocol to specify side effects when data are fetched or specialize the PutWrappedValue protocol to specify side effects when data are stored.

The default behavior for GetWrappedValue is to return the value in the localState. The default behavior of PutWrappedValue is to store the new value in the localState. As is discussed later, accessing data in the localState may trigger additional side effects if active values are nested.

Property Annotations

The second kind of annotated value in Loops is property annotation. Property annotations can be installed on the value of any object variable or property. Properties are useful for describing the relationship between the value of an object variable and the object itself. They also provide a mechanism for storing derived values that can be cached locally.

The idea of property annotations in Loops was motivated by several applications to knowledge programming. Property annotations provide a way of attaching extra descriptions to data for guiding its interpretation. Instance Truck-37, shown below, contains several kinds of annotations that have been used in knowledge engineering applications.

Truck-37
    owner PIE   *doc (*Owner of truck.)*
    highway I66   *doc (*Route number of the highway.)*
                                           preHighway I9

    milePost 276   *doc (*Location on the highway.)*
                                       dataType Integer

    totalWeight 10   *doc (*Current weight of cargo in tons.)*
                                       upperLimit 12
    stoppingPlace FortWorth   *reason AuditRecord 12*
    arrivalTime 1400   *certaintyFactor .8*

Properties can be used to keep a history of values for a variable. The variable highway has a property prevHighway to record the previous value for the variable. Properties can also be used to save data type information for dynamic checking of programs. This is illustrated by the variable milePost.

Properties can be used to save constraints on values, such as the upperLimit property of totalWeight. In some knowledge engineering applications it is important to save a record of program inferences. For example, the certaintyFactor property of arrivalTime records a measure of the confidence in the estimate of arrival time, and the reason property of stoppingPlace saves a record of the reasoning step that led to this choice of a place to stop.

These properties have no special significance to the Loops kernel. Loops just provides a way of associating the property lists with data so that application programs can find them starting with the data and interpret them appropriately.

We have also considered an implementation in which the properties are stored on an object-wide basis and are separated from the annotated value. This has the disadvantage that the collection of properties of a variable cannot be manipulated as a single entity. The advantage is that variable access is not slowed down by the presence of properties.

Like active values, the idea of extendible property lists for variables has its historical roots in frame languages. Alternative ways of annotating values have been tried in actor and constraint languages (Steele, 1980, is one example). The major variations in Loops are that property annotations are objects that are created on demand, can be recursively nested, and share much of the implementation of active values.

Recursive Annotations

Annotated values can be nested. Nested property notations enable what we loosely call descriptions of descriptions. Nested active values allow the programming of multiple, independent side effects. Both kinds of annotated values have an instance variable, conventionally named localState, used to hold the data.

When annotated values are nested, they are arranged in a chain so the outermost annotated value points to an inner one through its localState and so the innermost annotated value contains the ultimate datum.

When active values are nested, then GetWrappedValue methods or Put-WrappedValue methods are procedurally composed. Getting a value eventually causes all of the GetWrappedValue methods to be invoked. Similarly, putting a value causes all of the PutWrappedValue methods to be invoked.

The first step in this sequence is that a PutWrappedValue message is sent to the outermost active value. The outer PutWrappedValue method then performs a computation and at some point needs to store the data in its localState.

This step involves checking whether the localState contains an annotated value. If not, the data is stored directly in localState. If yes, a PutWrappedValue message is sent to the nested annotated value using the same protocol as the outermost active value.

The code for performing this test and storing the data is inherited from AnnotatedValue and is invoked using ← Super as shown below. The PutWrapped-Value method invoked by the ← Super is inherited from the class ActiveValue.

[LAMBDA (self newValue object varName path type)
(* *This is a specialized*
PutWrappedValue method
for....)
(* *Specialized side effect code*
invoked before nesting goes here.)
...
(* *This ← Super stores localState*
or invokes a nested active value.)
(← Super)
  (* *Specialized side effect code*
  invoked after nesting goes here.)
...]

For multiple active values, the net effect is that all of the specialized PutWrappedValue methods for all of the nested active values will be invoked, and the data will ultimately be stored in the localState of the innermost one.

GetWrappedValue methods are based on a similar procedural template. Depending on how these procedural templates are filled out, a PutWrappedValue method or GetWrappedValue method can perform its side effects before accessing data in localState, after accessing data in localState, or in some combination of the two.

Language support for attached procedures has historically aspired to provide a discipline for controlling interactions among multiple attached procedures. To this end, two issues have been addressed: classifying the kinds of trigger conditions and specifying the order[2] and conditions of execution for multiple procedures.

For example, FRL provided event categories for triggering such as *if-needed, if-added,* and *if-removed.* In Loops, the only triggering events are the fetching

---

[2]Loops allows programmatic control of the order of access to localState of an activeValue and other operations. Different common applications require variations in the time ordering of the side effect and accessing the localState.

For applications like checking a constraint, it is appropriate to check the constraint before the new value is stored. For applications such as computing the sum of the new localState and other data (for example, to maintain a derived value for the sum of a set of figures), one first gets data and then does the summation. A more extensive set of examples is summarized as:

Operation	Order of Side Effect	Side Effect for Application
Put	Side effect first	Check a constraint
Put	Side effect second	Update a gauge
Get	Side effect first	Check access privileges
Get	Side effect second	Combine with other data

and storing of data. Specialization of fetching and storing must be programmed in the access methods of the active values. Other events, such as object creation, are handled by methods on objects that can be specialized (thus taking advantage of the integration with the object-oriented paradigm).

Frame languages have taken various approaches to specifying the order of invocation for multiple procedures. KL-One distinguished between three types of triggers: pre, post, and after. Other frame languages have used an ordered list to specify the order, with exceptions indicated by the use of special tokens returned by the procedures as they are executed.

We have found these sublanguages unnecessary for the common case of composed procedures—and too weak for the exceptional cases of complex ordering. Loops avoids introducing a sublanguage for control by using nesting of active values for the common case of functional composition and by using the control structures of LISP inside the methods for the complex cases.

Programming languages like Flavors (Weinreb and Moon, 1984) and Smalltalk-80 (Goldberg and Robson, 1983) support specialized access methods for variables. However, these methods are applicable to all instances of a class. No language support is provided for dynamically attaching (and detaching) methods to individuals.

Applications of Access-Oriented Programming

Access-oriented programming in Loops started out not as a programming paradigm, but rather as a minor variation of an implementation for attached procedures. As we have tried new applications, we have looked for ways to change Loops that would simplify our applications. These changes and simplifications led to the development of the access-oriented paradigm. This section presents a sampling of applications that have shaped the development of the paradigm.

Gauges

When a technician fixes a broken piece of electronic equipment, he brings to the task a collection of measuring tools, such as voltmeters and oscilloscopes. These tools enable him to observe the behavior of a circuit as registered by a probe that he attaches to the circuit paths.

An analogous set of instruments is available in Loops that uses active values as probes for data. For example, one can attach a fuel-gauge active value to the contents of the fuel tank of some truck in the traffic simulator. This active value connects the truck object to a gauge object. Whenever the simulator changes the value of fuel in the truck, the gauge object updates the image on the screen.

The use of a gauge in Loops is very much like taking a meter off the shelf and attaching its probe to a circuit. One simply creates an instance of the appropriate gauge and sends it a message telling it to attach itself to the desired object variable. Figure 2 pictures the object hierarchy for the set of gauges standardly available in Loops and the set's screen representation.

A gauge is connected to the monitored variable through an active value, an instance of the GaugeProbe class. The important features of GaugeProbe are its variable myGauge and its specialized PutWrappedValue method. Its variable myGauge is analogous to the wire that connects a physical probe to its display instrument. This arrangement also works for attaching multiple gauges on a single datum.

In an earlier implementation of gauges, the active values used fixed properties of the monitored variables to save state, such as pointers to their associated gauges. In that arrangement, special precautions were necessary to keep multiple gauges from interfering with each other.

We now recognize that multiple gauges have independent purposes and should have independent resources. By representing GaugeProbes as Loops objects and using their own state for storing state information, we eliminate an unwanted path of interaction among multiple probes.

This principle simplifies the correct implementation of independent monitoring processes. It is one of the most important differences between active values and attached procedures.

We use gauges as a tool for instrumenting programs. Although gauge-like displays have been used in computer programs for years, their special attraction in Loops is that they can be attached to data in arbitrary programs without changing the program.

To instrument data in most programming languages, it is necessary to find all of the places in the source program that can change the data and then add code at each place to invoke a display package. Access-oriented programming makes it possible to annotate the program in only one place: the variable to be monitored.

This makes gauges considerably more practical as debugging aids. Gauges provide a more focused way of monitoring program states, with independent views of different aspects.

Traps for Variables

Access traps are another application of active values that is generally useful for debugging. They are used to suspend program execution when some variable is referenced. The usual action wanted in a trap is an invocation of a debugging executive, such as the Interlisp break package. Such traps are an important tool for identifying the conditions in a large program when some data are erroneously changed.

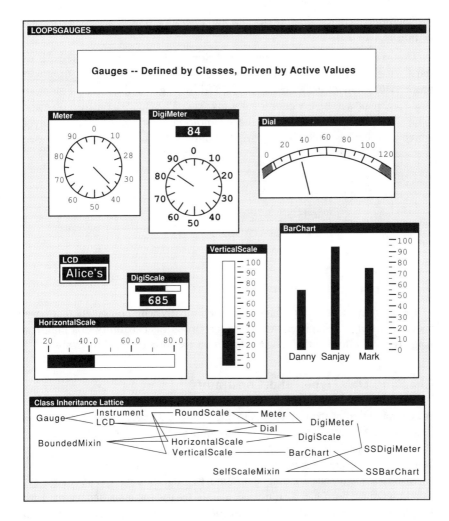

These gauges display the value of the variable to which they are attached. The gauges are updated when the variables are changed. Some, like the vertical scale on the left, can rescale themselves if the value exceeds the gauge limit.

Figure 2. Gauges in Loops

Loops provides several kinds of traps:

- GetTraps, which detect when a program fetches a value,
- PutTraps, which detect when a program stores a value,
- AccessTraps, which detect both stores and fetches, and
- ConditionalTraps, which perform a trap operation only if an auxiliary condition is satisfied.

The example below shows the annotation of the object Truck-37 with two traps. Truck-37 has traps on the value of stoppingPlace and on the upperLimit property of totalWeight. When a program tries to change the value of stopping-Place, a break will be unconditionally invoked. The ConditionalTrap on upper-Limit illustrates the use of an auxiliary condition to determine when to invoke a break. In this case, the break is invoked only if the new value for the property is greater than 15.

```
Truck-37
    totalWeight #[ConditionalTrap 12
                 when (GREATERP newValue
                       (@ containingObject
                          totalWeight::upperLimit))]
        upperlimit 15
    stoppingPlace #[PutTrap Fort Worth]
```

Historically, access traps have been used mostly with computers that have a special built-in trap register. Active values bring this capability to a high-level language and allow multiple variables to be monitored simultaneously.

Checking Data Types and Constraints

A generalization of the trap idea is to check new data against constraints before it is stored. An important kind of constraint is a check of the type of data being stored. This kind of specification is of central importance in strongly-typed computer languages, where types are checked at compile time.

However, in a late-binding exploratory programming environment, type checking must be done at run-time and is easily implemented using active values. The example below illustrates some type checking notations in Loops.

In this example, the instance variable milePost has a property datatype with the value Integer used by various graphics programs, interpreters, and compilers. Since there is no active value on milePost, it will not be automatically checked during an arbitrary store operation. In contrast, the variable totalWeight has a CheckDataType active value.

During a store operation, this active value will detect an error (or trap) if the new value is not an integer. The case for the arrivalTime instance variable is similar, except that the property datatype has an IntegerSpecification as its value.

These specifications are special objects put on the property list of the variable. These objects have methods for checking more complicated kinds of constraints, such as numeric ranges. The stoppingPlace instance variable has a specification that checks the class lattice to verify that the value is an instance of a city in Texas. These specification objects are put on the property list (not inside the active value) because they are also used for other purposes, such as intelligent editing of the instance Truck-43.

```
Truck-43
    milePost 276 datatype Integer
    ...
    totalWeight #[CheckDataType 10] datatype Integer
    arrivalTime #[CheckDataType 1400]
        datatype #$IntegerSpecification289
    stoppingPlace #[CheckDataType FortWorth]
        datatype #$CityInTexasSpecification
    ...
```

Indirection

Some computers have a way of tagging a memory location as containing an indirect address. Any attempt to fetch data from such a location causes data to be fetched instead from the indirect address. Storing data works analogously.

Active values provide an implementation for this idea so that fetches and stores on data cause references to some other object. The IndirectReference class of active values provides for referencing data indirectly in another object. It stores an access path to the real storage location.

This indirection example is fundamentally different in an important way from the gauge examples cited earlier. For gauges, when there are multiple active values, the order of nesting doesn't matter much. Side effects are independent and it is enough to ensure that they are all carried out.

The case is different for IndirectReference. These active values do not expect other active values to be more deeply nested. Their correct operation requires that they be the most deeply nested values so they will have the last GetWrappedValue or PutWrappedValue operation.

To support this need, active values follow a protocol of informing nested active values when they are installed. This enables active values whose placement is critical to adjust the order of nesting.

Truckin' and the Track Announcer

One of the largest programs written in Loops is the Truckin' knowledge game. The Truckin' program and related programs make extensive use of access-oriented programming.

Truckin' is a board game inspired in part by Monopoly. Figure 3 shows a snapshot of a Truckin' game board. The board has road stops arranged along a highway (which implicitly loops along the edges of the board). The players in the game drive trucks around, buying and selling commodities. Their goal is to make a profit. The game is based on a relatively complicated simulation that includes such things as road hazards, perishable and fragile goods, bandits, gas stations, and weigh stations.

An unusual feature of Truckin' is that the players are actually computer programs developed by the students taking a course on knowledge programming in Loops (Stefik, Bobrow, Mittal, and Conway, 1983). We use the game as a rich and animated environment for teaching principles of knowledge programming.

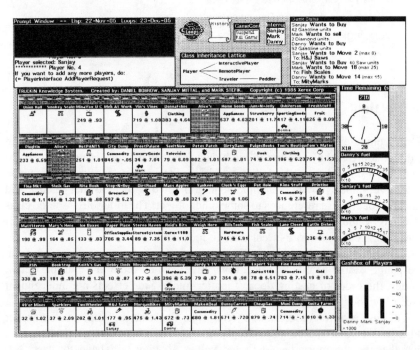

This is a display from the Truckin' game. Trucks are controlled by user programs. They must buy and sell goods and must avoid the bandits in black cars. The display is maintained by active value probes into the simulation.

Figure 3. Display from Truckin'

One of the design issues faced in implementing Truckin' was to find a way to ensure that the picture of the game board is always up to date with the underlying simulation. Several people were involved in writing the Truckin' simulator. There are many places where the values in the road stops could be changed either by direct action of the game master or by the need to maintain some constraints.

As it was in the simulator/display controller example cited earlier, our approach was to connect the screen image of each road stop to the underlying object variables. Each road stop image in the display is a sort of gauge monitoring part of the simulator.

A related program is the Truckin' Track Announcer, written by Martin Kay. The visual display of Truckin' changes quite rapidly during a competition. One of the ideas that came up during the Loops courses was to augment the display with a sort of radio announcer, an automatic program that would generate interesting spoken commentary about the competition as it unfolded.

The design of the Track Announcer had some of the same constraints as the game display. It needed to be informed about relevant changes in the progress of the game. Furthermore, it needed to be developed separately from Truckin' at a time when Truckin' itself was still evolving. Figure 4 illustrates the basic

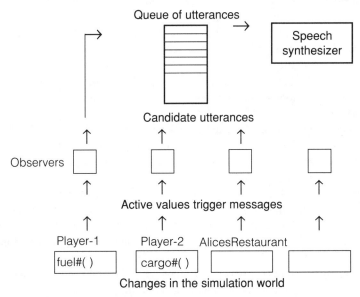

Observer demons watch for interesting patterns in the Truckin' game that can be converted to utterances. A new observer can be inserted at any time using an active value probe.

Figure 4. Truckin' Game Observers

architecture of the design. Active values were used to connect the Track Announcer to key variables in the players and road stops. These active values sent messages to a collection of objects called *observers*.

Observers are responsible for detecting interesting patterns of change in the game and then generating comments about them. These comments are placed on a queue of candidate utterances. A priority scheme is then used to select the next utterance to, for example, send it to a speech synthesizer device.

The observers in the Track Announcer are like *demons* in the Planner language (Hewitt, 1969). Demons are programs triggered whenever specified conditions become satisfied. A key implementation consideration for demons is finding an efficient way to monitor the demon conditions.

While Loops does not currently support demons, the Track Announcer example suggests how active values could be used in their implementation. For example, a demon compiler could convert a source description of demon conditions and generate an appropriate set of active values installed on the necessary variables.

Conclusion

Access-oriented programming is based on annotated values that associate annotations with data. These annotations can be dynamically attached to and removed from object variables and can be nested recursively. Loops provides the following three language features that accommodate the dynamic addition and deletion of annotations.

The first feature is that annotated values are invisible to programs that are not looking for them. Annotations can be added to programs without causing them to stop working.

The second feature is that annotated values are recursive. They can be added to data that are already annotated. Nested properties support the notion of descriptions of descriptions. Nested active values enable multiple, independent side effects on variable access.

The third feature is that annotated values are objects and have their own independent local variables for saving state. This contrasts with the technique of using variables or properties of the monitored object to save state. This language feature removes a path of potential interference among multiple active values intended to be independent.

These language features support the access-oriented paradigm. They provide concise expression of intent and facilitate program evolution.

References

Bobrow, D. G., & Winograd, T. (1977). An overview of KRL, a knowledge representation language. *Cognitive Science, 1(1),* 3–46.

Bobrow, D. G., & Stefik, M. J. (1983). *The Loops manual.* Palo Alto, CA: Xerox Corporation.

Brachman, R. J. (1979). On the epistemological status of semantic networks. In N. V. Findler (Ed.), *Associative networks: Representation and use of knowledge by computers.* New York: Academic Press.

Goldberg, A., & Robson, D. (1983). *Smalltalk-80—The language and its implementation.* Reading, MA: Addison-Wesley.

Hewitt, C. E. (1969). Planner: A language for proving theorems in robots. *Proceedings of the First International Conference on Artificial Intelligence* (pp. 295–302). Washington, DC.

Roberts, R. B., & Goldstein, I. P. (1977). *The FRL primer* (Technical Report AIM–408). Cambridge, MA: Artificial Intelligence Laboratory, MIT.

Sanella, M. (1983). *The Interlisp-D reference manual.* Palo Alto, CA: Xerox Corporation.

Steele, G. (1980). *The definition and implementation of a computer programming language based on constraints* (Technical Report AI–TR–595). Cambridge, MA: Artificial Intelligence Laboratory, MIT.

Stefik, M. J., Bobrow, D. G., Mittal, S., & Conway, L. (1983). Knowledge programming in Loops: Report on an experimental course. *AI Magazine, 4(3),* 3–13.

Weinreb, D., & Moon, D. (1980). *Lisp machine manual.* Cambridge, MA: Symbolics Corporation.

Part II

Tools and Techniques for Acquiring, Representing, and Explaining Knowledge

Chapter 3

An Evaluation of Expert System Development Tools*

Mark H. Richer
Mountain Lake Software, Inc.

In recent years there has been a great deal of interest in the commercial applications of *knowledge-based systems* (commonly called *expert systems*). Interest in these systems intensified with the development of programs that solve complex problems at an expert level (Hayes-Roth, Waterman, and Lenat, 1983; Buchanan and Shortliffe, 1984; Johnson, 1984; Waterman, 1986). In contrast with conventional software systems, knowledge-based systems generally represent domain and problem-solving knowledge explicitly in a database (called a *knowledge base*) that is separate from other program code (e.g., an interpreter or *inference engine*). Importantly, the knowledge base can be used for multiple purposes including problem solving, explanation, and instruction. Expert problem-solving knowledge can also be used in conjunction with a knowledge-based simulation to monitor or control a complex device or process (Fagan, Kunz, Feigenbaum,

*This chapter is a revised version of an article that appeared in *Expert Systems, 3(3)*, 166–183, 1986. It is reprinted here with the kind permission of the editors and the publisher.

Many people were helpful in the preparation of this chapter. A special thanks goes to Bruce Buchanan for his encouragement, support, and feedback throughout this project. Every effort was made to present a clear and accurate description of each system reviewed, but any errors, omissions, or views expressed in the chapter are solely the responsibility of the author. On the other hand, this chapter would not have been possible without the help of many individuals, who are or were employed at one of the four companies whose products are described in this chapter. They are Mike Dolbec, Rich Fikes, Gary Fine, Mike McFall, Donald Griest, David Hornig, Marie Markwell, Robert Noble, Daniel Sagalowicz, Doug Shaker, Tom Shelton, and Aaron Stern. In addition, Bill Clancey, Jay Ferguson, Susanne Humphrey, David Leserman, Robert Morgen, Mike and Osborner, 1984) or to instruct students in a dynamic setting (Brown, Burton, and de Kleer, 1982; Hollan, Hutchins, and Weitzman, 1984). Knowledge bases generally consist of symbolic structures such as rules (Hayes-Roth, 1985), frames (Fikes and Kehler, 1985), and logical expressions (Genesereth and Ginsberg, 1985). In addition, AI programming environments often include support for functional (LISP), object-oriented, and access-oriented programming.

Each of the software tools described in this chapter provides support for one or more of these representational and programming paradigms. Throughout the chapter the term "expert system" refers to a knowledge-based system that includes expert problem-solving knowledge.

Many AI applications share common methods for representing knowledge, controlling inference, and maintaining large systems. As a result, AI researchers have been able to generalize their methods by developing knowledge representation languages and expert system shells (Hayes-Roth, Waterman, and Lenat, 1983; van Melle, 1984; Shortliffe, and Buchanan, 1984; Johnson, 1984; Waterman, 1986; van Melle, Shortliffe, and Buchanan, 1981; Stefik, 1979). A *shell*, as used here, means an expert system development tool that provides standard ways for representing knowledge about a similar problem domain or task along with a standard inference procedure. Shells tend to be designed for solving a certain class of problem only, and are not as general and flexible as tools that allow the user to define their own representation and control mechanisms. However, they tend to be simpler and easier to learn than more general tools. All tools provide both a high-level language and an environment for creating, modifying, and testing systems.

Because of high start-up costs, the groups that are currently interested in purchasing the more expensive software tools include large corporations, major research labs, and government agencies that can afford the investment and who believe that the short- and long-term benefits can offset the initial high costs. For these clients, the high price tag is not much of a deterrent because they have already committed themselves to the technology, and the prospect of building

---

Walker, Arthur Seaton, Nancy Skooglund, and Don Waterman provided many valuable comments that improved the final presentation of this chapter.

This project would not have been possible without the cooperation of and resources provided by the Guidon and Sumex-Aim projects at the Knowledge Systems Laboratory, Computer Science Department, Stanford University. This evaluation of expert systems tools was partially undertaken for the purpose of accessing the state of the art in AI tools and techniques that could be applied to the Guidon Project. The Guidon project is funded in part by ONR Contract N00014–79C–0302 and the Josiah Macy, Jr. Foundation (Grant B852005). The original version of this chapter was prepared using facilities provided by the SUMEX-AIM facility (NIH Grant RR00785).

their own tools for less money is slight. In the near future, the cost of developing an expert system may decrease given changes in several factors:

• *The software and hardware that is required to develop expert systems must become substantially less expensive.* Although personnel costs dominate all other costs in current expert system projects, the cost of software and hardware is significant for the dissemination or resale of expert systems applications. The more powerful tools have traditionally required a LISP intepreter or compiler along with support for bit-mapped graphics and a pointing device (e.g., a mouse). The combined software system requires a powerful processor, a large address space and virtual memory, four or more megabytes of RAM, and a LISP interpreter and compiler.

Given the continuing decrease in hardware costs (e.g., inexpensive RAM, high-speed storage devices, 32-bit processors), it seems likely that there will be strong competition among vendors offering LISP environments. In particular, the emergence of 68020 and 80386 workstations, increased use of VLSI technology, and new developments such as LISP coprocessor chips or boards should mean that powerful computers will continue to drop in price at a dramatic rate. In addition, systems may be recoded in languages such as C that can run more efficiently on less expensive hardware. This is an important consideration for companies that want to use their existing computer systems.

• *The value of expert systems must be well demonstrated in several commercially viable application areas.* If there are successful off-the-shelf application products, then interest in this market will grow. This should lead to larger volume sales and increasing competition, which should eventually result in substantial price decreases for expert systems software tools, LISP environments, and the necessary hardware.

• *The cost of labor involved in program construction must be reduced.* Currently, both the AI programmers and experts that are needed to build expert systems are highly paid professionals. Although the companies that sell expert system tools claim that their tools dramatically increase software productivity, realistically it may take many person-years to complete a substantial application that can be used on a routine basis.

Given the high cost of developing and maintaining an expert system application, the current target audience for applications is limited to organizations with large financial assets. Often, these companies are developing systems in-house or contracting with the major expert systems tool vendors. A few startup companies are developing applications (e.g., financial and insurance underwriting applications), but they are planning to sell their products to large organizations.

If the development and maintenance costs can be decreased, then the technology could be cost effective for small businesses, schools, scientists, and other professionals with limited budgets. This is tied to the assumption that the hardware and software costs for AI applications will indeed approach the level of other application products. For example, database and spreadsheet technologies have become widely used because they are affordable, and a wide range of people are capable of building their own databases or spreadsheet models.

There are several reasons why it is difficult and time-consuming to build an expert system. To address this problem we need:

- a better understanding of how to obtain, organize, and represent expert knowledge (this is typically called *knowledge engineering*);

- a better understanding of what expert systems are;

- to know how to choose between alternative architectures and techniques;

- to know how to manage effectively a large expert system project including design, implementation, testing, documentation, training, and maintenance;

- more university classes in expert systems (especially project classes) that compare different system architectures, programming techniques, and knowledge engineering practices (e.g., interviewing techniques); and

- more software tools that are easier to learn, use, and modify.

The purpose of this chapter is two-fold: to propose the criteria for evaluating software tools for developing expert systems, and to describe several existing expert system development tools. The tools described in this chapter were chosen for review for several reasons. They are all serious development environments that run on high-performance workstations or common mini-computers (e.g., DEC® VAX®). Current tools that run only on microcomputers (e.g., IBM® PC) are not considered here. The tools chosen are all commercially available products. This eliminates research systems, even though they may be available as public-domain programs. Also excluded are in-house tools such as Schlumberger's STROBE (Smith, 1984; Schoen and Smith, 1983), and tools which are not fully supported by vendors, such as Xerox's Loops (Stefik, Bobrow, Mittal and Conway, 1983). The reason for focusing on fully supported commercial products is that the criteria for evaluating a software tool should include consideration of product support, training, documentation, and port-

DEC is a registered trademark of Digital Equipment Corporation.
VAX is a registered trademark of Digital Equipment Corporation.
IBM is a registered trademark of International Business Machines, Inc.

ability. The products described herein include ART® (Inference Corporation), KEE® (IntelliCorp), Knowledge Craft® (Carnegie Group Inc.), and S.1 (Teknowledge, Inc.).

Information on specific system tools was gathered from technical reports, magazine articles, user manuals, training materials, interviews with users, demonstrations, observations at various AAAI and IJCAI conferences, conversations with company representatives, and personal visits to several companies.

Criteria for Evaluation

It is difficult to evaluate any tool without proper consideration of the tool's intended use. A tool excellent for commercial use may be inadequate for research purposes, and vice versa. On the other hand, some of the commercial tools are being used for major research efforts, and they provide the advantage of better support and documentation. The features that a tool provides, including extensibility, are important factors for some research projects that need maximum flexibility.

The amount of training and support required to use a tool effectively can vary greatly. There are at least two kinds of training that may be required: an experienced AI programmer may only want to learn about the specific features of a system, whereas other programmers may need more general training in AI. However, in both cases excellent training, documentation, software support, and technical assistance are extremely important. In fact, many customers may find that the quality and quantity of training and support that they can expect to receive may be one of the more important considerations in choosing an expert system development tool.

The cost of the software is certainly an important factor, but in the long run calculating the cost effectiveness of one tool versus another is a complicated matter. The total cost of a tool includes the cost of training and support, the hardware, and personnel required. This must be weighed against the total gain. If the basic features of one system are such that you can more easily encode the knowledge that you are trying to capture in your expert system, then the extra cost of the software and required hardware may be more than offset by the time saved during knowledge engineering. However, the success of writing a program of any kind can often be determined as much by the programming environment as by the specific language features that are provided. The quality of

---

ART is a registered trademark of Inference Corporation.
KEE is a registered trademark of IntelliCorp, Inc.
Knowledge Craft is a registered trademark of Carnegie Group Inc.

the user interface, and the available editors and debuggers are critical components of any software development system. It is hard to evaluate any dimension in isolation from another because they can interact with each other. However, one way has been chosen to organize a set of dimensions (see Table 1 below) and each dimension is discussed in the subsections below.

Table 1
Criteria for AI Tools

Basic Features	Language features for representing or encoding knowledge; control and inference mechanisms available.
Development Environment	Explicit support for programmers or knowledge engineers during development, testing, and tuning of the knowledge base and program code; the programmer's interface.
Functionality	Ease of learning, ease of use, efficiency of development and run-time environment, and range of applications.
Support	Training, documentation, and support for answering technical questions.
Cost Factors	Cost of software, training, and hardware that may be required.

Basic Features

Expert system development tools generally provide support for representing symbolic knowledge. This knowledge can include facts, definitions, heuristic judgments, and procedures for doing a task or achieving a goal. Various formalisms or techniques are used to represent this knowledge including predicate calculus, logic programming, rules, semantic networks, and frames or schemata. Expert system development tools also provide built-in inference mechanisms which may include pure deduction, backward and forward chaining rule interpreters, and class inheritance. The LISP language has proven to be general and flexible enough to represent these kinds of knowledge and control structures. However, LISP programming can be painstaking and the resulting code can be opaque. Many researchers have chosen to use or develop knowledge representation languages that allow them to encode knowledge at a higher level, perhaps closer to how a person may conceptualize it. Often one or more of these methods have been combined in a single system.

It can be argued that certain kinds of knowledge are more easily or naturally represented in one formalism than in another. Heuristic knowledge for doing diagnosis can be represented naturally in rules, but some people claim that definitions and structural knowledge are more clearly represented in frames or relations. Predicate calculus relations provide a foundation in mathematical logic, but frames can be organized in a hierarchy providing the powerful mechanism of inheritance.

Different researchers with different biases and different problems to solve have often expressed a strong preference for one methodology over another. Recently there has been a trend toward hybrid programming systems (Bobrow and Stefik, 1986). IntelliCorp admits that there is a loss of simplicity and uniformity as a result of combining methodologies, but they argue that this is offset by gains in efficiency, flexibility, and the naturalness of the representation (Kunz, Kehler, and Williams, 1984). Certainly a system that is more general and more efficient over a range of problems can provide significant advantages to a system builder. However, hybrid systems may be more complicated to learn and use, and for some applications a simpler tool that provides more structure and less options and features may be sufficient and more cost-effective in practice. On the other hand, IntelliCorp argues that the limitations of a single representation system are often overcome by tricks which result in opaque or awkward representations. Kunz, et al. (1984) argue that the increased complexity of a hybrid system can be justified because "the designer [can] trade the effort to support and teach users to use the tricks with the effort required to support and teach users to use several methodologies." As more industrial case histories are reported, some light may be shed on which features are cost-effective for solving specific problems. In addition, continued research studies should help us classify problem types and problem-solving methods according to some dimensions that would indicate which representational frameworks are more appropriate for a given problem using a particular problem-solving method (Clancey, 1985).

The Development Environment

The development environment refers to the programmer's interface and the tools that facilitate development of an application, that is, features that may not be necessary in a run-time only application system. This includes knowledge base editors, rule compilers, knowledge base browsers, performance testing, and tuning tools.

Knowledge acquisition is often a difficult and time-consuming process. If a given tool provides most of the basic features needed to represent and solve a given problem, then it is likely that a large amount of the time on a project will be spent building and refining the knowledge base. In any case, explicit support for knowledge acquisition is crucial. Development software tools include knowledge base editors which help system builders enter knowledge into the system. An editor for a frame-based system can allow you to enter slots and values for individual objects. A package for displaying graphs helps the user visualize hierarchical relations in the knowledge base. Some systems simplify knowledge base construction by allowing a user to interactively add and edit nodes in a graph to update the knowledge base. If the system builder does not have to know about the underlying representation of objects in the program, then even domain experts may be able to use these tools to assist in knowledge base development.

Another class of tools that are useful for knowledge acquisition and validation are tools that check the integrity of the knowledge base to weed out contradictory facts or rules, discover missing or redundant information, and find syntactical errors. Spelling checkers can also be an invaluable aid because typographical or spelling errors can lead to knowledge base errors that may be hard to detect otherwise. A feature that allows running a large number of cases in batch mode facilitates testing and maintenance of a knowledge base. Also, automatic record keeping helps the maintainer of an expert system keep track of any changes in system performance on a given case. Such tools help avoid the introduction of subtle bugs into a knowledge base that could make a system fail unexpectedly on a case in which it previously performed well.

Interactive graphic displays are becoming a necessity in developing complex software systems (Model, 1979; Richer and Clancey, 1985). These graphic displays can be integrated with other debugging and monitoring aids, including high-level trace and break packages at the *knowledge base level* rather than at the level of the LISP stack. For example, the system builder should be able to set breaks when specified events occur (e.g., a certain rule is tried). In addition, programs that measure the execution speed of an application and help locate bottlenecks are also very important.

Although a system must perform correctly and efficiently, the end-user interface must be simple and effective. Tools that support the development of end-user interfaces, including graphic and textual displays of the system's state, explanations, requests, and decisions, can shorten development time. Some systems can be interfaced with other modules such as natural language interfaces. In the future, many toolkits may be available with expert system tools. Some of these toolkits are bundled with the system and some are available at an additional cost. Some may require additional hardware. These could include simulation kits, interfaces to interactive video, CD-ROM or other optical disk systems, and natural language interfaces, the latter including text recognition, text generation, explanation, sound generation, and voice recognition packages. Eventually, expert systems will be integrated with traditional software tools including popular word processors, spreadsheets, and communications programs. It seems likely that the future success of expert systems in the business or office market will depend on how well they can be integrated with existing systems.

Functionality

Functionality in this context refers to how the software actually works versus a description of the basic features, development environment, and support offered.

- How difficult is it to learn how to use the tool? What are the prerequisite skills, knowledge, or experience?

- How easy is the tool to use? Is it awkward or cumbersome for a programmer to do certain tasks (e.g., modify the knowledge base)?

- Is the product available on a range of hardware? What are the computational requirements for supporting the system (e.g., minimum memory needed)?

- What are the upper limits on the size of applications? Is there a maximum number of rules or a maximum number of frames that can be used for a given hardware configuration?

- How efficiently does the development software execute on a given hardware configuration? Is there a special run-time environment that is more compact, more efficient, or requires less memory during execution?

- Is the tool robust? For example, how good is the error handling, including error recovery and error messages? Is it difficult to build robust applications?

- What is the range of applications for which the tool is appropriate? Is the tool awkward for solving certain kinds of problems?

- Is the tool appropriate for research, prototyping, and/or end-user applications? Is the environment flexible and extensible? How easy is it to extend the language features?

Support

Product support includes training, documentation, phone assistance, mail support (including electronic mail), upgrades to software and documentation, and consulting arrangements. It is often interesting to know if other companies share equity in the tool vendor's company.

Until expert systems become more commonplace, a company that sells an expert system tool is also in the business of technology transfer. Therefore, many of the companies offer classes in building expert systems, programming in LISP, and so on. Additionally, expert system tools are often sold with an agreement to provide training and support. Often the customer sends one or more employees to the site of the software company for one or two weeks of training. This training can be a vital component for the successful use of a tool.

An important factor in evaluating a software development system is the quality and availability of written and on-line documentation. The kind and amount of documentation needed will vary depending on the design of the system, its intended purpose, its actual use, the people using it, and so on. Detailed documentation or source code may be needed in order to make major modifications and extensions to a system. Source code is often very expensive to obtain, and a non-disclosure agreement will commonly be required. This may be a problem for groups that are funded under government grants and wish to disseminate their systems for little or no charge.

An alternative to making in-house modifications to a tool is to hire the original software company (or someone else) to make custom modifications. In cases where this is a likely need, the product must be evaluated in the context of the availability and cost of custom work. Furthermore, it would be necessary to negotiate rights to any new products developed. Most software companies would like to retain the rights to any custom packages that they develop, but the contracting company may feel that they are paying a high price for this work and want to retain any licensing rights.

Some companies may prefer the company that supplies the tool also to produce the application system, including the encoding of expert knowledge, the process known as *knowledge engineering*. Many companies offer this service.

Cost Factors

These include the price of the software, support, training, and required hardware. Multiple copies of the software are usually sold at a reduced cost. However, the cost of developing an application and distributing it in-house or selling it as a product can be difficult to assess. For example, the cost of training is only one factor; related employee expenses can be considerable (e.g., travel expenses). A desirable alternative might be to set up an in-house training program and purchase instructional materials (books, videos, on-line systems) from the vendor if they are available.

When an application is intended to be widely disseminated, development costs can be distributed among many users. However, such systems are too costly unless they can be placed on low-end hardware configurations. The availability of a compact, robust, and efficient run-time environment may be necessary. An inexpensive licensing agreement for run-time only systems is highly desirable in such cases.

Once a system is developed, staff may be required just to maintain the system and support end users. These extra costs are not trivial (Bachant and McDermott, 1984). It would be nice if we could determine that a particular tool would facilitate building application systems that are more robust and easier to maintain and support than another tool; of course, this is difficult to determine at present.

Evaluation of Four Commercial Expert System Tools

The following four tools are reviewed in this chapter: S.1, KEE, Knowledge Craft, and ART. It is important to keep in mind that these tools are evolving, and future versions may include features that are absent in this description. The objective of this chapter is to develop a useful framework to evaluate current and future expert system tools. In the final analysis, an overall rating is not given to the systems reviewed because too many factors are involved for such a rating to be useful or accurate. The order in which the tools are described is convenient for describing and contrasting basic features, and does not imply anything beyond that. Because this chapter is not a tutorial on expert systems, common terms used to describe expert systems are not defined herein (see Waterman, 1986). Each tool is reviewed according to the criteria established in the previous section. A summary of features is presented in Table 2.

Important features that have been added to the four products since the original version of this chapter appeared are noted, but these new features are not described in detail. The following sections provide a good introduction to each tool's basic features as well as important advanced features. Because the information on pricing in the original article is out of date, and in general, the pricing of products can change frequently, specific dollar values are not included in this chapter. For a slightly different perspective on the evaluation of expert system development tools, see Mettrey (1987), which assesses the state of the art of expert system development tools in general and draws some examples from existing systems.

S.1 (Teknowledge, Inc.)

S.1 is a tool for developing rule-based consultation systems that are designed to solve structured-selection problems in which there is an enumerated set of solutions. The design of S.1 is based on the EMYCIN system (van Melle, 1981;

Table 2
Summary of Features

Tools	Basic Features
ART 3.1 (Inference)	**Rules**: many features including variables, complex pattern matching, and certainty factors; includes a rule compiler. **Logic**: propositions with certainty factors, logical dependencies, and extent. **Frames**: with taxonomic and user-definable inheritance, includes methods and active values, no slot value constraints. **Inference and Control**: backward and forward chaining, an agenda mechanism, assumption-based truth maintenance and hypothetical and temporal reasoning with ART Viewpoints. **Graphics Environment**: the ART Studio including browsers, a command monitor, and ARTIST, an icon drawing tool, and rule-based animation.
KEE 3.1 (IntelliCorp)	**Rules**: variables, fully integrated with frame system; includes a rule compiler. **Frames**: many features including taxonomic and user-definable inheritance, methods, active values, and slot value constraints; well integrated with object-oriented programming system. **Logic**: TellAndAsk language integrated with rules and frames. **Inference and Control**: forward and backward chaining, an assumption-based truth maintenance system and hypothetical and temporal reasoning with KEEworlds. **Graphics Environment**: multi-window and menu-based interface for programmers with browsers and editors, ActiveImages, an icon development package, and Common Windows and KEEpictures, which provide portable windowing and 2-D graphics routines for programmers.
Knowledge Craft 3.1 (Carnegie Group)	**Rules**: OPS5 rule language that can reference frames (separate product). **Logic**: PROLOG-equivalent language (separate product). **Frames**: many features including taxonomic and user-definable inheritance, methods, demons, contexts, and slot value constraints; object-oriented programming. **Inference and Control**: forward and backward chaining, contexts, and an agenda mechanism. **Graphics Environment**: Schemata Network Editor, CRL, CRL-PROLOG and CRL-OPS workcenters, schema-based 2-D graphics package based on the CORE standard.
S.1 (Teknowledge)	**Rules**: include object-attribute-value triplets and certainty factors. **Frames**: very limited, no inheritance, not easily extended. **Inference and Control**: backward chaining with uncertainty, control blocks (a very high-level procedural language), subsumption-based reasoning. **Graphics Environment**: browsers

Buchanan and Shortliffe, 1984) and includes control blocks as found in the original Oncocin system (Shortliffe, Scott, Bischoff, Campbell, van Melle, and Jacobs, 1984). Users are expected to be computer professionals with some AI training (which could be provided by Teknowledge). S.1 is a less complex tool than KEE, Knowledge Craft, or ART, partly because its use is constrained to a structured-selection problem-solving strategy. Teknowledge claims that many applications can be developed without using LISP or C programming. S.1 is not appropriate for all problems, but Teknowledge claims that a large class of diagnosis, catalog selection, and engineering design problems are amenable to S.1 techniques. The development version of S.1 described here is release 2.1 and the delivery system is release 2.0. Additional information on S.1 and Teknowledge can be found in Hayes-Roth (1984a), Teknowledge (1986), and Schindler (1986a).

More recently Teknowledge has developed a tool called Copernicus™. Copernicus contains many features that are absent in S.1. Copernicus is designed as a modular environment that integrates well with conventional software systems. Although Teknowledge continues to support S.1, Copernicus is intended to be a replacement for S.1 for the development of knowledge-based systems. However, Copernicus is not described in this chapter.

Basic Features of S.1

Rules. Rules in S.1 are similar to EMYCIN rules in that variables are not allowed, certainty factors can be added, procedural attachment is allowed, and backward chaining is the control mechanism used during rule interpretation. The basic component of a rule clause is an object-attribute-value triplet (e.g., "site of the infection is blood"), but certainty factors can be attached.

Control Blocks. High-level, algorithmic or procedural knowledge for controlling problem solving is represented in control blocks. This provides a structured high-level language for representing procedures. A control block statement can create an object, determine the value of an attribute, display text to the user, or invoke another control block. A consultation is started by invoking a top-level control block.

Frame System. Teknowledge says that assertions about objects and relationships between objects are represented in a specialized *frame system.* Users can define classes and attributes. However, in contrast to the other systems reviewed here, there is no explicit support for general class inheritance, run-time slot value

---

Copernicus is a trademark of Teknowledge, Inc.

type-checking, methods, or demons. However, S.1 frames do support propagation of subsumption relations during reasoning.

Uncertainty. Facts and rules in S.1 can be modified by certainty factors based on the certainty factor model developed in MYCIN (Shortliffe, 1976; Shortliffe and Buchanan, 1984).

LISP or C Programming. By using control blocks or procedural attachment in rule clauses, the knowledge programmer can access the underlying programming system to execute arbitrary function calls.

S.1 Development Environment

User Interface and Graphics Support. The user interface in S.1 is mostly menu-driven and the user can use a mouse device to make selections. The use of the menus, multiple windows, and the mouse found on current workstations provides a consultation system that is relatively easy for end users to learn and use. For example, the user can select commands and valid responses to questions from menus that are on the screen. Keyboard commands and input are also allowed at any time, in which case, abbreviations that uniquely specify the input can be used. S.1 has a help and status window which describes the current question, commands, and options.

Objects in the knowledge base have associated text strings. This allows S.1 to generate English text for questioning, explanation, and other purposes. Rules can be automatically translated into English if-then statements using these translations and some knowledge of correct grammar.

The S.1 environment does not provide advanced tools for the user to create graphic displays and interfaces, but these can be programmed using the underlying LISP or C graphics tools.

Knowledge Base Editing, Testing, and Debugging. When the user exits the S.1 knowledge base editor, the system automatically checks for syntax and consistency errors. Test cases can be saved and used again for system testing. S.1 allows the user to override the answer to a question in a saved case.

Graphic displays allow the knowledge engineer to browse the knowledge base and the dynamic state of execution during a consultation. The user, for example, can trace and break a variety of events when a rule fires. An event tree can be displayed in a trace window. Nodes in this tree can be selected to get explanations of system behavior, to find out values and certainty factors, and to obtain English translations.

Explanation. S.1 can generate English text to answer "how" and "why" questions by referring to the history of rules that have been applied.

End-User Systems. A consultation-only system can be created which prevents end users from modifying the knowledge base.

Functionality of S.1

The C version of S.1 is available on many systems including the DEC VAX, Apollo®, SUN®, IBM PC-RT, HP 9000s, and NCR® Tower. A version for the IBM 370 has been announced. A development version of S.1, written in LISP, is available on the Xerox 1100s and Symbolics™ machines. Delivery (or run-time only) systems are available on all the machines except the LISP machines. In addition, S.1 delivery systems are available on the AT&T® 7300 and the IBM PC-AT. Teknowledge claims that the C versions of S.1 run up to ten or more times faster than the LISP machine versions, and a C run-time system in S.1 is substantially more compact. In this sense, S.1 may provide a level of performance and functionality on a wider range of (less expensive) hardware than may be possible with the other systems.

In general, Teknowledge asserts that S.1 is appropriate for structured-selection (or classification) problems which include diagnosis, catalog selection, and engineering design problems. S.1 applications include: Analyst—General Motors Acceptance Corporation (Teknowledge, 1988), an expert system for analyzing GM dealers' financial statements to determine the overall financial health of a dealership; DEPICT™—National Patent Analytical Systems (Teknowledge, 1988), an expert system for interpreting the results of a drug and alcohol test-ing system; The Drilling Advisor—Elf-Acquitaine (Hayes-Roth, 1984a, b; Teknowledge, 1988), a system for diagnosing why an oil drill mechanism is sticking; DS4—Texas Instruments Industrial Systems Division (Teknowledge, 1988), a process monitoring and control system for data interpretation and diagnosis; ESPm—NCR® (Teknowledge, 1986; 1988), a remote field service consultant for computer maintenance; Maintenance Advisor (MAD)—Bell Northern Research (Teknowledge, 1988), a prototype expert

---

Apollo is a registered trademark of Apollo Computer, Inc.
SUN is a registered trademark of Sun Microsystems, Inc.
Symbolics is a trademark of Symbolics, Inc.
AT&T is a registered trademark of American Telephone and Telegraph.
DEPICT is a trademark of National Patent Analytical Systems, Inc.
NCR is a registered trademark of National Cash Register, Inc.

system for diagnosing and repairing problems with certain digital switches; Motor Expert—GM Delco Products (Teknowledge, 1988), an expert system that designs components of custom motors to conform with continually changing space, weight, and power constraints; Press Lineup Advisor—Rockwell International, Graphics Systems Division (Teknowledge, 1988), a decision support system that plans the positioning of printing plates during newspaper production (for The Los Angeles Times); and Vibration—General Motors (Teknowledge, 1988), a system to assist customer service technicians in the diagnosis of automotive noise and vibration problems.

Support for S.1

Teknowledge specializes in consulting and developing custom systems using S.1, M.1, Copernicus and other custom Teknowledge tools as well as products offered by other vendors. Although the company is no longer stressing sales of its tools, customers can purchase S.1 and other Teknowledge products along with full support. Support includes phone assistance, electronic mail, and software and documentation upgrades. It seems likely that Copernicus will replace S.1 as the preferred tool at Teknowledge.

Teknowledge also offers classes in knowledge engineering methodology as well as training on its own products. Teknowledge is a public corporation with several significant equity partners: General Motors, FMC, Proctor and Gamble, NYNEX, Elf-Acquitaine (France), and Frametome (France).

Cost of S.1

At this time, Teknowledge offers only site and corporate (multi-site) licenses for S.1 and other products. Maintenance, including upgrades and continued support, must be purchased annually. Sales of single units of their products have been discontinued so that the company can focus on custom system development and consulting. Universities can still purchase S.1 at a discount.

KEE (Knowledge Engineering Environment®, IntelliCorp, Inc.)

KEE is a hybrid tool integrating several AI methodologies into a single system. It provides support for frame-based knowledge representation with taxonomic inheritance, rule-based reasoning, logic representations, data-driven reasoning,

---

Knowledge Engineering Environment is a trademark of IntelliCorp, Inc.

object-oriented programming, interactive graphics, and LISP functional programming. KEE 3.1 include KEEworlds™, a mechanism for doing hypothetical and temporal reasoning based on de Kleer's assumption-based truth maintenance system (de Kleer, 1986). KEEworlds is not discussed here, but a detailed description can be found in the next chapter. In addition, Common Windows and KEEpictures™ are now included in the basic KEE product. Common Windows is a portable Common LISP window system that is used in all implementations of KEE. KEEpictures is an object-oriented 2-D graphics package that is integrated with KEE. It includes several sophisticated graphics objects and operations as well as basic line and curve drawing functions. Together Common Windows and KEEpictures provide a consistent and portable graphics and user interface platform for KEE developers. Release 3.1 of KEE also includes a rule compiler, which IntelliCorp claims will improve performance by as much as a factor of thirty. SimKit, a simulation toolkit built in KEE, is described in detail in Chapters 8 and 9. KEEconnection™, a database connection between KEE and SQL databases, is described in Chapter 11. For additional information on KEE and IntelliCorp, see Kunz, Kehler, and Williams (1984), Fikes and Kehler (1985), IntelliCorp (1985), Linden (1985), Nado, Bock, and Fikes (1985), Schindler (1986b), Fraser (1987a, b), and Grégoire (1988).

Basic Features of KEE

Frames. Frames are called *units* in KEE. Units are a data structure consisting of a unit name and a set of *attribute* descriptions, each defined by a *slot*. Associated with each slot is the attribute's *value*, constraints that the value must satisfy, procedures that are called whenever the slot is accessed or its value changes, and the source of any inherited value. Values of attributes can be stored, inherited from other frames, computed by executing LISP code, or deduced from a specified set of rules.

Slots describe an attribute of an object that is either *declarative* (e.g., represents a fact or relation) or *procedural* (e.g., invokes a method). Attribute values can be constrained to a certain class (e.g., LAWYERS) or a Boolean combination of class descriptions (e.g., UNION.OF. NOT.ONE.OF), an enumerated set (e.g., RED, YELLOW, BLUE), a data-type (e.g., integer), a range (e.g., between 1 and 100), and a minimum and maximum cardinality (e.g., 0, 10). Support for a partial description of a valid slot value provides type checking, a way to deduce certain facts (e.g., "Joe is not the mother of Bob because Joe is male"), and a way to represent some disjunctive and negative facts.

KEEworlds is a trademark of IntelliCorp, Inc.
KEEpictures is a trademark of IntelliCorp, Inc.
KEEconnection is a trademark of IntelliCorp, Inc.

Units can describe either a class of objects (e.g., PIPES) or an individual (e.g., PIPE.3). An individual can be described as an *instance* or member of one or more classes. In KEE, a distinction is made between *member* slots and *own* slots. Member slots are used to describe attributes of class members (either a subclass or instance), while own slots are used to describe the class or instance itself. For example, the own slots of the class PIPES might include lightest, longest, smallest, and oldest. These could be member slots of the class PHYSICAL.OBJECTS.-CLASSES.[1] Member slots of the class PIPE would probably include length, weight, height, and age. An instance of class PIPE would have length, weight, height, and age as own slots.

Units form class taxonomies with the property of inheritance. Units include classes, subclasses, and individuals. Any unit can have multiple parents. A subclass or an individual inherits the properties of the classes it belongs to according to a specified inheritance method. Inherited properties can be restricted by use of an OVERRIDE option. For instance, you could make 3-wheel-cars a subclass of cars which have 4 wheels by default by using OVERRIDE to change only the number-of-wheels attribute to 3. There are a number of inheritance options supplied with the system; in addition, user-defined inheritance options are also supported.

Rules. Rule clauses can include logical expressions with conjunctions, disjunctions, and negations, as well as arbitrary LISP s-expressions. Rules are represented as units that form a rule class hierarchy. KEE provides backward and forward chaining rule interpreters. User-supplied functions can tailor rule interpretation to specify depth-first, breadth-first, or other search strategies for backward chaining, and resolve conflicts in forward chaining when more than one rule is applicable. Although the KEE rule language is adequate for many problems and richer than the S.1 rule language, it is not a complete procedural programming language. For example, you cannot express iteration operations over a rule set in the rule language itself.

An example KEE rule that could be "used to determine which feedstock bin can supply alkali to a reactor whose PH level is lower than desired" (IntelliCorp, 1985) is shown below:

```
NEEDS.ALKALI RULE
    (IF ((?SOME.PLANT IS IN CLASS PLANTS)
    AND
    (A REACTOR OF ?SOME. PLANT IS ?SOME.REACTOR)
    AND
    (THE PH.STATE OF ?SOME.REACTOR IS LOW)
```

---

[1]The class PIPES is a subclass of PHYSICAL.OBJECTS, but it is a member (or instance) of PHYSICAL.OBJECTS.CLASSES, which in turn is its *metaclass*.

```
AND
(A FEED.STOCK.INPUT OF ?SOME.REACTOR IS ?SOME BIN)
AND
(THE CONSTITUENT OF ?SOME.BIN IS ALKALI))
THEN
(THE NEW.CONSTITUENT.BIN OF ?SOME.PLANT IS ?SOME.BIN))
```

Logic. Logical (Boolean) expressions are used in KEE to state constraints on slot values. Logical expressions are also used in rule clauses. This is integrated with a database assertion and query language based on a subset of predicate calculus, called TellAndAsk™ (Nado et al., 1985). For example, you can enter:

```
(ASSERT '(THE FLOW OF (THE FEEDWATER.PUMP OF R1) IS LOW))
```

This will result in storing the value LOW (if it's a legal value) in the FLOW slot of the feedwater pump unit associated with the R1 reactor unit. Retrieval requests can specify a pattern with a variable. To determine which objects have a feedwater pump with a low flow rate, the user could request:

```
(QUERY '(THE FLOW OF (THE FEEDWATER.PUMP OF ?X) IS LOW))
```

If the earlier assertion above had been made, then R1 would have been returned as an object that satisfied the user's query. The assertion and retrieval functions know how to store and access values in frames as well as how to store and retrieve facts that have no frame in which to be stored. These facts are placed in an *unstructured facts list.* This can be used as a debugging aid because it indicates to the developer those facts that the system has no way of representing in frames. QUERY and ASSERT can apply a rule set, providing a mechanism for backward or forward reasoning. A RETRACT construct allows removal of facts or slot values from the knowledge base. The TellAndAsk language provides relations that are commonly needed, but the user can add his or her own relations. The TellAndAsk language is defined in a KEE knowledge base as an inheritance network of units.

Graphical Representation. An icon can represent a KEE object or the value of an object attribute. This graphical representation is linked to the underlying frame representation of the object in the knowledge base as an active slot value. Manipulating the graphical images interactively updates the values in the knowledge base. Likewise, changes in the value of the slot by other means are reflected on the screen by appropriate changes in the icon's appearance. For example, fluid level in a device could be changed simply by dragging the mouse to move the level up or down. During a simulation any changes in the level

---

TellAndAsk is a trademark of IntelliCorp, Inc.

would be reflected in the icon's display. This capability is part of KEE's ActiveImages™ package which is included with the system. It is particularly effective for interactive simulations where several parts of a system are interconnected and changes in one subpart or device affect the whole system. KEE can propagate these changes automatically (on the screen and in the knowledge base) if the necessary relationships and actions have been represented in the knowledge base (ActiveImages is now implemented using KEEpictures).

Object-Oriented, Access-Oriented, and Functional Programming. KEE allows the programmer to integrate several programming paradigms including LISP, object-oriented, and access-oriented programming. Access-oriented programming in KEE is supported through the use of *active values* which allow procedural behavior to be invoked through a function call or by applying a set of rules when a slot value is retrieved or changed. This can be used to support data-driven reasoning. ActiveImages can be connected to slots with active values, allowing control of the system via a direct manipulation interface.

KEE Development Environment

User Interface and Graphics Support. KEE was designed to provide a powerful, flexible, and usable user interface for system developers. In addition, explicit support is provided to the developer for creating user interfaces for end-user applications (e.g., the ActiveImages package). In general, IntelliCorp has achieved this goal with respect to experienced programmers using the system. However, the knowledge engineering interface may still be complex for non-programmers. The application designer must pay careful attention to creating a usable system, though this applies to most general purpose tools.

The ActiveImages package provides direct support for dynamic applications that use graphics for display and interaction with the user. The KEE developer can create...

> graphical displays for both viewing and controlling KEE objects. Images such as histograms, thermometers, switches, push-buttons, plots, meters, pipes, and valves can be attached to the slots of KEE objects. ActiveImages also includes facilities for creating and attaching icons to objects, for collecting and saving collections of active images within control panels, and for customizing images and control panels through reshaping, annotation, and modification of descriptive parameters. Because the ActiveImages package is implemented as a KEE knowledge base, it can easily be extended by the user to create new kinds of images (IntelliCorp, 1985).

ActiveImages is a trademark of IntelliCorp, Inc.

Knowledge Base Editing, Testing, and Debugging. Many users feel that KEE makes the most sophisticated use of interactive graphics in the programmer's interface, and many prefer this style of interaction. Most frame-based systems allow the user to display trees and lattices that show class and object hierarchies. KEE also allows the user to edit the knowledge base interactively via selection of the nodes in a taxonomy graph with a mouse. A graphical knowledge base editor for creating and modifying frames is also provided.

KEE can explain how the value of an attribute is determined or why information is requested from the user. There is a *Backward Chainer Explanation Window* that displays a graph that shows the links between object attributes (the top goal or a rule premise) and the rules that conclude about the attributes during backward chaining. Rules are marked and boxed to distinguish them from the other nodes in the graph. The boxing makes it easier to see which premises (object-attribute-value triples written in English syntax) were concluded from rules and which were derived from facts in the knowledge base.

KEE uses rule class graphs to display the static relationships between rules in a class. Similar to the backward chaining window described above, these graphs have links between a premise and the rules that may conclude about the premise. KEE also includes a *How* graph showing the derivation tree for any conclusion. Also, the user can ask why a question is being asked during rule interpretation. KEE allows tracing of the rule interpreter during forward and backward chaining, and break commands for interrupting the rule interpreter to facilitate more detailed debugging. Active values and active images are useful for displaying reasoning steps as part of an explanation.

Functionality of KEE

KEE is supported on a wide variety of hardware platforms that support Common LISP including LISP machines, UNIX® workstations including 80386 configurations, minicomputers, and mainframes.

KEE is designed for a wide range of applications. It has been used primarily for diagnostic, planning, scheduling, configuration, and process-control applications. Example applications include: Cell Design Aid—Arthur Andersen & Co., an automated tool to aid in the intial design, fine tuning, and continued evaluation and modification of manufacturing work cells (IntelliCorp, 1987); CFD—Vitro, a Circuit Fault Diagnosis system (IntelliCorp, 1987); ELOISE (English Language-Oriented Indexing System for EDGAR)—Arthur Andersen & Co. (IntelliCorp, 1987), a system that assists in using EDGAR, which electronically receives SEC filings directly from filing companies; FIXER (Fault Isolation

---

UNIX is a registered trademark of AT&T Information Systems.

eXpert to Enhance Reliability)—NASA, automated fault analysis and management for life support systems (IntelliCorp, 1987); FSA—Arthur Andersen & Co., a financial statement analyzer; NEMESYS—GTE, a diagnostic system to improve maintenance of central office (telephone) switches (Macleish, Thiedke, and Vennergrund, 1986); PLEXSYS™—EPRI, a package of extensions to KEE for mechnical, electrical, and nuclear engineers and plant operators (IntelliCorp, 1987); Synapse—AT&T, an expert system for VLSI design (Subrahmanyam, 1986); Trade advisor—Maufacturer's Hanover Trust Co., an expert system to assist currency traders (Alper, 1988); Truck Routing Assistant—Arthur Andersen & Co (IntelliCorp, 1987); and several other applications described in Faught (1987). SimKit™, a discrete event simulation toolkit, is offered as an add-on to KEE and provides an interactive graphics interface for developing domain-specific simulation toolkits. It is currently available on several hardware platforms. The PC/Host is a distributed delivery environment that allows the KEE interface to run on an IBM PC compatible while the rest of KEE executes on a DEC VAX under VMS™.

Support for KEE

IntelliCorp offers basic and advanced training courses in KEE. Support services provided include phone support, electronic mail support, and software and documentation upgrades. IntelliCorp also offers consulting and custom development contracts. IntelliCorp is a public corporation and has no equity arrangements with other companies. However, Unisys Corporation has a nonexclusive right to market KEE.

Cost of KEE

Pricing for KEE varies according to the hardware platform. Discounts are available for multiple copies. Basic training and support are available at an additional cost. Basic training is provided for two people for seven days at IntelliCorp's headquarters. Support includes phone assistance or electronic mail support and software and documentation updates. Discounts for multicopy support are available.

Consulting and apprenticeship programs are available. IntelliCorp also offers a tutorial package including video- and-text based training materials. Universities can purchase KEE at a discount. SimKit is available as an additional product

---

PLEXSYS is a trademark of Electric Power Research Institute.
SimKit is a trademark of IntelliCorp, Inc.
VMS is a trademark of Digital Equipment Corporation.

with its own price structure for the software, support, and training. The PC/Host system, including a copy of KEE for the DEC VAX and one PC interface along with support, is also available at an additional cost. Additional copies of the PC interface can be purchased separately. The PC/Host is intended for delivery of applications only.

Knowledge Craft (Carnegie Group Inc.)

Knowledge Craft is a hybrid tool with features similar to KEE. It combines frame-based, rule-based, logic-based, object-oriented, and LISP programming in one system. In addition, it provides an agenda mechanism, a schema-based graphics interface, and a multi-user database facility for very large applications (currently available only on a DEC VAX). Knowledge Craft is implemented in Common LISP. Knowledge Craft was formerly called SRL+ and is based on the SRL (Schema Representation Language) originally developed at Carnegie-Mellon University (Fox, Wright, and Adam, 1985). Knowledge Craft refers to the entire programming environment, and CRL™ (Carnegie Representation Language™) refers to the representation language, but Knowledge Craft will be used herein to refer to both. The current version of Knowledge Craft is release 3.1, but release 3.2 is expected shortly. Carnegie Group asserts that the newer versions of Knowledge Craft have many enhancements. Important improvements include increased performance and robustness, a more powerful programming interface including knowledge acquisition editors and tracers for debugging, and improved graphics facilities for building end-user interfaces. CRL-OPS™ and CRL-PROLOG™, described below, are now offered as separate products.

Carnegie Group is interested in developing application shells written in Knowledge Craft that are targeted at solving recurring industrial problems. Simpak™ and Graphpak™ are two modules that combine to form a simulation package that is written in Knowledge Craft. Graphpak includes an object-oriented programming interface with gauges and graphs, and Simpak includes calendar management of events along with a simulation engine and statistics capabilities. TestBench™ is a family of products for developing and delivering diagnostic systems. TestBuilder™ is a diagnostic development system that runs

---

CRL is a trademark of Carnegie Group Inc.
Carnegie Representation Language is a trademark of Carnegie Group Inc.
CRL-OPS is a trademark of Carnegie Group Inc.
CRL-PROLOG is a trademark of Carnegie Group Inc.
Simpak is a trademark of Carnegie Group Inc.
Graphpak is a trademark of Carnegie Group Inc.
TestBench is a trademark of Texas Instruments Inc. and Carnegie Group Inc.
TestBuilder is a trademark of Texas Instruments Inc. and Carnegie Group Inc.

on the TI Explorer™. End-user applications are delivered on the Explorer or on PC-ATs. Testbridge™ is used to move applications to the AT platform, and TestView™ is needed as a run-time environment on each AT running a TestBuilder application. In addition, the Carnegie Group sells Language Craft®, an integrated open-architecture environment for constructing natural language interfaces. Additional information on Knowledge Craft and Carnegie Group can be found in Buday (1986), Carnegie Group (1986), Kingston (1987a, b), and Pepper and Kahn (1987).

Basic Features of Knowledge Craft

Frames. Frames in Knowledge Craft are called *schemata*. A schema in Knowledge Craft is composed of a schema name, a set of slots, and a value for each slot. Slots are used to describe attributes of an object or a class. The value of a slot can be any LISP expression. Most objects in the Knowledge Craft system are represented as schemata, with the notable exception of CRL-OPS and CRL-PROLOG statements. Below is an example of a Knowledge Craft schema, reprinted from Carnegie Group (1986), that might be used in an application for developing circuit boards:

```
{{ make-cpu1-board-spec
   IS-A: engineering-activity specification-development
   SUB-ACTIVITY-OF: develop-board-cpu1
   INITIAL-ACTIVITY-OF: develop-board-cpu1
   EXPECTED-COMPLETION-DATE: "August 8, 1985"
   INITIATED: t
   COMPLETED: nil
   DESCRIPTION: "Develop specifications for the cpu board" }}
```

Restrictions can be placed on slot values, multiple inheritance is supported, and a programmer can define complex search paths to be used during inheritance. Knowledge Craft also contains a dependency mechanism that identifies the source of inherited values. Knowledge Craft allows the user to define inheritance differently for any arbitrary relation. For example, inheritance for a part-of relation can be defined so that the attribute location is inherited, but the attribute size is not. The *scope* of a relation specifies for which objects the relation can apply. In the example above, the value of the SUB-ACTIVITY-OF slot or relation must be an ACTIVITY. The user can also define the *transitivity* of a relation. For

Explorer is a trademark of Texas Instruments Inc.
Testbridge is a trademark of Texas Instruments Inc. and Carnegie Group Inc.
TestView is a trademark of Texas Instruments Inc. and Carnegie Group Inc.
Language Craft is a registered trademark of Carnegie Group Inc.

example, SUB-ACTIVITY-OF can be defined so that if $\mathcal{B}$ is the value of the SUB-ACTIVITY-OF slot of $\mathcal{A}$ and C is the value of the SUB-ACTIVITY-OF slot of $\mathcal{B}$, Knowledge Craft can automatically infer that "C is a SUB-ACTIVITY-OF $\mathcal{A}$" is true. Knowledge Craft differs from KEE in that *meta-information* about an attribute value (such as value restrictions) is stored in a separate schema, called a *meta-schema*. In KEE, the value class, datatype, and cardinality are stored as *facets* in the same slot structure as the attribute value.

Rules. CRL-OPS, based on OPS5 (Forgy, 1981; Brownston, Farrell, Kant, and Martin, 1985), provides a forward chaining rule-based language that is integrated into the Knowledge Craft environment. CRL-OPS rules can reference schemata, and take advantage of the inheritance automatically provided. CRL-OPS is compatible with OPS5 programs, except for a few minor changes that are necessary for compatibility with Common LISP. CRL-OPS rules are not currently represented as schemata for compatibility with OPS5. However, CRL-OPS rules can be fired when a schema slot is accessed. Below is a sample CRL-OPS rule (Carnegie Group, 1986) that could be used to indicate that when an engineering activity is completed, each activity which is subsequent, or enabled by it, should be initiated:

```
(p enabling-rule
    { <activity>
    (engineering-activity ^completed t
     ^schema-name <completed-activity> )}
    {^<next-activity>
    (engineering-activity
     ^enabled-by <completed-activity>
     ^initiated nil)}
    —>
    (modify <next-actiivity> ^initiated t))
```

Logic Programming. CRL-PROLOG provides a logic programming capability with backward chaining. Except for straightforward syntactic differences between Common LISP and PROLOG, this version of PROLOG is very similar to DEC-20 PROLOG. Again, to maintain compatibility with PROLOG, CRL-PROLOG statements are not represented as schemata.

Object-Oriented, Access-Oriented, and Functional Programming. Object-oriented, access-oriented, and LISP functional programming are integrated with Knowledge Craft's schema-based system. Although, Knowledge Craft uses object-oriented programming in its system code, this style of programming is not emphasized in Knowledge Craft as much as it is in KEE. As in KEE, objects are represented as frames (called schemata in Knowledge Craft) and methods as slot values. CRL-DEMONS in Knowledge Craft provide support for access-oriented programming by allowing procedural behavior to be invoked when a slot value is added, deleted, or modified. Demon functions can be used to initiate or return control to CRL-PROLOG or CRL-OPS programs.

Event Scheduler. CRL-AGENDA, a multi-queue event manager, can be used to schedule events to occur using either a simulated or a real clock. Events are represented as schemata, and are placed on an agenda. Event slots may include the event's assigned queue, its ordering within the queue, and the prescribed time the event will take place. This provides direct support for event-based simulations of complex processes.

Contexts and Hypothetical Reasoning. Contexts allow alternative solutions to be tested when solving a problem. Each schema name can be associated with multiple instantiations of the schema depending on the current context. The same schema in a different context may contain different slot values. Schema contexts form strict trees with inheritance. Explicit support is not provided for truth maintenance, but it can be added by a programmer. Carnegie Group takes the stance that the use of truth maintenance varies widely among systems, and no one solution would be generally satisfactory.

Knowledge Craft Development Environment

User Interface and Graphics Support. A CORE (GSPC, 1977; 1979) and schema-based graphics package for constructing 2-D graphics displays is provided. This is a device-independent package that provides functions for manipulating multiwindow displays. Graphic interfaces in Knowledge Craft are created and manipulated using *canvas*, *window*, and *viewport* schemata. A canvas schema is an abstract display stream with infinite extent in a user-coordinate space. Windows are rectangular areas within a canvas, and do not correspond to the rectangular boxes on the screen that are often called windows. Instead viewports refer to rectangular areas of the screen where part of the canvas is visible.

All graphics objects, including lines and text, are represented as schemata. The canvas consists of one or more graphic or textual objects that can be scaled to any size in a viewport. A canvas can contain multiple windows. This means that the same part of a canvas can be displayed in two windows simultaneously at different scalings (e.g., one can be a zoom view), and changes to an object in the canvas can be automatically reflected in each window where the object is visible because there is only one underlying schemata that represents the object on the canvas. Another advantage of a schema-based representation of graphic objects is that it facilitates the development of programs that can draw, edit, and reason about graphic objects on the screen.

Knowledge Craft provides support for building interfaces that use key words or control characters to execute commands. Escape-key string-completion is available to simplify entry of key words. User interfaces can easily be developed which provide keyboard commands equivalent to mouse-driven menu commands. Support for developing on-line help is also provided. The command system is hierarchically structured and represented as schemata.

Knowledge Base Editing, Testing, and Debugging. The *Schema Network Editor* supplied in the CRL-Workcenter can display schemata in a tree, allowing the user to add or delete a schema or modify a schema's attributes. Schemata are modified using an EMACS-like schema editor. The CRL-PROLOG Workcenter supplies axiom editing, listing, and tracing (e.g., If the fact "Fred is a bird" is displayed, the user can select the fact to discover that this was derived from the fact that "Fred is a canary"). A trace window of the goal tree is provided, and each node of the tree can be expanded to show the clause which generated the goal and the instantiations of relevant variables. The CRL-OPS Workcenter allows rule editing, listing of working memory and conflict set, and a step-by-step display of the CRL-OPS rules that fire and the changes they cause in the conflict set.

User-Defined Error Handling. Knowledge Craft provides a schema-based error-handling mechanism. Default error responses are available, but a programmer can specify a different response by supplying a function in the slot value for a particular error condition.

Version Management. Using the context mechanism, different versions of a knowledge base can be created and saved.

Database Support. On the DEC VAX a multi-user database system is available that can store a very large number of schemata. This makes it possible to separate schemata from a virtual memory file, and have needed schemata loaded on demand only. Temporary changes by local users are cached in memory and do not change the shared database.

Functionality of Knowledge Craft

Knowledge Craft is written in Common LISP and is currently available on several hardware platforms. Applications of Knowledge Craft include: APES—DEC (Carnegie Group, 1988), a system for the automated design of digital circuits; CLASS—Boeing (Carnegie Group, 1988), a composite shop planning and scheduling system; Dispatcher—DEC (Buday, 1986; Carnegie, 1988), a system that manages an automated material handling system in a DEC factory; Forge Shop Scheduler—Ellwood City Forge Corporation (Schreiber, 1987; Carnegie Group, 1988), a production scheduling system based on a knowledge-based finite capacity scheduler; BLAST—DEC (Carnegie Group, 1988), a network design assistant that makes recommendations for making networks perform to specifications; Production Planner—DEC (Carnegie Group, 1988), a knowledge-based production planning and simulation system; and SBDS—Ford Motor Company (Carnegie Group, 1988), a system for troubleshooting faulty automobile powertrains.

SRL, the prototype of Knowledge Craft that was developed at Carnegie-Mellon, has been used for several applications that have been described in the literature, including Callisto (Sathi, Fox, Greenberg, and Morton, 1985; Sathi, Fox, and Greenberg, 1985), a product management system which focuses on the semantic representation of activities and product configuration; Isis (Fox, 1983; Fox and Smith, 1984), a production management system which models, schedules, and monitors activities; Rome (Kosy and Dhar, 1983; Kosy and Wise, 1984), a quantitative reasoning system for long-range planning; DS (Fox, Wright, and Adam, 1983), a rule-based architecture for the sensor-based diagnosis of physical processes; and INET (Reddy and Fox, 1983), a technique for corporate distribution analysis based on the knowledge-base simulation approach to modeling and simulation.

Support for Knowledge Craft

Carnegie Group offers a variety of courses on Knowledge Craft, Language Craft, and other topics in AI. They will make arrangements to teach courses either at the customer's site or at their headquarters in Pittsburgh. One person must be trained with the first copy of Knowledge Craft. Additional training is optional and will be provided at an additional cost.

The Carnegie Group emphasizes its experience in building custom systems and claims its expertise lies in four major areas: (1) automated engineering design (CAD/CAM/CAE) including VLSI and metal products design aids; (2) production management including factory shop floor management; (3) sensor-based machine control and diagnosis management of flexible manufacturing systems components and robotics; and (4) project and product management engineering and software products.

The following companies have an equity relationship with Carnegie Group: Ford Motor Company, Digital Equipment Corporation, Texas Instruments, Boeing Company, and US West.

Cost of Knowledge Craft

The first copy of Knowledge Craft includes product support for one year. Additional copies on the same hardware at the same site are discounted. A first copy at a second site or on different hardware is also discounted, but at a lower rate. Universities and non-profit institutions can purchase any number of copies at a discount.

ART (Automated Reasoning Tool®, Inference Corporation)

ART is an integrated tool based on a powerful rule-based language that supports hypothetical reasoning and other features. ART integrates rules, frames, logic, and LISP functional programming into one system. A sophisticated display package facilitates the development of end-user iconic displays. The current version is release 3.1 which includes an object-oriented and access-oriented programming system. The object-oriented system supports *multi-methods* which allows the method selected in message passing to be determined by (a vector of) multiple objects rather than just the receiving object of a message (see Chapter 1 for a more detailed explanation of multimethods). An advance in ART 3.1 is an extension of the pattern matching technology in ART's rule compiler so that rules are now *joined* from right to left, as well as the customary left to right. This results in improved performance because less comparisons are necessary during pattern matching. ART 3.1 also includes a *file compiler,* which compiles an ART knowledge base into a binary format, greatly speeding up the loading of large knowledge bases. In addition, Inference claims ART 3.1 has eliminated 99% of garbage collection in the system by using explicit deallocation of storage. Additional information on ART and Inference Corporation can be found in Williams (1984a, b), Clayton (1985a, b, c, d), Schindler (1986c, d), Inder (1987a, b; 1988), and Grégoire (in press).

Basic Features of ART

Propositions, Facts, and Patterns. A *proposition* in ART expresses declarative knowledge including general relations (e.g., "dogs are mammals") and situation-specific relations (e.g., "the dog is sick"). A *fact* in ART consists of a proposition and an *extent*, that is, in what situations or *Viewpoints*™ the proposition is valid. ART differentiates between facts that are explicitly stated to be false and facts

---

Automated Reasoning Tool is a registered trademark of Inference Corporation.
Viewpoints is a trademark of Inference Corporation.

that are unknown (not known to be true or false). This is supported by allowing ART propositions to have truth values associated with them. In addition, ART supports logical dependencies which allows facts to be retracted if it is found that supporting facts are actually known to be false at a later point. For example, ART allows rules of the form While A is true, B is true.

In ART, *patterns* are propositions with variables. Patterns may also include wild cards, literal values, logical connectives, as well as arbitrary predicates and procedural restrictions encoded in LISP. *Goal* patterns, in ART, define the conditions for which the known data might suggest actions or changes in the propositional database. The set of active goals are stored in a goal base. Strategy patterns represent the conditions under which the system's current goals suggest a particular processing or inference approach to occur. A strategy pattern can describe relationships among entries in the *goal base*. Strategy patterns are stored in a strategy base.

Schemata. Schemata in ART allow the user to describe objects and classes of objects. Multiple inheritance is used and is integrated with the rule language; that is, rules can refer to schemata. Slots are represented as schemata and rules can reason about slots. ART 3.1 supports attaching procedural actions to slots, that is, methods and active values. However, ART still lacks explicit support for stating constraints on slot values (in constrast to KEE). Users may define relations in the system with their own inverses and transitivity properties. Relations may introduce other new relations automatically and users may define their own inheritance relations.

Below is a sample compiled ART schema (Clayton, 1985b):

```
(DEFSCHEMA DOG
    "schema for all dogs"          ;comments can be inserted here
    (HAS-INSTANCES FIFI)           ;ART automatically inserts
    (HAS-INSTANCES FIDO)           ;HAS-INSTANCES slots
    (VOCALIZATION BARK)
    (SOCIAL-ENVIRONMENT PACK)
    (OFFSPRING PUPPIES)
    (BODY-COVERING FUR)            ;inherited from MAMMAL schema
    (BIRTH LIVE)                   ;inherited from MAMMAL schema
    (IS-A MAMMAL))
```

Object-Oriented, Access-Oriented, and Functional Programming. In addition to LISP functional programming, ART 3.1 provides explicit support for object- and access-oriented programming styles. Methods in the form of LISP functions are attached to schema objects using the defaction function. There are four types of methods in ART: primary, before, after, and whopper. Whopper methods can be executed partly before and partly after the other kinds of methods with the use of whopper-continue statements that are used to pass control to other method types. Another class of actions in ART are *active values* which provide an access-oriented programming facility. These are also defined using defaction. Active values can be invoked either before or after the put, get, modify, and retract operations.

Rules. Rules are used in ART to encode procedural knowledge. ART allows for general purpose, hypothetical, constraint, and belief rules. ART provides a rich pattern matching language which is used to create and apply rules. Forward and backward chaining is possible by combining goals and facts within a rule. The conflict resolution strategy may be defined by the user. Arbitrary function calls are allowed in the condition and action statements of a rule. ART also includes a rule compiler to produce more efficient run-time applications. Below are some sample ART rules (Williams, 1984a):

- Forward chaining rule

  English: Any expression raised to the zero power can be simplified to 1.

  ART: (**Defrule** Exponent-Zero (is ?X (expt ? 0)) => (**assert** (is ?X 1)))

- Backward chaining rule

  English: If you want to know whether person A and person B are cousins, verify that some combination of their parents are siblings.

  ART: (**Defrule** Cousin
  (cousins ?A ?B)
  <=
  (parent ?parent1 ?A)
  (parent ?parent2 ?B)
  (sibling ?parent1 ?parent2))

ART differentiates between inference and production rules. Inference rules add facts to the knowledge base while production rules change facts (e.g., the value of an object attribute). An example production rule is printed below in English only.

AND-Gate-Rule:
If the output of an AND-gate is 1, and one of its inputs goes to 0, change the output to 0.

Viewpoints. The most sophisticated feature in ART is the robust implementation of *Viewpoints,* a mechanism designed for hypothetical reasoning. ART can process a very large number of Viewpoints "simultaneously." The Viewpoint mechanism supports logic programming without backtracking, temporal reasoning, and assumption-based truth maintenance. Viewpoints are similar in functionality to de Kleer's assumption-based truth maintenance system (de Kleer, 1986). Viewpoints are hierarchically organized and multiple inheritance or *merge* Viewpoints are allowed. ART automatically checks for inconsistencies. The Viewpoint structure can be inspected by the user and referenced by a rule. In addition, logical dependencies can be used within a Viewpoint.

Uncertainty. Each Viewpoint can have a confidence rating associated with it that gives a numeric estimate of a Viewpoint's validity. Numerical certainty factors can also be associated with individual facts in the knowledge base.

ART Development Environment

User Interface and Graphics Support. The ART Studio™ includes knowledge base browsers, an execution monitor, and a graphics package. ART has a built-in help system which is available to the user at any time, and is designed to explain system commands and language features. The user can use either a mouse-based menu system or equivalent keyboard commands to browse through the system. Command entry in ART is facilitated by spelling correction and command abbreviations.

ART includes a graphics package called ARTIST™ (ART Image Synthesis Tool) that assists a developer in creating iconic and animated displays for end users. Icons are represented as schemata, but the code is generated automatically by ARTIST when the programmer uses the structured graphics editor to create the icons. Rules can operate directly on the representations of the graphic objects allowing for rule-based animation.

Knowledge Base Editing, Testing, and Debugging. Graphical representations of hierarchical knowledge structures can be automatically displayed as graphs with elliptical nodes. A structured knowledge base editor is also provided. ART 2.0 does not provide a schema editor equivalent to KEE's graphical unit editor.

A program monitor allows the developer to observe and debug program behavior in execution. There are schema, rule, and Viewpoint browsers included in the system. The debugging environment allows tracing execution, setting breakpoints, and examining the state of execution. The users can manually enter

---

ART Studio is a trademark of Inference Corporation.
ARTIST is a trademark of Inference Corporation.

or alter facts while the system is running. The mouse can be used to facilitate user input.

Functionality of ART

ART is written in Common LISP and is currently supported on several LISP and UNIX workstations. ART is a powerful programming environment and is appropriate for solving a large class of problems. A goal of Inference is to make ART a general purpose AI programming language and environment that allows for LISP or C programming, but does not require it. Although a carefully written ART program can run efficiently for a real-time application, it may require more computational resources than the other systems.

Examples of ART applications include: The Authorizer's Assistant— American Express Corporation (Inference, 1986), an interactive authorization support system; The Expert Cabling System—Ferranti Computer Systems, Limited (Inference, 1986), an expert system for cabling configuration of computer systems; CSI Expert Publishing System—Crossfield CSI (Inference, 1986), a newspaper publishing system; EROS—Ferranti Computer Systems, Limited (Inference, 1986), a system for battlefield radio signal analysis; FFAST—Coopers & Lybrand (Inference, 1986), a financial expert system development framework; The Foreign Exchange Advisory System—The Athena Group (Inference, 1986); MEDCHEC—Lockheed (Inference, 1986); MIRAGE—Hughes Aircraft Company (Inference, 1986), a 64-bit microcode emulator; MSU—Westinghouse Electric Corporation (The Waggener Group, 1987), a knowledge-based production scheduler; NAVEX—NASA (Maletz, 1985; Inference, 1986), a navigation system for coordinating space shuttle radar tracking during re-entry, a task normally performed by trained NASA staff; NEXPERTS—Composition Systems (The Waggener Group, 1985), a distributed decision network for automated newspaper layout that consists of ten cooperating expert systems running on different hosts connected by a network; The Portfolio Management Advisor—The Athena Group (Inference, 1986), an expert system for managing institutional investment portfolios; and TIARA—The Equitable (Inference, 1986), an internal audit risk accessor.

Support for ART

Basic and advanced training courses, phone assistance, software and documentation upgrades, and custom development services are available to ART customers. The ART tutorial materials are well-written and comprehensive. Inference is privately owned with several corporate investors including Lockheed and Ford Motor Company.

Cost of ART

The cost of ART varies depending on the hardware platform on which it is used. Multicopy discounts are also available. In addition, run-time only versions of ART are considerably less expensive than complete development systems. The first copy of ART includes technical support (e.g., phone assistance) and maintenance (software and documentation updates) for one year. Training is not included and can be obtained for an additional per person fee. Training is available for two people for two weeks at Inference's Los Angeles headquarters. On-site and phone consulting are also available. After the first year, maintenance, including support and software and documentation upgrades are available at an additional fee. Educational institutions can purchase ART at a discount.

Conclusion

S.1 is a rule-based development and delivery system that includes object-attribute-value triplets, certainty factors, backward chaining, control blocks, and subsumption-based reasoning. S.1 is designed for using a structured-selection problem-solving strategy. Teknowledge has a great deal of experience in developing systems of this kind. S.1 is also less expensive and easier to learn than the other systems. It comes closest to fitting the definition of a shell, that is, an expert system development tool that provides a standard method for representing domain knowledge and problem-solving strategies.

ART, KEE, and Knowledge Craft are all similar in that each supports a variety of AI techniques. They are all flexible and general purpose AI programming environments. The interactive graphics facilities for these three systems are fairly sophisticated, though KEE provides the most complete graphically-oriented interface for the programmer. KEE is also very well integrated with an object-oriented programming system.

ART provides a sophisticated mechanism for hypothetical and temporal reasoning through the use of multiple Viewpoints. Knowledge Craft provides a less powerful context mechanism, but it is hard to compare the features because they exist for different reasons. The current version of KEE includes KEEworlds, an assumption-based truth maintenance system that provides similar functionality to ART's Viewpoints. KEEworlds is described in detail in the next chapter.

ART can be viewed as an extended rule-based system, whereas KEE and Knowledge Craft are best viewed as extended frame-based systems. In other words, the integration of a fully complete rule, frame, and logic system probably does not yet exist. However, there is no agreement as to whether this is necessary or desirable. A key issue is whether or not choosing among alternative methods is a matter of style or makes an appreciable difference in solving real problems.

Although Knowledge Craft is a general expert system tool, Carnegie Group has chosen to focus their efforts on industrial manufacturing applications. Carnegie Group is also pursuing an interesting line of development by using Knowledge Craft as the foundation for several application shells. Although IntelliCorp's SimKit is not an application shell, it can be viewed as a simulation shell or toolkit in the sense that it provides much of the standard functionality required for simulation modeling (SimKit is described in Chapters 8 and 9). If an organization plans on developing different kinds of applications, then there is an advantage in using one basic system with a shell for each application rather than purchasing, maintaining, and training people in multiple systems.

All four products are well supported. However, there is still much room for improvement with regard to general usability, power, and flexibility. The products have become more reliable and robust and the vendors are committed to improving them, particularly according to user needs. However, these tools are still expensive at this time, and therefore, for the present, they are out of the reach of many potential customers. Many of the companies that are working on expert systems applications are still very discrete about applications that have been completed or are in development, in order to maintain a competitive edge. In the next few years, as more information becomes available on systems that are in routine use, it should become clearer how useful and cost effective the expert systems approach is for a broad range of real-world applications.

References

Alper, A. (1988). Brokerage seeks to trade on AI. *Computerworld, May 23,* 1988.

Bachant, J., & McDermott, J. (1984). R1 Revisited: Four years in the trenches. *AI Magazine, 5(3),* 21–32.

Bobrow, D., & Stefik, M. J. (1986). Perspectives on artificial intelligence programming. *Science, 231,* 951–957.

Brown, J. S., Burton, R. R., & de Kleer, J. (1982). Pedagogical, natural language, and knowledge engineering techniques in SOPHIE I, II, and III. In D. Sleeman & J. S. Brown (Eds.), *Intelligent tutoring systems* (pp. 227–282). London: Academic Press.

Brownston, L., Farrell, R., Kant, E., & Martin, N. (1985). *Programming expert systems in OPS5: An introduction to rule-based programming.* Reading, MA: Addison Wesley.

Buchanan, B. G., & Shortliffe, E. H. (1984). *Rule-based expert systems.* Reading, MA: Addison-Wesley.

Buday, R. (1986). Carnegie: Schooled in expert systems. *Information Week, April 28, (63),* 35–37.

Carnegie Group. (1986). *Knowledge Craft overview.* Pittsburgh, PA: Carnegie Group Inc.

Carnegie Group. (1988). *Knowledge Craft application notes.* Pittsburgh, PA: Carnegie Group Inc.

Clancey, W. J. (1985). Heuristic classification. *Artificial Intelligence, 27,* 289–350.

Clayton, B. (1985a). *ART programming primer.* Los Angeles, CA: Inference Corporation.

Clayton, B. (1985b). *ART programming tutorial, Volume 1: Elementary ART programming.* Los Angeles, CA: Inference Corporation

Clayton, B. (1985c). *ART programming tutorial, Volume 2: A first look at Viewpoints.* Los Angeles, CA: Inference Corporation.

Clayton, B. (1985d) *ART programming tutorial, Volume 3: Advanced topics in ART.* Los Angeles, CA: Inference Corporation.

de Kleer, J. (1986). An assumption-based TMS. *Artificial Intelligence, 28(2)*, 127–162.

Fagan, L., Kunz, J., Feigenbaum, E., & Osborner, J. (1984). Extensions to the rule-based formalism for a monitoring task. In B. G. Buchanan & E. H. Shortliffe (Eds.), *Rule-based expert systems* (pp. 397–423). Reading, MA: Addison-Wesley.

Faught, W. S. (1986). Applications of AI in engineering. *Computer, 19(7)*, 17–27.

Fikes, R., & Kehler T. (1985). The role of frame-based representation in reasoning. *Communications of the ACM, 28(9)*, 904–920.

Forgy, C. (1981). *OPS5 user's manual* (Technical Report CMU–CS–81–135). Pittsburgh, PA: Carnegie-Mellon University.

Fox, M. (1983). *Constraint-directed search: A case study of job shop scheduling* (Technical Report CMU–RI–TR–83–22). Pittsburgh, PA: Carnegie-Mellon University.

Fox, M., Lowenfeld, S., & Kleinosky, P. (1983). Techniques for sensor-based diagnosis. *Proceedings of the International Joint Conference on Artificial Intelligence*, IJCAI-83. Karlsruhe, W. Germany.

Fox, M., & Smith, S. (1984). ISIS: A knowledge-based system for factory scheduling. *Expert Systems, 1(1)*.

Fox, M., Wright, J., & Adam, D. (1985). *Experience with SRL: An analysis of a frame-based knowledge representation* (Technical Report CMU–RI–TR–85–10). Pittsburgh, PA: Carnegie-Mellon University.

Fraser, J. (1987a). Learning KEE in Munich, *Airing, 1*, 15–16. Scotland: AIAI, University of Edinburgh.

Fraser, J. (1987b). Some aspects of programming in KEE, *Airing, 3*, 11–15. Scotland: AIAI, University of Edinburgh.

Genesereth, M., & Ginsberg M. (1985). Logic programming. *Communications of the ACM, 28(9)*, 933-941.

Grégoire, E. (in press). Evaluation of expert system tools KEE & ART: A case study. *International Journal of Applied Artificial Intelligence.*

GSPC (1977). Status report of the graphics standards planning committee. *Computer Graphics, 11*.

GSPC (1979). Status report of the graphics standards committee. *Computer Graphics, 13(3)*.

Hayes-Roth, F. (1984a). The industrialization of knowledge engineering. In W. Reitman (Ed.), *Artificial intelligence applications in business.* Norwood, NJ: Ablex Publishing Corp.

Hayes-Roth, F. (1984b). The knowledge-based expert system: A tutorial. *Computer, 17(9)*, 11–28.

Hayes-Roth, F. (1985). Rule-based systems. *Communications of the ACM, 28(9)*, 921–932.

Hayes-Roth, F., Waterman, D., & Lenat, D. (Eds.). (1983). *Building expert systems.* Reading, MA: Addison-Wesley.

Hollan, J. D., Hutchins, E. L., & Weitzman, L. (1984). Steamer: An interactive inspectable simulation-based training system. *AI Magazine, 5(2)*, 15–27.

Inder, R. (1987a). The State of the ART, part 1. *Airing, 1*, 8–14. Scotland: AIAI, University of Edinburgh.

Inder, R. (1987b). The State of the ART, part 2. *Airing, 2*, 7–15. Scotland: AIAI, University of Edinburgh.

Inder, R. (1988). The State of the ART, part 3. *Airing, 4*, 13-20. Scotland: AIAI, University of Edinburgh.

Inference. (1986). *ART application notes*. Los Angeles, CA: Inference Corp.

IntelliCorp, Inc. (1985). *The knowledge engineering environment*. Mountain View, CA: IntelliCorp, Inc.

IntelliCorp, Inc. (1987). *Artificial intelligence application notes*. Mountain View, CA: IntelliCorp, Inc.

Johnson, T. (1984). *The commercial application of expert systems technology*. London: Ovum, Ltd.

Kingston, J. A. (1987). Knowledge Craft training in Pittsburgh and Knowledge Craft European user group. *Airing, 2*, 18–23. Scotland: AIAI, University of Edinburgh.

Kingston, J. A. (1987a). Technical overview of Knowledge Craft, part 1. *Airing, 3*, 6–20. Scotland: AIAI, University of Edinburgh.

Kingston, J. A. (1987b). Technical overview of Knowledge Craft, part 2. *Airing, 4*, 9–12. Scotland: AIAI, University of Edinburgh.

Kosy, D., & Dhar, V. (1983). *Knowledge-based support system for long range planning* (Technical Report CMU). Pittsburgh, PA: Carnegie-Mellon University.

Kosy, D., & Wise, B. (1984). Self-explanatory financial planning models. *Proceedings of the National Conference on Artificial Intelligence* (pp. 176–181). AAAI-84. Austin, TX.

Kunz, J. C., Kehler, T. P., & Williams, M. D. (1984). Applications development using a hybrid AI development system. *AI Magazine, 5(3)*, 41–54.

Linden, E. (1985). IntelliCorp: The selling of artificial intelligence. *High Technology*, 22–25.

Macleish, K. J., Thiedke, S., & Vennergrund, D. (1986). Expert systems in central office switch maintenance. *IEEE Communications Magazine, 24(9)*, 26–33.

Maletz, M. (1985). *NAVEX: Space shuttle navigation expert system*. Los Angeles, CA: Inference Corporation.

Mettrey, W. (1987). An assessment of tools for building large knowledge-based systems. *AI Magazine, 8(4)*, 81–89.

Model, M. (1979). *Monitoring system behavior in a complex computation environment* (Technical Report STAN–CS–79–701). Stanford, CA: Computer Science Department, Stanford University.

Nado, R., Bock, C., & Fikes, R. (1985). *An assertion and retrieval interface for a frame-based representation system*. Mountain View, CA: IntelliCorp, Inc.

Pepper, J., & Kahn, G. (1987). Knowledge Craft: An environment for rapid prototyping of expert systems. *A Review of Products, Services & Research* (pp. 72–79). AAAI-87 Conference Materials. Seattle, WA.

Reddy, Y., & Fox, M. (1983). INET: A knowledge-based simulation approach to distribution analysis. *Proceedings of the IEEE Computer Society Trends and Applications*. Washington, DC: National Bureau of Standards.

Richer, M. H., & Clancey, W .J. (1985). Guidon-Watch: A graphic interface for viewing a knowledge-based system. *IEEE Computer Graphics and Applications, 5(11)*, 51–64.

Sathi, A., Fox, M., Greenberg, M., & Morton, T. (1985). *Callisto: An intelligent project management system* (CMU Technical Report). Pittsburgh, PA: Carnegie-Mellon University.

Sathi, A., Fox, M., & Greenberg, M. (1985). The application of knowledge representation techniques to project management. *Transactions on Pattern Analysis and Machine Intelligence.*

Schindler, P. (1986a). Tools pick up pace of expert system. *Electronic Design, July* .

Schindler, P.(1986b). At Teknowledge, knowledge is first. *Information Week, 63, April 28*, 26–27.

Schindler, P. (1986c). IntelliCorp holds KEE to the market. *Information Week, 63, April 28*, 30–32.

Schindler, P. (1986d). The ART of Inference: Power and flexibility. *Information Week, 63, April 28*, 38–39.

Schoen, E., & Smith R. G. (1983). Impulse, a display-oriented editor for Strobe. *Proceedings of the National Conference on Artificial Intelligence* (pp. 356–358). AAAI-83. Washington, DC.

Schreiber, R. R. (1987). Gaining the upper hand with AI. *CIM Technology, May.*

Shortliffe, E. H. (1976). *Computer-based medical consultations: MYCIN.* New York: Elsevier.

Shortliffe, E. H., Scott, A., Bischoff, M., Campbell, A., van Melle, W., & Jacobs, C. (1984). An expert system for oncology protocol management. In B. G. Buchanan & E. H. Shortliffe (Eds.), *Rule-based expert systems* (pp. 653-665). Reading, MA: Addison-Wesley.

Shortliffe, E. H., & Buchanan, B. G. (1984). A model of inexact reasoning in medicine. In B. G. Buchanan & E. H. Shortliffe (Eds.), *Rule-based expert systems* (pp. 233–262). Reading, MA: Addison-Wesley.

Smith, R. G. (1984). *Structured object programming in STROBE* (AI Memo No. 18). Ridgefield, CT: Schlumberger-Doll Research.

Stefik, M. J. (1979). An examination of a frame-structured representation system. *Proceedings of the Sixth International Joint Conference on Artificial Intelligence.* IJCAI-79. Tokyo, Japan.

Stefik, M. J., & Bobrow, D. G. (1989). Object-oriented programming: Themes and variations. In M. H. Richer (Ed.), *AI tools and techniques.* Norwood, NJ: Ablex Publishing Corp.

Stefik, M. J., Bobrow, D., & Kahn, K. (1988). Integrating access-oriented programming into a multiparadigm environment. In M. H. Richer (Ed.), *AI tools and techniques.* Norwood, NJ: Ablex Publishing Corp.

Stefik, M. J., Bobrow, D. G., Mittal, S., & Conway, L. (1983). Knowledge programming in Loops: Report on an experimental course. *AI Magazine, 4(3)*, 3–13.

Subrahmanyam, P. A. (1986). Synapse: An expert system for VLSI design. *Computer, 19(7)*, 78–89.

Teknowledge. (1986). *NCR Corporation builds computer maintenance expert system using Teknowledge S.1 product.* Palo Alto, CA: Teknowledge, Inc.

Teknowledge. (1988). *S.1 application notes*. Palo Alto, CA: Teknowledge, Inc.

The Waggener Group. (1985). *Profile of an expert system application for newspaper publishing*. Los Angeles, CA: Inference Corporation.

The Waggener Group. (1987). *An expert system for production scheduling*. Los Angeles, CA: Inference Corporation.

van Melle, W. (1981). *System aids in constructing consultation programs*. Ann Arbor, MI: UMI Research Press.

van Melle, W., Shortliffe, E. H., & Buchanan, B. G. (1984). EMYCIN: A knowledge engineer's tool for constructing rule-based expert systems. In B. G. Buchanan & E. H. Shortliffe (Eds.), *Rule-based expert systems* (pp. 302–313). Reading, MA: Addison-Wesley.

Waterman, D. A. (1986). *A guide to expert systems*. Reading, MA: Addison-Wesley.

Williams, C. (1984a). Software tool packages the expertise needed to build expert systems. *Electronic Design, August,* 153–167.

Williams, C. (1984b). *ART the advanced reasoning tool—conceptual overview*. Los Angeles, CA: Inference Corporation.

Appendix A: AI Companies Whose Products Are Described

Carnegie Group Inc.
5 PPG Place
Pittsburgh, PA 15222
(412) 642-6900

Inference Corp.
5300 W. Century Blvd., 3rd floor
Los Angeles CA 90045
(213) 417-7997

IntelliCorp, Inc.
1975 El Camino Real West
Mountain View, CA 94040-2216
(415) 965-5500

Teknowledge, Inc.
1850 Embarcadero Road
P.O. Box 10119
Palo Alto, CA 94303
(415) 424-0500

Chapter 4

Reasoning with Worlds and Truth Maintenance*

Robert E. Filman
IntelliCorp, Inc.

Broadly speaking, computers are information transducers. They read data, manipulate it in some computational process, and display the results. The mapping we create between the input data, manipulation and output data, and the external world is part of what makes computers valuable. The payroll program that takes wage rates and hours worked, multiplies and figures deductions, and prints the values for net paychecks is useful because the wage rates and hours worked, computations, and net checks correspond to the real hours and rates of the company's workers. Traditionally, computers have been limited to modeling only those parts of the world where regularity dominates exception. That is, because workers are paid the product of their wage rate and hours worked, less deductions computed by simple formulas and table look-ups, it is straightforward to write a computer program that computes paychecks. Because a company has many workers which it repeatedly pays by the same algorithm, it is worthwhile for it to have such a program written. To the extent that the underlying

*This is a slightly revised and expanded version of an article that appeared in *Communications of the ACM, 31(4)*, 382–401, April 1988. Copyright © 1988, Association for Computing Machinery, Inc. It is reprinted here with the kind permission of the editors and the publisher.

I would like to thank William Faught, Richard Fikes, Peter Friedland, Paul Morris, Robert Nado, Anne Paulson, Marilyn Stelzner, and Eric Weiner for their insightful comments on the drafts of this chapter. The KEEworlds/ATMS system was designed and implemented by IntelliCorp's Research Department: Richard Fikes, Robert Filman, Phillip McBride, Paul Morris, Robert Nado, Anne Paulson, Richard Treitel, and Martin Yonke.

This research was supported by the Defense Advanced Research Project Agency under Contract F30602–85–C–0065. The views and conclusions reported here are those of the author and should not be construed as representing the official position or policy of DARPA, the U.S. government, or IntelliCorp, Inc.

world is more complex, the program required for the modeling becomes more complex, and takes (perhaps exponentially) more skill to design, more time to write, more effort to debug, and more devotion to maintain. A pay system based, for example, on the complexity of task performed, the external demand for the objects produced, predictions about future economic conditions, and the artistic quality of the work is beyond the reach of conventional programming technology. Dealing with that degree of complexity requires more sophisticated systems than are currently available.

The goal of knowledge-based systems (KBS) technology is to expand greatly the horizon of "reasonable-to-build" applications. Using KBS technology simplifies modeling a large class of complex situations involving symbolic reasoning and eases stating complicated things about irregular domains. Nevertheless, even this expressiveness would not be useful without the tools to make it accessible—inspection and modification mechanisms to reveal the state of the model, and input and display mechanisms to easily translate between computer and human-understandable forms. Towards this end, several *knowledge-based system development environments* have been developed, both in research institutions and commercially. These environments use technologies such as pattern-action rules (EMYCIN [van Melle, Scott, Bennett, and Peairs, 1981], OPS5 [Brownston, Farrell, Kant, and Martin, 1985], ART® [Williams, 1984], and S.1 [Hayes-Roth and London, 1985]), frames (Units [Stefik, 1979], and KL-One [Brachman and Schmolze, 1985]), variants of procedural attachment—that is, demons and object-oriented programming (Smalltalk-80 [Goldberg and Robson, 1983], and Flavors [Symbolics, 1985]), and integrations of the above (Loops [Stefik, Bobrow, Mittal and Conway, 1983], and KEE® [Fikes and Kehler, 1985]). Such environments provide not only the internal representational structures of their chosen paradigm, but also interface facilities that understand and can manipulate these structures.

Recently, we have extended the KEE environment to include both a *truth maintenance system* (TMS) (based on de Kleer's work on the Assumption-based Truth Maintenance System [ATMS] [de Kleer, 1986]) and a context or *worlds system* (Morris and Nado, 1986). We call these extensions KEEworlds™. A world represents a set of related facts—for example, a situation, a simulation checkpoint, a belief set, or a hypothetical state of a problem solver. A world is characterized by a set of *assumptions*. The TMS remembers the assumptions on which each deduced fact is based. A world sees a deduced fact if and only if the world's assumptions are a superset of the assumptions that support that deduction.

The integration of a conventional object-oriented representation environment with worlds and truth maintenance is a novel combination. It requires modifying

ART is a registered trademark of Inference Corporation.
KEE is a registered trademark of IntelliCorp, Inc.
KEEworlds is a trademark of IntelliCorp, Inc.

the system's internal representation structures and constructing a new rule system to manipulate world and ATMS entities. Similarly, discovering how best to exploit these new facilities requires further research and experimentation. This chapter presents some of our early experiments with the new system.

The primary activity of a KEE system user is first to construct a *model* of an underlying domain and then to build one or more reasoning components that manipulate that model. Thus, KEE is a tool that enables *model-based reasoning*. In this chapter, we develop several examples of reasoning with KEEworlds, all centered around a common domain of scheduling shipments.

An Overview of Truth Maintenance

In general, reasoning is the process of deriving new knowledge from old. If the underlying knowledge never changes, if we never explore hypothetical spaces and if our knowledge is free of internal contradictions, the accumulation of knowledge is straightforward—we just add the results of our reasoning to our pile of knowledge. Unfortunately, few problems are so simple. We usually find ourselves reasoning under a set of assumptions that may be withdrawn or changed. Often the entire reasoning process is focused on identifying preferred assumption sets. Ideally, when the assumptions change, we would like to withdraw those conclusions that are no longer valid, retaining those that are still true. This requires attaching *justifications* or *dependencies* to derived facts, that is, reasons for belief in these facts.

Historically, the need for dependencies first arose in the context of the *frame problem* (McCarthy and Hayes, 1969)—the problem of determining what has not changed over an event or series of events. For example, we imagine situation S, where a monkey is in a room with a red box located at position $\langle x, y \rangle$. The action of the monkey, A, *pushing the box to* $\langle x', y' \rangle$ creates a new situation, S'. How is our computer system to know that the color of the box is still red in S'? It is not the case that the color of the box is constant over all actions. Instead, if A had been the action *painting the box green,* then the color of the box would be different in S'. Our system must somehow incorporate the knowledge that the action of moving an object does not change its color.

Systems such as STRIPS (Fikes and Nilsson, 1971) and PLANNER (Hewitt, 1971) approached the frame problem by associating with each action lists of facts that were added by the action and those that were deleted by the action. The problem with this approach was that to be correct the operators that changed system state had to modify all facts that had been derived on the basis of the now-to-be-deleted facts. That is, if in state S, above, we had concluded that the box at $\langle x, y \rangle$ was under a bunch of bananas, and action A was moving the box, we needed to withdraw this conclusion in S'.

One of the first systems to associate dependencies with derivations was Stallman and Sussman's system for circuit analysis, EL (Stallman and Sussman, 1977). Their goal was to find those faulty assumptions responsible for producing contradictions. They introduced the idea of *dependency-directed backtracking*. Traditionally, many systems have relied on *chronological backtracking*, that is, considering all the possibilities for the most recent choice before revising any earlier decision. Chronological backtracking has the advantage that it is simple to implement with a stack.

We illustrate the disadvantages of chronological backtracking with a variant on the monkey and bananas problem. In the traditional monkey and bananas problem, a monkey is in a room, the room has a bunch of bananas hanging from the ceiling, and there is a box on the floor. The monkey wants to get (and then eat) the bananas. To achieve this goal, the monkey must push the box under the bananas, climb the box, and grab the bananas. In our problem, our monkey comes into the room with several boxes and several bunches of hanging bananas. The monkey's goal is once again to obtain a comestible bunch. The monkey proceeds to select a bunch of bananas, select a box, push the box under the bananas, and climb and grab. But to the monkey's surprise, the bananas are not edible. The monkey has a failure. Chronologically backtracking, the monkey reconsiders his last decision, the box selection. So the monkey picks another box, climbs down, pushes the first box away, pushes the new box under the same bunch of bananas, and so forth. Only after the monkey has exhausted all the boxes in the room does the chronologically backtracking monkey reconsider his choice of which bunch of bananas to pursue. A monkey using dependency-directed backtracking would notice that the edibility of the bananas depended only on the bunch choice (independent of the box choice) and would revise that choice instead. That is, in dependency-directed backtracking, the choice to be revised is not simply the last choice made, but a choice that contributed to the failure. To be able to do this we must keep the dependencies of derivations. (There are, of course, other salutary effects from retaining dependencies for conclusions. The most important of these is that we are keeping the information required to explain the derivation and validity of those conclusions.)

Doyle (1979) and, independently, London (1978) were the first to recognize that the facilities for recording dependencies—dependency-directed backtracking and "currently believing" particular assumptions—could be incorporated into a system independent of an overarching reasoning mechanism. Doyle called his system a truth maintenance system or TMS (the term has stuck, though he currently favors the phrase *reason maintenance system.*) In addition to dependencies, Doyle's system incorporated the idea that particular assumptions could be *in* (currently believed) or *out* (not currently believed); a particular derivation would be valid, for example, if assumptions X and Y were *in*, but Z, *out*. In-ness and out-ness enable both modeling varying "current worlds" (worlds being assignments of in and out to assumptions) and basing beliefs on the out-ness of facts (in the spirit of PLANNER's THNOT [Hewitt, 1971]). Issues in the implementation of TMSs arise in the algorithms for revising the beliefs of the system when assumptions go in and out. In general, algorithmic and semantic difficulties can ensue when revising beliefs that have (circularly) come to support themselves.

Truth maintenance systems have been a fertile field for AI research, for example, in the work of de Kleer, Doyle, Steele, and Sussman (1979), McAllester (1982), McDermott (1983), and Martins and Shapiro (1983). In our work, we have been extending de Kleer's (1986) assumption-based truth maintenance system (ATMS) to include contextual mechanisms (worlds), nonmonotonicity (assumption-retraction), and integration with an underlying frame system.[1]

An Object-Centered Domain Description

We illustrate our discussion of knowledge representation and reasoning with examples from the problem of building tools to aid the dispatcher of the hypo-thetical Big Giant Trucking Company. Big Giant serves 24 cities in Indiana and Illinois (an area we call Mid.Continent [Figure 1]), moving shipments of various materials over particular highways in certain trucks driven by specified drivers. The tables in Appendix A present typical local data for the primary primitive domain objects in our example.

The dispatcher wants to devise a *schedule*—a collection of *trips* (an assign-ment of a truck and a driver to a particular itinerary) such that all shipments are picked up at their origins and delivered to their destinations. The dispatcher's job is complicated by the fact that he or she is working under a set of con-straints—restrictions about what constitutes a legal schedule. These constraints range from those of common sense, for example, "The driver of a trip has to be in the same city as the truck," and "You can't put more on a truck than it can hold"; through the legalities of this particular domain, "Union drivers can't drive more than 11 hours a day," and "You need the right kind of license to drive the bigger trucks"; and on to the absurdities that characterize so much of the real world, for example, "Driver White is wanted by the police in Illinois, and can't be sent there." Ideally, the dispatcher would like to *optimize*—to construct a near-minimal cost schedule—but in a highly constrained situation he is usually lucky just to find a *feasible* (legal) schedule.

---

[1]In the first two respects, our system appears similar in behavior to the Viewpoints™ facility of ART (Williams, 1984). As little has been published about the algorithms of that system, it is difficult to make detailed comparisons.

Viewpoints is a trademark of Inference Corporation.

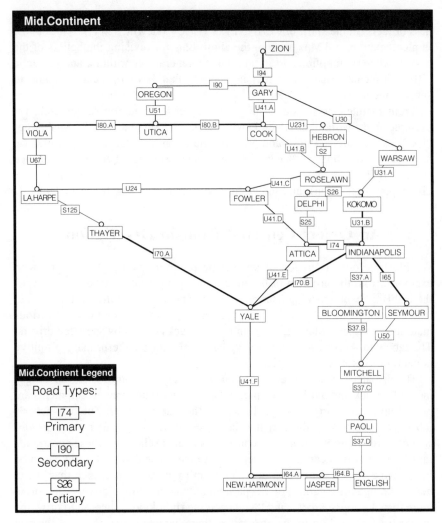

Figure 1. Mid.Continent

Although Big Giant is just a simple example developed to illustrate the points of this chapter, it shares a complex texture of regularity punctured by exceptions found in real problems. Such a combination of regularity and exception characterizes domains most appropriate for knowledge-based techniques: The regularity of the domain enables us to actually build something, whereas the exceptions foil conventional programming technology.

We represent the objects of the domain as *units* (frames) and arrange these units in a class hierarchy; thus, the class of trucks has *subclasses* big.trucks, medium.trucks, and small.trucks. Individual trucks are *members* of these classes (Figure 2). For example, truck Piper is a member of the class of small.trucks. Both classes and members are represented as units; a given unit can represent both a class and a member of a class.

Relationships between objects and values are represented as *slots* in the units that represent the objects. There are two kinds of slots: *own* slots and *member* slots. An own slot expresses a relationship involving its unit as an individual. Thus, the statement that the value of the own slot location in unit Piper is Gary is the assertion that "the location of Piper is Gary." Member slots occur only in class units. A member slot expresses a relationship involving the members of the class. The statement that the value of the member slot location in unit trucks is Indianapolis is (to a first approximation) the assertion that the location of any member of the class of trucks defaults to Indianapolis. *Facets* are annotations of slots to express additional information about that slot. The facets of member slots inherit along with the slot itself. Typical facets are *inheritance role* (the rule used to combine values from the unit's parents with the unit's local values), *valueclass* (type), and *min.cardinality* and *max.cardinality* (restrictions on the number of values a slot can have.)

KEE provides a number of standard inheritance roles, such as *union* (the value in an inherited slot is to be the union of the local values and the inherited values), *override.values* (if there is a local value in the slot, it is the value of the slot; otherwise, the values inherited from some parent are used), and *method* (a mechanism for assembling functions from fragments, similar to the mixins of Flavors [Symbolics, 1985]). Users can describe additional inheritance roles of their own. Although KEE provides a variety of inheritance mechanisms (and allows user-defined extensions to this set), in these examples we use inheritance only to specific locally overridable default values.

Valueclass information is used to deduce type violations, to determine the semantic classes for values, to coerce ambiguous notation to the appropriate datatype and to organize particular interface mechanisms. Cardinality information is similarly used to detect contradictions. The behavior of the system on detecting a valueclass or cardinality violation (coercing the value to the new class, interrogating the user, or noticing a contradiction) is controlled by the setting of a global switch.

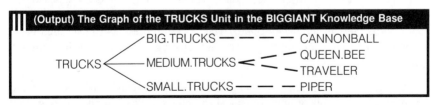

Figure 2. **The Trucks Hierarchy**

Since the task of the dispatcher is to create trips, it seems useful to reify the concept of a trip. We have a class of trips, and members of that class that are particular trips. Conceptually, the dispatcher believes that a trip has been composed when he or she has told a particular driver to drive around in a specific truck doing certain things. We represent these components of a trip as slots in the trip unit: driver, truck, and itinerary. We represent an itinerary as a sequence of *actions*, where each action is a triple: a city in which the action takes place, an object for the action (one of the shipments or nil), and the particular action to be taken (originating in that city, taking that shipment on or off the truck, or just visiting the city). This representation is strong enough to specify the route of a trip to the individual highway segment level, but flexible enough to allow us the more minimal specification of only the key actions of the trip, permitting the driver to take the usual (shortest) route between any two cities. From the specification of a driver, truck, and itinerary for a trip (and the weather), it is possible to derive other facts about a trip—for example, how long it takes and how much it costs. We also store such derived information in slots of the trip. Figure 3 shows the information in trip Example.trip partway through a problem-solving process.

Worlds and Truth Maintenance

In general, problem solving is the discovery of some set of beliefs—be they the values of some variables, a complex data structure, or a collection of formulas in a theorem prover. In systems that search, different sets of beliefs are believed at different points in the problem-solving process. That is, we may start by believing X, conclude Y, and then switch context to believing Z. On the other hand, the entire search process proceeds against a background of a fixed set of facts—a model of the unchanging underlying world. Thus, if our task is to generate itineraries through the cities of Mid.Continent, we have at various points beliefs about partially assembled itineraries and the costs and consequences of these itineraries. On the other hand, facts such as the connectivity network of cities and highways, the capacity of trucks, and the license class of drivers are constant throughout the problem-solving process. These *background facts* are true in every context. (Of course, if our problem solving included the possibility of improving drivers' licenses or adding routes to our territory, these would cease to be facts in the background.) The system represents (most) such background facts more economically, without incurring the space and time costs of truth maintenance.[2]

---

[2]Background facts are not to be confused with defaults—defaults are a mechanism for easily expressing a bulk of information and exceptions for that information. In general, a particular default may or may not be true in the background.

(Output) The EXAMPLE.TRIP Unit in BIGGIANT Knowledge Base in the START WORLD

Unit: **EXAMPLE.TRIP** in knowledge base **BIGGIANT** in world **START**
Created by FILMAN on 14-Apr-86 13:03:12
Modified by FILMAN on 14-Apr-86 13:04:10
Member Of: **TRIPS**

Own slot: **DISTANCE** from **EXAMPLE.TRIP**
Values: 360

Own slot: **DRIVER** from **EXAMPLE.TRIP**
Values: **GRAY**

Own slot: **DRIVER.COST** from **EXAMPLE.TRIP**
Values: UNKNOWN

Own slot: **DRIVER.COST.PER.HOUR** from **EXAMPLE.TRIP**
Values: UNKNOWN

Own slot: **DURATION** from **EXAMPLE.TRIP**
Values: UNKNOWN

Own slot: **ITINERARY** from **EXAMPLE.TRIP**
Values: ((**INDIANAPOLIS** NIL ORIGIN) (**SEYMOUR COMPUTERS** ON) (**THAYER COMPUTERS** OFF))

Own slot: **MAX.VOLUME** from **TRIPS**
Values: UNKNOWN

Own slot: **MAX.WEIGHT** from **TRIPS**
Values: UNKNOWN

Own slot: **ORIGIN** from **EXAMPLE.TRIP**
Values: **INDIANAPOLIS**

Own slot: **SHIPMENTS.HANDLED** from **EXAMPLE.TRIP**
Values: **COMPUTERS**

Own slot: **TOTAL.COST** from **EXAMPLE.TRIP**
Values: UNKNOWN

Own slot: **TRUCK** from **EXAMPLE.TRIP**
Values: **PIPER**

Own slot: **TRUCK.COST** from **EXAMPLE.TRIP**
Values: UNKNOWN

Figure 3. Example.trip

The ATMS is primarily concerned with those expressions that have different values in different contexts—the fodder of search. The ATMS records the justifications for beliefs, propagates justifications on the basis of new derivations, and ensures that exactly the appropriate derived facts are visible at any time. To accomplish this, the ATMS incorporates three basic concepts: *facts* (also called propositions or nodes), *assumptions*, and *justifications*.[3]

Formally, the ATMS manipulates *assumptions* and *propositions*. Each assumption corresponds to a primitive decision or choice. We use assumptions primarily either to hypothesize the existence of some context or to believe some particular fact. Each proposition has an associated *datum;* its content for the users of the ATMS. However, the datum is not itself used by the ATMS operations. (Thus, each own-slot value and unstructured fact that has been noticed by the ATMS is the datum for its own unique proposition. Background facts economize by going without propositions.) We use the notation $\mathcal{P}$ to represent the proposition associated with fact P, and the notation $\ddot{\mathcal{P}}$, to represent the assumption of P—the choice of believing $\mathcal{P}$.

Propositions may be *justified* in terms of assumptions or other propositions. Justifying proposition Z by X and $\mathcal{Y}$ $(X, \mathcal{Y} \vdash Z)$ is the assertion that whenever X and $\mathcal{Y}$ are believed, Z is to be believed, too.

Viewing the justification of a proposition by a set of assumptions and propositions as a single proof step, we see that the justification structures for a particular proposition form proof trees for that proposition. An *environment* is the set of assumptions obtained by transversing such a justification structure back to a well-founded set of assumptions. The *label* of a proposition is the set of minimal environments that support that proposition. The label can be seen as a summary of the necessary assumptions required for believing the associated datum. The primary operation in the ATMS is the addition of a justification to a proposition. This causes the ATMS to update the labels of all affected propositions. That is, if we discover another set of assumptions that supports the belief in proposition $\mathcal{P}$, we consider for each proposition directly justified by $\mathcal{P}$ whether that set of assumptions is part of a new minimal support for it. This process ensures that the label of a proposition always reflects every minimal set of assumptions that imply that proposition.

---

[3]There are various ways that information can be stored in the KEE system: as the values of own and member slots and facets, in the inheritance links between units, and in unstructured facts (arbitrary data structures). The ATMS maintains the truth of only the values of own slots and unstructured facts. We have not implemented truth maintenance on statements such as (Cannonball is in class large.trucks) (class membership) and (The transmission of all trucks is automatic) (member-slot values). Some of our recent work has produced Opus, a KEE-like system in which all facts are accessible to the ATMS (Fikes, Nado, Filman, McBride, Morris, Paulson, Treitel, and Yonke, 1987).

It is convenient to identify "assuming a datum in a context" with the proposition structure of that datum and with the datum itself. Data are distinguished from propositions because propositions include more information—proofs of the datum and summaries of the supporting assumptions of those proofs. Assumptions are distinguished from propositions because (a) propositions can acquire other justifications than just the decision to assume them, and (b) assumptions are used for the system's context mechanism. On the other hand, it is convenient in most situations to think of facts as identical with their propositions (and, occasionally, with the assumption of those facts).

Let us consider an example in greater detail. Suppose we come to justify the fact

The truck.cost of some.trip is 452 $(\mathcal{A})$

on the basis of the facts

The truck of some.trip is Traveler $(\mathcal{B})$

and

The itinerary of some.trip is... (C)

This belief might arise, for example, from the application of a rule about computing truck costs. In any context where we come to believe $\ddot{\mathcal{B}}$ and $\ddot{C}$, we also believe $\mathcal{A}$. If our beliefs in $\mathcal{B}$ and C are based on assumptions $\ddot{\mathcal{B}}$ and $\ddot{C}$, then the structure for the proposition whose datum is $\mathcal{A}$ is the justification structure to $\mathcal{B}$ and C, and the label, $\{\{\ddot{\mathcal{B}}, \ddot{C}\}\}$ (Figure 4).

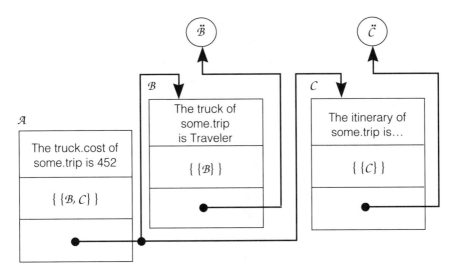

Figure 4. The Proposition Structure of $\mathcal{A}$

We might also come to justify $\mathcal{A}$ on the basis of facts C and

The truck of some.trip is Queen.Bee, $\qquad\qquad$ (𝒟)

𝒟 similarly supported by assumption $\ddot{\mathcal{D}}$. The label of $\mathcal{A}$ would then be $\{\{\ddot{\mathcal{B}}, \ddot{\mathcal{C}}\}, \{\ddot{\mathcal{C}}, \ddot{\mathcal{D}}\}\}$. Our justification structure grows to that of Figure 5. If we discover a justification of $\mathcal{A}$ that traces back to assumptions $\ddot{\mathcal{B}}$, $\ddot{\mathcal{C}}$, and $\ddot{\mathcal{E}}$, this new justification is not included in the label of $\mathcal{A}$, as it is subsumed by the environment $\{\ddot{\mathcal{B}}, \ddot{\mathcal{C}}\}$.

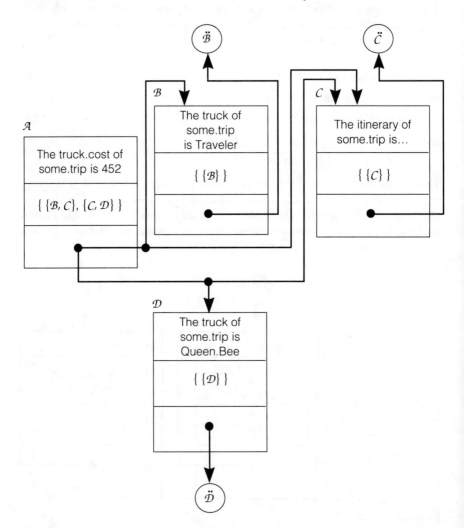

Figure 5. The Proposition Structure of $\mathcal{A}$ with a Second Justification

The ATMS treats the fact false specially. A set of assumptions is inconsistent (*nogood*) if we can derive false from it. Traditionally, inference is the process of extending a set of beliefs by applying inference procedures to those beliefs. The use of classical propositional logic illustrates this point: If I believe α and I believe $\alpha \supset \beta$, then I'm entitled to believe β. If that process produces a contradiction, one of our original assumptions must itself be wrong. The ATMS relies on this principle. It marks as inconsistent all sets of assumptions from which contradictions have been derived and removes derivations based on such assumption sets from its working memory. In the KEE system, contradictions can be created not only by explicitly deriving false, but also by conclusion of both α and (not α) and by cardinality and valueclass violations. However, for simplicity's sake, in most of our examples we induce contradictions only by explicitly deriving false.

Using the ATMS as a foundation, we have built a context mechanism, much in the spirit of the contexts of QA4 (Rulifson, Derksen and Waldinger, 1972) and Conniver (McDermott and Sussman, 1973). We call each context a *world*. Worlds can be created interactively through the user interface, by the actions of the rule system, or programmatically. Figure 6 shows the KEEworlds Browser, a graphical representation of the worlds extant at any time. The browser shows a single world, start. When creating a world, the user can specify a parent world or worlds. The newly created world has, as a default, all the assumptions (and hence, derived facts) of its parent worlds.

A world is characterized by a set of assumptions—both the assumptions of the existence of that world and its ancestor worlds, and the assumptions of facts explicitly asserted and deleted in that world. Testing the context-relative belief in a proposition is straightforward: If the assumptions of a world are a superset of any of the environments in the label of the proposition, that proposition is believed in that world. The system treats as believed in a world not only those assumptions explicited asserted into that world, but also any fact that has a derivation based on those assumptions. Thus, if in world ψ we believe $\mathcal{B}$ and C, we also believe $\mathcal{A}$, because C has been shown to be a consequence of $\mathcal{A}$ and $\mathcal{B}$.

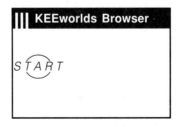

Figure 6. KEEworlds Browser of Start

This belief carries over into this world even though the justification $\mathcal{B}, C \vdash \mathcal{A}$ may have been made when the system was "focused" on some other world, or perhaps even before ψ was created. We do not have to rederive $\mathcal{A}$, because the ATMS preserves this derivation.

Rules and Justifications

We have spoken of the system creating justifications. In most applications, the primary source of justifications is the instantiation of *deduction rules* (although one can also explicitly add justifications). The KEE system has two kinds of rules, *deduction rules* and *action rules*. Deduction rules express the theories of

COMPUTE.TOTAL.COST
 while
   (the truck.cost of ?t is ?vc)
   (the driver.cost of ?t is ?dc)
 believe
   (the total.cost of ?t is (+ ?dc ?vc))

COMPUTE.TRUCK.COST
 while
   (the cost.per.mile of (the truck of ?t) is ?x)
   (the distance of ?t is ?d)
 believe
   (the truck.cost of ?t is (* ?x ?d))

COMPUTE.DRIVER.COST
 while
   (the driver.cost.per.hour of ?t is ?w)
   (the duration of ?t is ?d)
 believe
   (the driver.cost of ?t is (* ?d ?w))

COMPUTE.DRIVER.COST.PER.HOUR
 while
   (the wage.rate of (the driver of ?t) is ?w)
 believe
   (the driver.cost.per.hour of ?t is ?w)

COMPUTE.DURATION
 while
   (the itinerary of ?t is ?i)
   (the truck of ?t is ?v)
   (the weather of mid.continent is ?w)
 believe
   (the duration of ?t is (compute.duration ?i ?v ?w))

Figure 7.   Cost.Computation.Rules

a particular domain representation—truths believed in every world. Action rules create contexts and change the assumptions of particular contexts.[4]

When a deduction rule is instantiated, a justification is created. The justifications ensure that whenever facts matching the premise of the rule are believed, the system believes the corresponding conclusions. Thus, if a deduction rule is invoked that concludes $X, Y \vdash Z$, we do not necessarily know Z in any specific world. Instead, the ATMS has built a structure, the justification, that enables the system to recognize that if we ever come to believe both X and Y in a world, we also believe Z in that world. Figure 7 shows the deduction rules for computing the cost of trips in our example domain.

Truth Maintenance Across Worlds

The interaction of truth maintenance with worlds may seem clearer with an example. In this section we show how facts computed in one world are visible in other worlds that share the appropriate assumptions. We begin by asserting four facts in world start:

The driver of example.trip is Gray $(\mathcal{E})$

The truck of example.trip is Piper $(\mathcal{F})$

The itinerary of example.trip is
'((Indianapolis nil origin) $(\mathcal{G})$
(Seymour computers on)
(Thayer computers off))

The weather of Mid.Continent is snow $(\mathcal{H})$

Thus, world start includes, in its characteristic assumption set, assumptions for each of $\mathcal{E} - \mathcal{H}$. Let us call these assumptions $\ddot{\mathcal{E}}$, $\ddot{\mathcal{F}}$, $\ddot{\mathcal{G}}$, and $\ddot{\mathcal{H}}$.

---

[4]The system allows any rule to be used both for reacting to assertions (forward chaining) and answering queries (backward chaining). Rules in KEE are written in KEE's rule language, which itself is based on the extensible query and assertion language TellAndAsk™. In our examples, the clauses of rules are either the assertion or deletion of facts, the evaluation in the underlying LISP system of some expression, or the unification of a variable with an underlying evaluation. Unmarked facts are interpreted as assertions and ununified LISP expressions as Boolean tests. For the examples used in this chapter, the reader need only understand that a statement of the form (the location of Cannonball is Thayer) refers to one value of the location slot in unit Cannonball as Thayer and that a statement of the form (Cannonball is in class trucks) means that Cannonball is a member of some class in the transitive closure of the subclass relation on trucks. TellAndAsk allows embedding of subexpressions (e.g., (the transmission of (the truck of trip.1) is automatic)) and unifies variables ("?" symbols).

TellAndAsk is a trademark of IntelliCorp, Inc.

(Output) The EXAMPLE.TRIP Unit in BIGGIANT Knowledge Base in the START WORLD

Unit: **EXAMPLE.TRIP** in knowledge base **BIGGIANT** in world **START**
Created by FILMAN on 14-Apr-86 13:03:12
Modified by FILMAN on 14-Apr-86 13:04:10
  Member Of: **TRIPS**

Own slot: **DISTANCE** from **EXAMPLE.TRIP**
  Values: 360

Own slot: **DRIVER** from **EXAMPLE.TRIP**
  Values: **GRAY**

Own slot: **DRIVER.COST** from **EXAMPLE.TRIP**
  Values: 114.07498

Own slot: **DRIVER.COST.PER.HOUR** from **EXAMPLE.TRIP**
  Values: 13.5

Own slot: **DURATION** from **EXAMPLE.TRIP**
  Values: 8.449999

Own slot: **ITINERARY** from **EXAMPLE.TRIP**
  Values: ((**INDIANAPOLIS** NIL ORIGIN) (**SEYMOUR COMPUTERS** ON)
             (**THAYER COMPUTERS** OFF))

Own slot: **MAX.VOLUME** from **TRIPS**
  Values: UNKNOWN

Own slot: **MAX.WEIGHT** from **TRIPS**
  Values: UNKNOWN

Own slot: **ORIGIN** from **EXAMPLE.TRIP**
  Values: **INDIANAPOLIS**

Own slot: **SHIPMENTS.HANDLED** from **EXAMPLE.TRIP**
  Values: **COMPUTERS**

Own slot: **TOTAL.COST** from **EXAMPLE.TRIP**
  Values: 308.47498

Own slot: **TRUCK** from **EXAMPLE.TRIP**
  Values: **PIPER**

Own slot: **TRUCK.COST** from **EXAMPLE.TRIP**
  Values: 194.40001

Figure 8. Example.trip in Start after Query

When we query the system to determine the total.cost of example.trip in world start (using the cost.computation.rules), it runs the rules, deducing the fact

The total.cost of example.trip is 308.475   (1)

At this point, proposition *I* includes in its label the environment $\{\ddot{E}, \ddot{F}, \ddot{G}, \ddot{H}\}$. As these assumptions are a subset of the characteristic assumptions of world start, fact *I* is believed in start. Figure 8 shows a display of the unit example.trip relative to world start after this query. Since in deriving this value we derived several other intermediate values (such as the truck.- and driver.costs), the unit display also shows these values. Correspondingly, these facts have justification structures including subsets of $\{\ddot{E}, \ddot{F}, \ddot{G}, \ddot{H}\}$. (This display is a condensation [eliminating facets] of the display obtained by selecting Display Unit from the browser menu. In general, the user interface allows the user to browse and edit the knowledge base relative to worlds.)

Because the ATMS creates justification structures for derived facts, the justifications for beliefs are available to system and user programs. One such facility is invoked by selecting explain from the browser menu. Figure 9 shows the result of this selection—the *explanation graph* (proof tree) for the value of the total.cost of example.trip.

We can now create another world, other.world, asserting the same four facts *E–H* in it. Thus, the characteristic assumptions of other.world include $\{\ddot{E}, \ddot{F}, \ddot{G}, \ddot{H}\}$; other.world sees any fact (such as *I*) that is justified by this set. Figure 10 shows the browser and the facts of other.world. If we remove, say, assumption *E* from the characteristic set of other.world, the belief in the consequences of that deduction in other.world is withdrawn. In Figure 11 we see the beliefs of other.world after we have retracted assumption $\ddot{E}$ from other.world. The beliefs dependent on the driver being Gray (such as the driver.cost and total.cost of example.trip) are no longer present. However, beliefs that do not depend on the driver (such as the truck.cost of example.trip) are still there.

Contradictory Worlds

If the ATMS has been given a derivation for false that is justified by assumptions believed in a particular world, then that world is contradictory and is considered nogood. Figure 12 shows the browser after we have asserted a second truck for example.trip in other.world. Since the maximum cardinality of the truck slot is 1 and we have asserted two different trucks for example.trip, we have a contradiction, and other.world is nogood. Nogood worlds appear in the browser with solid boxes in their centers.

When the ATMS detects that a particular set of assumptions are mutually inconsistent, it propagates that information throughout the justification structure. This can result in some worlds becoming nogood. The rule system ignores

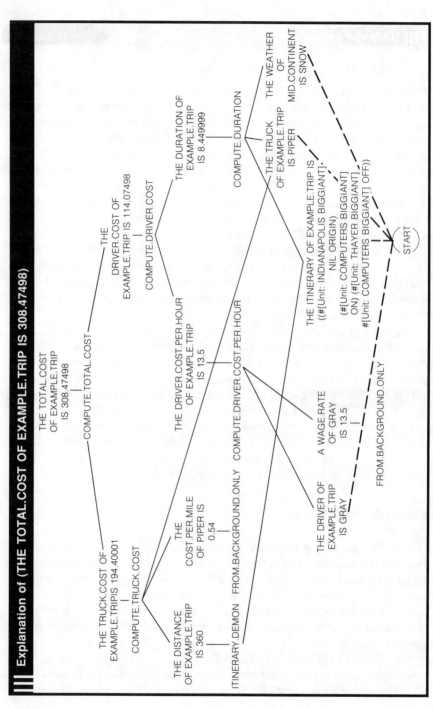

Figure 9. Explanation of the Total.Cost of Example.Trip

124

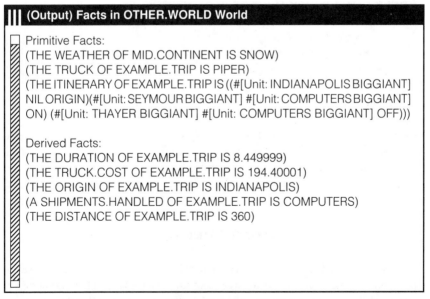

||| (Output) Facts in OTHER.WORLD World

Primitive Facts:
(THE WEATHER OF MID.CONTINENT IS SNOW)
(THE DRIVER OF EXAMPLE.TRIP IS GRAY)
(THE TRUCK OF EXAMPLE.TRIP IS PIPER)
(THE ITINERARY OF EXAMPLE.TRIP IS ((#[Unit: INDIANAPOLIS BIGGIANT]
NIL ORIGIN) (#[Unit: SEYMOUR BIGGIANT] #[Unit: COMPUTERS BIG-
GIANT] ON) (#[Unit: THAYER BIGGIANT] #[Unit: COMPUTERS BIGGIANT]
OFF)))

Derived Facts:
(THE DURATION OF EXAMPLE.TRIP IS 8.449999)
(THE DRIVER.COST OF EXAMPLE.TRIP IS 114.07498)
(THE TOTAL.COST OF EXAMPLE.TRIP IS 308.47498)
(THE DRIVER.COST.PER.HOUR OF EXAMPLE. TRIP IS 13.5)
(THE TRUCK.COST OF EXAMPLE.TRIP IS 194.40001)
(THE ORIGIN OF EXAMPLE.TRIP IS INDIANAPOLIS)
(A SHIPMENTS.HANDLED OF EXAMPLE.TRIP IS COMPUTERS)
(THE DISTANCE OF EXAMPLE.TRIP IS 360)

Figure 10. The Beliefs of Other.World

||| (Output) Facts in OTHER.WORLD World

Primitive Facts:
(THE WEATHER OF MID.CONTINENT IS SNOW)
(THE TRUCK OF EXAMPLE.TRIP IS PIPER)
(THE ITINERARY OF EXAMPLE.TRIP IS ((#[Unit: INDIANAPOLIS BIGGIANT]
NIL ORIGIN)(#[Unit: SEYMOUR BIGGIANT] #[Unit: COMPUTERS BIGGIANT]
ON) (#[Unit: THAYER BIGGIANT] #[Unit: COMPUTERS BIGGIANT] OFF)))

Derived Facts:
(THE DURATION OF EXAMPLE.TRIP IS 8.449999)
(THE TRUCK.COST OF EXAMPLE.TRIP IS 194.40001)
(THE ORIGIN OF EXAMPLE.TRIP IS INDIANAPOLIS)
(A SHIPMENTS.HANDLED OF EXAMPLE.TRIP IS COMPUTERS)
(THE DISTANCE OF EXAMPLE.TRIP IS 360)

Figure 11. The Beliefs of Other.World after Retracting the Driver

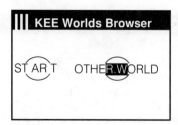

Figure 12. Browser with Other.World Nogood

nogood worlds in choosing rules to apply. We can exploit this behavior with rules that produce contradictions (for example, by deducing false) in the worlds that violate domain constraints, are logically inconsistent, undesirable, or just plain unlikely to occur in the modeled domain. Thus, deductions of contradictions can be used as a tool for controlling the reasoning process.

Constraints

We express the domain-specific constraints as deduction rules whose conclusion is false. For example, the dispatcher errs in assigning driver d to truck v, when d and v are in different cities. We express this constraint with the rule:

DRIVER.AND.TRUCK.MUST.BE.IN.SAME.CITY
  while
      (the location of (the driver of ?t) is ?dl)
      (the location of (the truck of ?t) is ?vl)
      (not (equal ?dl ?vl))
  believe
      false

If we run this rule in a world where Gray (located in Gary) and Queen.Bee (located in Indianapolis) are the driver and truck of example.trip, we deduce false, making the world nogood. Appendix B presents typical constraint rules for Big Giant.

World Structures

The dispatcher is faced with a difficult problem: satisfying an irregular set of constraints while working in a large combinatorial space. This problem has aspects of "interpretation construction" (i.e., the assignment of values to a few variables) in the selection of drivers, trucks and itineraries for trips. However, itineraries are themselves complex objects, not amenable to simple optimization. In these next three sections, we describe a series of tools for the dispatcher: first, the *dispatcher's advice taker*, a manual approach that illustrates the use of the system to record the dispatcher's decisions and check them for constraint violations; second, a *dispatcher's apprentice* that, using the rule system, demonstrates a division of work—giving the dispatcher the hard problem of determining itineraries and allowing the system to complete the more mechanical details of truck and driver assignments; and third, a *dispatcher's replacement* that programmatically solves the entire problem. Our intent is to illustrate the interaction between problem solving, the ATMS, and the worlds system. Clearly, we are not presenting an interface for a dispatcher so much as the tools a system builder could use in constructing a problem solver for the dispatcher.

Problem solving is typically an exploratory, incremental process. One starts with a set of beliefs about the world and recursively considers alternative choices that modify those beliefs. Usually, the modifications to a set of beliefs are incremental; by and large, we retain most of the original assumptions of the initial state, adding or deleting only a few at each step. Thus, the dispatcher who starts with the problem of completing an empty trip may choose among trucks, drivers, and itineraries to get to the next problem state; once in that state, he may modify the itinerary or focus on an earlier point in the problem-solving process. KEEworlds allows us to reflect the structure of the search space in the structure of a worlds graph. That is, one can model alternatives or changes to a particular world by creating *child* worlds. By default, these worlds inherit the assumptions (and therefore, the derived facts) of their parents. The user, however, is also allowed to change (add and delete) assumptions in the children (often in the creation process). Thus, we might model the action in world ψ_p of sending Queen.Bee from Indianapolis to New.Harmony by creating ψ_c, a child world of ψ_p and, in ψ_c, changing Queen.Bee's location to New.Harmony. If (as an assumption) the driver of Queen.Bee in ψ_p is Green, Queen.Bee's driver will still be Green in ψ_c.

Similarly, a common problem-solving tactic is to break a problem into subproblems, solve the subproblems independently, and finally merge the subproblem solutions (if compatible) into a global solution. We model this structure by placing the original problem in a world, ψ, and then creating children worlds $\psi_{c_1}, \ldots, \psi_{c_n}$, each of which encodes one of the subproblems. When we have a set of descendant worlds, $\psi_{d_1}, \ldots, \psi_{d_m}$, that solve the subproblems, we try to merge them into a solution world. In the dispatcher's advice taker, we model the solution of the entire problem of schedule creation by breaking the problem into the tasks of defining a trip for each itinerary in its own separate world, and then merging these worlds (building a child world with these worlds as parents) when all tasks have been solved. This merge can fail even though each subproblem solution is itself consistent. For example, two itineraries can in themselves be consistent, but together be inconsistent because they use the same driver. We model dead ends and failures as nogood worlds.

Formally, the worlds exist in a directed, acyclic graph over the "parent-child" relation. Loosely, the assumptions true in a particular world, ψ, are those that have been explicitly added at ψ, and those assumptions in the parents of ψ that have not been explicitly deleted in ψ.[5]

The Dispatcher's Advice Taker

The dispatcher's advice taker leaves the decisions about trip composition to the dispatcher, but checks those decisions for consistency with the constraints of the problem space. That is, the dispatcher decides who to assign to what, and the advice taker checks to see if that assignment breaks any of the dispatching rules. (Thus, the advice taker acts in the spirit of McCarthy's Advice Taker [1968]— able to converse about the domain and verify assertions, but not able to make decisions.) As described above, we express constraints as deduction rules whose conclusion is false.

A typical interaction with the dispatcher's advice taker might go as follows. We have three itineraries, $iter_1$, $iter_2$, and $iter_3$, for which we seek to make simultaneous truck and driver assignments:

$iter_1$ = ((Indianapolis nil origin)
       (Seymour computers on)
       (Thayer computers off))
$iter_2$ = ((Gary nil origin)
       (La.Harpe toys on)
       (Viola carpet on)
       (Oregon toys off)
       (Cook carpet off))
$iter_3$ = ((Indianapolis nil origin)
       (Kokomo refrigerators on)
       (Warsaw refrigerators off)
       (Roselawn bicycles on)
       (Gary typewriters on)
       (Attica typewriters off)
       (Bloomington bicycles off))

---

[5]This description is a simplification of the true situation, where a more elaborate conflict-resolution strategy is used when a particular assumption has been both added and deleted in different ancestors. For the details of the conflict-resolution strategy, the reader is referred to Morris and Nado's article (1986).

We create a world, origin, and describe the weather of Mid.Continent as fair in that world. We then create three child worlds of origin worlds one, two, and three—making trips trip.1, trip.2, and trip.3 have itineraries of *iter₁*, *iter₂*, and *iter₃*, respectively in those worlds (Figure 13). Effectively, we have broken the problem of finding compatible drivers and trucks for these trips into the sub-problems of finding a driver and truck for each trip. We represent partially completed solutions to these problems in worlds. When each subproblem is completely solved, we merge the solutions to see if they are mutually consistent.

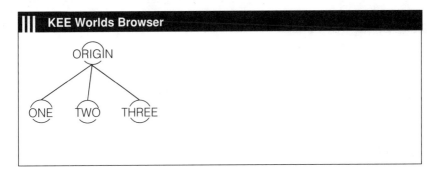

Figure 13. Worlds **One, Two,** and **Three**

We try assigning Gray to trip.1 by creating Gray/one, a child world of one, asserting "the driver of trip.1 is Gray" in that world and running the constraint rules in the new world. These rules render that world nogood. Examination of the explanation reveals that Gray, based in Gary, is unsuitable as a driver for a trip that starts in Indianapolis (Figure 14). Abandoning that world, we build

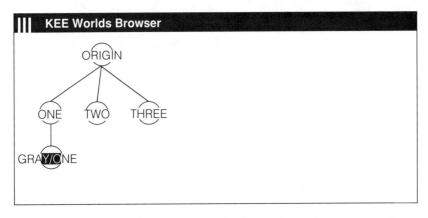

Figure 14. **Gray Should Not Drive Trip.1**

Green/one and Queen.Bee/Green/one, where Green drives Queen.Bee on trip.1. Running the constraint rules in these worlds shows them free of contradictions (Figure 15). We continue in a similar fashion, finding a place for Gray driving Piper on trip.2, and for White driving Queen.Bee on trip.3. In Figure 16 we see that an attempt to merge the three leaf worlds has failed because we have assigned the same truck (Queen.Bee) to two different trips. We correct this with a new truck for trip.1 leading to a successful merge (Figure 17). This world cumulates the facts of its parents to form a solution.

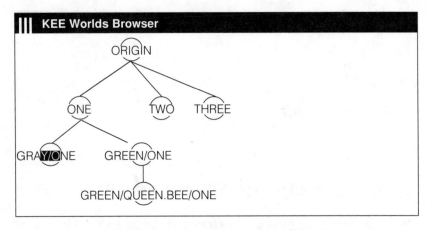

Figure 15. After Assignment to Trip.1

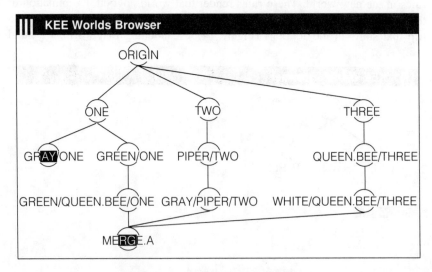

Figure 16. Failure of Merge.a

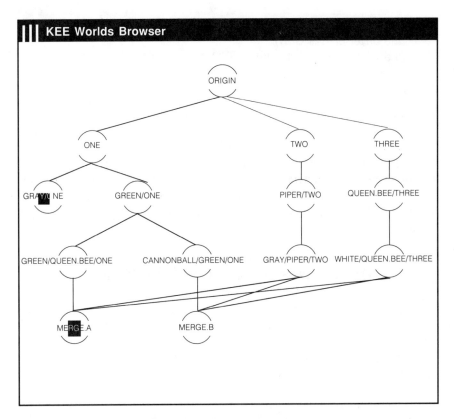

Figure 17. Successful Merge

Modifying the Knowledge Base

Because we are in a dynamic, symbolic, and interactive environment, it is straightforward to modify the representation structures to reflect new concepts and constraints. If, for example, we wish to introduce the idea that (a) trucks have transmissions that are typically manual, (b) Piper has an automatic transmission, and (c) Driver Gray refuses to drive any truck with an automatic transmission, we could

1. Create member slot transmission in class unit trucks, giving it value manual;

2. Assert (the transmission of Piper is automatic); and

3. Create another member of the class of constraint rules whose external form is:

while
  (the driver of ?t is Gray)
  (the transmission of (the truck of ?t) is automatic)
believe
  false

Running the constraint rules now makes world merge.b nogood.

This description of the dispatcher's advice taker is interesting not as an interface one would actually want to provide to a working dispatcher, but because it illustrates parent and child relationships between worlds and shows the use of the world system to reflect problem partitioning and recombination. Worlds express problem-solving state; that state can be used for things such as segmenting knowledge, checkpointing changes, and preserving search state at the discretion of the system developer.

The Dispatcher's Assistant and the Rule System

Most problems require more action on the part of the system than simple state preservation and constraint checking. We usually want the computer to actually solve something, not merely represent it. KEE provides several different mechanisms for problem solving, such as active values (demons), methods (object-oriented programming), and conventional programming. One such mechanism is the rule system. We have already seen examples of deduction rules—declarative expressions of universal truths. Deduction rules create justifications for facts; the ATMS ensures that worlds find those facts that are true in them. *Action rules* cause the system to change its view of the state of some world. That is, like the programmatic assignment of a value to a variable, action rules change the state of the system.[6]

The two kinds of action rules are *same-world action rules* and *new-world action rules*. As the name suggests, same-world rules run in a particular world; they make changes to (additions to and deletions from) the beliefs (characteristic assumptions) of that world. For a same-world rule to run in a world, all the

---

[6]The deduction/action rule division roughly corresponds to the traditional dichotomy in AI between declarative and procedural knowledge (Winograd, 1975). Often in AI the use of rules as facts is jumbled with their procedural interpretation. Deduction rules express universal truths and can be understood independently of their context. Action rules are, in many ways, like the procedures of a program. Independently understanding their behavior can be as difficult as understanding the import of an isolated program statement, separated from its programming context. Recognizing this difference between these two varieties of rules clarifies the issue of why rule-based systems can seem both straightforward to understand and more complicated than ordinary programming languages.

premises of the rule must be true in that world. New-world rules create a new world. This world can have multiple parents. That is, the rule system searches for a set of compatible parent worlds where the facts have been added that satisfy the premises of the rule. For each such set, it builds a world that has that set as its parents. That new world inherits all the assumptions (and therefore deductions) of its parents. The changes implied by the action part of the rule then take place in the new world. Syntactically, new-world rules include the keyword in.new.world (or in.new.and.world) to indicate new-world creation. We distinguish action rules by the use of the keywords if and then in place of the deduction rule's while and believe.

We trust the conclusions of the ATMS because it implements a simple monotonic propositional logic. Theorems about that logic assure us that subsumption and elimination of contradictory derivations are valid operations. To preserve this clean semantics, the premises of deduction rules must be either facts known to the ATMS or state-independent LISP computations. Action rules express programmatic change, and we make no pretense of expressing a declarative semantics of programs. We can therefore be more liberal about premises for action rules, allowing operators such as THNOT, quantified subexpressions, mixed forward and backward chaining, and reference to non-ATMS facts (such as class membership and member slots).

The ability of a new-world action rule to gather clauses from different worlds in creating a new child world can make it difficult to develop particular world topologies. It is often the case that the children of a world are meant as mutually exclusive alternatives. Such worlds (and their descendants) should never merge. To simplify expressing this idea, the system provides *exclusion sets:* sets of incompatible child worlds. Each world can have one or more exclusion sets. Two worlds in an exclusion set are treated as mutually contradictory and cannot share descendants. Exclusion sets can be created through the user-interface, programmatically, or by the rule system. As a default, if world ψ_c, a child of world ψ_p, was created by the rule system, then ψ_c is in ψ_p's default exclusion set. It will be excluded from the other worlds created by running rules on ψ_p. Rules specified with the keyword in.new.and.world create worlds that are not in any exclusion set. Exclusion sets are displayed on the browser with the symbol $\boxtimes$.

The Dispatcher's Assistant

In this section we illustrate the dispatcher's assistant, a five-action-rule system that, given a set of itineraries, determines a compatible and legal set of driver and truck assignments for those itineraries. To run the assistant, we start by creating a world, begin, and, for each itinerary, making it the itinerary of a trip in begin. We make a list of these trips, the trip.list of assistant, in begin. That is, in the world begin, we assert the following facts:

```
The weather of Mid.Continent is fair
The itinerary of trip.1 is ((Indianapolis nil origin)
                           (Seymour computers on)
                           (Thayer computers off))
The itinerary of trip.2 is ((Gary nil origin)
                           (La.Harpe toys on)
                           (Viola carpet on)
                           (Oregon toys off)
                           (Cook carpet off))
The itinerary of trip.3 is ((Indianapolis nil origin)
                           (Kokomo refrigerators on)
                           (Warsaw refrigerators off)
                           (Roselawn bicycles on)
                           (Gary typewriters on)
                           (Attica typewriters off)
                           (Bloomington bicycles off))
The itinerary of trip.4 is ((Gary nil origin)
                           (Oregon books on)
                           (Cook newsprint on)
                           (Indianapolis newsprint  off)
                           (Mitchell books off))
The trip.list of assistant is   (trip.1 trip.2 trip.3 trip.4)
```

Understanding the behavior of the assistant requires understanding the scheduling algorithm of the rule system. A rule system cycles through a three-step process of (a) determining which instantiations of rules are eligible to fire, (b) selecting a particular instantiated rule to fire, and (c) taking the actions required by that firing. Collectively, the set of instantiated rules that are eligible to fire at any cycle is that cycle's *conflict set*. A rule system's *conflict-resolution algorithm* decides which element of the conflict set fires. The conflict-resolution algorithm of the rule system is based on an agenda. When an element of the conflict set is discovered, it is added to the agenda; at each step, one of the rule instantiations on the agenda is selected for firing. The rule system's default agenda mechanism divides enabled rule instantiations into three classes: deduction rules, same-world action rules, and new-world action rules. It fires all the rules in the earlier classes before firing any in the later classes; rule instantiations in each class are kept on a stack. Thus, the default rule system behavior implements depth-first search. It tries to expand the consequences of the latest discovery first; if that fails, the system focuses on earlier situations and tries their alternatives. The rule system provides agenda functions for backward chaining using breadth-first and best-first searches, and forward chaining using combinations of rule priorities and premise complexity. Users can write their own agenda mechanisms to implement strategies such as blackboards (Nii, 1986).

Figure 18 shows the additional rules for the dispatcher's assistant. The system consists of five action rules in addition to the constraint rules discussed earlier. The assistant keeps its local search state on the candidate.trucks, candidate.drivers, trip.list, pending.trip, and problem slots of the assistant unit. At any point in the search, the candidate.trucks and candidate.drivers slots contain the available, but not-yet-assigned trucks and drivers, and the trip.list slot contains a list of the trips that have not yet been filled. We note a trip that has had a truck assigned, but does not yet have a driver as a pending.trip. We mark the problem of the assistant as solved when all trips have trucks and drivers in a consistent world.

MAKE CANDIDATE.TRUCKS   *Collect possible trucks as candidate.trucks.*
if
    (?v is in class trucks)
then
    (a candidate.truck of assistant is ?v)

MAKE.CANDIDATE.DRIVERS   *Collect possible drivers as candidate.drivers.*
if
    (?d is in class drivers)
then
    (a candidate.driver of assistant is ?d)

ASSIGN.TRUCK   *Assign a truck to this trip.*
if
    (the trip.list of assistant is ?1)
    (equal ?first (car ?1))
    (a candidate.truck of assistant is ?v)
then in.new.world
    (delete (a candidate.truck of assistant is ?v))
    (the truck of ?first is ?v)
    (a pending.trip of assistant is ?first)

ASSIGN.DRIVER   *Assign a driver to this trip.*
if
    (the trip.list of assistant is (list.of (?first . ?rest)))
    (a pending.trip of assistant is ?first)
    (a candidate.driver of assistant is ?d)
then in.new.world
    (delete (the trip.list of assistant is (list.of (?first . ?rest))))
    (the trip.list of assistant is ?rest)
    (delete (a candidate.driver of assistant is ?d))
    (the driver of ?first is ?d)
    (delete (a pending.trip of assistant is ?first))

STOP ASSISTANT   *Stop when you've got a solution.*
if
    (the trip.list of assistant is NIL)
then
    (the problem of assistant is solved)
    (lisp (stop.forward.chaining))

Figure 18. The Dispatcher's Assistant Rules

We invoke the rule system on these rules (and, of course, the constraint rules), focusing its attention on the world begin. This causes the following behavior:

1. None of the constraint rules matches the data, but the first two same-world action rules (make.candidate.trucks and make.candidate.drivers) fire repeatedly, accumulating all trucks and drivers as values of the candidate.trucks and candidate.drivers slots of assistant in world begin. Because all same-world rules are run before any new-world rules, all the trucks and drivers are noticed before any assignment of a truck or a driver to a trip.

2. The new-world action rules then come into effect. Assign.truck selects the first trip in the trip.list of the current world, finds a candidate truck and, in a new world, (a) makes that truck the truck of the trip, (b) marks that trip as the trip that is "pending" a driver, and (c) removes that truck from the set of candidate trucks. (Thus, this algorithm implicitly enforces the constraint that a truck can't be used in more than one trip.)

3. The constraint rules then get their turn. If they fail to make this world nogood (fail to find a contradiction), assign.driver continues by finding the unique pending trip, the trip.list, and a candidate driver, and, once again in a new world, by (a) making that driver be the driver of the trip, (b) removing that driver from the candidate drivers, (c) resetting the pending trip, and (d) setting the trip.list to the rest of the previous trip list. Once again the constraint rules run.

In each case (2) and (3), we have selected one of several possible candidate trucks or drivers. In fact, the rule system would be perfectly happy to match these rules against every candidate truck and driver. However, since the agenda is a stack, these other elements of the conflict set are postponed until after the consequences of the first assignment have been pursued. The system stops producing children on a particular branch when either (a) the constraints mark a world nogood, keeping the action rules from pursuing its consequences; or (b) all the possible choices at that world have been exhausted.

4. The system, as described thus far, eventually finds all legal truck and driver assignments. The fifth rule stops the system after the first solution (literally by clearing the agenda). After execution, the browser shows a tree of worlds with root begin, each world corresponding to a decision point in the search. Figure 19 shows the browser after a run of the assistant.

Programmatic Solution: The Dispatcher's Replacement

Solving the entire dispatching problem (creating itineraries and assigning compatible trucks and drivers to them) is considerably more difficult than

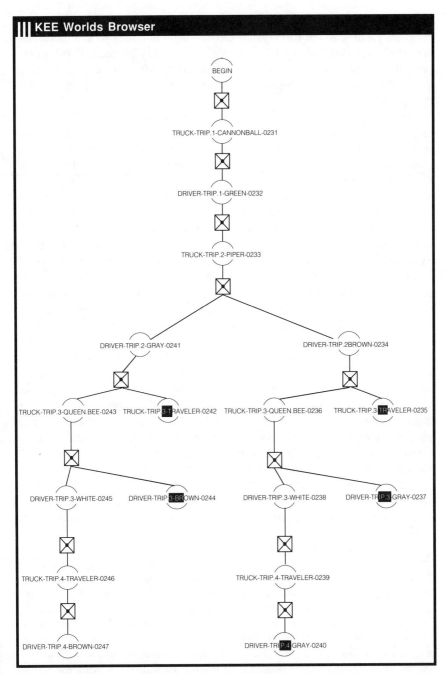

Figure 19. Worlds After the Dispatcher's Assistant

the previous task. For this task we turn to a programmatic solution: a LISP program, running in the KEE system environment, that uses KEE's representation structures and invokes KEE system functionality as needed. We want a program that finds a feasible solution—one that satisfies the constraints. Since this is designed as a demonstration system, we also want a program that does this quickly.

Our strategy is to create a set of trips with compatible drivers and trucks and empty itineraries (or, more precisely, itineraries whose sole element is that they originate in the location of their trip's driver and truck.) Thus, if we have four drivers and four trucks, our set might include four trips, but incompatibilities between the available drivers and trucks might limit us to a smaller set (e.g., if all the trucks are in one city and all the drivers in another, our maximal compatible set is empty). We then consider each shipment in turn, looking for the best way to extend the itinerary of some trip to include it. If we are unable to find a way of extending some itinerary within the problem constraints, we start the itinerary extension process over with a (randomly) different ordering of shipments. (If several such tries all fail, we look for a different set of compatible trucks and drivers and repeat the entire process.)[7] Our algorithm is extremely heuristic— we have sacrificed optimality and completeness for simplicity and speed.

We use worlds to preserve the state of our search. That is, each time the search process makes a choice, it creates a world embodying the effect of that choice. (If a world with the same information already exists, we reuse it.) Since many choices violate the constraint rules, we run the constraint rules immediately after world creation. If they deduce that the just-created world is nogood, we consider other alternatives. We consider which rule produced this nogood in deciding which other alternatives to consider. Worlds are data structures for the program; the program explicitly calls the system functions that create worlds, create exclusion sets, run the rule system, and examine the justifications of facts. Figure 20 shows the browser after running the dispatcher's replacement.

We wrote a program that searches for a feasible solution. It is natural to ask why we did not produce a more optimal algorithm, and why we have not employed the algorithmic methods of operations research, such as linear and

---

[7]Our algorithm thus combines elements of generate-and-test and depth-first search. This is in contrast to a pure depth-first search, where the failure to place a shipment suggests trying a different alternative for the previous shipment. In our algorithm, a successful placement of a shipment is not revoked unless we are trying an entirely different solution to the problem. We chose this combination in the belief that there are likely to be many solutions in the search space, but that many parts of the space lack any solutions. Hence, we want a search strategy that repeatedly samples a narrow radius over a wide area, rather than one that does a concentrated search in one place. That is, if a descent from a particular spot doesn't work out, it is better to try something completely different than to look too long in the same neighborhood.

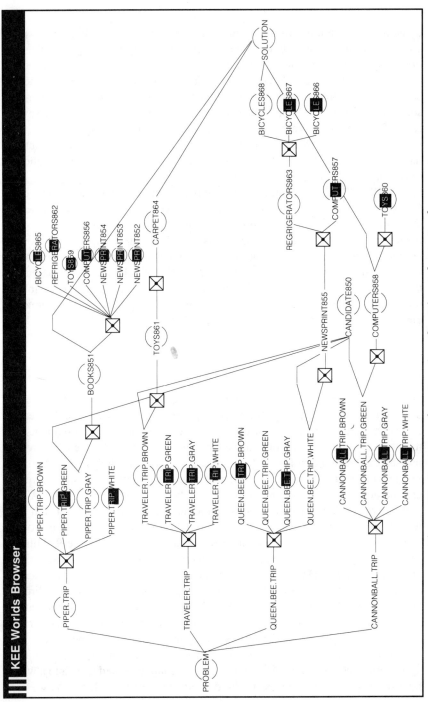

Figure 20. Browser after Running the Dispatcher's Replacement

dynamic programming, to reach this goal. Optimizing algorithms are usually considerably more computationally expensive than simply finding feasible solutions, especially in irregular domains. Our goal was not to explore the space of numerical optimization. Of course, if a close-to-optimal schedule were necessary, one could apply optimization methods, such as exchanging components of solutions and hill-climbing itinerary variations, to the results of one or several runs of the main program. Operations research methods require restating the problem in formal, mathematical terms. They make assumptions about the nature of the underlying space, for example, linearity and convexity, and are most suited to modifying an existing solution, rather than creating one from scratch. We allow any arbitrary constraints on valid solutions (e.g., "you can't ship goats and cabbage at the same time, unless you are also shipping farmers"). Our symbolic approach leaves both the problem and its solution in a form that is comprehensible to the nonexpert. It is a trivial matter, for example, for the user to define a new concept and integrate constraints that use that concept (as we showed with the transmission example). The symbolic, model-based approach makes the computational transformations of the system accessible to nonwizards. A fertile topic for research is the integration of mathematical optimization algorithms with symbolic problem expressions.

Discussion

In this small example, we have been able to illustrate only a few of the potential uses of truth maintenance and the worlds system. The ATMS is a tool for search. Its primary attributes are that it preserves deductions across environments and that it retains the justifications for deductions. The first of these enables reducing search—facts do not need to be rederived, even if the system is pursuing several different alternatives simultaneously; constraints are easily expressed and automatically propagated throughout the knowledge base. The ATMS particularly lends itself to situations where the same conclusion or search state would be otherwise repeatedly rediscovered. The second allows the use of the justifications for processes such as user explanation (as in Figure 9), guiding search (as used by the dispatcher's replacement), and (though not illustrated) probabilistic and evidential reasoning. Thus, because the justification structures exist, it is straightforward to do search strategies such as dependency-directed backtracking. On the other hand, the ATMS is less appropriate for situations where non-redundant information is never derived and old contexts rarely continued—using the ATMS requires storing information that is never retrieved.

The worlds system provides both a conceptual contexting mechanism and a systematic access to the ATMS. By reifying a group of related facts into a world, the user acquires direct access to the consequences of those facts. As we have seen, worlds can be used for state preservation and checkpointing, incremental solution construction, hypothetical reasoning, and reasoning with incomplete information. A more exhaustive list would include items such as reasoning about time and events and representing belief structures. Because the ATMS supports the world system, derivations in one context automatically propagate to all other appropriate contexts. The ATMS also allows the worlds system a straightforward implementation of the notion of merging contexts.

We hope that the concentration of this chapter on examples of reasoning about scheduling under constraints has not obscured our broader point—that choosing appropriate representations and tools vastly expands the set of things a computer system can conveniently process. By using an integrated and symbolic underlying representation we can easily model a complex domain; by employing the integrated computational tools of our system, we can easily reason about different aspects of that domain. We started with the domain of "helping the dispatcher of a trucking company." We have shown one (of the many) ways of representing the data and knowledge of that domain symbolically. Because the system is symbolic, we have been spared most of the intellectual burden of coding and translating between mental concepts and machine-understandable form. Because the system provides an appropriate set of representational primitives—objects, rules, demons, messages, truth maintenance, and worlds—it is straightforward to represent the relationships in the trucking world and reason about them. Because the representation is semantically clear, we can take the same model and use it in different ways—such as a state preserver, problem solver, user-interface basis, and simulation system. We have performed model-based reasoning.

References

Brachman, R. J., & Schmolze, J. G. (1985). An overview of the KL-ONE knowledge representation system. *Cognitive Science, 9(2)*, 171–216.

Brownston, L., Farrell, R., Kant, E., & Martin, N. (1985). *Programming expert systems in OPS5*. Reading, MA: Addison-Wesley.

de Kleer, J. (1986). An assumption-based truth maintenance system. *Artificial Intelligence, 28(2)*, 127–162.

de Kleer, J., Doyle, J., Steele, G. L., & Sussman, G. J. (1979). Explicit control of reasoning. In P. H. Winston & R. H. Brown (Eds.), *Artificial intelligence: An MIT perspective*. Cambridge, MA: MIT Press.

Doyle, J. (1979). A truth maintenance system. *Artificial Intelligence, 12(3)*, 231–272.

Fikes, R., & Kehler, T. (1985). The role of frame-based representation in reasoning. *Communications of the ACM, 28(9)*, 904–920.

Fikes, R., & Nilsson, N. J. (1971). STRIPS: A new approach to the application of theorem proving to problem solving. *Artificial Intelligence, 2(3–4)*, 189–208.

Fikes, R., Nado, R., Filman, R., McBride, P., Morris, P., Paulson, A., Treitel, R., & Yonke, M. (1987). *OPUS: A new generation knowledge engineering environment. Phase 1 final report.* Mountain View, CA: IntelliCorp, Inc.

Goldberg, A., & Robson, D. (1983). *Smalltalk-80: The language and its implementation.* Reading, MA: Addison-Wesley.

Hayes-Roth, F., & London, P. (1985). Software speeds expert systems. *System Software, 71,* 71–75.

Hewitt, C. (1971). *Description and theoretical analysis (using schemata) of PLANNER: A language for proving theorems and manipulating models in a robot.* Unpublished doctoral dissertation, Mathematics Department, MIT, Cambridge.

London, P. (1978). *Dependency networks as representation for modeling in general problem solvers* (Technical Report 698). College Park, MD: Department of Computer Science, University of Maryland.

Martins, J. P., & Shapiro, S. C. (1983). Reasoning in multiple belief spaces. *Proceedings of the 8th International Joint Conference on Artificial Intelligence* (pp. 370–372). Karlsruhe, W. Germany.

McAllester, D. (1982). *Reasoning utility package user's manual* (AIM 667). Cambridge, MA: Artificial Intelligence Laboratory, MIT.

McCarthy, J. (1968). Programs with common sense. In M. Minsky (Ed.), *Semantic information processing.* Cambridge, MA: MIT Press.

McCarthy, J., & Hayes, P. (1969). Some philosophical problems from the standpoint of artificial intelligence. In B. Meltzer & D. Michie (Eds.), *Machine intelligence 4.* Edinburgh, UK: Edinburgh University Press.

McDermott, D. V. (1983). Contexts and data dependencies: A synthesis. *IEEE Transactions on Pattern Analysis and Machine Intelligence, 5(3),* 237–246.

McDermott, D. V., & Sussman, G. J. (1973). *The Conniver reference manual* (Memo 259). Cambridge, MA: Artificial Intelligence Laboratory, MIT.

Morris, P. H., & Nado, R. A. (1986). Representing actions with an assumption-based truth maintenance system. *Proceedings of the 5th National Conference on Artificial Intelligence* (pp. 13–17). Philadelphia, PA.

Nii, H. P. (1986). The blackboard model of problem solving. *AI Magazine, 7(2),* 38–53.

Rulifson, J. F., Derksen, J. A., & Waldinger, R. J. (1972). *QA4: A procedural calculus for intuitive reasoning* (Technical Note 7). Menlo Park, CA: Artificial Intelligence Center, Stanford Research Institute.

Stallman, R. M., & Sussman, G. J. (1977). Forward reasoning and dependency-directed backtracking in a system for computer-aided circuit analysis. *Artificial Intelligence, 9(2),* 135–196.

Stefik, M. J. (1979). An examination of a frame-structured representation system, *Proceedings of the 6th International Joint Conference on Artificial Intelligence* (845–852). Tokyo, Japan.

Stefik, M. J., Bobrow, D. G., Mittal, S., & Conway, L. (1983). Knowledge programming in Loops: Report on an experimental course. *AI Magazine, 4(3),* 3–13.

Symbolics, Inc., (1985). *User's guide to Symbolics computers* (Vol. 4). Cambridge, MA: Symbolics, Inc.

van Melle, W., Scott, A. C., Bennett, J. S., & Peairs, M. A. (1981). *The EMYCIN manual* (Technical Report HPP–81–16). Stanford, CA: Heuristic Programming Project, Stanford University.

Williams, C. (1984). *ART: The advanced reasoning tool—Conceptual overview.* Los Angeles, CA: Inference Corporation.

Winograd, T. (1975). Frame representations and the declarative/procedural controversy. In D. G. Bobrow & A. Collins (Eds.), *Representation and understanding.* New York: Academic Press.

Appendix A

Big Giant Data

The following tables list the more important slot values of the central objects of the Big Giant domain. Values in braces indicate (potentially) multivalued slots. That is, a given shipment originates in only one city, but any city may have several shipments originate there.

SHIPMENTS	origin	destination	weight	volume	loading.time	unloading.time
bicycles	Roselawn	Bloomington	500	100	.20	.25
books	Oregon	Mitchell	1000	50	.20	.25
carpet	Viola	Cook	3500	300	.20	.25
computers	Seymour	Thayer	1000	150	.20	.25
newsprint	Cook	Indianapolis	6000	400	.20	.25
refrigerators	Kokomo	Warsaw	9000	600	.20	.25
toys	La.Harpe	Oregon	1000	100	.20	.25
typewriters	Gary	Attica	1000	200	.20	.25

DRIVERS	class	location	license.class	max.drive	wage.rate
Brown	union.drivers	Gary	class.3	11.0	13.00
Gray	nonunion.drivers	Gary	class.1	12.5	13.50
Green	union.drivers	Indianapolis	class.3	11.0	13.00
White	nonunion.drivers	Indianapolis	class.2	12.5	13.50

TRUCKS	class	location	license.class	cost.per.mile	volume.capacity	weight.capacity
Cannonball	big.trucks	Indianapolis	class.3	1.2400	1280	32000
Piper	small.trucks	Gary	class.1	.5400	400	5000
Queen.bee	medium.trucks	Indianapolis	class.2	.9000	640	10000
Traveler	medium.trucks	Gary	class.2	.9000	640	10000

CITIES	roads	origin.shipments	destination.shipments	state
Attica	{I74, U41.E, U41.D, S25}		{typewriters}	Indiana
Bloomington	{S37.B, S37.A}		{bicycles}	Indiana
Cook	{U231, I80.B, U41.B, U41.A}	{newsprint}	{carpet}	Indiana
Delphi	{S25, S26}			Indiana
English	{I64.B, S37.D}			Indiana
Fowler	{U41.D, U41.C, U24}			Indiana
Gary	{I94, I90, U41.A, U30}	{typewriters}		Indiana
Hebron	{S2, U231}			Indiana
Indianapolis	{I74, I70.B, I65, U31.B, S37.A}		{newsprint}	Indiana
Jasper	{I64.B, I64.A}			Indiana
Kokomo	{U31.B, U31.A, S26}	{refrigerators}		Indiana
La.Harpe	{U67, U24, S125}	{toys}		Illinois
Mitchell	{U50, S37.C, S37.B}		{books}	Indiana
New.Harmony	{I64.A, U41.F}			Indiana
Oregon	{I90, U51}	{books}		Illinois
Paoli	{S37.D, S37.C}		{toys}	Indiana
Roselawn	{S2, U41.C, U41.B}	{bicycles}		Indiana
Seymour	{I65, U50}	{computers}		Indiana
Thayer	{I70.A, S125}		{computers}	Illinois
Utica	{I80.B, I80.A, U51}			Illinois
Viola	{I80.A, U67}			Illinois
Warsaw	{U31.A, U30}	{carpet}		Indiana
Yale	{I70.B, I70.A, U41.F, U41.E}	{books}	{refrigerators}	Illinois
Zion	{I94}			Illinois

HIGHWAYS

	connects	grade	length	state
I64.A	{New.Harmony, Jasper}	primary	60	{Indiana}
I64.B	{Jasper, English}	tertiary	30	{Indiana}
I65	{Seymour, Indianapolis}	primary	60	{Indiana}
I70.A	{Thayer, Yale}	primary	150	{Illinois}
I70.B	{Yale, Indianapolis}	primary	90	{Indiana, Illinois}
I74	{Attica, Indianapolis}	primary	60	{Indiana}
I80.A	{Viola, Utica}	primary	100	{Illinois}
I80.B	{Utica, Cook}	primary	90	{Indiana, Illinois}
I90	{Gary, Oregon}	secondary	100	{Illinois, Indiana}
I94	{Zion, Gary}	primary	60	{Indiana, Illinois}
S125	{La.Harpe, Thayer}	tertiary	80	{Illinois}
S2	{Hebron, Roselawn}	tertiary	10	{Indiana}
S25	{Delphi, Attica}	tertiary	40	{Indiana}
S26	{Delphi, Kokomo}	tertiary	30	{Indiana}
S37.A	{Indianapolis, Bloomington}	secondary	50	{Indiana}
S37.B	{Bloomington, Mitchell}	tertiary	30	{Indiana}
S37.C	{Paoli, Mitchell}	tertiary	10	{Indiana}
S37.D	{Paoli, English}	tertiary	10	{Indiana}
U231	{Cook, Hebron}	tertiary	20	{Indiana}
U24	{Fowler, La.Harpe}	secondary	180	{Illinois, Indiana}
U30	{Gary, Warsaw}	secondary	70	{Indiana}
U31.A	{Warsaw, Kokomo}	secondary	70	{Indiana}
U31.B	{Indianapolis, Kokomo}	primary	40	{Indiana}
U41.A	{Gary, Cook}	secondary	20	{Indiana}
U41.B	{Cook, Roselawn}	secondary	20	{Indiana}
U41.C	{Roselawn, Fowler}	secondary	30	{Indiana}
U41.D	{Fowler, Attica}	secondary	30	{Indiana}
U41.E	{Attica, Yale}	secondary	90	{Indiana, Illinois}
U41.F	{Yale, New.Harmony}	secondary	70	{Indiana, Illinois}
U50	{Seymour, Mitchell}	tertiary	30	{Indiana}
U51	{Oregon, Utica}	secondary	40	{Illinois}
U67	{Viola, La.Harpe}	secondary	50	{Illinois}

Appendix B

Constraint Rules

These are typical constraint rules for the Big Giant system. The first three form the subclass of FORBIDDEN.MIXED.TRIP.RULES (rules about combining two or more trips together); the remainder are the subclass FORBIDDEN.SINGLE.-TRIP.RULES. One heuristically interesting aspect of these rules is that they impose equiprevalent pairwise constraints between all combinations of drivers, trucks, and itineraries. That is, there are driver-truck, driver-itinerary, and truck-itinerary combinations that are illegal, and they occur with roughly similar frequency. Had one of these been lacking or improbable, the task of building the dispatcher's replacement would have been easier, as we could have focused on selecting the most constrained item first.

ONE.TRIP.PER.DRIVER   *A given driver can only drive a single trip.*
   while
       (the driver of ?tl is ?d)
       (the driver of ?t2 is ?d)
       (not (equal ?tl ?t2))
   believe
       false

ONE.TRIP.PER.SHIPMENT   *Any given shipment can only be handled on a single trip.*
   while
       (a shipments.handled of ?tl is ?s)
       (a shipments.handled of ?t2 is ?s)
       (not (equal ?tl ?t2))
   believe
       false

ONE.TRIP.PER.TRUCK   *A given truck can only go on one trip in a given world.*
   while
       (the truck of ?tl is ?v)
       (the truck of ?t2 is ?v)
       (not (equal ?tl ?t2))
   believe
       false

CANT.EXCEED.VOLUME.LIMITS   *The cargo carried at any time on this trip can't exceed the volume limit of this truck.*
> **while**
>> (the volume.capacity of (the truck of ?t) is ?w)
>> (the max.volume of ?t is ?m)
>> (lisp (> ?m ?w))
> **believe**
>> false

CANT.EXCEED.WEIGHT.LIMITS   *The cargo carried at any time on this trip can't exceed the weight limit of this truck.*
> **while**
>> (the max.weight of ?t is ?m)
>> (the weight.capacity of (the truck of ?t) is ?w)
>> (lisp (> ?m ?w))
> **believe**
>> false

COMPUTE.DURATION   *This rule computes the duration of a trip, given the truck, weather, and itinerary.*
> **while**
>> (the itinerary of ?t is ?i)
>> (the truck of ?t is ?v)
>> (the weather of mid.continent is ?w)
> **believe**
>> (the duration of ?t is (compute.duration ?i ?v ?w))

COMPUTE.VOLUME   *This rule computes the maximum volume used on a particular itinerary.*
> **while**
>> (the itinerary of ?t is ?i)
> **believe**
>> (the max.volume of ?t is (compute.max.volume ?i))

COMPUTE.WEIGHT   *Compute the maximum weight of a particular itinerary.*
> **while**
>> (the itinerary of ?t is ?i)
> **believe**
>> (the max.weight of ?t is (compute.max.weight ?i))

DRIVER.AND.TRUCK.MUST.BE.IN.SAME.CITY   *The driver and the truck of a trip must be in the same city.*
> **while**
>> (the location of (the driver of ?t) is ?dl)
>> (the location of (the truck of ?t) is ?vl)
>> (not (equal ?dl ?vl))
> **believe**
>> false

DRIVER.MUST.BE.WHERE.TRIP.STARTS *The driver of a trip must be in the same city as the origin of the itinerary.*
  while
    (the origin of ?t is ?l)
    (the location of (the driver of ?t) is ?dl)
    (not (equal ?dl ?l))
  believe
    false

DRIVER.MUST.HAVE.RIGHT.LICENSE.RULE *If a driver does not have the appropriate license for this trip, then the trip is no good.*
  while
    (the not.can.be.driven.by of (the license.class of (the truck of ?t))
      is (the license.class of (the driver of ?t)))
  believe
    false

TRIP.CANT.LAST.TOO.LONG *The duration of the trip can't be greater than the time this driver is allowed to drive.*
  while
    (the duration of ?t is ?m)
    (the maximum.driving.time of (the driver of ?t) is ?w)
    (lisp (> ?m ?w))
  believe
    false

TRUCK.MUST.BE.WHERE.TRIP.STARTS *The truck has to be where the itinerary originates.*
  while
    (the origin of ?t is ?l)
    (the location of (the truck of ?t) is ?vl)
    (not (equal ?vl ?l))
  believe
    false

WHITE.CANT.DRIVE.IN.ILLINOIS *White is wanted by the police in Illinois, and can't be sent on any trips there.*
  while
    (the driver of ?t is White)
    (the itinerary of ?t is ?i)
    (lisp (is.in.illinois ?i))
  believe
    false

Chapter 5

AQUINAS: A Knowledge-Acquisition Workbench*

John H. Boose
Jeffrey M. Bradshaw

Knowledge Systems Laboratory, Boeing Advanced Technology Center

Acquiring knowledge from a human expert is a major problem when building a knowledge-based system. Aquinas, an expanded version of the Expertise Transfer System (ETS), is a knowledge-acquisition workbench that combines ideas from psychology and knowledge-based systems research to support knowledge-acquisition tasks. These tasks include:

- eliciting distinctions,
- decomposing problems,
- combining uncertain information,
- incremental testing,
- integration of data types,
- automatic expansion and refinement of the knowledge base,
- use of multiple sources of knowledge, and
- providing process guidance.

*This chapter was originally published under the title, "Expertise transfer and complex problems: using AQUINAS as a knowledge-acquisition workbench for knowledge-based systems," *International Journal of Man-Machine Studies* (1987), *26*, 3–28. It is reprinted here with the kind permission of the editors and the publisher.

Thanks to Roger Beeman, Miroslav Benda, Kathleen Bradshaw, William Clancey, Brian Gaines, Cathy Kitto, Ted Kitzmiller, Art Nagai, Doug Schuler, Mildred Shaw, David Shema, Lisle Tinglof-Boose, and Bruce Wilson for their contributions and support. Aquinas was developed at the Knowledge Systems Laboratory, Advanced Technology Center, Boeing Computer Services in Seattle, Washington.

Aquinas interviews experts and helps them analyze, test, and refine the knowledge base. Expertise from multiple experts or other knowledge sources can be represented and used separately or combined. Results from user consultations are derived from information propagated through hierarchies. Aquinas delivers knowledge by creating knowledge bases for several different expert system shells. Help is given to the expert by a dialog manager that embodies knowledge-acquisition heuristics. Aquinas contains many techniques and tools for knowledge acquisition; the techniques combine to make it a powerful testbed for rapidly prototyping portions of many kinds of complex knowledge-based systems.

Obtaining and Modeling Expertise

Expertise Transfer System

The Expertise Transfer System (ETS) has been in use at Boeing for more than three years. Hundreds of prototypical knowledge-based systems have been generated by ETS. The system interviews experts to uncover key aspects of their problem-solving knowledge. It helps build very rapid prototypes (typically in less than two hours), assists the expert in analyzing the adequacy of the knowledge for solving the problem, and creates knowledge bases for several expert system shells (S.1, M.1, OPS5, KEE®, and so on) from its own internal representation (Boose, 1984, 1985, 1986).

The tools in ETS are now part of Aquinas, a much larger system. Aquinas was developed to overcome ETS's limitations in knowledge representation and reasoning (Figure 1). Due to these limitations, ETS was usually abandoned sometime during the knowledge-acquisition process. Typically, project approaches were explored or feasibility was assessed for several days or a week, and then development continued in some other expert system shell. While the use of the tool in this way saved substantial time (typically 1 or 2 calendar months from a 12- to 24-month project), it was desirable to explore new approaches for making the system more powerful.

Aquinas Tasks and Tool Sets

Aquinas is a collection of integrated tool sets. They share a common user interface (the dialog manager) and underlying knowledge representation and database (Figure 2). Each set of tools addresses a general knowledge-acquisition task and embodies sets of strategies that support the task. Many of these strategies will be illustrated later.

KEE is a registered trademark of IntelliCorp, Inc.

Improved process efficiency:
- Rapid feasibility analysis
- Multiple alternative testing with little resource expenditure
- Expert enthusiasm
- Easier to learn expert-system and knowledge-engineering concepts
- Group knowledge elicitation and decision making

Faster knowledge-base generation
- Very rapid prototyping
- Vocabulary identification
- Solution elicitation
- Trait elicitation through triads and other methods
- Hierarchies
    Problem decomposition
    Reasoning at varied levels of abstraction

Improved knowledge-base quality
- Embedded testing and feedback during the knowledge elicitation process
- Multiple knowledge representations
- Multiple methods for handling uncertainty based on needed precision, convenience
- Tools for comparing knowledge from different experts to show similarities and differences
- Consultation systems giving consensus and dissenting opinions from multiple sources of knowledge
- Analytic tools

Better knowledge-base maintenance and comprehensibility
- Case-based and knowledge source-based elicitation, structure, analysis
- Knowledge at higher levels of abstraction
- Single central source generation of expert system shell knowledge bases
- Knowledge libraries

Extensions to personal construct theory methods
- Manipulation of rating grids in hierarchies
- Multiple variable scale types
- Many analytic tools in a single framework
- Interactive testing and debugging of rating grid knowledge

Aquinas is a knowledge-acquisition workbench that provides a variety of capabilities.

Figure 1. Features of Aquinas

Dialog manager						
ETS Repertory grid tools	Hierarchical structure tools	Uncertainty tools	Internal reasoning engine	Multiple scale type tools	Induction tools	Multiple expert tools
Object-oriented DBMS						
CommonLoops/Common LISP						

The Aquinas workbench is a collection of integrated tool sets that support various knowledge-acquisition tasks.

Figure 2. The Aquinas Workbench

Task: Elicit Distinctions

Gaines (1987) has characterized knowledge acquisition as "the modeling of events enabling adequate prediction and action." In this view, a distinction is the primitive concept underlying the representation of knowledge and the formal theory of modeling. Systems that acquire problem-solving knowledge seek to establish qualitative and quantitative distinctions that lead to effective prediction and action, while weeding out distinctions that are redundant or inconsequential.

Eliciting Distinctions with Aquinas. Personal Construct Psychology. George Kelly's personal construct theory (Kelly, 1955) provides a rich framework for modeling the qualitative and quantitative distinctions inherent in an expert's problem-solving knowledge. ETS (Expertise Transfer System) is a set of tools used by the expert to elicit, analyze, and refine knowledge as rating grids. In a rating grid, problem solutions—*elements*—are elicited and placed across the grid as column labels, and traits of these solutions—*constructs*—are listed alongside the rows of the grid (see Figure 3, taken from the Programming Language Advisor). Traits are first elicited by presenting groups of solutions and asking the expert to discriminate among them. Following this, the expert gives each solution a rating showing where it falls on the trait scale.

Many of the strategies used in building a rating grid are extensions of ideas in the work of Kelly and in the PLANET system (Gaines and Shaw, 1981; Shaw and Gaines, 1987a, b). These strategies include triadic elicitation, corner filling, and multiple analysis and display tools. Aquinas can analyze a rating grid in many ways to help the expert refine useful distinctions and eliminate those that are inconsequential or redundant. Distinctions captured in grids can be converted to other representations such as production rules, fuzzy sets, or networks of frames.

Task: Decompose Problems

Experts building large knowledge bases face the task of decomposing their problem in ways that enhance efficiency and clarity. In our previous work using ETS, the difficulty of representing complex problems in a single rating grid became clear. First, a single rating grid can represent only flat relations between single solutions and traits. No deep knowledge, causal knowledge, or relationship chains can be shown. A second limitation was that only solutions or traits at the same level of abstraction could be used comfortably in a single grid. Finally, large single grids were often difficult to manipulate and comprehend.

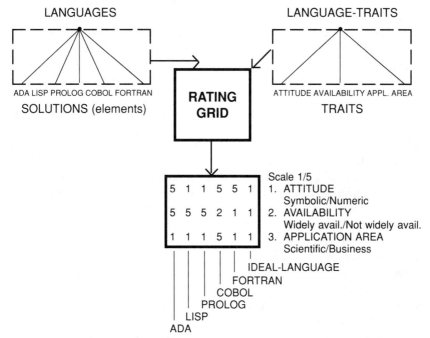

Rating values in different hierarchies combine to form *rating grids*. The children of a node in a *solution hierarchy* supply the solutions along the top of the grid; the children of a node in a *trait hierarchy* supply the traits down the side of a grid.

Figure 3. Rating Grid

Problem Decomposition Strategies in Aquinas. Hierarchies. Hierarchical tools in Aquinas help the expert build, edit, and analyze knowledge in lattices and hierarchies. These hierarchies allow the expert to break up complex problems into pieces of convenient size and similar level of abstraction. Hierarchies in Aquinas are organized around *solutions, traits, knowledge sources* (i.e., *experts*), and *cases.*

Nodes in the four hierarchies combine to form rating grids. In the most simple case, the children of a node in a solution hierarchy supply the solutions along the top of a grid; the children of a node in a trait hierarchy supply the traits down the side of a grid. Rating values within the grid provide information about the solutions with respect to each trait (Figure 3).

In eliciting knowledge for complex problems it is sometimes difficult for the expert to identify conclusion sets whose members are at similar, useful levels of granularity. For instance, in an engine diagnostic system, the expert may include the repair solutions engine, battery, ignition coil, and electrical system. Engine and electrical system are at more general levels of structural and functional abstraction than battery and ignition coil. Mixing more general and more specific solutions in the same rating grid causes problems during trait elicitation, since traits useful in differentiating engine from electrical system problems are not necessarily those useful in discriminating ignition coil from battery problems.

Solution hierarchies. Solutions are grouped in specialization hierarchies within Aquinas. This structure aids experts in organizing large numbers of solutions that may exist at different levels of abstraction. For example, a solution class named vehicle is a superclass (parent or prototype) to car and truck subclasses. The car class can serve, in turn, as a parent to a class of specific car models or to a particular instance of a car.

Trait hierarchies. Characteristics of a particular level in the solution hierarchy can be structured in trait hierarchies. For instance, in a knowledge base for a transportation advisor, the solutions exist in hierarchies of vehicles. Each level in the solution hierarchy has a trait hierarchy that contains information needed to select solutions at that level. A trait hierarchy attached to the vehicle abstraction level of a solution hierarchy, for instance, may contain information about general use type, relative speed, cost, and so forth for the types of vehicles in the hierarchy. The car subclass is attached to a car trait hierarchy that contains information useful in selecting a particular car.

Two other hierarchies are formed in Aquinas (see Figure 4).

Expert hierarchies. Expert hierarchies represent multiple knowledge sources as structured groups. Each node in the expert hierarchy may represent an individual, an aspect of an individual, a group, or an independent knowledge source. Information from multiple experts may be independently elicited and analyzed, then weighted and combined to derive joint solutions to problems. Analyses can be performed that show similarities and differences among experts. Experts each

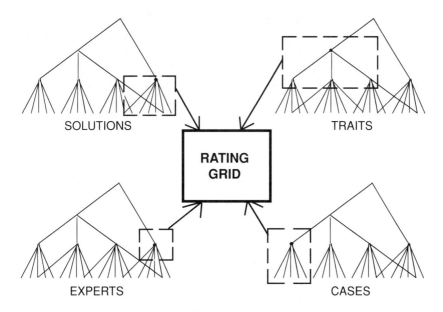

Values from *expert* and *case hierarchies,* as well as solution and trait hierarchies, are combined in many ways to form rating grids. Relationships between nodes do not have to be strictly hierarchical; lattices may be formed when more than one parent points to the same child.

Figure 4. Rating Grid with Expert and Case Hierarchies

have their own solution and trait hierarchies, which may or may not overlap those of others. Each expert's unique problem-solving strategies and information are preserved.

Case hierarchies. Case hierarchies define subsets of the knowledge base appropriate to solving a particular class of problems. For example, in a knowledge base of information about vehicles, a user may want to include different knowledge for selecting a vehicle for going over land than for going over water. A land case and a water case may be created, each drawing on a subset of the expert pool knowledgeable in those areas. Additional levels may be created for short or long land trips, cost considerations, and so on. A hierarchy of cases allows the knowledge base to be developed, modified, and maintained based on specific classes of situations. Eventually the lower leaves in case hierarchies become specific consultation instances when the knowledge is tested and used to solve a specific problem.

From hierarchies to rating grids. A rating grid is built by combining values associated with nodes in each of the four basic hierarchies. Relationships between nodes do not have to be strictly hierarchical; lattices may be formed when more than one parent points to the same child. The expert defines the current rating grid by selecting appropriate nodes in the hierarchies.

Figure 5 shows selected map nodes (case: K-ACQUISITION; expert: WEC; solution: WEC.ELEMENT; trait: WEC.ELEMENT.TRAIT) that define the rating grid of Figure 3. Each different collection of nodes (at least one from each hierarchy)

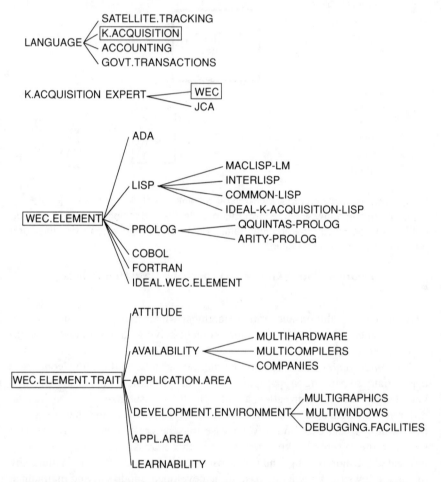

Each cell in a rating grid is described by a unique set of four hierarchy nodes. Aquinas users specify rating grids by selecting sets of nodes (either the nodes themselves or their children).

Figure 5. Hierarchy Nodes for Rating Grid of Figure 3

describes a rating grid. A rating grid could be a single column or row, or even a single cell. Inversely, each cell in a rating grid is uniquely described by its location in the four hierarchies.

In a sense, each rating grid is four dimensional. Any two of these dimensions are shown at once as rows and columns in a given grid. Usually solutions and traits are shown, but sometimes it is useful to show other combinations. For instance, a grid could display the ratings of several experts across the top with particular solutions down the side. The associated trait and case nodes would be shown to the side of the grid. Often the ratings displayed summarize or generalize information from different nodes in the hierarchies; this issue is discussed later in the chapter.

Techniques for defining and exploring hierarchies. Strategies for helping the expert build and refine hierarchies in Aquinas include laddering, cluster analysis, and trait value examination. Some of these strategies will be demonstrated in the section describing the Programming Language Advisor.

Task: Specify Methods for Combining Uncertain Information

A major limitation of most current knowledge engineering tools is that they do not allow experts to specify how specific pieces of information should be combined (Gruber and Cohen, 1987). Most tools either tend to use fixed, global numeric functions to compute values or restrict the expert to purely symbolic representations of uncertainty. Ideally, flexibility and comprehensibility could be achieved by allowing experts to specify how information should be combined locally, either by selecting from a set of commonly accepted combining functions (e.g., as done by Reboh and Risch, 1986; Reboh, Risch, Hart, and Duda, 1986) or by defining their own method.

Combining Uncertain Information in Aquinas. In Aquinas, uncertain knowledge, preferences, and constraints may be elicited, represented, and locally applied using combinations of several different methods. These methods may be classified into three main types: absolute, relativistic, and probabilistic.

Absolute reasoning. Absolute (categorical) reasoning involves judgments made with no significant reservations. It "typically depends on relatively few facts, its appropriateness is easy to judge, and its result is unambiguous" (Szolovitz and Pauker, 1978). For example, in selecting a programming language, users may be able to say with certainty that they would be interested only in languages that run on an Apple Macintosh or that they will not consider a language that costs more than $400, regardless of other desirable characteristics. Experts can also build these types of absolute constraints into the knowledge associated with an Aquinas rating grid.

Relativistic reasoning. Unfortunately, not all judgments can be absolute. Many involve significant trade-offs, in which information and preferences from several sources must be weighed. Even if criteria for the ideal decision can be agreed upon, sometimes it can be only approximated by the available alternatives. In these cases, problem-solving information must be propagated in a relativistic fashion. Aquinas incorporates a variety of models and approaches to relativistic reasoning, including MYCIN-like certainty factor calculus (Adams, 1985), fuzzy logic (Gaines and Shaw, 1985), and the Analytic Hierarchy Process (AHP, Saaty, 1980).

Probabilistic and user-defined reasoning. In the current version of Aquinas, some limited propagation of probabilistic information is made possible by allowing discrete distributions on rating values. Future versions of Aquinas will have more complete models for the elicitation (Alpert and Raiffa, 1982; Spetzler and von Holstein, 1984; Wallsten and Budescu, 1983) and analysis of probabilistic information including Bayesian (Howard and Matheson, 1984; Cheeseman, 1985; Henrion, 1987; Pearl 1986; Spiegelhalter, 1986), Dempster-Shafer (Shafer, 1976; Gordon and Shortliffe, 1985), and other approaches (Shastri and Feldman, 1985). Users may also define their own methods for combining and propagating information.

The availability of different inference methods within a single workbench allows users and experts flexibility in adapting Aquinas to the problem at hand. Methods are currently selected based on the cost of elicitation, the precision of the knowledge needed, convenience, and the expert's preference. Future research will suggest heuristics for helping experts select appropriate methods and designs for particular types of questions (e.g., Shafer and Tversky, 1985). These heuristics will be incorporated into the Aquinas dialog manager.

Task: Test the Knowledge

McDermott (1986) has emphasized the inseparability of acquired knowledge from the role it plays in problem solving. Within a given knowledge acquisition tool, the problem-solving method must be available to the expert as the knowledge base is being constructed so that incremental testing and refinement can take place.

Testing Knowledge in Aquinas. A mixed-initiative reasoning engine within Aquinas supports consultations. The model of problem solving currently used in Aquinas is that of multiple knowledge sources (experts) that work together in a common problem-solving context (case) by selecting the best alternatives for each of a sequential set of decisions (solutions). Alternatives at each step are selected by combining relevant information about preferences (relativistic reasoning), constraints (absolute reasoning), and evidence (probabilistic reasoning).

For many structured selection problems, a more specialized version of this model seems adequate. After analyzing several expert systems for classification, Clancey (1986) suggested that many problems are solved by abstracting data, heuristically mapping higher-level problem descriptions onto solution models, and then refining those models until specific solutions are found (Figure 6). This is also similar to the establish-refine cycle used in CSRL (Bylander and Mittal, 1986; Chandrasekaran, 1986; Bylander and Chandrasekaran, 1987). In the version of Aquinas described in this chapter, data abstraction is carried out within hierarchies of traits, and solutions are refined as information is propagated through solution hierarchies.

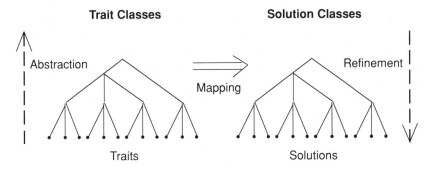

Clancey studied structured selection systems and built an abstraction and refinement model (1986). Inference in Aquinas typically occurs in a bottom-up fashion through the trait hierarchies and in top-down fashion through the solution hierarchies.

Figure 6. Abstraction and Refinement Model

While the current version of Aquinas works best on those problems whose solutions can be comfortably enumerated (such as those amenable to the method of heuristic classification), we are interested in generalizing Aquinas to incorporate synthetic (constructive) problem-solving methods such as those in SALT (Marcus, 1987).

Task: Integrate Diverse Data Types

Problem solving in knowledge-based systems often involves combining symbolic and numeric information. Qualitative and quantitative aspects are complimentary rather than opposing considerations, so knowledge acquisition tools need to represent such information flexibly and conveniently. In our work with ETS, we found that it was inconvenient to represent certain types of problem-solving information solely using Kelly's constructs. Unordered variables, such as a set of computer types, had to be represented as a series of bipolar traits (VAX/NOT-VAX, IBM/NOT-IBM, and so on) when it would have been easier to combine them into a single nominal trait (a COMPUTER trait whose values are VAX, IBM, and so on).

Experts also apply different levels of precision at different points in the knowledge-acquisition process. For example, in some instances it might be sufficient to know that an object is hot or cold. At a later point, it may be important to know the exact temperature of the object. Levels of precision must also be appropriately flexible. ETS only deals with ordinal ratings on a scale from 1 to 5, not with probabilities or exact numeric values.

Integrating Data Types Within Aquinas. In Aquinas, various trait (attribute) scale types can be elicited, analyzed, and used by the reasoning engine. Traits are currently described according to the level of measurement of their rating scales, which is determined by the expert. The level of measurement depends on the presence or absence of four characteristics: *distinctiveness, ordering in magnitude, equal intervals,* and *absolute zero* (Coombs, Dawes, and Tversky, 1970). These four characteristics describe the four major levels of measurement, or types of traits: nominal (unordered symbols), ordinal, interval, and ratio (Figure 7). The additional information about trait types gives increased power to analytical tools within Aquinas and allows experts to represent information at the level of precision they desire.

RATING SCALE	DESCRIPTION	EXAMPLES
Nominal	Unordered set	LANGUAGE: {ADA COBOL LISP}
Ordinal	Ordered set	COLD/HOT: {1 2 3 4 5} SIZE: {SMALL MEDIUM LARGE}
Interval	Ordered set with measurable intervals	SMALL-INTEGERS: {1 2 3 4 5 6 7} F-TEMP: {32...112}
Ratio	Ordered set with measurable intervals and an absolute origin	HEIGHT: {0.0' 1.0'...}

Aquinas expands the knowledge representation capability of rating grids from personal construct theory by allowing the use of several types of rating scale values. Scale types are selected for convenience, precision, or efficiency of value entry.

Figure 7. Rating Scales

Ratings may be generated through two methods:

1. *Direct.* An expert directly assigns a rating value for a trait and an element. If an exact value is unknown, Aquinas helps the expert derive an estimate (Beyth-Marom and Dekel, 1985). If fine judgments are needed, Aquinas can derive a set of ratio-scaled ratings from a series of *pairwise comparisons* (Saaty, 1980). Aquinas also contains tools for encoding of probability distributions on specific values. The value with the highest probability is displayed in the grid, but all appropriate values are used in reasoning and may be edited with graphic distribution aids.

2. *Derived.* Incomplete grids can be automatically filled through propagation of rating values from another grid through the hierarchies (e.g., from lower to higher level grids, different experts, or different cases).

Precision and cost. Increased precision and specificity in knowledge acquisition allow increased problem-solving power, but usually at some cost (Michalski and Winston, 1985). This cost is reflected in both the amount of work needed to elicit the additional information and the increased complexity and greater number of steps in the reasoning process. Aquinas tries to minimize this cost by eliciting more precise information only when it is needed to solve critical portions of the problem. If, for example, Aquinas finds that it cannot sufficiently discriminate between solutions from simple rating values between 1 and 5, it may suggest that the user perform a series of pairwise comparisons to increase the sensitivity of judgments.

Task: Automatic Expansion and Refinement of the Knowledge Base

Knowledge acquisition tools can increase their leverage by suggesting appropriate expansions and refinements of the knowledge based on partial information already provided by the expert. Michalski (1986) has discussed the advantages of incorporating learning strategies within conventional knowledge acquisition tools.

Expanding and Refining Knowledge with Aquinas. Several types of tools make inductive generalizations about existing knowledge. Generalizations can be examined by the expert and used to refine the knowledge, and they are used by the reasoning engine. Sometimes, Aquinas may suggest that traits be deleted after analyzing the knowledge through a process that is similar to the simplification of decision tables (Hurley, 1983; Michalski, 1978) and decision trees (Quinlan, 1983).

Learning strategies in Aquinas include simple learning from examples (selective induction on lower level grids to derive values for higher level grids), deduction (inheritance of values from parents), analogy (derivation of values based on functional similarity of traits), and observation (constructive induction based on cluster analysis). The dialog manager (described below) also contains various learning mechanisms.

Task: Use Multiple Sources of Knowledge

Future knowledge acquisition systems can neither assume a single source of expertise nor a closed world. In ETS, we began experimenting with strategies for manually combining ETS knowledge from several domain experts (Boose, 1987). Others in our laboratory have been involved in developing methods for cooperative problem-solving (Benda, Jagannathan and Dodhiawala, 1986).

Using Multiple Sources of Knowledge in Aquinas. Knowledge from multiple experts (or other knowledge sources) can be analyzed to find similarities and differences in knowledge, and the degree of subsumption of one expert's knowledge over another (Gaines and Shaw, 1981). Information from analyses can be used to guide negotiation among experts. The reasoning engine uses knowledge from user-specified and weighted sources and gives consensus and dissenting opinions.

Task: Provide Knowledge-Acquisition Process Guidance

As knowledge acquisition tools become more sophisticated and knowledge bases grow larger, the complexity of the knowledge engineering task increases. One approach to managing this complexity is to implement some form of apprenticeship learning program that is available to the expert (e. g., Wilkins, Clancey, and Buchanan, 1987).

Providing Process Guidance in Aquinas. A subsystem called the *dialog manager* contains pragmatic heuristics to guide the expert through knowledge acquisition using Aquinas. Its help is important in the use of Aquinas, given the complexity of the Aquinas environment and the many elicitation and analysis methods available to the expert. The dialog manager makes decisions about general classes of actions and then recommends one or more specific actions, providing comments and explanation if desired. This knowledge is contained in rules within the dialog manager in Aquinas. A session history is recorded so that temporal reasoning and learning may be performed (Kitto and Boose, 1987).

Using Aquinas: Building a Programming Language Advisor

Aquinas is written in Interlisp and runs on the Xerox® family of LISP machines. Subsets of Aquinas also run in an Interlisp version on the DEC® Vax® and a C/UNIX®-based portable version. The Aquinas screen is divided into a typescript window, map windows showing hierarchies, rating grid windows, and analysis windows (Figure 8 below). Experts interact with Aquinas by text entry or by mouse through pop-up menus.

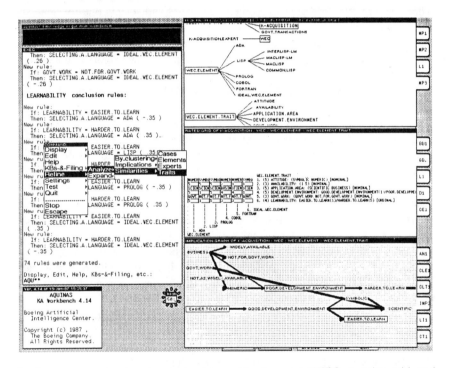

Aquinas screen showing developing hierarchies for expert WEC, a rating grid, and an implication analysis graph of the grid.

Figure 8. Aquinas Screen

The following are the steps in an Aquinas session in which an expert is building a Programming Language Advisor. Novice software engineers and project managers would use such a system to help select programming languages for application projects. Aquinas guides the expert in putting knowledge into Aquinas's knowledge base, and continues through the making of a knowledge base for the S.1 expert system shell. These steps are:

1. Elicit Cases and the Initial Grid (Solutions, Traits, and Ratings)

The expert is first asked to specify the behavior of Aquinas's dialog manager. Then the expert enters several problem test cases and selects one for analysis. The *knowledge-acquisition language case* is selected (satellite tracking, accounting, and government transaction cases are also entered). The cases are added to the case hierarchy and appear in the map window (Figure 8; upper right corner). Eventually, experts may be able to select and modify grids and cases from a library; we hope that in several years this library will contain hundreds of hierarchies of grids.

The expert chooses to think about a language for developing a knowledge acquisition testbed, and enters potential candidates (Figure 9). After five languages are entered, Aquinas adds an *ideal language* for this problem. This would be an ideal solution for the knowledge acquisition case. The languages are added to the solution hierarchy as children. Then Aquinas asks the expert to enter traits based on differences and similarities between languages. This is the heart of Kelly's interviewing methodology; Aquinas uses it in several different ways as knowledge is expanded through elicitation and analysis.

Aquinas initially assumes that traits will be bipolar with ordinal ratings between 1 and 5. The expert is asked to rate each solution with regard to each trait, but the expert may specify different rating scales (unordered, interval, or ratio). Aquinas later assists in recognizing and changing types of rating scales. Aquinas also elicits information about the importance of each trait. This knowledge is used later in the decision making process.

2. Analyze and Expand the Initial, Single Grid

Once a grid is complete, an analysis is performed to show *implications* between various values of traits (see the lower right-hand window in Figure 8). Implications are read from left to right, and the thickness of the arc shows the strength of the implication (HARDER.TO.LEARN implies POOR. DEVELOPMENT.ENVIRONMENT). A method similar to ENTAIL (Gaines and Shaw, 1985; Shaw and Gaines, 1987) derives implications: rating grid entries are used as a sample set and fuzzy set logic is applied to discover inductive implications between the values. This method uncovers higher-order relationships among traits and later helps build trait hierarchies. The expert can also use an interac-

---ELICITING ELEMENTS---
Please enter a list of LANGUAGE elements for K-ACQUISITION, one to a line. When you're done, enter a RETURN. Try to include at least one LANGUAGE that would NOT be good for K-ACQUISITION (a counter example).
AQU** **ADA**
AQU** **LISP**
AQU** **PROLOG**
AQU** **COBOL**
AQU** **FORTRAN**
AQU** **(CR)**
Can you imagine a new ideal LANGUAGE for K-ACQUISITION?
AQU** **YES**
For now, it will be called IDEAL K-ACQUISITION-LANGUAGE.

---BUILDING TRAITS BY TRIADS---
When answering the following questions, remember to keep the K-ACQUISITION case in mind.

Think of an important attribute that two of ADA, LISP, and PROLOG share, but that the other one does not. What is that attribute?
AQU** **SYMBOLIC**
What is that attribute's opposite as it applies in this case?
AQU** **NUMERIC**
What is the name of a scale or concept that describes SYMBOLIC/NUMERIC?
AQU** **ATTITUDE**

Think of an important trait that two of LISP, PROLOG, and COBOL share, but that the other one does not. What is that trait?
AQU** **WIDELY AVAILABLE**
What is that trait's opposite as it applies in this case?
AQU** **NOT AS WIDELY AVAILABLE**
What is the name of a scale or concept that describes WIDELY-AVAILABLE/NOT-AS-WIDELY-AVAILABLE?
AQU** **AVAILABILITY**

---FILLING IN RATINGS---
Please rate these things on a scale of 5 to 1, where 5 means more like SYMBOLIC and 1 means more like NUMERIC. If neither one seems to apply, enter N(either). If both seem to apply, enter a B(oth). If you would like to change the range or type of scale, enter C(hange scale).
    SYMBOLIC(5) NUMERIC(1)
        ADA** **5**
        LISP** **1**
        PROLOG** **1**
        COBOL** **5**
        FORTRAN** **5**
        IDEAL-K-ACQUISITION-LANGUAGE** **1**

Aquinas asks the expert for an initialsSet of potential solutions to the first problem case. Then, the solutions are presented in groups of three, and the expert gives discriminating traits. Ratings are entered for each solution for each trait.

Figure 9. Dialog with Expert

tive process (implication review) to analyze and debug this information; the expert may agree or disagree with each implication. If the expert disagrees, the knowledge that led to the implication is reviewed, and the expert can change the knowledge or add exceptions that disprove the implication (Boose, 1986). Certain types of *implication patterns* are also uncovered. Discovery of *ambiguous* patterns, for example, may mean that traits are being used inconsistently (Hinkle, 1965; Boose, 1986).

After the initial grid is complete, the dialog manager suggests a method to help the expert expand the grid. The method depends on the size of the grid, analysis of information in the grid, session history, and so on. The dialog manager inserts the appropriate command on the screen. The expert may change this recommendation or accept it by entering RETURN.

3. Test the Knowledge in the Single Grid

The dialog manager next recommends that the grid knowledge be tested by running a consultation. The expert is asked to provide desirable values for the traits associated with an instance of the case under consideration. These values may be appended with a certainty factor and/or the tag ABSOLUTE to show an absolute constraint. Consultation questions are ordered according to a computed benefit/cost ratio that depends on both the generated system (e.g., entropy of a given trait, Quinlan, 1983) and the specified expert (e.g., cost of obtaining information) parameters. The questions may also be be ordered according to an arbitrary specification given by the expert. Performance is measured by comparison of experts' expectations with Aquinas consultation results.

Two methods are available in Aquinas for turning rating values in grids into solution recommendations. One approach involves mapping this information onto certainty factor scales. Each rating in the grid is assigned a certainty factor weight based on its relative strength (a 5 is stronger than a 4), the *relative weight* the expert has assigned to the trait, and any *absolute constraints* that the expert has specified for the trait. In the test consultation, EMYCIN's certainty factor combination method (Adams, 1985) is used to combine the certainty factors. The result is a rank-ordered list of solutions with certainty factor assignments. These certainty factors are also used when rules are generated for expert system shells.

Another available approach employs Saaty's Analytic Hierarchy Process to order a set of possible solutions. Grid information obtained through pairwise comparisons or through regular rating grid methods is mapped onto *judgment matrices*. The *principal eigenvector* is computed for each matrix; the eigenvectors are normalized and combined to yield a final ranking of the solutions. Each solution has a score between 0.0 and 1.0. In a knowledge base consisting of multiple grids, these values are propagated through the hierarchies.

4. Build Hierarchies (Structured as Solutions and Traits in Multiple Grids) from the First Grid

Next, the dialog manager recommends that the expert expand the trait and solution hierarchies by performing a *cluster analysis* (Figure 10). Aquinas uses a method of single-link hierarchical cluster analysis based on FOCUS (Shaw and Gaines, 1987) to group sets of related solutions or traits. The junctions in the clusters can be seen as conjectures about possible new classes of solutions or traits. These more general trait or solution classes may be named and added to the hierarchies.

Laddering is also often used to find traits at varying levels of abstraction (Boose, 1986).

"Why?" questions are used to find more general traits:

What is a new trait that says why you think GOOD-DEVELOPMENT-ENVIRONMENT should be true of a LANGUAGE for K-ACQUISITION?

AQU** FASTER SYSTEM DEVELOPMENT

"How?" questions help find more specific traits:

How could a language for K-ACQUISITION be characterized by WIDELY-AVAILABLE?

AQU** RUNS ON MULTIPLE HARDWARE
AQU** MANY COMPILERS AVAILABLE
AQU** MANY COMPANIES OFFER

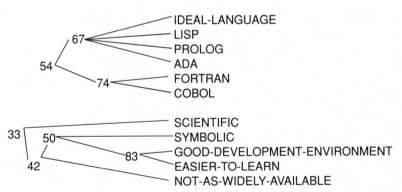

Solution and trait clusters are formed from information in rating grids. The expert is asked to label nodes and expand clusters where possible; new traits are used to expand the hierarchies.

Figure 10. Solution and Trait Clusters

Experts stop expanding the trait hierarchies when they are able to provide direct grid ratings at these more specific trait levels. Ratings need not be explicitly given at each level of the trait and solution hierarchies, but can often be inferred from other grids in the knowledge base (e.g., induction from more specific examples or inheritance from more general ones) (Lieberman, 1986).

5. Use Several Rating Value Types (Transform Ordinal Ratings to Nominal and Interval Ratings) to Represent Knowledge

Aquinas helps the expert convert a trait with ordinal values (DELIVERY-COST: HIGH-COST(5) / LOW-COST(1)) into a trait with ratio scaled rating values (DE-LIVERY-COST: (1500 - 60000) DOLLARS-US). The expert rerates the solutions in terms of the new values and these values appear on the grid. Aquinas provides several forms of estimation help. Four estimation procedures are provided: START-&-MODIFY, EXTREME-VALUES, DECOMPOSITION, and RECOMPOSI-TION (Beyth-Marom and Dekel, 1985). In this instance, the EXTREME-VALUES procedure first asks for the least and greatest DELIVERY-COST one could imagine for the type of LISP being considered. Through a series of questions, Aquinas helps shrink this range until a satisfactory estimate is given.

Aquinas also helps the expert change trait scale types by checking values associated with particular kinds of traits. For instance, bipolar traits that receive only extreme ratings (e.g., RUNS.ON.VAX/RUNS.ON.IBM) may be better represented with an unordered trait (e.g., COMPUTER.TYPE).

6. Test Knowledge in Hierarchies; Test Knowledge from Multiple Experts

Another expert adds knowledge about programming language selection to the knowledge base and tests it. In the first consultation (Figure 11), the user is interested in selecting a particular version of LISP, Prolog, or ADA for a knowledge acquisition project. Because of the many potential solutions, the user is given the opportunity to specify a subset for consideration. The solutions in this subset are called *solution candidates*.

Aquinas then asks for a set of absolute and preferred trait values for this consultation. The user enters an absolute constraint that only languages with a delivery cost of less than $30,000 will be considered. Patterns of constraints may be entered by using key words such as AND and OR. The user may accept default values entered in a previous consultation by pressing the RETURN key. If a default value has not been previously specified and the user types RETURN, that trait will be ignored in the inference process for this consultation. The user's preference for HARDWARE type is partitioned among three manufacturers by pairwise comparison (Figure 12), which generates a ratio-scaled set of preferences (Saaty, 1980).

---TEST CONSULTATION---

Would you like to run an EXISTING or NEW consultation?
AQU** **EXISTING**
What is the name of this existing consultation?
AQU** **LISP-PROLOG-ADA-ONLY**
This test consultation is named K-ACQUISITION.LISP-PROLOG-ADA-ONLY.

Which K-ACQUISITION alternatives would you like to consider in this consultation
(LISP-PROLOG-ADA-ONLY). Enter them one to a line. If you wish all solutions to be
considered, type ALL. When done, press RETURN.
AQU** **MACLISP-LM**
AQU** **INTERLISP**
AQU** **COMMON-LISP**
AQU** **QUINTUS-PROLOG**
AQU** **ADA-1**
AQU** **(CR)**
The following experts know about MACLISP-LM, INTERLISP, COMMON-LISP,
QUINTUS-PROLOG, and ADA-1: WEC JCA. Would you like to exclude or weight
any of these experts?
AQU** **NO**

Please indicate the desired trait selection values for LISP-PROLOG-ADA-ONLY
solutions. Press RETURN to indicate agreement with the default values, or type in
a new value. Values may be appended with a certainty factor in the form '.8' and/or
the word ABSOLUTE to indicate that the value is an absolute constraint when
selecting a type of LANGUAGE for K-ACQUISITION.
(WIDELY-AVAILABLE(5), 1.0)** **(CR)**
(GOOD-DEVELOPMENT-ENVIRONMENT(5), 1.0)** **(CR)**
(LOW-COST(<45000 DOLLARS-US),1.0, ABSOLUTE) (NOTE: THIS INCLUDES
HARDWARE FOR A WORKSTATION)** **<30000 DOLLARS-US 1.0 ABSOLUTE**

The expert tests the knowledge by running a consultation. The expertise of two
experts is used and consensus and dissenting solutions are given (see Figure 12).

Figure 11. Running a Consultation

The results of the consultation are presented to the user. For each solution, the
consensus recommendation of the experts consulted is presented, followed by
the weight of each expert that contributed to the recommendation. With multiple
experts, it may sometimes be useful to examine a set of recommendations from
a *dissenting* expert or group of experts. Since WEC's recommendations differed
most from the consensus, these are listed as a dissenting opinion.

A general model illustrating the inference propagation path was shown in
Figure 6. For each expert consulted and for each level in that expert's solution
hierarchy, a partial problem model is constructed, evaluated, and abstracted in

(COMPANIES(VAX .33, IBM .33, ATT .33), 1.0)** **PAIRWISE**
Please compare these values of HARDWARE with regard to their importance in contributing to an overall high score for a particular type of LANGUAGE for K-ACQUISITION in the context of LISP-PROLOG-ADA-ONLY.
Please compare **VAX** and **IBM**. Enter:
VAX=IBM if VAX and IBM are **equally** important
VAX>IBM or VAX<IBM if one of the pair is **weakly** more important
VAX>>IBM or VAX<<IBM if one is **strongly** more important
VAX>>>IBM or VAX<<<IBM if one is **demonstrably** or very strongly more important
VAX>>>>IBM or VAX<<<<IBM if one is **absolutely** more important
AQU** **VAX<IBM**

Please compare **VAX** and **ATT**. Enter:
VAX=ATT if VAX and ATT are **equally** important
VAX>ATT or VAX<ATT if one of the pair is **weakly** more important
VAX>>ATT or VAX<<ATT if one is **strongly** more important
VAX>>>ATT or VAX<<<ATT if one is **demonstrably** or very strongly more important
VAX>>>>ATT or VAX<<<<ATT if one is **absolutely** more important
AQU** **VAX>>>>ATT**

Results for test consultation K-ACQUISITION.LISP-PROLOG-ADA-ONLY:
    1: INTERLISP (.47: (WEC .5, JCA .5))
    2: QUINTUS-PROLOG (.40: (WEC 1.0))

Would you like to see the dissenting opinion for this consultation?
AQU** **YES**

The following dissenting opinion was given by WEC:
Overall agreement with consensus: .79
1: QUINTUS PROLOG (.40)
2: INTERLISP (.39)

The expert specifies "run-time" values for traits, entering an absolute cost constraint, and performing a pairwise comparison task to derive relative values for hardware. Consensus and dissenting opinions are given along with the weighted contributions of each expert.

Figure 12. Test Consultation (Continued)

a bottom-up fashion through the trait hierarchy of that solution level. Through this process the solution is refined as the children of the best solutions are chosen for continued evaluation. Bottom-up abstraction takes place again in the trait hierarchy at the new solution level, and the cycle continues until all remaining solution candidates have been evaluated. Then an ordered list of solution candidates is obtained and combined with the results from other experts.

This information from a single case may then be combined, if desired, with information from other cases to derive a final ranking of solution candidates. Users may override this general model of inference propagation by specifying explicit inference paths and parameters.

7. Edit, Analyze, and Refine the Knowledge Base, Building New Cases

Once the experts have entered information about one case, they then describe additional cases. They could start from scratch by entering a list of relevant solutions and traits, but that would be inefficient if there were significant overlap in those required by a previously entered case and a new one (Mittal, Bobrow, and Kahn, 1986). Aquinas allows an expert to copy pieces of hierarchies (and, optionally, their associated values) between cases. Information copied in this way can be modified to fit the new context. This facility may also be used to copy pieces of hierarchies between experts.

8. Further Expand and Refine the Knowledge Base

Hierarchies and rating grids continue to be used during the session to expand and refine the knowledge base. Work in progress has been shown in Figure 8. Aquinas contains a variety of other tools to help analyze and expand the knowledge base.

- *Comparison of Experts (Sources).* The MINUS tool (Shaw and Gaines, 1987) compares grids on the same subject from different experts and points out differences and similarities. This information has been used to manage structured negotiation between experts (Boose, 1986). SOCIOGRIDS features (Shaw and Gaines, 1987) will be available in the future to display networks of expertise. Nodes and relations in these networks will show the degree of subsumption of one expert's grid over grids from other experts.

- *Incremental Interviewing.* Aquinas can use an incremental dialog to elicit new traits and solutions, one at a time, from the expert (Boose, 1986). This is useful when the expert does not have a list of solutions to start a grid and in other situations during knowledge refinement.

- *Trait Value Examination.* New solutions can be identified by asking the expert to fill in holes in the values of trait ranges. For instance, no solution may exist with a rating of 2 on some ordinal trait scale; the expert is asked if one can be identified:

  What is a new LANGUAGE that would receive a value of 2 on the scale SCIENTIFIC(5)/BUSINESS(1)?

New traits can also be identified by forming triads based on ratings: if LISP and PROLOG are rated 5 on SCIENTIFIC(5)/BUSINESS(1), and ADA is rated 4, the expert is asked,

What is a new trait having to do with SCIENTIFIC/BUSINESS that makes LISP and PROLOG similar yet different from ADA?

- *Trait Range Boundary Examination.* Important traits can frequently be identified by exploring the boundaries of trait ranges:

You said that the range of DELIVERY-COST for LISP for the K-ACQUISITION case was 1500 to 60000 DOLLARS-US. Can you think of any conditions in the future that might make DELIVERY-COST LESS THAN 1500?

AQU** **YES**

Enter conditions in terms of traits, one to a line; enter a RETURN when done.
AQU** **HARDWARE BREAKTHROUGH - LISP ON A CHIP**
AQU** **(CR)**

Can you think of any conditions in the future that might make DELIVERY-COST GREATER THAN 60000?

AQU** **YES**

Enter conditions in terms of traits, one to a line; enter a RETURN when done.

AQU** **VERY POWERFUL HARDWARE**
AQU** **PARALLEL ARCHITECTURES AVAILABLE**
AQU** **(CR)**

- *Completeness Checking.* A single grid can be used as a table of examples. If the table is incomplete, the expert is asked to fill in additional examples (Boose, 1986).

- *Combine Similar Traits.* Sometimes different labels are used for the same underlying concept. This can be discovered when a similarity analysis is performed (functionally equivalent traits with different labels may be uncovered). If the expert cannot think of a new solution to separate identical traits, then the traits may be combined into a single trait.

9. Generate Rules for Expert System Shells

The expert is the judge of when the point of diminishing returns has been reached within Aquinas. When such a point is reached, a knowledge base is generated for an expert system shell, and development continues directly in that shell. Similarity and implication analyses allow experts to determine whether traits or solutions can be adequately and appropriately discriminated from one another. The system provides correlational methods for comparing the order of Aquinas recommendations to an expert's rankings.

Aquinas can generate knowledge bases for several expert system shells (KEE, KS-300/EMYCIN, Loops, M.1, OPS5, S.1, and others). The knowledge contained in grids and hierarchies is converted within Aquinas into rules, and the rules are formatted for a particular expert system shell. Appropriate control knowledge is also generated when necessary. Rules are generated with screening clauses that partition the rules into subsets. An *expert clause* is used when expertise from multiple experts is weighted and combined together. A *case clause* controls the focus of the system during reasoning.

Four types of rules are generated:

- *Implication rules* are generated from arcs in the implication graph and conclude about particular traits. The conclusion's certainty factor is proportional to the strength of the implication. The use of implication rules restricts search and lessens the number of questions asked of users during consultations.

- *Solution rules* conclude about a particular solution or solution class. The conclusion's certainty factor is derived from a combination of the *grid rating strength* and the *trait weight*.

- *Absolute rules* are generated when the expert places an absolute constraint on a trait's value. Sometimes information about absolute constraints is included elsewhere when knowledge bases for expert system shells are generated.

- *Specialization/generalization rules* are derived from information in the hierarchies and are used to propagate hierarchical information.

Discussion

General Advantages and Disadvantages of Aquinas

Improved Process Efficiency and Faster Knowledge Base Generation. Aquinas inherits the advantages of ETS: rapid prototyping and feasibility analysis, vocabulary, solution and trait elicitation, interactive testing and refinement during knowledge acquisition, implication discovery, conflict point identification, expert system shell production, and generation of expert enthusiasm (Boose, 1986). It is much easier for users to learn knowledge-based system concepts by using

Aquinas than by reading books or attending classes (i.e., rules are automatically generated and used dynamically in consultations; new vocabulary is incrementally introduced).

ETS, still in use at Boeing, has been employed to build hundreds of single-grid prototype systems. Single grids as large as 42 x 38 (1596 ratings) have been built. Alternative approaches may be tested with little expenditure of resources. Knowledge bases have been generated for expert system shells that contain over two-thousand rules. Typically, something on the order of a 15 x 10 grid is built that generates several hundred rules.

Over 30 prototype systems have been built during the development of Aquinas (an AI book consultant, an AI tool advisor, a course evaluation system, a customer needs advisor, a database management system consultant, an investment advisor, a management motivation analyzer, a personal computer advisor, a personality disorder advisor, a product design and impact advisor, a robotic tool selector, a Seattle travel agent, and a wine advisor, among others). Some of these systems contain thousands of ratings arranged in hierarchical grids. The Programming Language Advisor session took less than two hours with each of the two experts.

Improved Knowledge Base Quality. Aquinas offers a rich knowledge representation and reasoning environment. We believe that Aquinas can be used to acquire knowledge for significant portions of most structured selection expert system problems. Hierarchies help the expert break down problems into component parts and allow reasoning at different levels of abstraction. Varying levels of precision are specified, with multiple types of rating scales when needed. Multiple handling methods for combining uncertain information are available based on needed precision and convenience. Knowledge from multiple experts may be combined using Aquinas. Users may receive dissenting as well as consensus opinions from groups of experts, thus getting a full range of possible solutions. Disagreement between the consensus and the dissenting opinion can be measured to derive a *degree of conflict* for a particular consultation. The system can be used for cost-effective group data gathering (Boose, 1987).

Analytic tools help uncover inconsistencies and circularities in the growing knowledge base.

Better Knowledge Base Maintenance and Comprehensibility. Elicitation, structuring, analysis, and testing of knowledge is based on specific cases. When knowledge in Aquinas is updated, it is done so with respect to a specific case. Addition of new knowledge in this way can be strictly controlled by the expert; the tendency for local changes to degrade other cases is thus curbed.

The expert builds and refines knowledge in rating grids and hierarchies—not directly in production rules. As a result, knowledge at this higher level of abstraction is more compact, comprehensible, and easier to maintain.

The growing collection of rating grids and case knowledge represents an important resource for building a variety of knowledge-based systems. Knowledge is stored explicitly with associated problem cases, making knowledge bases easier to update and maintain.

Currently, a user may copy and change any portion of the Aquinas knowledge base during a consultation. In the future, each expert will be able to protect areas of knowledge. The expert may believe protection is necessary because some knowledge should not be changed or because the knowledge has commercial value.

Extensions to Personal Construct Theory Methods. Aquinas significantly extends existing Personal Construct Theory methods. Rating grid knowledge can be tested and used interactively to make decisions; rating grid information may be arranged and coupled in hierarchies; multiple rating scale types are available (not just bipolar ordinal scales); and many grid analysis tools are available in a single workbench.

Process Complexity. Aquinas is not as easy to use as was ETS using single grids. There are many elicitation and analysis tools for a novice to understand; the decision-making process and inference engine can be set up to work in several different ways. We expect that continuing improvements in the dialog manager will help make the system more comprehensible and decrease the learning time for new users.

Theoretical Issues—Knowledge Elicitation

Personal Construct Psychology methods provide no guarantee that a sufficient set of knowledge will be found to solve a given problem. Aquinas attempts to expand the initial subset of solutions and traits based on problem-solving knowledge for specific cases. The goal is to solve enough cases so that the knowledge is sufficient to solve new cases. This is the methodology of knowledge engineering in general; Aquinas helps make the process explicit and manageable.

Hierarchical decomposition can be used to build intuitive, comprehensible models that seem to behave in reasonable ways. One disadvantage is that some problems do not easily fit the hierarchical model. It also may be true that a particular problem would best be represented by a *collection of conflicting hierarchies* (hierarchies for mechanical problems tend to model structure or function, not both, and both may be necessary).

The use of multiple rating value types provides more flexibility, convenience, and precision in representing knowledge. However, deciding a particular type of variable to use can be a complex task. The dialog manager offers some assistance, but the expert usually must learn appropriate usage of rating types through experience.

Experts develop Aquinas knowledge bases serially. In the future, we would like to build a participant system in which many experts could dynamically share rating grids and hierarchies (Chang, 1985).

Analysis and Inference

Multiple analysis tools and elicitation methods in Aquinas help the expert think about the problem in new ways and tend to point out conflicts and inconsistencies over time. Lenat (1982) argues that knowledge representations should shift as different needs arise. This should lead to better problem and solution descriptions, and, in turn, to better problem solving.

Inference in Aquinas is efficient because the problem space is partitioned. Information in the trait hierarchies is attached to particular levels of solutions. Although no formal studies have been conducted, consultation results using the methods described above seem reasonable.

Rule generation for expert-system shells is straightforward. Development of the knowledge base can continue in an expert system shell that may offer advantages of speed, specialized development and debugging facilities, and inexpensive hardware.

Future Directions

We intend to build a knowledge-acquisition environment that includes specific domain knowledge for specialized application areas and can acquire knowledge for synthetic problems, combining features from other knowledge-acquisition tools such as MDIS (Antonelli, 1983), DSPL (Brown, 1984), MORE (Kahn, Nowlan, and McDermott, 1985), MOLE (Eshelman, Ehret, McDermott, and Tan, 1987), and TKAW (Kahn, Breaux, Joeseph, and DeKlerk, 1987).

Presently Aquinas works best on those problems whose solutions can be comfortably enumerated (*analytic* or *structured selection* problems such as classification or diagnosis), as opposed to problems whose solutions are built up from components (*synthetic* or *constructive* problems such as configuration or planning). Simple classification can be thought of as a single decision problem (handled by ETS). Complex structured selection problems may require a set of linked data abstraction/solution refinement decisions (Aquinas). The next step may be to generalize this process to acquire and represent knowledge for planning, configuration, and design problems where the order of linked decisions in solution hierarchies may represent precedence of events or goals rather than just solution refinement. In these problems, hierarchies may be assembled at consultation time rather than constructed totally in advance as they are currently. Grid cells might sometimes contain an arbitrary computation rather than a rating. These would include results of functions (such as found in spreadsheets) or database retrievals. Deeper models of the structure and function of physical systems could be modeled.

An important step in expanding the knowledge-acquisition workbench concept is the linking together of other specialized tools. At the Boeing Knowledge Systems Laboratory we are investigating ways of integrating diverse knowledge representations from different laboratory projects so that this may be more easily accomplished. In the domain of knowledge acquisition, we feel that the approach used in SALT (Marcus, McDermott, and Wang, 1985; Marcus and McDermott, 1986; Marcus, 1987) is particularly promising. SALT is a system that interviews experts to build knowledge bases for certain types of constructive problems (its first use was to configure elevators). We are also interested in generating knowledge sources for BBB, a blackboard system that has been successfully applied to a variety of problems (Benda, Baum, Dodhiawala, and Jagannathan, 1986).

Development of the Aquinas workbench will continue in an incremental fashion. Techniques will be continuously integrated and refined to build an increasingly more effective knowledge-acquisition environment.

References

Adams, J. (1985). Probabilistic reasoning and certainty factors. In B. G. Buchanan & E. H. Shortliffe (Eds.), *Rule-based expert systems: The MYCIN experiments of the Stanford Heuristic Programming Project*. Reading, MA: Addison-Wesley.

Alpert, M., & Raiffa, H. (1982). A progress report on the training of probability assessors. In D. Kahneman, P. Slovic, & A. Tversky (Eds.), *Judgment under uncertainty: Heuristics and biases*. New York: Cambridge University Press.

Antonelli, D. (1983). The application of artificial intelligence to a maintenance and diagnostic information system (MDIS). *Proceedings of the Joint Services Workshop on Artificial Intelligence in Maintenance*. Boulder, CO.

Benda, M., Baum, L. S., Dodhiawala, R. T., & Jagannathan, V. (1986). Boeing blackboard system. *Proceedings of the High-level Tools Workshop*. Ohio State University, Columbus, OH.

Benda, M., Jagannathan, V., & Dodhiawala, R. (1986). On optimal cooperation of knowledge sources. *Workshop on Distributed Artificial Intelligence*, Gloucester, MA.

Beyth-Marom, R., & Dekel, S. (1985). *An elementary approach to thinking under uncertainty*. London: Lawrence Erlbaum Associates.

Boose, J. H. (1984). Personal construct theory and the transfer of human expertise. *Proceedings of the National Conference on Artificial Intelligence*, AAAI-84 (pp. 27–33). Austin, TX.

Boose, J H. (1985). A knowledge acquisition program for expert systems based on personal construct psychology. *International Journal of Man-Machine Studies, 23*, 495–525.

Boose, J H. (1986). *Expertise transfer for expert system design*. New York: Elsevier.

Boose, J. H. (1987). Rapid acquisition and combination of knowledge from multiple experts in the same domain. *Future Computing Systems Journal, 1(2)*, 191–216.

Brown, D. E. (1984). *Expert systems for design problem-solving using design refinement with plan selection and redesign*. Unpublished doctoral dissertation, Ohio State University, Columbus.

Bylander, T., & Chandrasekaran, B. (1987). Generic tasks in knowledge-based reasoning: the "right" level of abstraction for knowledge acquisition. *International Journal of Man-Machine Studies, 26(2)*, 231–244.

Bylander, T., & Mittal, S. (1986). CSRL: A language for classificatory problem solving and uncertainty handling. *AI Magazine, 7(3)*, 66–77.

Chandrasekaran, B. (1986). Generic tasks in knowledge-based reasoning: High-level building blocks for expert system design. *IEEE Expert, 1(3)*, 23–30.

Chang, E. (1985). *Participant systems*. Unpublished manuscript. Alberta Research Council Advanced Technologies, Calgary, Alberta.

Cheeseman, P. (1985). In defense of probability. *Proceedings of the Ninth International Joint Conference on Artificial Intelligence*, IJCAI-85 (pp. 1002–9). Los Angeles, CA.

Clancey, W. (1986). Heuristic classification. In J. Kowalik (Ed.), *Knowledge-based problem-solving*. New York: Prentice-Hall.

Coombs, C. H., Dawes, R. M., & Tversky, A. (1970). *Mathematical psychology*. Englewood Cliffs, NJ: Prentice-Hall.

Eshelman, L., Ehret, D., McDermott, J., & Tan, M. (1987). MOLE: a tenacious knowledge acquisition tool. *International Journal of Man-Machine Studies, 26(1)*, 41–54.

Gaines, B. R. (1987). An overview of knowledge acquisition and transfer. *International Journal of Man-Machine Studies, 26(4)*, 453–472.

Gaines, B. R., & Shaw, M. L. G. (1981). New directions in the analysis and interactive elicitation of personal construct systems. In M. L. G. Shaw (Ed.), *Recent advances in personal construct technology*. New York: Academic Press.

Gaines, B. R., & Shaw, M. L. G. (1985). Induction of inference rules for expert systems. *Fuzzy Sets and Systems 8(3)*, 315–328.

Gordon, J., & Shortliffe, E. H. (1985). The Dempster-Shafer theory of evidence. In B. G. Buchanan & E. H. Shortliffe (Eds.), *Rule-based expert systems: The MYCIN experiments of the Stanford heuristic programming project*. Reading, MA: Addison-Wesley.

Gruber, T., & Cohen, P. (1987). Design for acquisition principles of knowledge system design to facilitate knowledge acquisition. *International Journal of Man-Machine Studies, 26(2)*, 143–160.

Henrion, M. (1987). Propagating uncertainty by logic sampling in Bayes' networks. In J. Lemme & L. N. Kanal (Eds.), *Machine intelligence and pattern recognition*. Amsterdam: Elsevier, North Holland.

Hinkle, D. N. (1965). *The change of personal constructs from the viewpoint of a theory of implications.* Unpublished doctoral dissertation. Ohio State Univ., Columbus.

Howard, R. A., & Matheson, J. E. (1984). Influence diagrams. In R. A. Howard & J. E. Matheson (Eds.), *Readings on the principles and applications of decision analysis.* Menlo Park, CA: Strategic Decisions Group.

Hurley, R. (1983). *Decisions tables in software engineering.* New York: Van Nostrand Reinhold.

Kahn, G., Nowlan, S., & McDermott, J. (1985). MORE: An intelligent knowledge acquisition tool. *Proceedings of the Ninth Joint Conference on Artificial Intelligence,* IJCAI-85 (pp. 581–584). Los Angeles, CA.

Kahn, G. S., Breaux, E. H., Joeseph, R. L., & DeKlerk, P. (1987). An intelligent mixed-initiative workbench for knowledge acquisition. *International Journal of Man-Machine Studies, 27(2),* 167–180.

Kelly, G. A. (1955). *The psychology of personal constructs.* New York: Norton.

Kitto, C., & Boose, J. H. (1987). Heuristics for expertise transfer: The automatic management of complex knowledge-acquisition dialogs. *International Journal of Man-Machine Studies, 26(2),* 183–202.

Lenat, D. (1982). The nature of heuristics. *Artificial Intelligence, 19(2),* 189–249.

Lenat, D., Prakash, M., & Shepard, M. (1986). CYC: Using common sense knowledge to overcome brittleness and knowledge acquisition bottlenecks. *AI Magazine, 6(4),* 65–85.

Lieberman, H. (1986). Using prototypical objects to implement shared behavior in object-oriented systems. *Proceedings of the Object-Oriented Programming Systems, Languages and Applications Workshop* (pp. 214–223). Portland, OR.

Marcus, S. (1987). Taking backtracking with a grain of SALT. *International Journal of Man-Machine Studies, 26(4),* 383–398.

Marcus, S., & McDermott, J. (1987). *SALT: A knowledge acquisition tool for propose-and-revise systems* (Carnegie-Mellon University Department of Computer Science Technical Report CMS–CS–86–170). Pittsburgh, PA.

Marcus, S., McDermott, J., & Wang, T. (1985). Knowledge acquisition for constructive systems. *Proceedings of the Ninth Joint Conference on Artificial Intelligence* (pp. 637–639). Los Angeles, CA.

McDermott, J. (1986). Making expert systems explicit. *Proceedings of The IFIP Congress.* Dublin, Ireland.

Michalski, R. S. (1978). *Designing extended entry decision tables and optimal decision trees using decision diagrams.* Urbana, IL: Intelligent Systems Group, Artificial Intelligence Laboratory, Department of Computer Science, University of Illinois.

Michalski, R. S., (1986). *Machine learning.* Plenary talk at the AAAI Knowledge Acquisition for Knowledge-based Systems Workshop, Banff, Canada.

Michalski, R. S., & Winston, P. (1985). *Variable precision logic* (Artificial Intelligence Laboratory Memo 85). Cambridge, MA: Massachusetts Institute of Technology.

Mittal, S., Bobrow, D., & Kahn, K. (1986). Virtual copies: At the boundary between classes and instances. *Proceedings of the Object-Oriented Programming Systems, Languages, and Applications Workshop* (pp. 159–166). Portland, OR.

Pearl, J. (1986). *Fusion, propagation and structuring in belief networks* (Technical report CSD–850022, R–42–VI–12). Los Angeles, CA: Cognitive Systems Laboratory, Computer Science Department, University of California.

Quinlan, J. R. (1983). Learning efficient classification procedures and their application to chess end games. In R. S. Michalski, J. G. Carbonell, & T. M. Mitchell (Eds.), *Machine learning—An artificial intelligence approach, 1*. Palo Alto, CA: Tioga.

Reboh, R., & Risch, T. (1986). SYNTEL: Knowledge programming using functional representations. (Vendor presentation). *National Conference on Artificial Intelligence, AAAI-86*. Philadelphia, PA.

Reboh, R., Risch, T., Hart, P. E., & Duda, R. O. (1986). Task-specific knowledge representation: a case study. *Proceedings of the High-level Tools Workshop*. Ohio State University, Columbus, OH.

Saaty, T. L. (1980). *The analytic hierarchy process*. New York: McGraw-Hill.

Shafer, G. (1976). *A mathematical theory of evidence*. Princeton, NJ: Princeton University Press.

Shafer, G., & Tversky, A. (1985). Languages and designs for probability judgment. *Cognitive Science, 9*, 309–339.

Shastri, L., & Feldman, J. (1985). Evidential reasoning in semantic networks: A formal theory. *Proceedings of the Ninth International Joint Conference on Artificial Intelligence*, IJCAI-85 (pp. 465–474). Los Angeles, CA.

Shaw, M. L. G., & Gaines, B. R. (1988). PLANET: A computer-based system for personal learning, analysis, negotiation and elicitation techniques. In J. C. Mancuso & M. L. G. Shaw (Eds.), *Cognition and personal structure: Computer access and analysis*. New York: Praeger Press.

Shaw, M. L. G., & Gaines, B. R. (1987). Techniques for knowledge acquisition and transfer. *International Journal of Man-Machine Studies, 27(3)*, 251–280.

Spetzler, C., & von Holstein, C. (1983). Probability encoding in decision analysis. In R. Howard & J. Matheson (Eds.), *Readings on the principles and applications of decision analysis, 2*. Palo Alto, CA: Strategic Decisions Group.

Spiegelhalter, D. J. (1986). Probabilistic reasoning in predictive expert systems. In L. N. Kanal & J. Lemmer (Eds.), *Uncertainty in artificial intelligence*. Amsterdam: North-Holland.

Szolovitz, P., & Pauker, S. (1978). Categorical and probabilistic reasoning in medical diagnosis. *Artificial Intelligence, 11*, 115–144.

Wallsten, T., & Budescu, D. (1983). Encoding subject probabilities: A psychological and psychometric review. *Management Science, 29*.

Wilkins, D. C., Clancey, W. J., & Buchanan, B. G. (1987). Knowledge base refinement by editing abstract control knowledge. *International Journal of Man-Machine Studies, 27(3)*, 281–294.

Chapter 6

Knowledge Representation in NIKL*

Raymond L. Bates
Robert Mac Gregor

USC Information Sciences Institute

The purpose of this chapter is to give the reader an understanding of NIKL and related knowledge representation languages. To do this, some basic issues will be discussed concerning knowledge representation and knowledge representation languages. These issues include what to expect from a knowledge representation language, how to use NIKL in building Artificial Intelligence (AI) systems, and the advantages and disadvantages of using NIKL in these systems. A prognosis for the future is included as well.

NIKL implements sets of functions that can be used to represent knowledge in a computer. As opposed to the commercially supported products described in Chapter 3 which also contain knowledge representation languages, NIKL is missing features such as a graphical user interface, a rewrite rule system, and a customer support group. In contrast to these systems, however, NIKL exclusively uses formal methods to manipulate knowledge.

AI programs that store and use knowledge (e.g., expert systems) must have a formal or informal way in which to manipulate this knowledge. Using an

*Many of the articles cited in this chapter appear in *Readings in Knowledge Representation* (Brachman and Levesque, 1985). For their contributions to NIKL and Loom, the authors wish to thank Thomas Kaczmarek, William Mark, Thomas Lipkis, Norman Sondheimer, Ronald Brachman, Sheila Coyazo, and Marc Vilain.

This research is supported by the Defense Advanced Research Projects Agency under Contract Number MDA903–81–C–0335. Views and conclusions contained in this paper are the authors' and should not be interpreted as representing the official opinion of DARPA, the U.S. Government, or any person or agency connected with them.

informal method to represent or manipulate knowledge is prone to errors. Informal methods tend to be ad hoc, and they address the immediate problem at hand instead of the whole problem. These methods must be carefully controlled when manipulating knowledge, or they will "fire" under the wrong circumstances. The designers of NIKL believe that formal methods help create systems that are simpler to program and easier to maintain and scale up.

Demonstration systems tend to have just enough knowledge to accomplish their task. When a demonstration system is scaled up, unpredictable results may arise due to the increased knowledge required. Any new item of knowledge has the potential of making a major impact on the rest of the knowledge base. Furthermore, informal methods tend to be coded to work in one application area and in general are not transferable. Therefore, it is not always clear what is being represented. The resulting complexities make it impractical for a programmer to be aware of or to understand the potential ramifications of every change to the knowledge base. Formal methods can make this problem more manageable by relieving the programmer of some of the burden.

In response to this problem, KL-One and NIKL (New Implementation of KL-One) were designed to provide formal methods for representing knowledge. These methods provide a more efficient way to build AI systems that are less prone to error, more complete, and easier to evolve and maintain. Obviously KL-One and NIKL are not the only languages for solving knowledge representation problems, but their designers believe that they are capable of providing the most efficient solutions.

The basic outline of this chapter is as follows: an overview of NIKL; an overview of KL-One; a discussion of the KL-One and NIKL classifiers; a section on the history of NIKL; some unique applications of NIKL and of KL-One; a discussion of the future of NIKL (Loom); and the conclusion.

Knowledge representation can be a controversial subject. This chapter will attempt to clarify some of the issues and benefits of using a language like NIKL so that a potential user can make a rational choice as to its appropriateness for a specific application.

Overview of NIKL

NIKL is one of the members of the KL-One (Brachman, 1978) family of knowledge representation languages (KL-One is discussed below). NIKL has been in use for several years at a variety of sites. This exposure has led to various improvements and extensions to the system. Although the experiences discussed are particular to the use of NIKL, the requirements that have been discovered are relevant to any intelligent system that must reason about terminology.

A general goal of AI is to produce an intelligent entity. This entity must be capable of recognizing new objects in its environment and discerning properties of these objects. This recognition can be aided by a *terminological base*.

Work on NIKL has been motivated by a desire to build a *principled* knowledge representation system. The word "principled" is used to indicate that the system has a predetermined set of actions. NIKL can be used to reason about terms in a variety of applications, thus providing *terminological competence* (every term has an explicit definition). To this end, it is currently used for the following applications: natural language processing, expert systems, and knowledge-based software. The research methodology followed at USC Information Sciences Institute (ISI) is to allow application needs, rather than theoretical interests, to drive the continued development of the language. This methodology has allowed us to perform an empirical evaluation of the strengths and weaknesses of NIKL. It has also helped to identify general requirements for *terminological reasoning* (i.e., reasoning about terms) in intelligent systems.

The KL-One System

Ronald Brachman designed KL-One to "circumvent common expressiveness shortcomings" (Brachman, 1978). This language embodies the principles that concepts are formal representational objects and that epistemological relationships between formal objects must be kept distinct from conceptual relations between the things represented by those formal objects. The concept of a man (what properties men have: 0 to 2 arms, 0 to 2 legs, a proper subset of the concept of a person) should be separated from particular instances of men (Bill, John, etc.). If a knowledge representation language fails to make an explicit separation between what it means to be a man in general and the properties of a particular man, the distinction may be confused. Humans, using common sense, have no difficulty in understanding this distinction, but computers lack this ability. The distinction is important in recognizing new individuals versus generic properties of all individuals in a group. KL-One can be defined as an "epistemologically explicit representation language to account for this distinction" (Brachman, 1978).

Brachman describes a KL-One concept as "a set of functional roles tied together by a structuring gestalt." His first technical report on KL-One (Brachman, 1978) defines concept definitions to "capture information about the functional role, number, criteriality and nature of potential role fillers; and 'structural conditions,' which express explicit relationships between the potential role fillers and give functional roles their meaning." For a recent overview of the KL-One system, see Brachman and Schmolze (1985).

The KL-One and NIKL Classifiers

An important consequence of the well-defined semantics of KL-One is that it is possible to define a classification procedure to determine the subsumption relationship for concepts in a KL-One network. A detailed description of the semantics of the KL-One classifier is provided in Schmolze and Lipkis (1983). The classifier for KL-One deduces "that the set denoted by some concept necessarily includes the set denoted by a second concept but where no subsumption relation between the concepts was explicitly entered" (Schmolze and Lipkis, 1983). The classifiers for NIKL and KL-One have been developed both at ISI and at Bolt Beranek and Newman, Inc. (BBN).

The desirable properties for a classification algorithm are soundness (no incorrect inference must be made), completeness (all correct inferences must be made), and totality (the algorithm must always halt). Theoretical analysis (Brachman and Levesque, 1984) has determined the limits on the expressiveness of KL-One-like languages, if completeness of the classification algorithm is to be maintained. Work on NIKL has concentrated on the issue of soundness, foregoing completeness in favor of increased expressiveness. There is a fundamental choice: the classifier can make all possible deductions by using a very restrictive language, or the system can be allowed to miss some deductions in favor of greater expressiveness of the language. An efficient implementation of NIKL has also been a goal, and the NIKL classifier is in fact nearly two orders of magnitude faster for large networks than the KL-One classifier.

The importance of the NIKL classifier is that the user need not recognize the class of an instance for each application (see the example in the section on Classification-Based Reasoning). NIKL's classifier can also be used to recognize new instances of concepts and to place them in the appropriate location in the network. The user need not worry about such issues as tractability (the system will arrive at an answer in a reasonable length of time), soundness, and completeness; this work has already been done. The reasoning component of NIKL is not ad hoc, as it can be in the commercial systems KEE® and ART®. The ad hoc nature can come from the user of ART or KEE having to duplicate some of the functionality of the classifier in his code.

The Development of NIKL from KL-One

NIKL and KL-One bear a strong family relationship. The designers of NIKL took a pragmatic view of knowledge representation and attempted to design a

---

KEE is a registered trademark of IntelliCorp, Inc.
ART is a registered trademark of Inference Corporation.

practical system. Many of the differences between NIKL and KL-One were directly influenced by work on KRYPTON, another knowledge representation language (Brachman, Fikes, and Levesque, 1983). Close cooperation between the NIKL design team and the KRYPTON designers resulted in many system similarities, despite a strong distinction on the issue of completeness. The KRYPTON designers were interested in ensuring that their system made all possible inferences, even at the risk of limiting expressibility. The NIKL designers, on the other hand, were willing to accept compromises in completeness in order to increase expressibility and make the system more usable.

A significant difference between NIKL and KL-One involves the representation and use of *roles*. In both NIKL and KL-One, a role is a relationship between two concepts. At the time NIKL was designed, use of KL-One had uncovered a need for revisions in the semantics of roles. For example, in NIKL, explicit structural conditions are not used to define the meaning of roles, because the KL-One formalization was found to be inadequate, and it was discovered that these conditions produced no useful results. Another difference between KL-One and NIKL concerns the way concepts and roles interrelate. In KL-One, the notation for relating roles within concepts (which includes relations such as *modifies, differentiates,* and *individuates*) is cumbersome. The designers of NIKL gave roles a much simpler notation and semantics. They interpreted roles as two-place relations and concepts as one-place relations. Because of this, roles took on a new significance. Roles in NIKL are defined as having a domain and a range. They are organized in a separate taxonomy, are thought of as representations of relations, and are assumed to be used consistently.

This enlightened view of roles was one of the lessons learned through the application of KL-One. It represents a case where something learned through the use of a specific tool has general applicability. Attributes of concepts should be formalized and should also have well-defined semantics. This discovery is not unique to the KL-One community—it is an adaptation of the ideas found in systems built around first-order logic. The rediscovery of this idea simply underscores its importance.

Applications of KL-One and of NIKL

The NIKL implementation was developed in 1982. Since then, NIKL has been in use principally at ISI and at BBN, which contributed to the design of the system. Several browsing, syntactic support, and graphing tools have been developed and used to construct and maintain knowledge bases. A natural language paraphraser, designed to assist users in understanding networks, was also developed, but it has not been heavily used. In addition, various inference mechanisms driven by the classifier have been implemented.

KL-One and NIKL have been applied in the areas of natural language processing (Bobrow and Webber, 1980; Mark, 1981; Bates and Bobrow, 1983; Sondheimer, Weischedel, and Bobrow, 1984; Sidner, 1985); expert systems (Neches, Swartout, and Moore, 1985); man-machine interfaces (Mark, 1986; Sondheimer, 1986); and software description (Kaczmarek, Mark, and Wilczynski, 1983; Wilczynski and Sondheimer, 1984). Large networks of NIKL and KL-One concepts, in excess of 1500 concepts, have been developed in these environments.

Classification-Based Reasoning

The NIKL classifier provides a general, weak method for categorizing descriptions of objects. It is insufficient as the sole inference mechanism for an intelligent system, but it can be used effectively (and efficiently) in what we have termed classification-based reasoning.

Most uses of KL-One and NIKL rely heavily on this type of classification-reasoning cycle. The application first creates a new description of some partial result and then classifies this into a static network describing knowledge of the problem domain. Based on the result of the classification, additional inferences are drawn about the partial result and a new description is constructed. These inferences are the result of some user-defined rule or procedure that examines the network, looking for inferences that the rule is capable of making. The resulting new description may achieve the goal of the reasoning cycle, in which case reasoning terminates. More typically, further classification and redescription are required, and the reasoning cycle begins again.

One way of evaluating this reasoning cycle is to think of the classifier as selecting applicable rules based on the terminology that is used to describe the task domain and the problem at hand. Selection of the rules is within the terminological system, that is, it is based on the definitions of terms. However, the rules are outside the terminological component and are expressed in some other language.

An example of classification-based reasoning can be found in the Consul application of NIKL (Mark, 1984). Consul uses classification extensively in the process of interpreting natural language requests for interactive computing services. For example, the user types the request, "Tell me about my afternoon meeting" (represented by user-request in Figure 1). Consul's natural language front-end will describe this request (in NIKL) as calling for a tell-about-action where the agent to be told is the logged-in-user and the object to be described is a meeting that is further described as being in the afternoon and in the possession of the same logged-in-user. Tell-about-action, user-request, meeting, afternoon, and logged-in-user are all defined as NIKL concepts. Object and agent-to-be-told are defined roles of the tell-about-action concept. Owner and time are roles of the concept meeting.

The description of the request will be classified into the NIKL knowledge base, which represents user expectations and system capabilities. Since Consul will not immediately understand how to execute this request, it will look for redescription rules (a rule that will enable the system to create a new concept that is a reformulation of the original concept). It will seek an applicable rule that is the most specific, as defined by the inheritance taxonomy. In this example, the description of the request is classified under the concept tell-the-logged-in-user, which is defined as a specialization of a tell-about-action whose agent must be the logged-in-user. The concept tell-the-logged-in-user has a rule attached to it which, when applied, causes a new concept to be created that is a redescription of the request (see Figure 2).

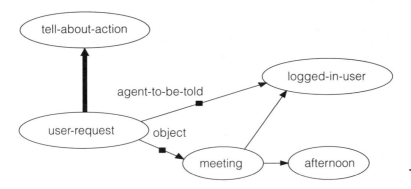

Figure 1. Initial Request

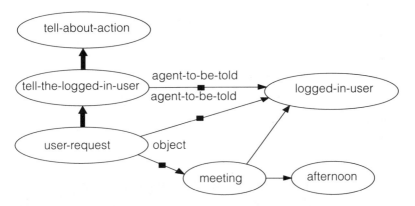

Figure 2. Request After Classification

Having performed this redescription, Consul will continue to refine the original request until it is redescribed as a composite operation. The final result will request the system to display the result obtained by retrieving a meeting with a time in a specific range from a particular file in the directory of logged-in-user.

The user of NIKL communicates to the system by entering a set of lists. Diagrams are not acceptable as input. The example input in Figure 3 captures most of the information depicted in Figure 2. (To express all the information in Figure 2 it would be necessary to give names to the unnamed role.) As previously indicated, the NIKL classifier classifies the concept user-request under the concept tell-the-logged-in-user.

It is apparent that the heart of the NIKL system is the classifier. However, there are many additional uses of the system. NIKL contains a protection mechanism that makes it impossible for the user to create an inconsistent network (as far as domain and range of roles are concerned). If an incompletely specified network is entered, NIKL automatically fills in the gaps by creating new concepts, thus circumventing the inconsistencies. In addition, the system is capable of comparing two concepts to determine any differences between them.

```
(defconcept tell-about-action primitive)

(defconcept logged-in-user primitive)

(defconcept meeting primitive)

(defconcept tell-the-logged-in-user
    (specializes tell-about-action)
    (res agent-to-be-told (vrconcept logged-in-user)))

(defconcept user-request
    (specializes tell-about-action)
    (res agent-to-be-told (vrconcept logged-in-user))
    (res object (vrconcept meeting)))

(defrole agent-to-be-told
    (domain tell-about-action)
    (range logged-in-user))

(defrole object
    (domain user-request)
    (range meeting))
```

Figure 3. Example of NIKL's Input Language

Other Applications

Both NIKL and KL-One have been used in a wide spectrum of applications. A fundamental test for any knowledge representation system is the variety of applications for which it will help the programmer achieve his goals. Some example applications are listed below.

Natural Language. Historically, research projects in knowledge representation and in natural language have supported each other. Natural language systems need a strong knowledge representation system to accomplish their tasks. One of the first uses of KL-One represented the syntactic and semantic structures needed to interpret the parses produced by the RUS parser developed at BBN (Bobrow and Webber, 1980). NIKL is also being used in Penman (Mann, 1983), a text generation system developed at ISI.

Database Retrieval. The RABBIT system (Tou, Williams, Fikes, Henderson, and Malone, 1982) is an intelligent database assistant, based on KL-One, which is designed to aid a user in formulating queries about databases. RABBIT is especially suited for users who have a limited knowledge of the content of the databases. The system has a novel approach to retrieval of data by using reformulation. It works by permitting the user to construct a description of what he is seeking. The basic mode of operation is a loop involving the user: the system returns an instance, and the user then has an opportunity to criticize this instance. The system repeats this loop until the user receives the required information. The semantics of the database are captured in a KL-One database. It is not possible for the user to create a semantically improper query.

Hybrid Representation Systems. KL-One-style systems, for example, KL-One, KL-Two (Vilain, 1984), KRYPTON, and BACK (von Luck, Nebel, Peltason, and Schmeidel, 1987), have traditionally divided their knowledge space into two partitions, called the *Terminological Box* (T-Box) and the *Assertional Box* (A-Box). They have utilized two distinct reasoners, one for each box, to carry out their inferences. KRYPTON and KL-Two are called *hybrid* systems, since they do not attempt the entire task with a single reasoner. In KL-Two, the A-Box, called PENNI (Vilain, 1984), uses McAllester's RUP system (McAllester, 1982). In KRYPTON, the A-Box is a version of Stickel's theorem prover. The T-Box in KL-Two is NIKL.

Man-Machine Interfaces. Another use of NIKL is in the field of User Interface Management Systems (UIMS). An ideal UIMS would provide a syntactically uniform interface to multiple computer applications, and would provide the applications programmer with tools to help him program his system. This system would reason about the underlying systems and about the user (what he knows, and how to present and gather information). Some of this research has begun at ISI in two projects: Integrated Interfaces (II) (Arens, Miller, and Sondheimer, 1988) and Single Interface to Multiple Systems (SIMS) (Pavlin and Bates, 1988). Both of these projects make good use of NIKL as a tool to achieve their aims.

Graphic Tools for NIKL

KL-One and NIKL have a rich tradition of graphics. The most convenient method to communicate the contents of a NIKL network is by graphic representations (pictures). This use has led to attempts at programming computers to draw these pictures. This has not always been successful.

One of the early attempts at graphical representation was KLONEDRAW. This program, which ran on Interlisp-D-style machines (developed at both Xerox and BBN), drew pictures very much like the user of KL-One would draw on a blackboard. Although KLONEDRAW is no longer in use, two active projects are now exploring some of the same basic problems.

ISI Grapher. The ISI Grapher (Robins, 1987) began as a tool for displaying subsumption links in a NIKL network. Because of its versatility, however, it has become a general-purpose tool for displaying arbitrary directed graphs. The ISI Grapher can be used to lay out a graph of subsumption links of NIKL concepts in linear time. It currently runs on Sun, Mac-II, TI, and Symbolics-type machines.

The rapid speed of the Grapher makes it a powerful tool for examining NIKL concept networks. It is the easiest method of visualizing the correctness of the NIKL concept network (that is, making sure that concepts have the correct parents and children).

KREME. The KREME Knowledge Editing Environment (Abrett and Burstein, 1986) is an attempt by Glenn Abrett and Mark Burstein of BBN to break a NIKL-like language from its batch mode. The current NIKL system is *batch*, so that the user must enter the network using a text editor and then load in the network and classify the concepts. Only after this may the user look for errors. The process must be started over from the beginning if an error is found.

The KREME system has an interactive editor and graph system. The user may add or subtract information about a concept and then see the result immediately. The knowledge representation language used in KREME is similar to NIKL.

Limitations of NIKL

Although many knowledge representation systems work for only a specific example system, NIKL can be used in a much wider range of applications. However, it is not appropriate for every problem. It is necessary to understand the costs of using NIKL and its limitations in order to determine whether or not it is appropriate for a specific application. NIKL can reason about terms, but has difficulty with instances. It is possible to represent "All men are persons" in NIKL, but representing "John is a man" is not palatable. NIKL cannot deal with exceptions. If the concept "All birds fly" is represented in NIKL, then either a penguin is not a bird or penguins fly. (A better NIKL model of the concept of birds is one with the concept bird and two concepts under it, flying birds and non-flying birds.) Negation is a function that NIKL had to sacrifice to make the system tractable. There is no simple way to represent that something is 90 percent certain of having a specific property. Fundamental difficulties exist in representing and reasoning about the real world.

Loom: Beyond NIKL

Loom (Mac Gregor and Bates, 1987) represents a recent entry into the KL-One family of knowledge representation systems. Loom directly succeeds the NIKL system. During NIKL's lifetime, the NIKL user community had requested a wide variety of extensions for future versions (Kaczmarek, Bates, and Robins, 1986). Loom's designers determined that these needs could best be achieved by redesigning and reimplementing NIKL. The result is a more flexible architecture that preserves the strengths of the original system while admitting some new and powerful forms of reasoning.

Loom's architecture strongly reflects the view that the variety of inference methods provided by a comprehensive knowledge representation system can best be performed by a well-integrated collection of specialized reasoning components, rather than by a single, general-purpose reasoner. As mentioned before, KL-One-style systems have divided their knowledge space into a Terminological Box (T-Box) and an Assertional Box (A-Box). Loom's principal architectural contribution is to introduce two additional partitions—the *Universal Box* which contains assertions about classes of individuals, and the *Default Box* which contains knowledge about assumptions—each having its own associated reasoning component.

Complementing this increase in the number of domain-independent reasoners embedded in the system architecture is a growing library of domain-specific, *narrow-coverage* reasoners. Currently, these reasoners include facilities for computing or reasoning about transitive relations, sets, intervals, and patterns, as well as elementary forms of numeric reasoning. These reasoners can be invoked independently or called by the broad-coverage reasoners.

In order to integrate this collection of reasoners, it is necessary to develop a language for expressing knowledge that emphasizes the overall coherence and uniformity of the knowledge structures. Loom accomplishes this goal by building on the *concept-centered* view of knowledge employed in KL-One (and NIKL). Accordingly, all universal and default knowledge is attached to specific concepts. In a similar vein, sets, intervals, patterns, and relations (including transitive and composite relations) are all realized as specialized forms of concepts—their definitions share a uniform syntax, and each of them has its own sublattice within the concept taxonomy.

Conclusion

The KL-One-like classifiers have proven to be both versatile and useful in a wide variety of applications. The most important function of these classifiers is to provide the ability to recognize new objects in their environment and discern properties of these objects. The KL-One community has been able to achieve many of its accomplishments due to classifiers. These classifiers could only exist in systems with well-defined semantics and a formal basis.

KL-One-like languages continue to evolve to meet the demands of the user community. Through the years, KL-One and NIKL have addressed a wide variety of problems in AI. Since its development, NIKL has become the star in the KL-One family of languages, because it is more usable and available than KL-One. NIKL is likely to remain useful for many years, despite the fact that its successor, Loom, is on the horizon.

References

Abrett, G., & Burstein, M. (1986). The BBN laboratories knowledge acquisition project: KREME knowledge editing environment. *Proceedings of the Expert Systems Workshop* (pp. 1–8). Washington, DC: Defense Advanced Research Projects Agency.

Arens, Y., Miller, L., & Sondheimer, N. (1988). Presentation planning using an integrated knowledge base. *Architectures for Intelligent Interface: Elements and Prototypes* (pp. 93–107). ACM SIGCHI, Monterey, CA.

Bates, M., & Bobrow, R. (1983). Information retrieval using a transportable natural language interface. *Proceedings of the 6th Annual International ACM SIGCHI Conference on Research and Development in Information Retrieval* (pp. 81–86). ACM SIGCHI, Bethesda, MD.

Bobrow, R., & Webber, B. (1980). Knowledge representation for syntactic/semantic processing. *Proceedings of the National Conference on Artificial Intelligence* (pp. 316–323). AAAI-80, Austin, TX.

Brachman, R. (1978). *A structural paradigm for representing knowledge* (Technical Report 3605). Cambridge, MA: Bolt Beranek and Newman, Inc.

Brachman, R., Fikes, R., & Levesque, H. (1983). KRYPTON: A functional approach to knowledge representation. *Computer, 16(10)*, 67–73.

Brachman, R., & Levesque, H. (1984). The tractability of subsumption in frame-based description languages. *Proceedings of the National Conference on Artificial Intelligence* (pp. 34–37). AAAI-84, Austin, TX.

Brachman, R. & Levesque, H. (Eds.). (1985). *Readings in knowledge representation.* San Mateo, CA: Morgan Kaufman.

Brachman, R., & Schmolze, J. (1985). An overview of the KL-One knowledge representation system. *Cognitive Science, 9(2)*, 171–216.

Kaczmarek, T., Bates, R., & Robins, G. (1986). Recent developments in NIKL. *Proceedings of the National Conference on Artificial Intelligence* (pp. 978–985). AAAI-86, Philadelphia, PA.

Kaczmarek, T., Mark, W., & Wilczynski, D. (1983). The CUE project. *Proceedings of SoftFair: A Conference on Software Development Tools, Techniques, and Alternatives* (pp. 383–389). Arlington, VA.

Mac Gregor, R., & Bates, R. (1987). *The Loom knowledge representation language* (Technical Report ISI/RR–87–188). Marina del Rey, CA: USC Information Sciences Institute.

Mann, W. (1983). An overview of the Penman text generation system. *Proceedings of the National Conference on Artificial Intelligence* (pp. 261–265). AAAI-83. Washington, DC.

Mark, W. (1981). Representation and inference in the Consul system. *Proceedings of the Seventh International Joint Conference on Artificial Intelligence* (pp. 375–381). IJCAI-81. Vancouver, BC.

Mark, W. (1984). *The Consul project* (Annual Technical Report ISI/SR–85–150). Marina del Rey, CA: USC Information Sciences Institute.

Mark, W. (1986). Knowledge-based interface design. In D. A. Norman & S. W. Draper (Eds.), *User centered system design.* Hillsdale, NJ: Lawrence Erlbaum Associates.

McAllester, D. (1982). *Reasoning utility package user's manual* (Technical Report AI Memo 667). Cambridge, MA: Massachusetts Institute of Technology.

Neches, R., Swartout, W. R., & Moore, J. (1985). Explainable (and maintainable) expert systems. *Proceedings of the Ninth International Joint Conference on Artificial Intelligence* (pp. 382–389). IJCAI--85. Los Angeles, CA.

Pavlin, J., & Bates, R. (1988). *SIMS: Single interface to multiple systems* (Technical Report ISI/RR–88–200). Marina del Rey, CA: USC Information Sciences Institute.

Robins, G. (1987). *The ISI grapher: A portable tool for displaying graphs pictorially* (Technical Report ISI/RR–87-196). Marina del Rey, CA: USC Information Sciences Institute.

Schmolze, J., & Lipkis, T. (1983). Classification in the KL-One knowledge representation system. *Proceedings of the Eighth International Joint Conference on Artificial Intelligence* (pp. 330–332). IJCAI-83. Karlsruhe, W. Germany.

Sidner, C. (1985). Plan parsing for intended response recognition in discourse. *Computer Intelligence, 1(1)*, 1–10.

Sondheimer, N. (1986). Knowledge-base support of man-machine interfaces. R. Neches & T. Kaczmarek (Eds.), *AAAI-86 Workshop on Intelligence in Interfaces* (pp. 84–90). AAAI-86. Philadelphia, PA.

Sondheimer, N., Weischedel, R., & Bobrow. R. (1984). Semantic interpretation using KL-One. *Proceedings of Coling84* (pp. 101–107). Association for Computational Linguistics.

Tou, F., Williams, M., Fikes, R., Henderson, A., & Malone, T. (1982). RABBIT: An intelligent database assistant. *Proceedings of the National Conference on Artificial Intelligence* (pp. 314–318). AAAI-82. Pittsburgh, PA.

Vilain, M. (1984). *KL-Two, a hybrid knowledge representation system* (Technical Report 5694). Cambridge, MA: Bolt Beranek and Newman, Inc.

von Luck, K., Nebel, B., Peltason, C., & Schmiedel, A. (1987). *The anatomy of the BACK system* (KIT Report 41). Technische Universitat Berlin.

Wilczynski, D., & Sondheimer, N. (1984). *Transportability in the Consul system: Model modularity and acquisition* (Internal note from the Consul project). Marina del Rey, CA: USC Information Sciences Institute.

Chapter 7

On Making Expert Systems
More Like Experts*

William R. Swartout
Stephen W. Smoliar

USC Information Sciences Institute

Expert systems still lack the skill of an expert when it comes to providing explanations of the results of expert reasoning. This is because while such systems may implement knowledge which is sufficient to mimic the performance of an expert, they do not necessarily model the expertise upon which that performance is based. Such a model must include knowledge of that domain's terminology, knowledge of domain facts, and knowledge of problem-solving methods. The Explainable Expert Systems project has been exploring a new paradigm for expert system development that is intended to capture such missing knowledge and make it available for explanation. This chapter will discuss the principles behind this paradigm and consider two systems that employ it.

How does an expert's behavior demonstrate his expertise? At the very least, he must be able to solve problems within his domain. But we require more of human experts than just getting the right answer. First, an expert can adapt his problem-solving techniques to novel or unusual situations. Second, an expert can often determine on the basis of the statement of a problem whether or not it lies within the scope of his expertise. Finally, an expert can explain his

*This is a revised version of "On making expert systems more like experts," *Expert Systems*, (1987), *4(3)*, 196–207. It appears here with the kind permission of the editors and the publisher.

The research described in this chapter was supported under DARPA Grant #MDA 903–81–C–0335 and National Institutes of Health Grant #1 P01 LM 03374–01 from the National Library of Medicine. The authors would like to thank Robert Balzer, Lewis Johnson, Jack Mostow, Robert Neches, Ramesh Patil, Peter Szolovits and David Wile for their comments, suggestions, and discussions during the course of this research.

problem-solving behavior. This entails more than just playing back a trace of the steps that led to a solution; it also requires motivating those steps, justifying their validity, and relating them to general principles of the domain. The Explainable Expert Systems (EES) project has concentrated on capturing the knowledge that is needed to support the explanatory skills of an expert.

Early work on MYCIN advanced the claim that its behavior could be explained by paraphrasing its rules and their invocation, allowing the system to answer questions such as: "What rules fired when? What information caused a rule to fire? What were the consequences of the action associated with that rule? How was a conclusion reached?" Attempts to answer these questions were addressed by an explanation facility discussed in Davis (1976).

Figure 1 provides an example of the sort of explanation which may be provided by this approach. In this case, the expert system is one which provides advice on administering digitalis (Swartout, 1977). When the system requests the patient's serum calcium level, the physician using it asks why it wants this information. The system responds by describing those activities it is trying to perform. This explanation does suggest that serum calcium is a kind of sensitivity. However, in all probability, it would not be considered acceptable if it were given by an expert physician.

WHAT IS THE LEVEL OF SERUM CALCIUM?

ENTER NUMERICAL VALUE ====> **why?**

The user types "why?" indicating that he questions why he is being asked to supply the value of serum calcium.

MY TOP GOAL IS TO BEGIN THERAPY. ONE STEP IN DOING THAT IS TO CHECK SENSITIVITIES. I AM NOW TRYING TO CHECK SENSITIVITY DUE TO CALCIUM.

Figure 1. A Limited Justification for a Question

The problem is that one expects more from a human expert than a procedural account of how a problem is being solved. Our experience in both debriefing experts and building expert systems has revealed that expertise involves the ability to deal with a much broader range of questions (Swartout, 1986). In this chapter, we shall focus our attention on three classes of such questions:

1. Justifications:
   "Why is serum calcium an important factor in digitalis administration?"

2. Questions about terminology of the domain and its definition:
   "What is a 'sensitivity'?"

3. Questions about the intent behind a goal:
   "What does it mean to perform a diagnosis?"
   "What does it mean to check sensitivities?"

There are several reasons why it is important for an expert system to be able to answer questions such as these. First, a user is more likely to accept an expert system's recommendations if he can assure himself that the system's reasoning is based on a sound understanding of the underlying principles of the domain. Second, the answers to these questions can help a user understand how closely his understanding of the domain agrees with the system's. A wide disparity can serve as a warning that the expert system may be attempting to exceed the capabilities of the expertise it is modeling. Third, the ability to answer such questions may help educate inexperienced users about the fundamentals of the expert system's domain (Clancey, 1987).

The reason why these and similar questions, whose answers are so natural to an expert, are so problematical for an expert system is because most explanations, like the one in Figure 1, are based on knowledge that is only sufficient to mimic the performance of an expert. Thus, explanations can be provided of how a method works or is applied in a particular setting. However, no account can be given for why such activities have occurred or why the system is trying to achieve them. Also, the system cannot elaborate upon its use of the terms that it employs and the intent behind its goals because no explicit definitions have been provided in its knowledge base.

What has happened to the information required to deal with such questions? The knowledge that is needed to answer them is known by a system builder at the time he creates an expert system and is used by him in the process of deriving the expert system's rules or methods. But because that knowledge is not needed for the expert system to perform properly, it does not appear in the rules or methods of the expert system itself and hence is unavailable for explanation. Such knowledge includes not only the underlying principles and facts of the problem domain, but also knowledge of how those principles and facts are incorporated into a working expert system.

In the Explainable Expert Systems (EES) project, we have been exploring a new paradigm for expert system development that is intended to capture such missing knowledge and make it available for explanation. In our approach, system builders and domain experts collaborate to construct a high-level representation of knowledge in the domain that includes the normally missing knowledge that forms the basis for an expert system's rules or methods. System code is then derived automatically from this knowledge base. A trace of the derivation process is recorded which may then be used to associate the behavior of the system with the additional knowledge required to satisfy the needs of explanation.

In the remainder of this chapter, we discuss how the EES paradigm allows one to deal with questions such as those cited above. We begin the next section by considering in greater detail what knowledge must be provided explicitly in order to answer such questions. In the third section we consider how that knowledge may be represented. We then consider the construction of the actual expert system. We investigate two approaches to expert system construction. In the first, the supporting knowledge is treated as a specification from which an automatic programmer synthesizes the code for the expert system. In the second, the expert system is based on direct interpretation of the supporting knowledge. Finally, we discuss specific issues concerning explanation.

Knowledge to Support Explanation

Let us return to the questions considered in the first section and conjecture what might be satisfactory answers for them:

1. Justifications:
   "Why is serum calcium an important factor in digitalis administration?"

   Increased serum calcium causes increased automaticity, which may cause a change to ventricular fibrillation, a dangerous heart condition. Increased digitalis also causes increased automaticity. Thus, if the system observes increased serum calcium, it reduces the dose of digitalis due to increased serum calcium.

2. Questions about terminology of the domain and its definition:
   "What is a 'sensitivity'?"

   A drug sensitivity is an observable deviation in a patient that causes a dangerous condition, where the dangerous condition is also caused by the drug.

3. Questions about the intent behind a goal:
   "What does it mean to perform a diagnosis?"

   To perform a diagnosis is to find a set of diseases which account for the patient's symptoms.

   "What does it mean to check sensitivities?"

   Checking sensitivities to a drug involves altering the dosage level of that drug to compensate for the effect of the sensitivities.

In order to be able to furnish such explanations, the first step is to understand what kinds of knowledge or expertise need to be represented and how that knowledge should be partitioned. The current implementation of EES involves a knowledge base for the following three kinds of expertise:

Terminological Knowledge is knowledge of the concepts and relationships of a domain that experts use to communicate with one another. In expert systems, terminology forms a language that knowledge sources use to communicate with one another and to provide the building blocks from which representations for other kinds of knowledge are constructed. It also furnishes the basic vocabulary through which questions are comprehended and answers are formulated.

Domain Descriptive Knowledge can be thought of as the "textbook rudiments" which are required before one can turn to solving problems. In a medical domain, this would be primarily physiological knowledge, describing causal relations among physiological states and symptoms associated with diseases and the effects of various therapies.

Problem Solving Knowledge is "how to" knowledge. It supplies knowledge about how tasks (called *goals* in our system) can be accomplished. This is where knowledge about how to perform a diagnosis or how to administer a drug belongs.

We shall now discuss the representation of each of these types of knowledge and how they contribute to the implementation of an expert system which can address questions such as those cited above.

The Knowledge Base: Representation

Terminology

It may seem odd to think of terminology as a kind of expertise, but before one can begin to understand a domain, one must understand the terms that are used to describe it. During the first stages of building an expert system, when system builders are debriefing an expert about a domain, much of the time they spend together is concerned with understanding the terminology of the domain. Since terminology provides the building blocks out of which an expert system is constructed, it plays a pivotal role in the process of building an expert system.

Despite its importance, few expert systems have any representation for the definition of terminology. The terminology is known by the system builder, but it is not explicitly defined within the expert system itself. Instead, the terms used by the system implicitly acquire a definition based on how other knowledge sources in the system react to them and the operational mechanisms for recognizing instances of those terms. This can lead to problems both in explanation and maintenance of an expert system.

To illustrate the problem of implicit terminology briefly, suppose we define a simple rule for recognizing fever:

> If patient's temperature > 100
>   then conclude fever.

One might envision an explanation facility which, if faced with the need to define the concept of fever, would search for knowledge of how fever was recognized. It could then use this rule to reply that fever was a condition in which the patient had a temperature greater than 100 degrees.

Unfortunately, this approach confuses an operational means for recognizing fever with a definition for it. Suppose an expert system with this rule and explanation facility is actually deployed in the field. Under such circumstances it may yield many false positive results because some people drink hot coffee before their temperature is taken. This bug may be easily fixed by modifying the rule:

> If patient's temperature > 100
>   and patient has not recently drunk coffee
>   then conclude fever.

What will this do to the explanation facility? Since it depends on the modified rule, it will now include the consumption of coffee as part of its description of fever. The two predicates in the rule serve very different roles. The first is concerned with establishing criteria for recognizing fever, while the second insures the validity of the temperature measurement; but the expert system has no way to recognize this differentiation. Thus, a simple act of maintenance has caused it to lose the ability to explain the concept of fever.

Our representation of terminology provides explicit definitions for entities and binary relations expressed in a notation based on a typed predicate calculus. Following ideas pioneered in KL-One (Brachman and Schmolze, 1985), a classifier is used to arrange the entities in a generalization hierarchy based on subsumption relations among their definitions (Schmolze and Lipkis, 1983). In the domain of digitalis therapy, the entities will include physiological parameters such as increased serum calcium and decreased serum potassium, both of which are specializations of observable deviation. A drug sensitivity may then be characterized by its relationship to dangerous conditions and drug entities. A formal definition may be paraphrased as follows:

> *drug sensitivity*: an observable deviation in a patient that causes a dangerous condition, where the dangerous condition is also caused by the drug.

Domain Descriptive Knowledge

As was mentioned above, domain descriptive knowledge is the sort of knowledge that one typically finds in textbooks. It provides factual knowledge about the domain. Like definitions, such knowledge may be represented as declarative assertions. The domain descriptive knowledge for digitalis therapy included facts such as:[1]

Increased digitalis causes increased automaticity.
Decreased serum potassium causes increased automaticity.
Increased serum calcium causes increased automaticity.
Increased automaticity may cause ventricular fibrillation.[2]
Ventricular fibrillation is a dangerous condition.
Decreased serum potassium is an observable deviation.
Increased serum calcium is an observable deviation.

While causal knowledge is a central part of domain descriptive knowledge for this domain, it is important to emphasize that domain descriptive knowledge is not always causal. In well-understood domains, such as electronic circuit analysis, the domain descriptive knowledge might describe the circuit and its operation, while in poorly understood domains, the domain descriptive knowledge might merely consist of probabilistic associations between various states and state changes in the domain. What is not part of domain descriptive knowledge is knowledge of how to achieve various results: how to diagnose a patient or administer a drug. That knowledge is part of problem-solving knowledge.

Problem-Solving Knowledge

Problem-solving knowledge is represented as plans that express how tasks can be accomplished. Each plan has a *capability description* which describes what goals the plan can achieve. Each plan also has a *method* which is a sequence of substeps (which may themselves include subgoals) for accomplishing the goal. Capability descriptions are patterns and may include variables that are bound when the capability description is matched against a goal to be achieved. Plan capabilities and goals are represented using the terminology described above. The generalization hierarchy of terms induces a generalization hierarchy of plans which we use for finding candidate plans for achieving goals (see Neches, Swartout, and Moore [1985] for details).

As an example, consider a plan for compensating for drug sensitivities. It captures the common-sense notion that if a patient has a sensitivity to a particu-

---

[1]In the heart, *automaticity* refers to the degree to which muscle cells are likely to fire spontaneously, resulting in abnormal heart rhythms. *Ventricular fibrillation* is one such abnormal rhythm that is very dangerous because it indicates a condition in which the heart has ceased to pump blood.

[2]Recent medical results have suggested that other causal mechanisms in addition to automaticity may cause ventricular fibrillation.

lar drug, then the dose of that drug should be reduced. This plan may be paraphrased as follows:

Capability-description: Compensate drug dose for a drug sensitivity

Method: If the drug sensitivity exists in the patient, then reduce the drug dose because of the drug sensitivity

Note the generality of this strategy; nothing in this plan is specific to either particular sensitivities or, for that matter, to the drug digitalis. We feel this approach is a major improvement over the representation of problem-solving knowledge in terms of low-level production rules.

As we have already seen in the example of fever, rule-based systems tend to confound problem-solving knowledge and domain descriptive knowledge in a common representation. Consequently, a collection of rules may be required to capture a single problem-solving strategy. As an example, MYCIN must sometimes deal with the problem of being able to identify the genus of a microorganism but not its species. In this case, MYCIN assumes that the species is the one most likely for the particular genus. While this is a reasonable default strategy, it has been implemented as a collection of rules, each specific to a single genus. From the standpoint of explanation, this is bad because the system has no representation of the general strategy it is following; hence it cannot be explained.

Expert System Construction

Merely representing the knowledge described in the previous section is not sufficient to produce the explanations we want. That knowledge must be employed to create an expert system, and understanding how that takes place provides the critical link between expert behavior and the deep knowledge upon which it is based. Such knowledge is essential for explanation production.

In this section we present two approaches to expert system construction which capture that link. The first approach is illustrated in Figure 2. In that approach, a program writer is used to create an expert system from the three sources of knowledge described above. The design decisions it makes are recorded in a development history. This includes, among other things, the plans that were chosen to implement various facets of the system, alternatives that were rejected, and the reasons for acceptance or rejection. This development history, together with the expert system itself and the supporting knowledge base, provides information to accommodate queries concerned with justification.

Unfortunately, this approach failed to account for how a plan is supported by underlying domain knowledge, in the form of both definitions and domain facts, so that such support could not be explained. To address this need, we have

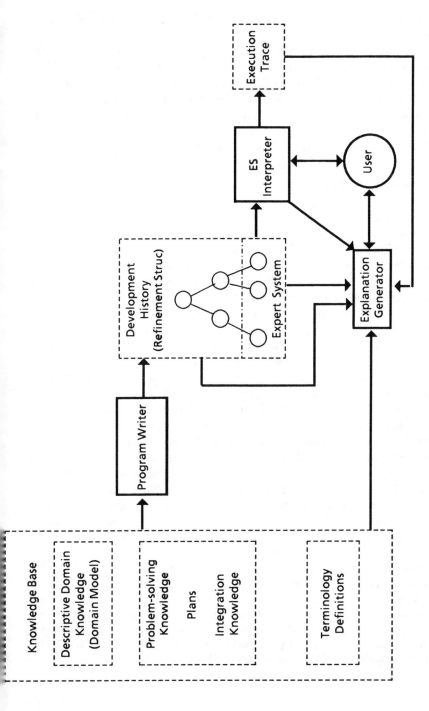

Figure 2. Architecture for EES Version I

205

introduced the modifications, shown in Figure 3, which address the relationship between problem-solving knowledge and terminological and domain knowledge. Terminological definitions and domain facts are employed by a transformation system which synthesizes domain-specific problem-solving plans. These plans are supplemented by domain-independent plans which we call *weak methods*. The resulting plans can now be interpreted directly to produce expert behavior. This approach provides an explanation facility with access to the factual underpinnings of the problem-solving knowledge and, as we shall see, with knowledge to address questions about intent.

The Program Writer

The program writer creates an expert system using goal refinement and reformulation. Starting with a high-level goal (such as administer digitalis), the writer searches through its hierarchy of plans for those plans whose capability descriptions subsume (that is, match) the goal. It selects one of the matching plans and instantiates its method. This results in the posting of subgoals in the method as further goals to be implemented, and the program writer searches for plans to implement those goals in turn. The writer continues in this fashion until all goals have been implemented in terms of primitive constructs.[3]

In the event that no plan is found for implementing a goal, the program writer attempts to reformulate, or transform, the goal into a goal or set of goals that can be implemented. In constructing the original version of the Digitalis Advisor, such a reformulation was performed (manually) with respect to the problem of checking sensitivities. The original problem was transformed into a set of subproblems specific to each individual sensitivity and a combining function for producing an overall adjustment to the dose. Because this process of *reformulation into cases* only occurred in the head of the programmer, that system could only produce the limited explanations in Figure 1, reflecting the result of the reformulation, but not the process behind it. Reformulation into cases is one of several different kinds of reformulations which have been identified (see Neches, Swartout, and Moore [1985] for a detailed discussion). We shall now consider how this particular example is handled by the EES automatic programmer.[4]

---

[3]These indicate constructs for setting a variable, conditional constructs, and the like, corresponding to LISP constructs such as SETQ, COND, and so forth.

[4]The example we present here was actually implemented using the XPLAIN framework (Swartout, 1983), which also produced the sample explanations that appear in Figure 4. XPLAIN was a precursor to the EES framework. It did not provide an explicit representation for terminology. We are presenting this example from the perspective of EES, rather than XPLAIN, because it provides a more understandable account of the program writing process.

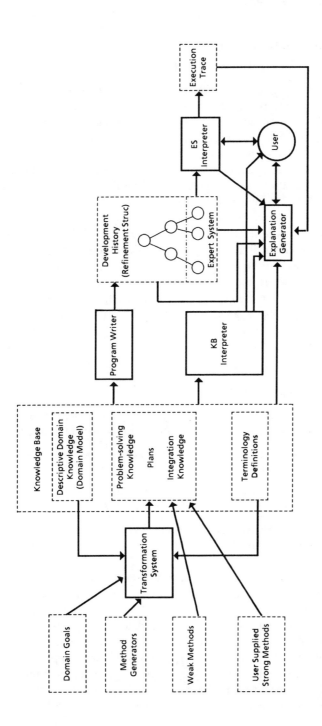

Figure 3. Architecture for EES Version II

207

At some point in the program writing process a goal is posted to:

Compensate digitalis dose for digitalis sensitivities

This is a goal to compensate the dose for all the digitalis sensitivities that are known to the system (by being represented in the domain descriptive knowledge) or that can be deduced by the system. The program writer searches the hierarchy of plans to find all the plans whose capability description subsumed the goal. In this case, none would be found. The plan in the previous section might seem to be directly applicable to this goal; but that plan can only compensate for an individual sensitivity, while the goal requires compensating for all the sensitivities. Thus, we must reformulate the goal into a set of goals over individual sensitivities before program writing may proceed. The system does that by making use of its terminological and domain descriptive knowledge. Consulting the terminological knowledge for the definition of sensitivity, it finds that a drug sensitivity is an observable deviation in a patient that causes a dangerous condition, where the dangerous condition is also caused by the drug. Specializing that term to *digitalis sensitivity* and using the domain facts, it finds two individual observable deviations that are digitalis sensitivities: *increased serum calcium* and *decreased serum potassium*. The writer then reformulates the original goal into two goals over individual digitalis sensitivities:

Compensate digitalis dose for increased serum calcium

Compensate digitalis dose for decreased serum potassium

The method described above can then be applied to each of these two goals. When that is done, the methods are instantiated to produce two code fragments:

If increased serum calcium exists in the patient then reduce the digitalis dose because of increased serum calcium

If decreased serum potassium exists in the patient then reduce the digitalis dose because of decreased serum potassium

The problems of determining whether increased serum calcium or decreased serum potassium exist and of reducing the dose are then posted as new goals for the system to implement.

An additional problem that confronts the program writer is to reason about how to combine the two code fragments. Since both fragments cause the dose to be reduced, the issue is to determine what should be done if both sensitivities co-occur. This is an example of what we refer to as an *integration problem:* how to integrate similar conclusions reached by multiple knowledge sources. In most expert systems this kind of problem is handled by some implicit mechanism built into the system's interpreter (like the certainty factor mechanism in MYCIN). Because the mechanism is built into the interpreter, it is convenient to use but also subject to abuse, since the assumptions that underlie it are never explicitly checked. Also, usually only one mechanism is provided, so system builders will attempt to apply that mechanism to as many situations as possible, even if its appropriateness is questionable. We argue that integration problems should be reasoned about explicitly by the program writer while the expert system is being created. Taking that approach allows the assumptions that underlie an integration technique to be checked. Also, several techniques may be represented, allowing the program writer to select the most appropriate one for the problem at hand. In this particular case, the system uses a piece of integration knowledge that tells it that the two program fragments can be chained together (that is, connect the outputs of one to the inputs of the next) if the causal relations that the fragments are based on are independent and additive (see Swartout [1983] for further details).

This entire process was recorded so that it could later be used to give richer explanations reflecting the causal underpinnings that the expert system was based on, as shown in Figure 4. The critical difference between that explanation and the one in Figure 1 is the second and third sentences of the first explanation which provide a causal reason for checking serum calcium. This explanation was produced by paraphrasing the causal relations involved in the reformulation.

Please enter the value of serum calcium: **why?**

The system is anticipating digitalis toxicity. Increased serum calcium causes increased automaticity, which may cause a change to ventricular fibrillation. Increased digitalis also causes increased automaticity. Thus, if the system observes increased serum calcium, it reduces the dose of digitalis due to increased serum calcium.

Please enter the value of serum calcium: **9**
Please enter the value of serum potassium: **why?**

(The system produces a shortened explanation, reflecting the fact that it has already explained several of the causal relationships in the previous explanation. Also, since the system remembers that it has already told the user about serum calcium, and because it knows that the same plan was used to generate the code for both serum potassium and serum calcium, it suggests the analogy between the two here.)

The system is anticipating digitalis toxicity. Decreased serum potassium also causes increased automaticity. Thus (as with increased serum calcium), if the system observes decreased serum potassium, it reduces the dose of digitalis due to decreased serum potassium.

Please enter the value of serum potassium: **3.7**

**Figure 4. A Causal Explanation of Why
Serum Calcium and Potassium are Checked**

Deriving Problem-Solving Knowledge

Primitive Actions

While the EES Version I framework allows us to capture the knowledge needed to explain the rationale that underlies an expert system, it still does not provide the capability to represent the intent behind a goal (the third question type in the first section). For example, it is not possible to answer the question: "What does it mean to administer digitalis?" Problem-solving knowledge about how to give digitalis can be retrieved; but it is not represented anywhere that the problem of digitalis administration is one of finding a dosage level of digitalis that produces satisfactory therapeutic results subject to the constraint of avoiding (or minimizing) toxic effects.

The problem of representing intent is really one of defining terminology, but specialized to defining verbs and verb clauses. To provide a basis for these definitions, we have attempted to uncover a core set of *primitive actions* in terms of which higher-level goals are defined and explained. Because these actions are *primitive*, they cannot be explained and hence must be chosen so that almost every user can be assumed to understand them readily. Our use of primitive actions has its roots in Pappus' discussion of solving mathematical problems which was analyzed at great length by Polya (1971). Pappus based his work on the observation that all mathematical problems could be reduced to the primitive actions of *finding* and *proving* and that problem solving was a matter of planning subgoals (also expressed in terms of those primitive actions) through which those actions could be achieved.

We have been exploring this approach in the context of a system for diagnosing digital circuits and adapted Pappus' two primitive actions to this domain:

1. determine-whether: establishes the truth of a given assertion

2. find: finds an object that matches a given description

Capturing the intent behind a domain level goal involves linking that goal to its definition in terms of these primitive actions. Thus, we would define the goal:

"diagnose decomposable digital system s"

as the problem:

"finding a primitive system p such that p is a subcomponent of s and p is faulty"

We acknowledge that the primitive actions find and determine-whether may not accommodate other areas of problem solving as readily as mathematics or circuit diagnosis. Thus, we believe that our set of primitive actions may grow as we gain more experience with this approach. For example, a canonical representation of the goal of administering digitalis might be expressed as finding a digitalis dosage level which satisfies a set of assertional constraints; but what are we to make of goals involving the verb "compensate"? Such an action might be expressed in terms of achieving (or avoiding) a patient state, and, certainly, achieving and avoiding are actions that are often found in problem solving. However, we are still in the process of investigating how such actions may best be represented as primitive actions.

Transformations

In addition to representing intent, the primitive actions delimit the kinds of problem-solving behavior that an expert system may exhibit. This provides a well-defined target for transformations which derive problem-solving knowledge from declarative domain knowledge, thereby facilitating the definition of such transformations. For a very simple example, if the knowledge base contains the assertion that A exists if and only if B exists, then it is possible to derive a plan that determines whether B exists by checking for the presence of A. Since the implication is two-way, it is also possible to derive another plan for checking for the existence of A by checking for B.[5]

More complex examples can be handled by our transformations. For example, in constructing a digital circuit diagnoser, the domain descriptive model included the following fact:

the expected output of an adder is equal to the sum of its expected inputs

Because this fact is about an equality relationship, it is used to derive a general plan which can find the expected output of an adder. This plan posts subgoals which find that adder's expected input values; if those subgoals succeed, it returns the sum of their results. Similar plans are derived which account for other devices.

Weak methods

It is also possible to define plans whose capability descriptions involve primitive actions in a domain-independent manner. For example, performing the determine-whether action on an assertion which is a conjunction does not involve any domain-specific knowledge. The method for such a plan would be based on

---

[5]Of course, care should be taken in interpreting such plans to avoid circular reasoning chains.

subgoals which perform the determine-whether action on each of the conjuncts. Thus, one may develop a set of plans for the determine-whether action corresponding to the different syntactic possibilities of an assertion whose truth is being determined.

Such plans are generalizations of the domain-specific plans which have already been considered. Any goal which matches the capability description of a domain-specific plan may also match the capability description of one or more of these more general plans. We call the domain-independent plans *weak methods;* they play two important roles:

1. They provide an operational semantics for primitive actions. Thus, the weak methods provide knowledge of how to determine-whether an assertion holds, regardless of that assertion's domain-specific content.

2. This semantic base allows the problem solver to apply "first principles" to any goal which cannot be accommodated by domain-specific knowledge. If no domain-specific plan has an appropriate capability description, one can always resort to the weak methods.[6]

Our view of weak methods differs from the more common use of the term, such as may be found in Laird and Newell (1983). This more familiar usage is based on a view of problem solving as the application of operators within a problem space. From this approach, weak methods serve as decision procedures for the selection of the most appropriate operators. In our approach a problem is represented not by a problem space, but by a primitive action which must be achieved, and the solution of a problem is the planning of subsidiary actions which will obtain this result. Weak methods, then, may be regarded as the most general plans for performing primitive actions, because they deal with the actions themselves, rather than with any problem-dependent objects affected by the actions. Nevertheless, our approach does share some common ground with the problem space view of weak methods. For example, the generate-and-test method of Laird and Newell (1983) is represented in our system as a weak method for dealing with the find action. Indeed, we conjecture that every weak method analyzed in Laird and Newell (1983) may be represented as the realization of some primitive action.

We recognize that due to limitations in our technology for automatically deriving plans, there may be desired expert behavior that we cannot achieve relying solely on mechanically derived plans and weak methods. For that reason, we have included the possibility of manually defining strong (domain-specific)

---

[6]Indeed, in our experiments with the digital circuit diagnoser, we once forgot to load a portion of the knowledge base. The system still successfully solved problems by relying only on knowledge of terminological definitions and weak methods.

methods and entering them directly into the plan hierarchy (Figure 3). Like other plans, these are organized in the hierarchy based on their capability descriptions. The program writer[7] retrieves and instantiates them just like other plans. The difference is that these plans are less explainable. They cannot be related back to underlying domain-descriptive knowledge, as with the mechanically derived plans. We feel that one of the strengths of our approach is that it permits us to approach explanation in this incremental fashion. We can derive some plans mechanically, but our inability to derive other plans does not preclude constructing a system. Thus, it is possible to build a system even if it cannot be fully explained, but the explanations will improve with our increased understanding of the relation between domain-descriptive and problem-solving knowledge.

As of this writing, we have constructed sets of transformations for the find and determine-whether primitive actions and have used them to derive plans in the domain of digital circuit diagnosis. We have also defined approximately 25 weak methods for the find and determine-whether actions. We have constructed an interpreter that can execute these plans to produce problem-solving behavior. We are currently in the process of integrating the transformational system with our program writer. We are also exploring the applicability of this approach in other domains, such as digitalis therapy. We feel that these explorations will lead to a better understanding of the kinds of primitive actions that are appropriate to model.

The Cost of Automated Construction

It is important to recognize that our approach imposes some additional demands on the system builder. Our framework intentionally makes it difficult to build a system in an ad hoc fashion. This may make it more difficult to construct an initial prototype of a system, because consideration of difficult representation problems is harder to postpone. Additionally, because our system employs a richer knowledge representation, the system builder must be more sophisticated in his understanding of knowledge-representation techniques. Thus, the up-front costs of using a framework like EES may be higher than those of a conventional framework. However, the major cost of expert systems, like other software, is in maintenance and evolution. Our approach lowers those costs in two important ways. First, our representation allows a system builder to modify the system at a higher level of abstraction. Second, we explicitly record the design underlying the expert system in the development history. This provides a maintainer with a better understanding of the intent behind the resulting implementation.

---

[7]The program writer is currently being adapted to the new structure of EES Version II.

Further Requirements for Explanation

In the preceding sections, we have argued that if a system is to explain its reasoning, it is necessary to model additional kinds of expertise that are normally left out of a performance-oriented expert system. We have described the nature of those additional kinds of expertise and our approach to capturing that expertise in an expert system. In this section, we return to the issue of explanation and describe some additional constraints that explanation imposes on the way that knowledge is structured and represented.

The Need for a Continuum of Abstraction

From the preceding sections it might appear that we feel that a more abstract or "deeper" representation for expertise is always best. In fact, it is important to have a variety of different levels of abstraction available for explanation and to select among them based on the experience and interests of the user. For example, we have argued that an explanation that is just based on performance-level expertise is probably not appropriate for many users because it leaves out the rationale that justifies it. But such an explanation may be very appropriate for an expert user who fully understands the rationale and is just interested in assuring himself that the system will take the correct actions in a particular set of circumstances.

Thus, it is not just a matter of reasoning with compiled, performance-level knowledge for efficiency while falling back to deeper knowledge for explanation. Instead, the explanation routines must be capable of selecting among knowledge expressed at different levels of compilation and of producing explanations from that knowledge. That implies that the different levels of compilation and the correspondences among them must exist together. In comparing our approach of compiling an expert system from deeper level expertise with an approach in which the compilation step is skipped and the deep knowledge is directly interpreted, we often argue for our approach on the basis of increased efficiency; but the explanation requirement for simultaneously existing multiple levels of compilation also argues for our approach.

Different Information for Different Users

Paris (1987) has observed that explanations for novices and explanations for more experienced people differ fundamentally in the kind of information that is conveyed, and not just in the level of detail, as had been previously thought (Wallis and Shortliffe, 1985). Paris studied descriptions of various devices in both junior and adult encyclopedias. She discovered that the entries in junior encyclopedias tended to emphasize the function of the device and the functional relations of its parts, while adult encyclopedias emphasized component/subcomponent relationships and the physical structure of the device. Presumably, functional information is left out of the adult entries because adults already know that information. While Paris has identified this phenomenon, she has not yet provided a theory that explains what kinds of knowledge will be included and what will be left out.

We feel that the compilation process in EES may be the beginning of such a theory, at least for expert systems. Explanations presented at different levels of compilation differ fundamentally in the kinds of knowledge that is presented. Explanations produced from uncompiled knowledge will include definitions of terminology, causal relations, and abstract descriptions of problem-solving strategies. That is all information that will probably be familiar to an expert (hence it is not necessary to explain to him), but that a novice is likely to want to know. Explanations produced from compiled knowledge will be most appropriate for experts because they will not contain the motivating knowledge that experts would already know.

Conclusion

We have argued that explanations produced solely from performance expertise will be inadequate, because such explanations leave out the rationale upon which the expert system's behavior is based. We described three kinds of expertise that must be modeled to provide adequate explanations: knowledge of terminology, domain-descriptive knowledge, and abstract problem-solving knowledge. In conventional expert systems, these different kinds of knowledge are confounded together in a relatively low-level representation, such as rules, if they are represented at all. Separating the different kinds of knowledge improves explanations because it allows the explanation routines to select just the right information to present to answer a user's questions, free of confounding factors. The separation also makes the system easier to maintain because it increases its modularity.

We presented a framework for expert system construction that employs an automatic programmer to integrate the different kinds of knowledge to produce a working expert system. The program writer leaves behind a record of the design decisions that underlie the expert system. These "mental breadcrumbs" are used by explanation routines to explain the workings of an expert system in terms of basic domain knowledge.

We presented our current research, which is concerned with both providing a representation for the intent of goals in terms of primitive actions and a better understanding of the relationship between domain-descriptive knowledge and

problem-solving knowledge. Finally, we presented some additional requirements that explanation imposes and showed how our approach supports them.
Clearly, much remains to be done before expert systems will be able to explain
themselves as lucidly as human experts. Nevertheless, our results so far encour-
age us in our future undertakings.

References

Brachman, R. J., & Schmolze, J. G. (1985). An overview of the KL-One knowledge
    representation system. *Cognitive Science, 9,* 171–216.
Clancey, W. (1987). *Knowledge-based tutoring: The GUIDON program.* Cambridge,
    MA: MIT Press.
Davis, R. (1976). *Applications of meta-level knowledge to the construction, maintenance,
    and use of large knowledge bases* (Technical Report AIM–283). Stanford, CA:
    Stanford University.
Laird, J., & Newell, A. (1983). *A universal weak method* (Technical Report,
    CMU–CS–83–141). Pittsburgh, PA: Carnegie-Mellon University, Department of
    Computer Science.
Neches, R., Swartout, W., & Moore, J. (1985). Enhanced maintenance and explanation
    of expert systems through explicit models of their development. *Transactions on
    Software Engineering, SE-11,* 1337–1351.
Paris, C. L. (1987). Combining discourse strategies to generate descriptions to users
    along a naive/expert spectrum. *Proceedings of the Tenth International Joint
    Conference on Artificial Intelligence* (pp. 626–632) IJCAI-87. Milan, Italy.
Polya, G. (1971). *How to solve it: A new aspect of mathematical method* (2nd. ed.).
    Princeton, NJ: Princeton University Press.
Schmolze, J. G., & Lipkis, T. A. (1983). Classification in the KL-One knowledge
    representation system. *Proceedings of the Eighth International Joint Conference
    on Artificial Intelligence* (pp. 330–332) IJCAI-83. Karlsruhe, West Germany.
Swartout, W. R. (1977). *A digitalis therapy advisor with explanations* (Technical Report
    TR–176). Cambridge, MA: Laboratory for Computer Science, MIT.
Swartout, W. R. (1983). XPLAIN: A system for creating and explaining expert consulting
    systems. *Artificial Intelligence, 21(3),* 285–325.
Swartout, W. R. (1986). Knowledge needed for expert system explanation. *Future
    Computing Systems, 1(2),* 99–114.
Wallis, J. W., & Shortliffe, E. H. (1985). Customized explanations using causal knowl-
    edge. In B. G. Buchanan & E. H. Shortliffe (Eds.), *Rule-based expert systems: The
    MYCIN experiments of the Stanford heuristic programming project.* Reading, MA:
    Addison-Wesley.

Part III

Specialized Tools and Techniques

Chapter 8

AI Tools for Simulation*

Alfred D. Round
Knowledge Systems Laboratory, Stanford University

This chapter will describe how AI tools and techniques can facilitate the development and execution of computer simulation models. The first section outlines what simulation is used for and the limitations of traditional simulation techniques. The second section shows how object-oriented programming in SIMULA and Smalltalk-80 can overcome some of these limitations. The third section discusses the contributions made by languages and tools that incorporate rule-based and access-oriented paradigms into object-oriented simulation programs. The fourth section focuses on one tool, SimKit™, which provides a complete environment for the development and execution of simulation models. The fifth section focuses on the ways that AI paradigms are used for building simulation models. The conclusion assesses the progress of knowledge-based simulation tools to date.

An Overview of Simulation

Simulation is the art of predicting the future state of a system given a model of the system and its current state. Computers are needed to help construct and simulate models in complex domains such as power plants, national economies, and ecosystems.

Simulation is often used to predict the outcomes of using alternative models of a system so that the best alternative can be chosen for a given set of goals. In designing a factory, for example, a number of configurations of parts, tools, and machines can be modeled and simulated in order to determine which config-

---

* The author would like to thank Harold Brown, Brian Drummond, and Peter Karp for discussions that clarified various issues on simulation and simulation systems.

SimKit is a trademark of IntelliCorp, Inc.

uration best satisfies the goals of maximum rate of production and minimum cost. If each alternative could actually be implemented with reasonable time and expense, or modeled exactly by a set of analytically solvable equations, then simulation would not be necessary. For most domains of interest, however, the alternatives are neither feasible to implement nor reducible to analytically solvable equations. Ideally, simulation generates predictions in a timely and affordable manner for such domains. It is important to emphasize that such predictions are estimates, since the input data to a simulation are usually probabilistic.

Systems such as banks and assembly lines involve a finite number of entities that arrive at the system, form queues, receive services, and depart from the system. Since each of these events occurs at a single point in time for each entity, the simulation of such systems is called *discrete-event* simulation. If the system state variables change continuously, as in a chemical processing plant, a bacterial cell, or an airplane in flight, then the corresponding technique is called *continuous* simulation. A combination of discrete and continuous approaches is appropriate in some cases, such as a chemical reaction that is subject to sudden changes in temperature or pH. This chapter will emphasize discrete-event simulation, because most existing simulation tools and languages support this type of simulation.

The Limitations of Standard Simulation Techniques

Prior to 1965, almost all simulations were implemented as programs written in a high-level language, such as FORTRAN (Law and Kelton, 1983). Specialized simulation languages such as GASP, SimScript, and GPSS reduce development time by including routines to process arrival and departure events, generate input data, and collect and report results (Law and Kelton, 1983). However, all these languages suffer from a number of limitations:

- The development of a simulation model requires the ability to program in the language in which it is coded.

- A modification to the model may require recompilation of the entire program, which slows the development process.

- It is often desirable to simulate a system at different levels of detail. As an example, consider the simulation of a factory. If the goal of a given simulation is to predict the total output of the factory, the entire plant must be simulated. If the goal of the simulation is simply to understand why a particular workstation is behind schedule, only that workstation needs to be simulated. Using conventional simulation techniques, a separate program would have to be written for each of these situations.

- The simulation is a black box from the end user's point of view. The user cannot pose a question, modify the model, or interact in any other way with the simulation while it is running. There are no facilities for animation and no other means of viewing changes in the system as the simulation progresses.

- There is no explanation capability, so it is impossible to trace the events that lead to an unexpected result. It is entirely up to the user of the simulation to interpret the meaning of its output.

In the following sections, object-oriented languages and AI tools that partially overcome these limitations are described.

Object-Oriented Simulation Tools: SIMULA and Smalltalk-80

SIMULA

SIMULA is an Algol-based language that was created to facilitate the development of discrete-event simulations (Birtwistle, Dahl, Myhrhaug, and Nygaard, 1983). A principal concept in SIMULA is the *class*. A class consists of three parts: a *heading*, a *data declaration* part, and an *action* part. A class that represents all customers in a post office simulation could be defined as in Figure 1.

Each customer is represented by a separate instance of the CUSTOMER class. Each instance inherits the data declarations and actions of the class definition. As soon as a new CUSTOMER instance is created, it immediately begins to execute the code in its action part. The different CUSTOMER instances can therefore be engaged in entirely different activities at the same time.

The data declaration part of a class can also contain procedures. Procedures can be grouped together in classes called *prefix* classes. For example, assume that class B is declared as A CLASS B. Then class B is prefixed by class A; that is, the action part of B can directly refer to procedures in A. An example of a prefix class is LINK, which is defined as part of the SIMULA language. LINK contains four procedures for manipulating queues: OUT for removing an object from a queue, INTO for inserting an object at the end of a queue, and PRECEDE and FOLLOW for inserting an object before or after another specified object in the queue. LINK is used as a prefix class to the class PROCESS, which is typically used to prefix simulation objects.

As an example, consider a car wash which employs n people (Birtwistle, et al., 1983). When a car washer is done servicing a car, he goes to the tea room and joins a queue there. If a car arrives and a car washer is available (i.e., the

```
BEGIN
        COMMENT      ***POST OFFICE SYSTEM DESCRIPTION
                     ***THE FIRST SECTION OF THE DESCRIPTION
                     ***CONTAINS THE CLASS DECLARATIONS OF
                     ***THE VARIOUS KINDS OF OBJECTS IN THE
                     ***SYSTEM;
        CLASS        CUSTOMER(NROFTASKS,OLDLADY);
                     INTEGER NROFTASKS; BOOLEAN OLDLADY;
        BEGIN declared list of tasks;
            REF(CUSTOMER)NEXT;
            REF(CUSTOMER)SERVICE;

            WHILE NROFTASKS > 0 DO
                BEGIN
                        assign value to SERVICE;
                        IF OLDLADY
                        THEN enter front of SERVICE.Q
                        ELSE enter tail of SERVICE.Q;
                        IF SERVICE.POSTOFFICER is free
                        THEN activate SERVICE POSTOFFICER
                        ELSE passivate;
                        participate in transactions
                        leave counter;
                        NROFTASKS:=NROFTASKS-1;
                END;
        END;
END;
```

Figure 1. SIMULA Post Office System Description

tea room queue is not empty), the first car washer in the tea room queue leaves
that queue and services the car; otherwise, the car joins a car queue. Car washers
are implemented as instances of a PROCESS-prefixed class called CARWASHER,
defined as

```
PROCESS CLASS CARWASHER;
WHILE TRUE DO
BEGIN
    leave the tearoom;
    WHILE there are no more customers DO
    serve the next;
    wait in the tearoom;
END;
```

The definition for the class CAR is shown below:

```
PROCESS CLASS CAR;
BEGIN
    drive into the waiting line;
    IF tearoom is not empty
    THEN activate a car washer;
    passivate;
    drive out of garage;
END;
```

The ACTIVATE statement shows that a CAR instance is responsible for reactivating a CARWASHER instance. The CAR instance itself gets reactivated when it has completed service, that is, after the PASSIVATE stage. There is also a class CARGEN that generates the cars in the first place, defined as

```
PROCESS CLASS CARGEN;
WHILE time < simperiod DO
BEGIN
    ACTIVATE NEW CAR;
    HOLD (time to next car arrival);
END;
```

The HOLD time is generated by sampling from a probability distribution.

Procedures such as ACTIVATE, PASSIVATE, and HOLD are defined as part of the class SIMULATION. The SIMULATION-prefixed class WASHINGCARS defines the entire car wash simulation as

```
SIMULATION CLASS WASHINGCARS(N); INTEGER N;
BEGIN
    PROCESS CLASS CARWASHER . . . . .;
    PROCESS CLASS CARGEN . . . . . . . .;
    PROCESS CLASS CAR . . . . . . . . . . .;
    REF(HEAD)WAITINGLINE, TEAROOM;
    generate the queues;
    enter N car washers into TEAROOM;
END;
```

The class concept in SIMULA facilitates both coding and understanding simulation models because behavior is directly associated with objects.

Smalltalk-80

The class concept introduced by SIMULA was adopted and generalized in Smalltalk-80 (Goldberg and Robson, 1983). A Smalltalk-80 class consists of a *class name, instance variables,* and *methods,* corresponding to the name, data part, and action part of a SIMULA class. Figure 2 shows the definition of the Smalltalk-80 class Point for representing points in the Cartesian plane (Goldberg and Robson, 1981).

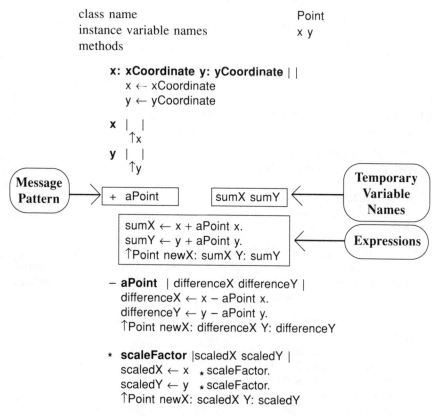

Figure 2. Class Template for the Class Point

All procedural and behavioral information is implemented in the form of methods. Objects interact by sending messages to each other. The object which receives a message attempts to match it against the message patterns of its methods; when a match is found, the corresponding method is executed. If a message of the form + offset is sent to a Point instance, the method whose message pattern is + aPoint will be invoked (see Figure 2). The code of this method computes and returns the sum of two points.

The entire Smalltalk-80 environment is implemented using classes that are defined in the Smalltalk-80 language. Two classes are provided specifically for performing simulations. The instances of class SimulationObject have a sequence of tasks that are performed when an object enters a simulation. The object proceeds through the simulation by receiving the messages startUp, tasks, and finishUp, in sequence. A number of predefined messages are made available to the Smalltalk-80 programmer to help implement the tasks. For example, holdFor:aTimeDelay suspends the execution of tasks for the amount of time specified by aTimeDelay.

A simulation is implemented in Smalltalk-80 as an instance of the class Simulation. Each Simulation instance maintains a queue of events and a clock set to the time of the next event in the queue. A simulation is started by sending the message initialize to a Simulation instance. The message defineArrivalSchedule causes an initial set of simulation objects to be added to the event queue. When a simulation object enters the simulation at its scheduled time, it begins executing its associated tasks. One of the tasks might be the scheduling of further events by sending the Simulation instance a message of the form scheduleArrivalOf: aSimulationObjectClass accordingTo: aProbabilityDistribution or scheduleArrivalOf: aSimulationObject at: aTimeInteger.

As an example, consider a simulation in which visitors enter a room, remain in the room anywhere from 4 to 10 time units, and leave the room. Visitor is created as a subclass of SimulationObject, and sends the following message as one of its tasks: self holdFor: (Uniform from: 4.0 to: 10.0) next. The term "self" refers to a particular Visitor instance, and Uniform indicates a probability distribution in which any value between 4 and 10 is equally likely to occur. The Simulation instance schedules the arrival of each Visitor with the message self scheduleArrivalOf: Visitor accordingTo: (Uniform from: 4 to: 8) startingAt: 3. According to these specifications, a Visitor will arrive every 4 to 8 units of simulated time starting at time 3, and stay between 4 and 10 simulated time units.

Smalltalk-80 extended the capabilities of SIMULA by allowing an instance to have any number of actions, each implemented as a method that responds to a specific message. This capability is enhanced by the fact that subclasses and their instances can add their own methods and override the method definitions of their superclasses. In addition, Smalltalk-80 provides classes that implement tools for browsing, editing, window manipulation, command menus, and other features that facilitate program development. The combination of message passing capabilities, built-in classes for simulation, and a large set of development tools, all implemented in classes defined in the Smalltalk-80 language, makes Smalltalk-80 the first truly integrated environment for developing and executing simulations.

Integrating AI Techniques into Simulation Tools

The object-oriented paradigms of SIMULA and Smalltalk-80 have remained a basis of subsequent simulation tools and languages. However, these later tools have further increased the ease of developing and using simulation models by

- integrating AI techniques such as rule-based inferencing and access-oriented programming into simulation, facilitating the development of simulation models by programmers and nonprogrammers alike;

- providing a highly interactive, graphical environment that allows "programming" by the manipulation of images on the screen and permits greater control over the simulation during run-time; and

- automating features such as data generation, statistics collection, and model verification.

This section discusses how several languages and tools use AI techniques to overcome some of the limitations inherent in traditional simulation methods.

ROSS

ROSS (McArthur, Klahr, and Narain, 1986) is a simulation language written in LISP that adopts the object-oriented programming paradigm of Smalltalk-80. Messages take the form (ask <object> <message>), where <message> must match the pattern for a method in the <object> to which it is sent. As an example, the class fixed-objects might create a subclass called fighter-base by issuing the following message:

(**ask** fixed-object **create generic** fighter-base **with**
position	(0,0)	;*position*
status	active	;*active or destroyed*
filter-center	nil	;*each base has one*
fighters-available	nil	;*list of free fighters*
fighters-scrambled	nil	;*occupied fighters*
fighters-destroyed	nil	;*its fighters lost*
scramble-delay	10	;*time to scramble once told*
alert-delay	10	;*delay to alert*
alert-duration	1800	;*how long to remain alert*
range	400.0)	;*how far its fighters can go*

A particular fighter-base can be created with the message (*ask* fighter-base *create instance* fighter-base1). A typical message that might be sent to fighter-base1 is (*ask* fighter-base1 send fighter2 guided by gci3 to penetrator4). The fighter-base method that would be executed in response to this message is

ask fighter-base **when receiving**
(send >fighter guided by >gci to >penetrator)
(ask !myself schedule after
!(ask myself recall your scramble-delay) seconds
tell !fighter chase !penetrator guided by !gci)
(ask !myself add !fighter to your list of fighters-scrambled)
(ask !myself remove !fighter from your list of fighters-available))

A major advantage of ROSS is its highly readable English-like syntax. This is possible because the message pattern of a method can be arbitrarily verbose. In addition, the programmer can customize the language by developing his own abbreviations. By using the abbreviations

(abbreviate '(ask !myself) 'you)
(abbreviate '(ask !myself recall your) 'your)
(abbreviate '(!) 'the)

the fighter-base method above could be written as

(**ask** fighter-base **when receiving**
(send >fighter guided by >gci to >penetrator)
(~you schedule after ~the (~your scramble-delay) seconds
tell ~the fighter chase ~the penetrator guided by ~the gci)
(~you add ~the fighter to your list of fighters-scrambled)
(~you remove ~the fighter from your list of fighters-available)

As in SIMULA and SmallTalk-80, ROSS provides a system clock for simulation. Instead of providing simulation classes directly, ROSS simply uses messages to schedule events in the future. The message (*ask* fighter-base1 *plan after* 20 seconds *tell* fighter1 chase penetrator2 guided by gci3) will cause fighter-base1 to send the embedded message to fighter1 after a delay of 20 seconds.

ROSS provides extensive interactive browsing and editing facilities. The data structures and methods of all classes and their instances are always inspectable. Users can therefore interrupt a simulation at any time to browse through the model or to make changes to the model. Screen-oriented editing capabilities are achieved by running ROSS as a process under the EMACS editor. ROSS can also be interfaced to a color graphics output device, thus permitting animated depictions of simulation objects on the screen.

An important feature of ROSS is the ability to record simulation events. The ROSS recording facility allows *traces* to be put on any number and combination of classes, instances, and messages, so that a historical trace of all references and changes to an object or all invocations of a method can be generated. Verbose English-language descriptions of methods are easily generated. These features of the recording facility help the user interpret the results of simulation runs.

Simulations have been written in ROSS for use by military strategists who are not programmers. For example, the air battle simulator SWIRL "encourages the user to explore a wide variety of alternatives and to discover increasingly effective options in offensive and defensive strategies" (McArthur, Klahr and Narain, 1986). ROSS has achieved this capability by extending the object-oriented, message-passing paradigm of Smalltalk-80 to include multiple inheritance, English-like syntax, an interactive run-time environment, and tracing facilities.

Truckin'

Both knowledge applications and simulations need to model systems. Expert system development tools such as Loops (Stefik, Bobrow, Mittal, and Conway, 1983) and KEE® (Kunz, Kehler, and Williams, 1984) integrate rules, access-oriented programming, methods, and LISP into a common environment for representing the structure and behavior of physical systems. The variety of representational techniques provided by Loops and KEE makes these tools useful for developing and executing simulation models, even though they are not simulation languages per se.

Researchers at Xerox PARC held two courses to test the performance of non-AI programmers in developing simulation models with Loops. Each student team developed a knowledge base to simulate the performance of a truck driver who moves along a game board and tries to maximize his profit by buying and selling commodities at various board stops. There are numerous obstacles along the route, such as bandits and bad roads. This domain was chosen for two reasons: a) it is easy to understand, and b) it provides challenges in developing strategical knowledge. Strategical knowledge is needed for resolving goal conflicts such as the trade-off between getting someplace fast and getting stopped for speeding.

A picture of the Truckin' game board is shown in Figure 3. The gauges to the right of the board display values selected by the player, such as fuel level and total cash, throughout the simulation. The top of the figure shows the internal state of the simulation. The upper left part shows the current rule that is being invoked. A trace of all events is provided in the top center window. The upper right window shows the browsing facility for the Truckin' knowledge base. The simulation can be interrupted at any time so that the user can pose queries about the current system state, such as why a truck made a particular stop.

Students learned about programming in Loops in one of two different courses. The students formed teams to develop and implement Truckin' strategies, and the teams competed against each other. The instructors received feedback in the

---

KEE is a registered trademark of IntelliCorp, Inc.

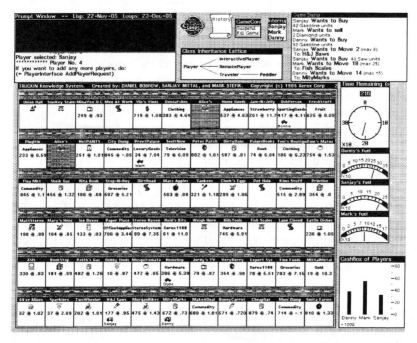

Figure 3. Display from Truckin'

form of performance on classroom exercises, the quality of play, and questionnaires about the courses. The students in the second course responded more favorably in all respects. The instructors concluded that the greater success of the second course was largely due to a greatly increased emphasis on using tools and techniques for debugging, monitoring, tracing, and explanation, as well as improved interactive graphics for browsing. Truckin' has therefore shown that the ability for non-AI programmers to rapidly develop powerful simulation models depends not only on a rich variety of paradigms in which to encode knowledge, but on the tools provided by the development and execution environment as well.

Steamer

SIMULA, Smalltalk-80, ROSS, and Loops facilitate the development, execution, and interpretation of simulation models, but knowledge of a programming language is required to code a simulation model in any of these environments. Sophisticated programming techniques are required to develop a Truckin' simulation, for example. In contrast, Steamer (Hollan, Hutchins, and Weitzman,

1984), which trains operators of steam propulsion systems, allows nonprogrammers (e.g., domain experts) to build complex, multi-level simulation models of a steam plant.

The color graphics interface is the principal Steamer tool that allows the user to interact with the system model and to control its simulation. One hundred views of the plant at different levels allows the display of the entire plant and its various subsystems. Within each view, icons represent system components, and gauges monitor the state of the components. For example, a pump is depicted as green if it is operating and red if it is not. Aspects of the plant's operation that normally are not directly inspectable, such as flow rates in pipes, can also be depicted. The graphics interface permits the user to control a simulation by selecting and manipulating the icons that represent plant components in a particular view. As an example, the user can simulate the effects of increasing the level of the deaerating feed tank (shown in the *Make-Up and Excess-Feed* view in Figure 4) by clicking the mouse at a higher level in the tank.

The different plant views are created using the Steamer graphics editor. A view is created by using this editor to select, refine, and integrate icons that will

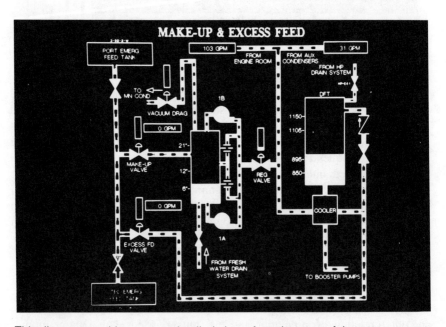

This diagram provides a more detailed view of a subsystem. Adequate coverage of the plant has required approximately 100 diagrams.

Figure 4. Make-Up and Excess Feed.

represent the components in the view. The icons are chosen from a standard set that includes abstract geometric entities such as lines and circles, gauges and graphs for depicting component states, and items such as pipes and valves that are specific to the steam propulsion plant domain. LISP code that represents the behavior of a component is automatically incorporated into the underlying model whenever the user creates an icon on the screen through the graphics editor. The underlying code for each view component is capable of sending and responding to messages from other components. This encoding of component behavior is completely transparent to the view developer.

The actual simulation was implemented in FORTRAN and written prior to the development of Steamer. The graphics editor is used to connect the icons that make up a view with the FORTRAN simulator through a process called *tapping*. This process uses pop-up menus to help map variables represented by icons onto variables in the FORTRAN simulator's mathematical model.

The tools provided by Steamer have added several capabilities to the simulation languages already discussed. Multiple levels of focus are provided in order to model and simulate the steam propulsion system at any level of detail. The construction and simulation of views does not require learning a programming language. Finally, the Steamer project has shown that traditional simulators written in FORTRAN can be successfully integrated into an intelligent development and run-time environment, thus enhancing the utility of the original simulation.

SimKit: An Integrated, Knowledge-Based Environment for Simulation

SimKit (Stelzner, Dynis, and Cummins, 1987) comprises a set of general-purpose modeling and simulation tools built on top of KEE, a frame-based expert system development tool, written in Common LISP. (See Chapters 3 and 4 for more details on KEE, and Chapter 9 for more details on SimKit.) Frames are called *units* in KEE. All facilities of KEE are available to SimKit users.

Modeling Structure

A SimKit *library* is a KEE knowledge base that contains definitions of object classes and the relationships between them. SimKit libraries are generally developed by programmers who use the programming facilities of KEE and LISP to define the behavior of objects. An example SimKit library, included with the basic system, is QLIB, which contains classes that define queueing objects and behaviors. The object classes in QLIB include SOURCES, SINGLE.SERVERS, and FIFO.QUEUES. In Simkit, relationships between objects are defined by a type of class called a *relation*. The only relation defined in QLIB is DOWN-STREAM.RELATION, which indicates that one object is downstream of another.

Sublibraries allow specialization of parent libraries to narrower domains. QLIB, for example, could be specialized by creating the sublibraries MANU-FACTURING.LIB, PUBLIC.SERVICE.LIB, and HIGHWAY.TRAFFIC.LIB. Each sublibrary inherits the classes and relations of its parent library. It can also add new object classes and relations, as well as override or delete those inherited from the parent library.

Libraries are created and modified using the SimKit *Library and Model Editor,* which defines the classes and relations in a library. The icons associated with each class and relation are displayed in the editor *viewports.* The left-hand viewport contains one icon to represent each of the classes defined for the library. The right-hand viewport contains icons representing relations between classes. The center or *design* viewport is used to construct, display, modify, and run a model.

A new relation is defined using the *Relations Editor* by giving its name, the name of its *inverse* relation, and its *domain* and *range.* The classes of domain and range objects must be defined (the relation [e.g., DOWNSTREAM.RELATION] goes "from" a domain object "to" a range object). All relations in the design viewport can be deleted or changed using the mouse.

Simulation models are created with the SimKit *Model Editor* by instantiating classes of physical objects from a library and specifying the relations between these instances. These library classes and relations are selected and moved with the mouse, so that nonprogrammers are able to construct simulation models. The model in Figure 5 shows the structure of a particular queueing system in terms of its objects and relations.

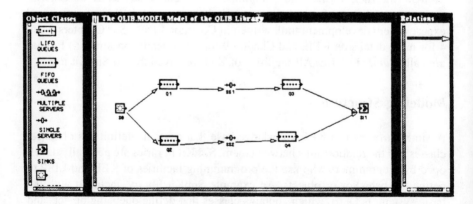

Figure 5. A Model of a Queueing System

Another useful modeling feature provided by SimKit is the *Composite Object Editor*. This editor allows the grouping of several object classes into a single composite class within a library. The model editor can then create instances of a composite class, just as it creates instances of single classes.

Modeling Behavior

As in Smalltalk-80, the objects in a SimKit simulation contain methods that are invoked by messages. Modeling behavior consists of defining the messages and the way that objects respond to them. The units that represent classes have special slots for containing methods, so object instances in simulation models automatically inherit these methods. A method usually consists of LISP code that is executed when a message is sent to the method slot (a method can also contain rules).

An example of a message protocol is provided by QLIB, whose four event types are implemented as four messages which can be sent to objects in a simulation model (such as servers and queues):

- When an item arrives at a component, an ITEM.ARRIVES! message is sent to the component.

- When an item starts an activity on a component, a START.ACTIVITY! message is sent to the component.

- When an item completes an activity on a component, a COMPLETE.ACTIVITY! message is sent to the component.

- When an item departs from a component, an ITEM.DEPARTED! message is sent to the component.

The COMPLETE.ACTIVITY! method in QLIB, which is fired upon receiving the COMPLETE.ACTIVITY! message, is defined as

```
(defun COMPLETE.ACTIVITY! (component item)
(let*((downstream.component
          (unitmsg component
          'determine.downstream.component item))
        (downstream.component.can.accept.item.p
          (unitmsg downstream.component 'accept.item?
            item)))
    (if downstream.component.can.accept.item.p
        (unitmsg component
        'move.to.downstream.component
            downstream.component item)
        (unitmsg component
        'wait.for.downstream.component
        downstream.component item))))
```

This function determines the downstream component of an item and whether that component can accept the item. If the downstream component can accept the item, then an ITEM.DEPARTS! message is scheduled for the current component and an ITEM.ARRIVES! message is scheduled for the downstream component. Otherwise, the current component puts itself into a waiting state until the downstream component becomes available.

Running a Simulation

The paradigm of sending messages to invoke specific behaviors through methods is incorporated into discrete-event simulation by scheduling the time at which messages are sent. Discrete-event simulation is implemented by the CALENDAR, CLOCK, and SIMULATOR units associated with each model.

The CALENDAR maintains an event queue in its FUTURE.EVENTS slot. When it is time for an event to occur, that event is deleted from the FUTURE.EVENTS slot and placed in the CURRENT.EVENT slot. An event is implemented as an instruction to the CALENDAR to formulate and send a message to the simulation object specified by CURRENT.EVENT. The method invoked within the receiving object might in turn produce another message that causes a new event to be added to the FUTURE.EVENTS queue. The CLOCK is always updated to the time of the current event. The simulation continues until one of the following occurs: there are no more events, a prespecified amount of time has elapsed, or the simulation is interrupted.

A model's SIMULATOR unit controls the simulation by initializing the model and starting and stopping simulation runs. The SIMULATOR unit contains a slot with the message INITIALIZE! which causes all objects in the simulation to return to a standard starting point or to a default state. The SIMULATOR unit also provides a menu that allows the user to control the simulation. The run option on this menu permits specification of the terminating conditions for a simulation run (e.g., when there are no more events). The user may step through a simulation, event by event, in order to debug the model or to better understand how the model works. The simulation can always be interrupted regardless of whether it is running continuously or one step at a time.

Generating Random Variables. The input data to a discrete-event simulation usually consists of random variables generated from a probability distribution. The creation of a sequence of random variables is handled by *generators* in SimKit. As each input value is used, a generator computes the next value in the sequence. SimKit provides a choice of six probability distributions for generating random variables, as well as a class of user-definable function generators. With these features, it is easy to generate input data about a simulation object (e.g., the lathe will fail, on the average, every six months; the failure rate will follow a normal distribution with a standard deviation of 2 months).

Collecting Simulation Statistics. The collection and display of statistics for variables in a simulation provides insight into the model that is being simulated. Some statistics are most meaningful when graphically displayed on the screen while the simulation is running (e.g., fluctuations in temperature of a chemical process plant). Other statistics summarize data over the entire simulation (e.g., the average time a car spends in a queue waiting to be washed).

SimKit provides units called *data collectors* that can be attached to simulation objects. Data collectors allow model developers to:

- gather various types of information about the simulation model, including numeric values, states, and time-weighted values;

- specify when data should be collected, including whenever a value changes, whenever a specified message is received, or whenever data collection is scheduled;

- filter or transform the data collected;

- display data on the screen in a graph or table;

- write data to a file for printing or further analysis; and

- analyze data as it is being collected.

Verification of Simulation Models. *Verification* is the process of ensuring that the computer model of a system correctly implements the specifications that define the system. There are usually a number of constraints on the structure and behavior of the system that must be reflected in the model. If a factory model includes two conveyor belts that head towards each other and intersect, then there is an error in the model. Many less obvious constraint violations may be present in a model, especially one of a highly complex system. Automatic verification of models would therefore be a highly useful feature of simulation development tools.

SimKit is one of the few simulation tools that offers a verification capability. A SimKit modeler can use the *value class* and *cardinality* mechanisms provided by KEE to maintain the consistency of *slot values* throughout libraries and models. The SimKit *KB Verifier* is an automatic verification tool which not only checks slots for value class and cardinality violations, but looks for references to deleted units and performs user-defined verification tests as well.

Where is the AI in AI-Based Simulation?

Simulation models built in environments such as Loops and KEE allow the programmer to make use of AI methods such as frames, rule-based inferencing, and access-oriented programming. SimKit illustrates how these AI methods facilitate the modeling of the structure and behavior of simulation objects. The slots in KEE frames have *facets,* such as cardinality and value class, which constrain the slot values. This provides for automatic consistency checking and aids in the verification of models. The value of a slot can consist of one or more entities (e.g., an integer, a color, or a data structure such as a list), or it can be a method. Methods are generally implemented as LISP functions; however, they can also apply a set of KEE rules instead. The ability to model the behavior of an object as LISP code or as rules eases the task of modeling, because some behaviors are more naturally modeled in mathematical or algorithmic terms (in LISP), while others are more easily expressed in a heuristic or declarative form (in rules).

A special kind of KEE method called an *active value* can be attached to a slot and fired whenever the slot value is accessed or modified. The active value facility is particularly useful in graphically displaying quantities that change during the course of a simulation. KEE provides a predefined set of active values called *active images* that support this capability. The temperature of a boiler might be graphically represented as a thermometer and internally represented as the temperature slot in the boiler unit. Whenever the value of the temperature slot changes, the active value attached to it is triggered and displays the new temperature in the thermometer image.

The methods that encode the behavior of objects in a SimKit simulation model are triggered only when a scheduled event sends a message to them. For some systems, only the sequence of states through which the modeled system passes is important, not the exact timing of events. In such cases, the behavior of simulation objects may be encoded entirely as rules. As an example, a knowledge base in the domain of molecular genetics was built for simulating the behavior of a virus (Meyers and Friedland, 1984). The purpose of the simulation is to predict which of two lifestyles (lytic or lysogenic) the virus will adopt when it invades a bacterium. The input to the simulation consists of a set of mutations to the virus. The simulation proceeds as a series of cycles in which forward chaining is applied to all rules that can be invoked under current experimental conditions. The simulation ends when one of the two virus lifestyles has been deduced. Another example is provided by IRIMS (Winkelbauer and Fedra, 1987), an integrated risk management system for managing hazardous substances in a chemical production plant. The simulation of a chemical process is performed by a forward-chaining inference engine that uses a set of knowledge bases containing rules about chemical processes and a set of information tables that dynamically store facts about the objects undergoing simulation. Further examples of simulation applications that use AI techniques can be found in Round (in press).

The experience to date suggests that most AI-based simulation models have been developed for specific applications such as the virus lifestyle predictor and the IRIMS integrated risk management system. The AI capabilities of tools such as SimKit are not being fully exploited, as these tools are often used by non-AI programmers who wish to rapidly build simulation models.

Conclusion

The languages and tools described in this chapter partially address the limitations of standard simulation techniques as listed in the introduction:

- Steamer and SimKit permit the development of simulation models without programming.

- Models can be developed in ROSS, Truckin', Steamer, and SimKit without having to recompile a program.

- Both Steamer and SimKit provide tools to facilitate the representation and execution of models at different levels of detail.

- ROSS, Truckin', Steamer, and SimKit provide graphical interfaces that can be used to control simulation runs. All have facilities that enable the user to stop a simulation run at any point in order to browse and query the model or to make changes to simulation objects. All provide means of visually depicting changing model parameters during the course of a simulation.

- The traces produced by ROSS can be used as a basis for interpreting simulation results. The environments which support Truckin' and SimKit (Loops and KEE, respectively) provide explanation capabilities which allows users to ask various how and why questions. Truckin', Steamer, and SimKit allow graphical depiction of variables on the screen during a simulation run, which helps the user understand the system being modeled, but it does not substitute for an interactive explanation capability.

While facilitating the development of simulation models, object-oriented and AI simulation tools still suffer from a number of limitations:

- The range of problems to which they have been applied is very narrow. Most systems that have been modeled with these tools are readily decomposable into well-defined objects and behaviors. This is one reason that a disproportionate number of SimKit applications are in the domain of factory modeling.

- The goal of creating models without writing code has only been partially achieved. Model builders who do not use the programming facilities of Steamer or SimKit are severely restricted in their ability to represent the behavior of objects.

- These tools do not provide general facilities for integrating simulations that have already been developed. Steamer does provide an interface to one particular FORTRAN mathematical simulator, but this feature has not been generalized for other simulators or other domains.

- Although these tools facilitate model development and execution, they provide no guidance about what to simulate. There may be many thousands of potential configurations of machines in a factory, in which case the main problem in optimizing the design lies in choosing which configurations to simulate. Such a problem is more amenable to analysis by expert systems, suggesting that the capabilities of simulation tools might be increased through integration with expert systems. SimKit is built on KEE, which is an expert system development environment, but most applications of SimKit have not made extensive use of KEE's inferencing and explanation capabilities.

More experience is needed in using the types of tools described in this chapter in order to understand how and when they are best applied to simulation problems. In addition, more research is needed to overcome the current limitations of AI-based simulation tools. Only with the acquisition of more experience and more powerful tools will we be able to judge the ultimate impact that AI techniques will have on simulation development.

References

Birtwistle, G. M., Dahl, O., Myhrhaug, B., & Nygaard, K. (1979). *SIMULA BEGIN*. Lund, Sweden: Studentlitteratur.

Goldberg, A., & Robson, D. (1981). The Smalltalk-80 system. *Byte Magazine, August*, 36–47.

Goldberg, A., & Robson, D. (1983). *Smalltalk-80: The language and its implementation*. Reading, MA: Addison-Wesley.

Hollan, J. D., Hutchins, E. L., & Weitzman, L. (1984). Steamer: An interactive inspectable simulation-based training system. *AI Magazine, 5(2)*, 15–36.

IntelliCorp (1986). *The SimKit system: Knowledge-based simulation tools in KEE, user manual, KEE Version 3.0* (Document Number 1.1–USK–1). Mountain View, CA: IntelliCorp, Inc.

Kunz, J. C., Kehler, T. P., & Williams, M. D. (1984). Applications development using a hybrid AI development system. *AI Magazine, 5(3)*, 41–54.

Law, A. M., & Kelton, W. D. (1982). *Simulation modeling and analysis*. New York: McGraw-Hill.

McArthur, D. J., Klahr, P., & Narain, S. (1986). ROSS: An object-oriented language for constructing simulations. In P. Klahr & D.A. Waterman (Eds.), *Expert systems: Techniques, tools, and applications*. Reading, MA: Addison-Wesley.

Meyers, S., & Friedland, P. (1984). Knowledge-based simulation of genetic regulation in bacteriophage lambda. *Nucleic Acids Research, 12(1)*, 1–9.

Round, A. D. (in press). Symbolic simulation. In A. Barr & E. Feigenbaum (Eds.), *The handbook of artificial intelligence* (Vol. 4), Morgan Kaufman.

Stefik, M. J., Bobrow, D. G., Mittal, S., & Conway, L. (1983). Knowledge programming in Loops: Report on an experimental course. *AI Magazine, 4(3)*, 3–13.

Stelzner, M., Dynis, J., & Cummins, F. (1987). *The SimKit system: Knowledge-based simulation and modeling tools in KEE*. Mountain View, CA: IntelliCorp, Inc.

Winkelbauer, L., & Fedra, K. (1987). Intelligent decision support for the management of hazardous substances: Symbolic simulation of chemical production processes. *Proceedings of the European Simulation Multiconference* (pp. 191–196). Vienna, Austria.

Chapter 9

SimKit: A Model-Building Simulation Toolkit*

Brian Drummond
Marilyn Stelzner
IntelliCorp, Inc.

Many knowledge-based applications require the formulation of qualitative models for problem solving or reasoning in the application domain. This is often referred to as *model-based reasoning* (Nardi and Simons, 1986). These models of domain knowledge map well onto an object-oriented programming paradigm because they involve detailed descriptions of objects and their relationships to one another.

Constructing these models is an iterative process for end users involving incremental definition, testing, and refinement. A user interface that supports model construction must provide tools that enable end users to rapidly build models. In the *toolkit style of interface*, exemplified by Bill Budge's Pinball Construction Set™ (Norman, 1986)

> the desired operations are done simply by moving the appropriate icons onto the screen and connecting them together. Connecting the icons is the equivalent of writing a program. There are no hidden operations, no syntax or command names to learn (Hutchins, Hollan, and Norman, 1986).

Relying on this *direct manipulation* user interface (Shneiderman, 1982), the user or *model builder* constructs a simulated pinball machine by selecting pieces such as "bumpers" and "paddles" from a "toolbox" and placing them on a board

---

*SimKit™ is the result of a team effort. Ed Payne, Bill Faught, Philip McBride, and Conrad Bock were responsible for SimKit's conceptual design. Then David Silverman, Fred Cummins, Dan Rabin, John Bailey, and Ken Cheetham made SimKit happen.

Pinball Construction Set is a trademark of Electronic Arts.

SimKit is a trademark of IntelliCorp, Inc.

which holds the pieces in place. At any time, the user can run the game and each piece behaves (more or less) like its real counterpart. When a "pinball" strikes an object, a realistic sound is heard and the ball appears to "bounce off" or "go through" the object as it would in an actual pinball machine.

With minimal training, the model builder can quickly build a complex structural and behavioral model. The user can then run the model to observe its behavior, and then modify the structure if desired. In the toolkit style of interface, the spatial relationships among objects seen on the screen allow the user to intuitively define a structural model. The model builder never needs to be aware of the complexities of the internal representations that actually support the model.

Borning has stated that the future of object-oriented programming lies in software toolkits that make flexible computing power available to a wide range of users, from professional programmers who create or refine toolkits to nonprogrammers who simply use the toolkits for model building (Borning, 1986). In the Pinball Contruction Set the user cannot create new kinds of objects with new behavior, and, therefore, a programmer cannot create or refine the toolkit. A key to the acceptance of a professional simulation toolkit environment is its ability to support both nonprogrammers (e.g, domain experts) who need to rapidly build models in an easy manner using parts from an existing toolkit, and programmers who need full access to all levels of the system including traditional programming facilities (e.g., LISP).

Having seen many efforts to build domain-specific simulation toolkits, such as Steamer (Hollan, Hutchins, and Weitzman, 1984), a steam-propulsion simulation training system, Intellicorp designed and implemented SimKit, a set of tools for building domain-independent simulation toolkits. SimKit is currently being used to construct toolkits and models in a range of knowledge-based simulation applications from factory scheduling to design of automated control systems to fault analysis in nuclear power plants. Figure 1 displays a SimKit model built for a sheet metal manufacturing application.

This chapter describes the specific objectives of the SimKit system, followed by a description of the approach taken to implement a set of tools that facilitate construction of kits in a wide range of domains. Several brief examples of domain-specific kits built with SimKit are then presented. Finally, there is a discussion of the limitations of the current implementation of SimKit, indicating directions for future development.

SimKit Design

Our objective in the design of SimKit was to build a set of tools that would help system developers build toolkit interfaces for a range of simulation domains.

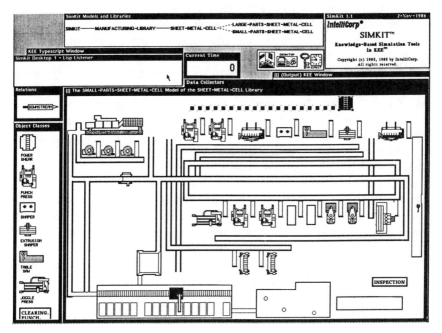

Figure 1. The SimKit System

The interface would facilitate graphical manipulation of objects and their relationships in a given domain. In the process of using a toolkit, the end user would build a model by moving and connecting icons on the screen that represent objects and relations in the domain model. Once a model is constructed, the user can run the model and observe a graphical animation of the system's behavior. Because this style of interface allows the user to manipulate the objects of interest directly, it is very transparent to the user and easy to learn.

For this style of user interface to be successful, the graphical representation of the domain model must always be consistent with the underlying application (knowledge base). As a result, much of the implementation effort required for SimKit was spent in developing facilities for establishing and maintaining the consistency of mappings between both domain objects and relations and their graphical representation.

When we examined the potential range of model behaviors that might be needed for different toolkits, we found common behavioral characteristics were shared among applications in different domains. For example, there are many discrete systems that exhibit *queueing* behavior. Queueing systems typically consist of networks of permanent components through which transitory items pass. Queues provide temporary storage when there are system backups.

Telecommunications networks, factories, and service operations such as the Department of Motor Vehicles can frequently be modeled as queueing systems. Because of the common behavioral characteristics (e.g., queueing behavior) exhibited in these domains, SimKit is designed to give users the ability to make specializations of a single toolkit describing shared (e.g., queueing) behavior. This methodology saves development time, simplifies the understanding and debugging of systems, and ensures compatibility across applications.

The conceptual design for SimKit is based on the distinction between a *model* and a *library*. A given model combines *structural* and *behavioral* components. The structural model describes a particular configuration of objects and the relations between those objects. The behavioral model is defined by *methods* that are stored in a class slot (in a library) as a LISP function or a set of rules. When a model is created by the user (from a library), the objects in the model inherit their behavior from an object class. The user sees the behavioral component of a model by running a simulation and by allowing system behavior to emerge through structural changes of the model objects.

A library consists of a collection of *object classes* and *relations* that can be used to build models. An object class is a generic object from which *instances* or *members* can be created. A relation is a user-definable connection between two or more objects in a model or library. Many different models can be constructed from the basic object classes and relations defined in a library. Models are often built by domain experts and other nonprogrammers using SimKit's direct manipulation interface, but library development generally requires programming skills. Libraries can be broad or narrow in their focus. For example, one library might deal with general queueing problems. That library might be specialized into a sublibrary for building manufacturing models, which in turn, might be further specialized into a sublibrary for printed circuit board manufacture with another for sheet metal manufacture. A model built using the printed circuit board library might represent a specific part of a factory as seen in Figure 1.

SimKit offers a set of graphical tools directly supporting structural model building. To support the definition of object behaviors, SimKit provides sample libraries defining the behavior of prototypical objects for a specific set of behaviors. To develop domain-specific object behavior, a kit builder can specialize a sample library that has similar behavior. Sample libraries, therefore, have a somewhat unique status; they fall halfway between the domain-independent tools in SimKit and the domain-specific library that is used to solve a particular problem.

Flexibility and ease of use are the major design tradeoffs encountered with SimKit. We want SimKit to be applicable to many different domains and at the same time, we want to give a developer as much help as possible in constructing a toolkit. The problem is to identify the subset of functionality that helps the system developer with a major portion of the task, but does not limit the toolkit's use to a narrow set of applications. SimKit can be thought of as a simulation and model building shell, into which the system developer adds domain knowledge.

SimKit Architecture

SimKit is a set of object-oriented tools implemented on top of the Knowledge Engineering Environment™(KEE®) (Kunz, Kehler, and Williams, 1986; also see Chapter 3). KEE is a frame-based system implemented in LISP, supporting object-oriented programming with inheritance across two types of links: *class/ subclass* and *class/member*. KEE also contains a rule system, active values (or *demons*) for data-driven programming, a multiple worlds facility for hypothetical reasoning (described in Chapter 4), an assumption-based truth maintenance system (de Kleer, 1986; described in Chapter 4), and tools for constructing end-user interfaces. Because SimKit is implemented on top of KEE, the user has full access to KEE's functionality, allowing the integration of knowledge-based applications with domain-specific toolkits developed using SimKit.

SimKit relies on an object-oriented programming paradigm, both for the representation of domain objects and for the implementation of SimKit tools. The basic components of object-oriented programming—classes, instances, and methods—are implemented as frames or *units* in a KEE knowledge base. Thus the major SimKit tools are each implemented as KEE knowledge bases accessible to the kit builder, ensuring a high degree of extensibility. For example, SimKit includes a facility for introducing stochastic variations, called *generators*, into a simulation.

The graphical requirements of SimKit's model editor led to the development of a general-purpose, object-oriented graphics package called KEEpictures™. KEEpictures provides special viewing areas or *viewports* with built-in scrolling and zooming facilities, and various classes of mouse-sensitive picture objects. Each viewport and picture is represented as a KEE unit with a large range of inherited attributes and behaviors. Pictures can be moved, reshaped, opened, closed, highlighted, and edited. As KEEpictures are represented using the same structures as other SimKit objects (i.e., KEE units), their presentations can be controlled by the same mechanisms used in the underlying application—methods and rules—thus preserving a tight integration between the application and its

---

Knowledge Engineering Environment is a trademark of IntelliCorp, Inc.
KEE is a registered trademark of IntelliCorp, Inc.
KEEpictures is a trademark of IntelliCorp, Inc.

graphic representation. In Figure 1, the largest window is a KEEpictures viewport, with each individual machine being a KEEpicture.

The major components of the SimKit system, as seen in Figure 2, are the *Model Editor*, which provides the generic toolkit interface, the *Library Editor*, which is used to define the domain-specific knowledge for a kit, and the *Library/Model Hierarchy* manager which manages the relationships between libraries, sublibraries, and models. In addition, a package of various simulation-specific tools is included in the basic system.

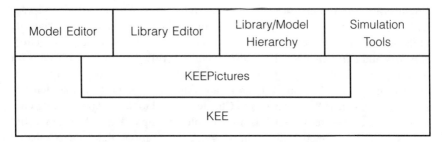

Figure 2. The SimKit Architecture

The Model Editor

SimKit's Model Editor is a graphic editor for creating instances of model classes, configuring them into graphic models, and defining relations between them. This is all accomplished by manipulating icons on the screen with a mouse.

The Model Editor, as shown in Figure 3, is composed of three windows, or viewports. The *Design Viewport* in the center window enables the user to zoom in and out on a model and to display its different parts by moving the viewport around the window. To the left of the Design Viewport is the *Object Classes Viewport* which displays icons representing each of the component classes in a library. Similarly, the *Relation Viewport* to the right of the Design Viewport displays the icons that represent relations between instances of model classes. Pop-up menus that are generated by selecting icons with the mouse enable the user to display and edit the underlying object definitions. Icons are also represented as objects, enabling the user to display and edit the bitmap image associated with an icon.

In order to construct a model, such as the one shown in Figure 3, the user first selects an icon in the Object Class Viewport, thereby selecting the class to be instantiated. An icon for the new object then appears, and the user positions it on the Design Viewport. At the same time a KEE unit representing the new object is created in the underlying application in the model knowledge base, inheriting its description from the selected class.

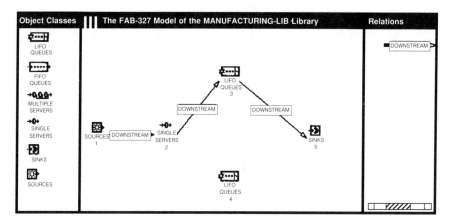

Figure 3. The SimKit Model Editor

After creating two or more objects, the user can define relations between two objects by first selecting the *domain* object with the mouse and then selecting the *range* object. If there is more than one relation displayed in the Relation Viewport, the relation that is currently highlighted is the one that will be asserted between the two objects. In Figure 3 there is only one relation defined, the DOWNSTREAM relation. SimKit relations are represented by attributes or *slots* of the objects involved, and are displayed on the viewport as an arrow, as seen in Figure 3 (to reduce screen clutter, the relation arrows may be selectively turned off). For example, if B is downstream from A, and inversely, A is upstream from B, then A will have a DOWNSTREAM slot whose value is B, B will have an UPSTREAM slot whose value is A, and there will be an arrow pointing from A to B on the viewport.

The user can modify other attributes of model objects by selecting the icon that represents an object and then selecting an item from a pop-up menu that displays the object's internal KEE representation in a new window. This window, shown in Figure 4, displays the attribute values for the chosen object and allows the user to pop up a menu of possible operations by clicking the mouse on any of the boldfaced names in the window. For example, one of the operations available on slot names allows the user to input the slot's value.

The behavior of SimKit objects is implemented using KEE's object-oriented programming facilities. Methods that describe an object's behavior are stored in slots in its class unit and are inherited by members of that class. In Figure 4 the COMPLETE.ACTIVITY! slot contains a method for activating behavior upon completion of an activity. Since the COMPLETE.ACTIVITY! method is part of a queueing library, this method commonly finds the next downstream object (such as another queue) which will accept an item sent from this object. Once a user has constructed a model, the user may decide to run the model. Running a model is usually initiated by sending a message to an object in the model, which sends one or more messages to other objects.

The user may decide to modify the model at any time. Selecting an icon pops up a menu that includes commands for deleting or moving the represented object. The relation arrows also can be selected to display a pop-up menu that includes commands for deleting the relation or for splicing another object between two related objects.

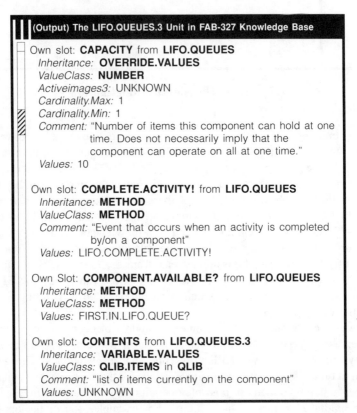

Figure 4. Display of a SimKit Object's Internal KEE Representation

The Library Editor

The kit builder uses the Library Editor to fill an empty Model Editor with the objects and relations that are used later to construct models in a specific domain. The Library Editor supports three major tasks for kit builders:

- creation of classes and the establishment of an object/icon mapping;

- definition of relations and the establishment of a relation/icon mapping; and

- specialized definition of part-whole relationships through the creation of objects representing compositions of arbitrary arrangements of other objects.

Library building is an iterative process, and the builder typically uses the Model Editor to construct models for testing additions to the library. KEE's frame system supports the addition of new attributes at the class level without making existing members of that class obsolete. Instead, the inheritance mechanism immediately "pushes" new attributes down to all members without any recompilation. This feature speeds up the library-building process because many changes made at the class level can be immediately tested on an existing model.

Several library editing commands are available to the library builder. One such command, called Create object class, prompts the user for a class name and a superclass, if any. It then creates a default icon for the class—the class name outlined in a box—and adds that icon to the Object Classes Viewport. This new class can be immediately instantiated in the Model Editor. Icon menus in the Object Class Viewport enable the user to edit the icon's bit map or to display the class object description. After displaying the class object description, as shown in Figure 4, the user can change the values of inherited attributes and add new attributes by creating new slots for the class.

In order to simplify the user interface for both kit builders and model builders, we assume reasonable default values for user inputs wherever possible, and make it easy for the user to change the default value. When an object class is instantiated, for example, it is assigned a system-generated name. However, a rename option is available on the object instance menu. When a kit builder defines a new object class, a default bit map for that class is created, but an option to edit a bit map is also available. We find this capability useful as both kit builders and model builders frequently prefer to be able to specify object descriptions incrementally, reformulating the original object, rather than having to provide the complete specification at the time an object is created.

Creating a new class relation follows a similar technique. The command to create a relation prompts the user for the name of the relation, the class of objects of which the domain object must be a member, the name of an inverse relation (if desired), and the class of objects of which the range object must be a member. Given this information, an object representing the new relation is created, inheriting slots and methods from a special object in the SimKit knowledge base where these definitions are stored. These default definitions supply functions for minimal relation activity, such as asserting, retracting, and splicing relations. A default icon for the relation—an arrow labeled with the name of the relation—is then added to the Relation Viewport, a slot with the same name as the relation is added to the domain object class, and a slot with the name of the inverse relation, if any, is added to the range object class. As with newly defined object classes, the new relation can immediately be used in asserting relations between objects in a model.

The kit builder has a number of options for customizing the relation icon: the line width can be changed, the line can have dashes, and the label can be modified or removed. The relation's behavior when it is asserted or retracted can also be modified by specialization of the appropriate method on the relation object. For example, the kit builder may wish to set the values of additional attributes on the objects involved when a relation is asserted or retracted.

Relations do not define object behavior, but they are used by the methods or rules which define object behavior. For example, a method that moved a part from one machine to the next would look at the value of the DOWNSTREAM slot in the first machine to determine the next destination for the part.

A powerful feature of the Library Editor is its capability to create new library object classes whose instances are arbitrary arrangements of instances of other object classes. The *composite* objects can further expedite the modeling of systems by representing part-whole relationships and permitting decomposition of systems into subsystems. The Model Editor enables the user to graphically view composites at different levels of abstraction. A factory, for example, might be viewed as a large number of interrelated machines, or alternately, as a smaller number of interrelated work cells containing individual machines.

The simplest way to define a composite object class is by example. The kit builder constructs a model with an example of the objects and the relations that will define the composite. After selecting the Create composite class by example command from the Library Editor pop-up menu, the user selects each object in the example. After ending the selection process, the user is prompted for a name for the composite object class. As with other object classes, an icon with the default bit map appears in the Object Classes Viewport and the composite class is immediately instantiable. The difference is that when a composite class is instantiated, instances of each of the component object classes are also created and the specified relations are asserted between the component objects. The user can also use menu commands to change the graphical representation from showing the composite object to showing the component objects and their relations.

The Library/Model Hierarchy

Both libraries and models in SimKit are implemented as KEE *knowledge bases,* named collections of objects that can be written to and reloaded from a file. Inheritance across knowledge base boundaries allows library knowledge bases to contain object class descriptions, while model knowledge bases contain instances of those classes. A SimKit user can manage the relationships between libraries and multiple sublibraries and models by displaying a Library/Model Hierarchy window as illustrated in Figure 5. In that graph, solid lines indicate a library/sublibrary relationship and dotted lines indicate a library/model relationship between knowledge bases. In Figure 5, SIMKIT is the root library with one sublibrary, the QLIB queueing library. QLIB in turn has one sublibrary, MANUFACTURING-LIB. The dotted lines in the graph that connect MANUFAC-TURING-LIB to FAB-409 and FAB-327 indicate that FAB-409 and FAB-327 are models that inherit properties from MANUFACTURING-LIB, QLIB, and SIMKIT, in that *precedence order.*

SimKit Models and Libraries

SIMKIT——QLIB———MANUFACTURING-LIB
FAB-409
FAB-327

Figure 5. Display of a Library/Model Hierarchy

The Library/Model Hierarchy has facilities that serve several purposes:

- Special default objects are created as new sublibraries and models are created. These default objects inherit from objects in the superlibrary.

- Users are prevented from loading a model or sublibrary unless the appropriate libraries are loaded.

- A mechanism is provided for specializing sample libraries for specific applications and for tailoring libraries for specific domains.

Simulation Tools

The SimKit system provides an assortment of discrete simulation tools that are well integrated with the modeling environment. Two objects that are critical to scheduling events are the calendar and the clock, which work together in controlling simulations. The calendar contains information on the current event being executed in addition to a list of events for future activation. Each event contains the following information: a clock time at which the event is to occur, a priority number which is used for ordering events scheduled for the same clock time, a message to be sent at activation time, and an object to receive the message. In a typical simulation, the first event is removed from the calendar's future event list and becomes the current event. The clock is then updated to the time at which the event takes place. This event is executed and the procedure is repeated with the next event on the future events list.

In a discrete event simulation, clock time jumps in varying increments. These increments represent the relative time periods between events which make changes in the system. Typically, one event will schedule one or more future events. When this happens, a new event is merged onto the calendar at the appropriate point in time.

SimKit also provides a set of generators for introducing variability into a simulation. Generators allow variance in time intervals between the creation of items at sources, types of items created at a source, time intervals between arrivals of items at objects, and service times of objects. Several types of generators are supplied, providing the following distributions: normal or Gaussian, lognormal, exponential, uniform, Poisson, and step or probability mass function. It is also possible to create a generator having a new distribution.

Another set of simulation tools provides data collection and analysis facilities. A special generic data.collectors object is provided which can be specialized for a particular domain. Basically, a data collector simply collects data (automatically) when attached to an interesting value or message. If the data collector is activated, first the data is converted to a more meaningful format if necessary, then it passes through a filter to weed out uninteresting values and from there it may pass through to various analyses or perhaps to storage or output. Many types of data collectors are available, including frequency counters, numeric collectors (showing such statistics as the mean, standard deviation, maximum and minimum values), history, and activity duration collectors.

Model Building Scenario

To illustrate the model building process in SimKit, a simple model called QLIB.MODEL has been constructed to which certain modifications will be made. This particular simulation model uses a specialized library called QLIB, which contains class objects specialized for handling queueing problems. As seen in Figure 6, several model objects have already been created in the Design Viewport. These objects are: a single source of data items called S1, four first-in-first-out (FIFO) queues labeled Q1 through Q4, two single-server queues named SS1 and SS2, and finally a data sink labeled SI1. Figure 7 shows these queueing objects as they exist in the underlying model knowledge base. Note that for each model component unit created, a corresponding image unit was also created.

In Figure 6, data items originate from the source S1, pass through the two queueing paths headed by the queues Q1 and Q2 (successive data items alternate

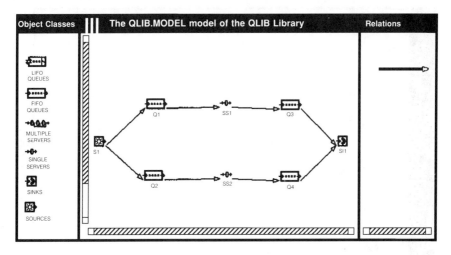

Figure 6. The Graphic Representation of QLIB.MODEL

between the two paths), and are consumed by the sink SI1. The task is (a) to add two new servers to the model, SS3, a single server, and MS1, a multiple server (a server capable of simultaneously processing more than one item at a time); (b) two new queues, Q5 and Q6; and (c) an additional sink, S12. A new downstream relation is to be asserted between SS1 and Q4, so that SS1 can push items to both of the servers SS3 and MS1. The resulting model will be shown in Figure 8.

First, the user clicks on the relation arrow between Q3 and SI1 and selects the Delete command from the *link commands* pop-up menu. To make more room for a new server and queue, the user uses the mouse to move SI1 further to the right; the assertion arrow connecting Q3 and SI1 automatically adjusts its length.

Next, a new single server is created, SS3, by clicking the mouse on the single server image in the Object Classes Viewport. A new graphic image representing a newly created single server appears and is positioned between Q3 and SI1 with the mouse.

SS3 is connected to Q3 and SI1 by clicking the mouse on the existing assertion image between the queue and the sink and then selecting the Splice command from a pop-up menu. The original relation is automatically retracted and two new relations are asserted together with the creation of two new assertion arrow images to graphically represent the asserted relations. This process is repeated to create Q5 and splice it between SS3 and SI1.

The process for asserting a new relation between existing components (rather than splicing in a new component) is only slightly different. To assert that Q4 is downstream from SS1, for example, the user clicks the mouse on SS1 which

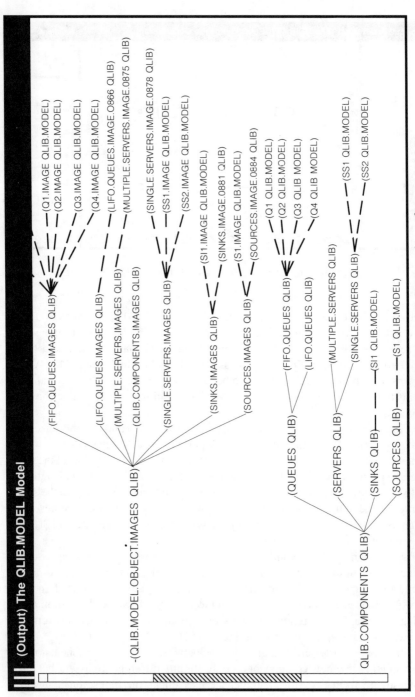

Figure 7. The Underlying Knowledge Base Representation of QLIB.MODEL

254

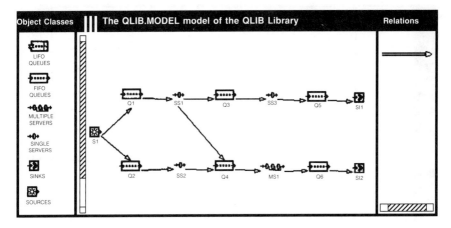

Figure 8. The QLIB.MODEL after Modifications

produces a rubber-band line whose arrowhead can be positioned over Q4, the intended range of the relation. Clicking the mouse again asserts the relationship between the server and the queue.

To complete the changes to the model, MS1, Q6, and SI2 are added and linked together through a combination of the processes described above. Figure 8 shows the Design Viewport after these changes have been made to the model. To illustrate how the automatic updating features of SimKit are employed, Figures 9 and 10 show how the values of the UPSTREAM and DOWNSTREAM slot of SS1 are automatically modified by SimKit to reflect the newly asserted relationships between the server and the queues.

At this point the user may elect to run a simulation using this graphic model description. This is easily accomplished by first initializing the model and then running it by selecting the appropriate commands from the system menus. As the simulation progresses, objects that are currently processing items highlight themselves in inverse video for clarity. The user may stop the simulation at any time, modify the model through mouse and menu actions, and then either continue or start the simulation again.

Experiences Using SimKit

SimKit currently has approximately one hundred users, building and using kits in a broad range of applications. Many of these kits are for queueing systems, because SimKit includes a sample library for this kind of system. The majority of these queueing systems are in manufacturing or telecommunications domains.

The SS1 Unit in QLIB.MODEL Knowledge Base

Unit: **SS1** in knowledge base **QLIB.MODEL**
Created by Drummond on 5-25-88 16:07:15
Modified by Drummond on 5-25-88 19:11:36
Member Of: **SINGLE.SERVERS** in **QLIB**

Own slot: **CONTENTS** from **SS1**
Inheritance: **VARIABLE.VALUES**
ValueClass: **QLIB.ITEMS** in **QLIB**
Cardinality.Max: 1
Comment: "list of items currently on the component"
Values: **SIMPLE.ITEMS.22**

Own slot: **DOWNSTREAM** from **SS1**
Inheritance: **OVERRIDE.VALUES**
Relation.For.Slot: **DOWNSTREAM.RELATION** in **QLIB**
Values: UNKNOWN

Own Slot: **IMAGE** from **SS1**
Inheritance: **VARIABLE.VALUES**
Comment: "The image unit that represents this frame object."
Values: **SS1.IMAGE**

Own slot: **UPSTREAM** from **SS1**
Inheritance: **OVERRIDE.VALUES**
ValueClass: (MEMBER.OF **QLIB.COMPONENTS** in **QLIB**)
Comment: "Components of which this component is a
downstream component."
Relation.For.Slot: **DOWNSTREAM.RELATION** in **QLIB**
Values: UNKNOWN

**Figure 9. The SS1 Unit Before
Relations are Asserted**

The SS1 Unit in QLIB.MODEL Knowledge Base

Unit: **SS1** in knowledge base **QLIB.MODEL**
Created by Drummond on 5-25-88 16:07:15
Modified by Drummond on 5-25-88 19:06:17
Member Of: **SINGLE.SERVERS** in **QLIB**

Own slot: **CONTENTS** from **SS1**
Inheritance: **VARIABLE.VALUES**
ValueClass: **QLIB.ITEMS** in **QLIB**
Cardinality.Max: 1
Comment: "list of items currently on the component"
Values: **SIMPLE.ITEMS.22**

Own slot: **DOWNSTREAM** from **SS1**
Inheritance: **OVERRIDE.VALUES**
Relation.For.Slot: **DOWNSTREAM.RELATION** in **QLIB**
Values: **Q4, Q3**

Own Slot: **IMAGE** from **SS1**
Inheritance: **VARIABLE.VALUES**
Comment: "The image unit that represents this frame object."
Values: **SS1.IMAGE**

Own slot: **UPSTREAM** from **SS1**
Inheritance: **OVERRIDE.VALUES**
ValueClass: (MEMBER.OF **QLIB.COMPONENTS** in **QLIB**)
Comment: "Components of which this component is a
downstream component."
Relation.For.Slot: **DOWNSTREAM.RELATION** in **QLIB**
Values: **Q1**

**Figure 10. The SS1 Unit After
Relations to Q1, Q3, and Q4 are Asserted**

A fairly typical application is the *control system* toolkit built by Allen-Bradley, a major vendor of factory control systems and controllers (Nielsen, 1987). The objective of this application is to allow a control system engineer to experiment with different design parameters for control systems, such as the number of levels in the control hierarchy of processors, the power of each processor in the hierarchy, the levels at which various types of data should be stored, and the level at which various types of control processing should be performed. With the model editor, the end user can build a model reflecting the control system hierarchy of processors and communications links. Special menus have also been added to facilitate experimentation with other design parameters.

SimKit has also been used as a framework for qualitative modeling of continuous processes. In this class of application, object classes might include pipes, tanks, and valves, and system developers would be trying to answer questions about, for example, the affects of a specific valve malfunctioning or a pipe breaking.

Another class of SimKit users have employed the graphics capabilities in a range of battle management applications. Their end goal is to develop AI planning systems, with a SimKit-based simulation demonstrating graphically the implications of various plans.

Levitt and Kunz (1985) have explored the application of knowledge-based techniques to the project management of large construction projects. The SimKit Model Editor was used to construct *critical path networks* of project activities indicating successor and predecessor relations between activities.

Limitations

Simkit's major limitation is that it provides little support for defining object behaviors, although the broad range of potential behaviors for SimKit toolkits makes the difficulty of creating a general behavior editor fairly obvious. Kit builders must currently develop a message protocol and implement the methods in LISP or rules. If a similar sample library is available, the library protocols can then be specialized. Unfortunately, this lack of support for developing behavioral models seems to be accentuated by the high degree of support that is provided for structural modeling.

Most SimKit users quickly find uses for composite objects, but soon want more complete support for composites. In particular, they want to be able to add composites once they have been defined, adding and removing components and relations. Interactive support for top-down decomposition of an object into its component parts is also very limited. Composition provides some challenging representational issues that we have only begun to solve.

Kit builders for battle management applications have asked for a model editor that recognizes and tracks relative positions of objects on a viewport. They would like to assign a coordinate scale to the viewport and then have object positions in that scale automatically calculated when objects are positioned or moved.

SimKit currently limits the user to using a single library to build a model, rather than being able to use members of classes from more than one library. This capability would be especially useful when more than one person is involved in building a kit.

Conclusions

The toolkit metaphor for user interfaces has broad applicability to knowledge-based applications requiring qualitative models. With the implementation of SimKit, we have demonstrated that a general set of tools can greatly facilitate the kit-building process. SimKit includes both a shell for creating graphical interfaces that construct structural models in a domain-specific manner, and tools that facilitate the addition of domain-specific knowledge to that shell. The end result of applying these tools is a graphical user interface for building simulation models in a specific domain.

References

Borning, A. (1986). Panel on the future of object-oriented programming. *OOPSLA '86*, Portland, OR.

de Kleer, J. (1986). An assumption-based truth maintenance system. *Artificial Intelligence, 28(2)*, 127–162.

Hollan, J. D., Hutchins, E. L., & Weitzman, L. (1984). Steamer: An interactive inspectable simulation-based training system. *AI Magazine, 5(2)*, 15–27.

Hutchins, E. L., Hollan, J. D., & Norman, D. A. (1986). Direct manipulation interfaces. In D. A. Norman & S. W. Draper (Eds.), *User centered system design*. Hillsdale, NJ: Lawrence Erlbaum Associates.

Kunz, J. C., Kehler, T. P., & Williams, M. D. (1984). Applications development using a hybrid AI development system. *AI Magazine, 5(4)*, 41–54.

Levitt, R. E., & Kunz, J. C. (1985). Using knowledge of construction and project management for automated schedule updating. *Applications of knowledge-based systems to engineering analysis and design* (pp. 67–80). Dearborn, MI: American Society of Mechanical Engineers.

Nardi, B. A., & Simons, R. K. (1986). Model-based reasoning and AI problem solving. In *Workshop on High Level Tools for Knowledge Based Systems*. Sponsored by AAAI, OLAIR, and DARPA, October 6–8, Columbus, OH.

Nielsen, N. R. (1987). The impacts of using AI-based techniques in a control system simulator. *Proceedings of the Conference on AI and Simulation, 18(3)*, 72–77. San Diego, CA: Society of Computer Simulation, Simulation Series.

Norman, D. A. (1986). Cognitive engineering. In D. A. Norman & S. W. Draper (Eds.), *User centered system design*. Hillsdale, NJ: Lawrence Erlbaum Associates.

Shneiderman, B. (1982). The future of interactive systems and the emergence of direct manipulation. *Behavior and Information Technology, 11*, 237–256.

Chapter 10

Transformational Synthesis Using REFINE*

Theodore A. Linden
Advanced Decision Systems

Lawrence Z. Markosian
Reasoning Systems, Inc.

Transformational synthesis is a paradigm for constructing programs, plans, or other complex conceptual objects by evolving them through small, relatively independent changes until a desirable result is achieved. The flow of control for making these changes is largely data directed; that is, each transformation may be invoked whenever a component of the evolving result matches the pattern specified in the transformation's preconditions. Transformational synthesis is a generalization of an approach to constructive problem solving developed during research on automatic programming; it has proven to be useful in developing other AI software that needs to be unusually flexible and extensible.

In *automatic programming,* programs are generated mechanically from functional specifications. When transformational synthesis is used for this purpose, the program is derived from the specifications by a series of small, independent changes or transformations. Transformational synthesis may be applied not only

*The research at Advanced Decision Systems on the application of transformational syntyesis to planning for the Autonomous Land Vehicle was supported by the Defense Advanced Research Projects Agency (DARPA) and the U.S. Army Engineer Topographic Laboratories (ETL) under subcontract #GH4–116847 from Martin Marietta Denver Aerospace, and it was also partially supported by IR&D funding from Advanced Decision Systems. A modified version of the sections in this chapter describing results from this contract, specifically the sections on results for reconnaissance mission planning and on the plan transformation, is also scheduled to appear in a future issue of *IEEE Expert.*

Sam Owre helped with the design and did most of the implementation work for the multi-vehicle ALV planner.

REFINE™ is a commercial product developed by Reasoning Systems, Inc.

REFINE is a trademark of Reasoning Systems, Inc.

to generating programs but also to constructing other complex objects such as relational database implementations of first-order logic queries, VLSI circuit designs, and detailed plans for robotic vehicles to achieve a set of military reconnaissance goals. The first half of this chapter describes transformational synthesis as embodied in the REFINE automatic programming system. REFINE is a software development environment that supports application of a number of programming styles, including transformational synthesis. In addition, REFINE is itself a transformational synthesis application—it is self-specified and uses transformational synthesis to generate new implementations of its specification.

The discussion of REFINE begins by examining the software life-cycle—both the traditional life-cycle for building and maintaining software and an alternative life-cycle called the *Specification-Based Software Life-cycle* that depends on a transformational approach to program generation. The third section of this chapter gives a brief, technical overview of the REFINE language and development environment and discusses related work.

The latter half of this chapter describes how transformational synthesis can be used to develop AI applications that are very flexible and extensible. This is done by representing the application problem in a knowledge base and using a set of transformations to construct the problem solution. With this approach, flexibility is achieved by having the control flow be driven by the knowledge base representations so that the application can adapt to widely varying problems and situations. Extensibility and maintainability of the application is enhanced to the extent that the application design achieves the goal of keeping the transformations independent.

The specific example that is described in this chapter deals with the generation of plans for multiple autonomous vehicles. The chief requirements of this application are (a) run-time flexibility in terms of the range of goals and situations for which the planner generates appropriate plans, and (b) maintainability through a wide range of future extensions. The transformations used in this application are described in order to illustrate the use of transformational synthesis, and implementation experience using REFINE is summarized. This application uses REFINE in three ways:

1. The REFINE syntax system is used to define a domain-specific language for specifying autonomous vehicle goals and plans.

2. The plan generator uses the same programming paradigm—transformational synthesis—as used by the REFINE compiler for automatic programming. The plan generator takes goal specifications as input and yields a plan defined in terms of primitive vehicle operations.

3. Domain-specific knowledge is managed by REFINE's integrated knowledge base, which also manages the documentation, parsed source code, and other information generated during the program development process.

The final section draws conclusions about the degree of flexibility and extensibility that can be achieved in AI applications software by using transformational synthesis and REFINE.

The Software Life-Cycle

Software development and maintenance is currently the major cost in most information processing systems, and these systems are becoming more and more complex. A knowledge-based approach to software development allows the environment to support all stages and aspects of the software life-cycle. Being *knowledge-based* means that most of the diverse logical materials of the programming process are factored out and represented formally in a knowledge base. In particular, such a knowledge base should have knowledge about programs, application domains, design histories of systems, and programming techniques.

Our aim is to have the software environment handle the details of programming and allow the programmers to concentrate on the application problem itself and its computational nature. This level of support requires a formalization of not only the products of programming but also as much as possible of the programming process. The software tools are integrated with the knowledge base providing the means for sharing of information. We give particular emphasis to lessening the cost of the maintenance phase of the software life-cycle because this has become the most expensive phase. A related theme is to increase the reuse of knowledge.

The life-cycle for large software projects is commonly divided into the following stages:

- *requirements* gathering and analysis,

- *specification* of the system's functionality,

- *validation* of the specifications against the requirements,

- *implementation* in a high-level language according to the specifications,

- *verification* to ensure that the specifications are met and the requirements fulfilled, and

- *maintenance* to fix errors that are found and to meet modified requirements.

Traditional Software Life-Cycle

In traditional software development as illustrated in Figure 1, the requirements and specifications are used during initial development, but maintenance and

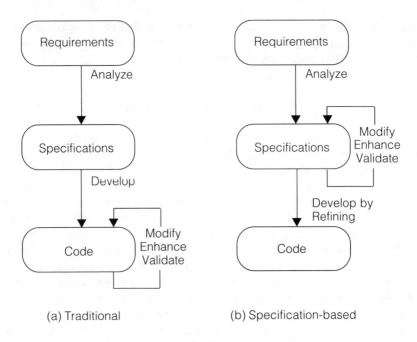

(a) Traditional   (b) Specification-based

Figure 1. Software Project Life-Cycles

verification are performed on the code. Even if there is some effort to maintain the requirements and specifications, this maintenance is separate from and incidental to program maintenance because the relationships among the requirements, specifications, and program are not available.

Several studies have shown that the cost to fix an error rises exponentially with how late in the life-cycle the error is discovered (Boehm, 1981). They have also measured the inevitable consequence of this fact, and together with the increase in size of software systems, software maintenance is taking a larger share of total project costs. It is now the dominant cost and it is increasing. We now look at two of the main reasons maintenance on high-level-language programs is so expensive: focusing on program code and failure to capture the development process.

Focus on Program Code. Ideally, specifications are well-factored and to the point. Efficient code, however, exploits interactions between logically separate pieces of knowledge and often requires complex data structures to realize simple abstractions. For example, a solution to a user's problem may be concisely expressed using a sequence; however, for efficiency the programmer implements it using a fixed-length array. Once the decision has been made to use the array, other uses for it may be found. Its scope is made global, and it quickly becomes an integral part of the program, related to other parts in complex ways. Such optimizations result in code that is efficient, but complex and tangled. This exacerbates the maintenance problem by making the program harder to understand, by increasing the dependencies among the program parts, and by delocalizing information. Minor changes in functionality now require extensive recoding. Data abstraction and program modularization strategies reduce complexity at the expense of efficiency.

Failure to Capture the Development Process. Traditional software tools deal primarily with the objects of programming—such as program text, specifications, and documentation—and not with the software development process. Because development steps are not represented, there is no good place to document design decisions. Thus, their rationale is frequently lost. Programmers are good at remembering such information for the short-term, but when returning to program code some time later, they often have difficulty in understanding the intent of their own code and in predicting the effects of modifying it. Furthermore, such knowledge is seldom transferred to other project members effectively.

Specification-Based Software Life-Cycle

The key feature of the specification-based approach is that maintenance is performed at a higher level—on abstract specifications—that are easier to understand than high-level-language code. This approach is illustrated in Figure 1(b). It bypasses the problem of determining the effects of changes to the program which is the biggest difficulty with the traditional approach and the source of the costliest errors. With this alternative approach the program must be redeveloped after each change to the specification. This is a more orderly problem than that of changing program code, and there is greater scope for providing automatic assistance. We present an automated transformational approach to this problem in the next section. Boehm (1988) calls this approach the *transform model* of the software development process.

   Knowledge-based techniques are the key to making the specification-based software life-cycle practical. In order to apply these techniques to the entire software process, it is necessary to formalize the processes involved as well as the products, and to have the machine capture the process. For example, all design decisions should be recorded. This allows them to be monitored, and policy enforcement and design review can more easily be achieved. During redevelopment, the previous design history can be examined to see what changes are necessary—with as much reused as possible.

Code Development by Transformation

Code can be developed by formal use of transformational synthesis—starting from the specifications, successive applications of formal refinement steps are made, in which each step embodies a distinct implementation decision. The important point is that these refinements are explicit in a knowledge base, that their rationale can be made explicit, and that there typically exist alternative refinements of a given specification. Successive selection among these alternatives is tantamount to searching a very large space of possible implementations, a task that requires significant expertise. Since different sequences of refinements generally result in different implementations of the same specification, a relatively small number of refinements can compactly encode a wide range of implementations. Each refinement is correctness-preserving so the final code is guaranteed to meet the specifications without further verification (determining the applicability of individual rules typically requires simple verification tests).

The transformation of specifications into program code can be more or less automated. At one extreme, the choice of transformations is made by the programmer, with the system recording the choices made and providing support for reusing previous transformation sequences. At the other extreme, the system performs analysis to decide the most efficient choices, translating the specification into efficient machine-level code that depends on usage and context. An intermediate position is currently taken by REFINE, with the system making the choices based on heuristics and some directives from the programmer. Because the REFINE language can be compiled and executed, it can be used as an *executable specification language*. Programmers gain the freedom to experiment with different high-level program designs since the task of refining a design into a procedural implementation is performed automatically by the compiler. This encourages a style of programming called *rapid prototyping* in which successive designs of a program are converted into prototype implementations in order to provide quick feedback for assessing the correctness and completeness of the design.

Several key system characteristics derive from the principle of transformational synthesis. First, a language is needed for expressing program specifications, low-level (or target-level) programs, and partially transformed specifications that contain a mixed range of constructs from very-high-level to low-level. This suggests the need for a *wide-spectrum* language. Second, a language is needed for representing transformations. Transformations can be formalized in terms of *transformation rules* that rewrite one fragment of code into another. The ability to state transformation rules succinctly requires the ability to express *program schemas* or *patterns* formally.

We next describe the REFINE system which has been built to support the specification-based software life-cycle.

The REFINE Language and Environment

The REFINE language (Reasoning, 1985) is a very high-level programming language; it contains constructs that allow programmers to express their programs in a fashion that is easy to write, understand, and modify. These very high-level constructs include operators from standard set theory (such as sets, sequences and mappings) and first order logic, a powerful state transformation operator (Westfold, 1984), and pattern matching constructs. Together, they facilitate the writing of programs at the specification level. Because a specification omits most implementation details, it is usually much shorter than a functionally equivalent program written in a standard language such as LISP or C.

REFINE has been designed to support *self-application* (Phillips, 1983; Green and Westfold, 1982). Since REFINE is a system for constructing programs, there is substantial leverage in applying REFINE to the task of building and extending itself. This principle has led to REFINE being *bootstrapped*—the REFINE system is written in the REFINE language and is used to synthesize itself. The specification of the REFINE system consists of about 40,000 lines of REFINE, which compile into about 1,000,000 lines of LISP.

The environment for REFINE program development includes several components in two groups. The first set, *language-oriented components,* includes the syntax system, type analyzer, compiler, knowledge base for representing programs and application domains, a customized text editor, and, of course, the REFINE language. The second set, *development tools,* includes the customized command interpreter, editor interface, context mechanism, documentation system, knowledge-base browsers, and graphics toolkit. In this chapter we are primarily concerned with the language-oriented components. REFINE is a very open system in that most of the components that are used in building REFINE itself are available to the user for building applications.

The *knowledge base* contains information about each construct in the REFINE language, including its syntax and its types of arguments. It also contains the internal representation for each REFINE program that has been parsed. Project management information (such as when the specification was compiled, what tests cases were run, etc.), documentation, test suites, and bug reports suggest the diversity of kinds of software knowledge captured in the knowledge base. All of the REFINE components use the knowledge base. The knowledge base is persistent; knowledge built up during a session can be saved and restored later.

REFINE contains an extensive *syntax system* that is fully integrated into the environment. A user can describe the surface and abstract syntax of a language using a syntax description language similar to, but higher-level than, BNF. The language being defined may be an extension to the basic REFINE language or it may be an entirely distinct language. An LALR(1) parser generator produces a parser from the syntax description. The parser converts syntactically correct

REFINE language statements into an abstract syntax tree representation in the knowledge base. The printer generates the text form from the internal representation. The *compiler* refines a very high-level specification into a high-level language by successive applications of program transformations. Most of the transformations are specified using a pattern language. Patterns arc used as schemas to match against the internal representation of programs in the knowledge base and to be instantiated to create the modified program representation.

The REFINE language is strongly-typed, but the burden of declarations and consistency is greatly relieved by the *type analyzer*. The type analyzer is more than a passive type checker. It combines information from user declarations, the knowledge base, and the use of data structures within the program to deduce the types of undeclared variables when enough contextual information is available to do so. The type analyzer also checks the consistency of declarations with actual usage.

One of the unique constructs in the REFINE language is the *transform*, which allows the user to specify state changes with declarative pre- and postconditions. Usually, transforms are written using the REFINE *pattern language*. Thus, the preconditions in the transform can be matched against structures in the knowledge base and, when a match is found, the structure is changed to match the pattern specified in the postcondition. The REFINE compiler itself consists primarily of transforms, most of which incrementally reduce specifications into procedural code.

The *context mechanism* maintains a hierarchy of states of the knowledge base. Previous states can be recreated. A variety of backtracking search algorithms can be easily implemented using this tool. Hence, under either program or user control, the context mechanism facilitates the consideration of a variety of program design ideas.

As stated above, most of the REFINE components are available for customization by the user. Thus, a user can define a domain-specific language using the syntax system and then write a precompiler for the new language using transformation rules and hooks into the REFINE compiler. The domain-specific language would thus compile into basic REFINE, and then into the target language.

Example of a REFINE Specification

We give an example of a REFINE specification to illustrate the very high-level, declarative character of the language. The example specification defines the set of deadlock states of a product state machine. The product state machine arises in the context of communications protocols, where it describes a system composed of protocol entities, each of which is modeled as Communicating Finite

State Automaton (CFSA). The individual CFSAs in the system communicate by sending messages across one-way channels. A deadlock state in such a system

- is a state,
- is not a final state,
- has no transitions out of it, and
- has all channels empty.

The REFINE specification of the set of all deadlock states of a product FSA reads as follows:

```
function Deadlock-States (pfsa : product-fsa) :
    set(product-state) =
{ ps | (ps : product-state)
    ps in pfsa.Q ∧
    ~ ps in pfsa.F ∧
    transitions-from-product-state(ps, pfsa) = {} ∧
    range( ps. channel-to-contents-map ) = { [] }
    }
```

Several points are worth noting about this simple specification. First, the specification is a line-for-line formalization of the preceding informal definition. (Several auxiliary definitions have been omitted that appear elsewhere in the complete application specification.) State machines are represented as tuples; Q selects the field that specifies the set of states and F selects the field that specifies the set of final states. Channel-to-contents-map is a map defined elsewhere in the application on each state of a product machine: for a particular state it maps each one-way channel to its contents, a sequence of messages that have been transmitted into the channel and are awaiting reception. To say that the range of this map for a particular product state contains only the empty sequence is to say that all the channels are empty.

What is almost more interesting than what is stated in this specification is what is omitted. There is no indication of how the various mathematical data structures (sets, sequences, and mappings) are to be represented in terms of low-level data types (they could be represented as linked lists, arrays, hash-tables, etc.) and how the set-theoretic operations (set membership test, set equality, etc.) are to be performed. These are implementation decisions that are left to the REFINE compiler. A discussion of the compilation of set-theoretic data types can be found in Kotik (1984).

Currently, the REFINE compiler generates the following Common LISP code to implement this specification:[1]

---

[1]The compiler does not generate the boldface formatting in the example.

```
(DEFUN DEADLOCK-STATES-OF (PFSA)
 (LET ((—SETVAR-275 (QUOTE NIL)))
 (LET ((STRUCTURE (NTH 1 PFSA))
 (STRUCTURE-336 (NTH 5 PFSA))
 (CV NIL))
 (LET ((SF-1068 NIL))
 (LOOP FOR PS IN STRUCTURE DO
 (IF! (SET-TO-LISP-LIST-1-SET-EQUAL-FN CV
 (TRANSITIONS-FROM-PRODUCT-STATE PS PFSA)
 (QUOTE TUPLE-EQUAL-FN**-5-1))
 THEN
 (LET ((APS (MEMBER PS STRUCTURE-336 :TEST
   (QUOTE TUPLE-EQUAL-FN**-3-1)))
 (APS-1804 (NTH 1 PS)))
 (IF! (AND (NOT APS) (EMPTY-CTC-MAP? APS-1804))
  THEN
 (PROGN
 (IF! (NOT SF-1068)
  THEN (SETQ SF-1068 T))
 (SETQ —SETVAR-275
 (ADJOIN PS —SETVAR-275 :TEST
  (QUOTE TUPLE-EQUAL-FN**-3-1)))))))
 (IF! SF-1068 THEN (PROGN))))
 —SETVAR-275))
(DEFUN SEQ-EQUAL-FN**-1-1 (ELT-1 ELT-2)
 (SEQ-TO-LISP-LIST-1-SEQ-EQUAL-FN ELT-1 ELT-2 (QUOTE EQ)))
(DEFUN TUPLE-EQUAL-FN**-2-1 (COMP-21 COMP-22)
 (TUPLE-TO-LISP-LIST-TUPLE-EQUAL-FN COMP-21 COMP-22 (QUOTE EQ)
 (QUOTE EQ)))
```

As expected, the main procedure of the Common LISP implementation alone is several times the length of the REFINE specification. Low-level procedural constructs (LOOP, IF-THEN, SETQ, etc.) have been used to implement the RE-FINE set-former.

However, the implementation is shorter than it might have been. The REFINE compiler has recognized opportunities for modularizing the implementation and has generated auxiliary functions to test equality among complex sequences and tuples. Several similar auxiliary functions are generated for the complete implementation of this specification. These functions are likely to be used by related specifications in this application.

Because the REFINE compiler is specified using sequences of program transformations, new optimizations and implementations are added relatively easily. Each transformation states the preconditions under which it is to be applied;

these may include the narrow context under which a particular optimization can be used. Because the transformations are applied in the order in which they occur in a sequence, the more powerful, but narrowly applicable, optimizations can be tested first, with more general ones following.

Related Work on Program Synthesis

One of the major recent thrusts for automatic programming in software development was initiated by Green, et al. (Green, Luckham, Balzer, Cheatham, and Rich, 1983), also reprinted in the collection by Rich and Waters (Rich and Waters, 1986). In addition, Rich and Waters (1986) contains an extensive collection of literature on the domain of program development by transformational synthesis. Barstow has written extensively on the design of the ΦNIX domain-specific automatic programming system (1985) and has commented extensively on the state-of-the-art in transformational programming (1987). Barstow has taken a knowledge-based approach to the specification and synthesis of programs in the domain of oil-well logging. REFINE provides a knowledge base and constructs for representing domain-specific knowledge in the form of program transformation rules. However, the emphasis in REFINE has been on providing a general specification and synthesis capability, together with tools that allow the user to extend that capability to a particular domain.

Many of the applications in REFINE focus on domains, such as communications, that have an accepted abstraction architecture that we believe is well suited to the transformational approach. The Explainable Expert Systems Project at USC Information Sciences Institute (Swartout and Smoliar, 1989) is directed toward providing knowledge-based and expert systems support for the programming process. In comparison, the REFINE approach emphasizes a general-purpose program specification language that allows mathematical (first-order logic and set-theoretic) specification of functionality together with automatic compilation of these specifications into executable code. We believe that a general and mathematically robust approach to specification and synthesis is a requirement for capturing and applying domain-specific problem-solving knowledge. Ladkin, Markosian and Sterrett (1988) demonstrate a domain-specific specification and synthesis environment for communication systems built "on top" of REFINE.

Applications of REFINE

In the remaining sections of this chapter, we discuss an application of the REFINE synthesis technology for deriving plans for robotic vehicles from high-level mission goals. In addition to this application, REFINE has been used in a diverse set of problem areas, including translation and compilation of program-ming languages; communication protocol specification, synthesis, validation and test generation; building language-specific software development environ-ments; discrete event simulation; and derivation of integration requirements from high-level product functionality. Common to all the applications is a *constructive* function: either automatically or interactively the applications assist the user in generating a complex, structured object. Robotic vehicle operation plans, software development environments and product integration specifica-tions are all constructed incrementally by refining abstract, relatively undetailed specifications and requirements. Each step in the transformation process repre-sents a distinct design decision; domain-specific design knowledge is codified in the form of REFINE transformation rules. The application of each rule adds greater detail and definition to the abstract structure. In some of the applications the synthesis process is completely automatic, with no human interaction. In others, the process requires human interaction. Where human interaction is required, AI techniques may be used to limit the number of options the user needs to consider and to maintain consistency of the structure under construc-tion, or at least to track the sources of inconsistency.

Using Transformational Synthesis to Develop AI Applications

Transformational synthesis is appropriate for use in applications software where there are no clear algorithmic solutions, where the output from the application is complex and varied, where the requirements are not well-defined in advance, and where flexibility and extensibility are important attributes of the software design. Applications that involve planning, design, interpretation, understand-ing, or situation assessment often have these attributes and are likely to benefit from the use of this paradigm. In later sections of this chapter, we describe how transformational synthesis has been used in a planning application—specifically planning reconnaissance missions for a group of autonomous vehicles. We have also experimented with this paradigm in a resource scheduling application, in the design of plans for an autonomous air vehicle application where rapid replanning is needed, and in the design of coordinated route plans for large aircraft fleets.

Features of the Transformational Synthesis Paradigm

The advantages of the transformational synthesis paradigm arise from the fol-lowing features:

1. By constructing the result in the knowledge base, the output from the application can have a complex structure, and the design paradigm does not depend on beginning with a rigorous specification of all outputs from the application.

2. Most approaches toward modularizing large systems require that the system's components and their interfaces be defined early in the system design process. Such forced early decisions often limit the future flexibility of the system. However, with transformations acting on a knowledge base, the knowledge base must be designed early, but other decisions about interactions between components (e.g., control decisions and parameter passing) may be deferred until later in the system development life-cycle.

3. Transformational synthesis is compatible with abstraction levels and information hiding techniques. The knowledge base can and should be designed with objects at multiple levels of abstraction. Each transformation should deal only with one or two adjacent levels of abstraction; and, ideally, it should be restricted from access to irrelevant parts of the knowledge base.

4. Searching is easily accommodated in the transformational paradigm. Alternative refinements can be constructed and evaluated by the transformations.

5. The use of a collection of transformations makes it relatively easy to extend the functionality of the software system by adding transformations.

6. The data directed control available with transformations allows decisions about the control flow among the transformations to be deferred until late in the development cycle or even until run-time. The binding of control decisions is one of many performance vs. flexibility tradeoffs involved in building flexible software systems. These decisions need to be made on a case by case basis and are likely to change as the system evolves toward operational use.

7. With the transformational synthesis paradigm, the evolution of results by the application software can be analogous to biological evolution—that is, very adaptable and flexible, but very slow. However, the paradigm also allows the software designer to introduce additional specialized transformations that optimize for the frequently encountered situations. Thus, transformational synthesis can accommodate many different points along the flexibility vs. efficiency tradeoff. Flexibility is usually important early in the application life-cycle and efficiency becomes increasingly important later in the life-cycle.

Transformational synthesis is not the right paradigm for all applications. When it does apply, there are two important goals to be achieved during the application's design.

1. The first and most critical part of a design using transformational synthesis is to find effective and general representations of intermediate plan states that occur as the problem is being solved. Clearly, it is important that all of the possible outputs from the application have natural representations in the knowledge base. The ability to adapt to additional output requirements depends on being able to extend the knowledge base representation easily. But the generality of the knowledge base representation needs to go beyond being able to represent any output. All of the possible intermediate stages in the evolution of those outputs also need to have natural representations. Usually it is harder to represent the partial and incomplete results at intermediate stages than it is to represent the final output. The representation should not require overcommitments at intermediate stages of the evolution. For example, at an intermediate stage it may be necessary to express a constraint about the possible values of an attribute even though it is clear that in any final output the attribute must have a specific value. (Most programming languages are good examples of representations that are good at expressing the final results of a development process, but are seriously inadequate at expressing what has been decided at intermediate stages of the development leading up to that result.) This representation problem is clearly hard; for some applications it may be so hard that the transformational synthesis paradigm becomes unfeasible.

2. Each transformation should be written without being dependent on the workings of the other transformations. The transformations do depend on the syntax and the semantics of the knowledge base representations. A major advantage of the transformational paradigm is that it can be used to minimize the assumptions made between pairs of transformations. The ideal is that transformations depend only on properties of the knowledge base, and that these properties can be made explicit. By making each processing module dependent only on the knowledge base, one eliminates the complexity involved in having potential dependencies between all possible pairs of transformations, thus giving hope that all properties on which modules depend can be made explicit.

The transformational synthesis paradigm can and should be used jointly with other programming paradigms. One of the strengths of the REFINE system, and the reason it was chosen for the application described in the next section, is that is does not lock the application designer into a single paradigm. Unlike AI tools, REFINE is a complete programming language and environment with full support for other programming paradigms such as procedural decomposition and object-oriented programming with inheritance.

Relationship with Other Techniques for Developing AI Applications

The application of transformational synthesis to planning problems has many similarities to the use of blackboard-based approaches to model planning as an incremental, opportunistic process; and it is strongly influenced by that work (Erman, Hayes-Roth, Lesser, and Reddy, 1980; Hayes-Roth, Rosenschein, and Cammarata, 1979; Hayes-Roth, 1985; Nii, 1986a, b). Transformations operating on a knowledge base are analogous to knowledge sources operating on a blackboard. The difference is that most blackboard-based work on planning uses an agenda mechanism to reason about and schedule the firing of knowledge sources. Thus far we have always found other simpler ways to control the firing of transformations. While we have proposed implementing metalevel planning (REFINE was selected partially because it would support reasoning about which transformation to apply next), in our actual applications we have been able to use heuristics in preconditions that select the appropriate transformations to apply without having to use run-time reflective reasoning about the control decisions. This seems to avoid the performance problems that have often been associated with blackboards.

Transformations are like rules in a rule-based system, and they have the same advantages in terms of modularity and extensibility that are usually claimed for rule-based systems. Transformations, however, are typically larger and more complex than the rules in most rule-based AI systems. They may specify substantial changes to the knowledge base, and they frequently perform complex algorithmic computations while determining the changes to make in the knowledge base. If rules correspond to relatively primitive deductions in an inferencing system, then transformations correspond to complex lemmas. Furthermore, the transformation concept as implemented in REFINE allows postconditions to be specified declaratively—in many rule-based systems the results of the rule must be defined algorithmically as an action that will accomplish the desired postconditions.

Results for Reconnaissance Mission Planning

This section summarizes the results achieved while applying the transformational synthesis paradigm to planning reconnaissance missions for a group of Autonomous Land Vehicles (ALVs). We believe these results are significant because the design paradigm allows us to combine multiple planning techniques in a flexible and extensible way and to generate effective plans that could not have been generated easily by other techniques. For a more complete description of these results and the planning methods used, see Linden (in press).

Multi-Vehicle Reconnaissance Missions

The ALV mission planning problem is to develop reconnaissance plans for a group of autonomous vehicles that are assigned to look for enemy vehicles in areas well in advance of friendly lines. A plan for these vehicles needs to select the observation points that are to be used, decide which vehicle will cover each observation point, and plan travel routes for each vehicle. All of these planning tasks are interdependent; for example, the choice of the observation points depends on how easy it is to get an available vehicle to the different possible ones. The plan should minimize risk while traveling to and hiding at the observation points. The plan needs to deal with constraints on fuel and time of arrival. In addition, we assume that the vehicle's knowledge of its own position will degenerate as it travels, and it will need to reestablish its approximate position periodically by passing near known landmarks. The planner does have information about potential observation points and routes—derived from a digital map— but all of this information is uncertain. A plan to have a vehicle move to an observation point at a specified time must deal with this uncertainty.

Abstraction Levels

Our current planner has the domain knowledge and heuristics to develop plans for these missions at the top three levels of abstraction; namely, the levels dealing with:

1. goals and evaluation criteria,

2. abstract plans that include selection among available observation points and assignment of ALVs to observation points, and

3. route plans down to the level of intermediate waypoints.

The transformational synthesis design paradigm will allow the planner to be extended down to lower levels of abstraction and thus be integrated with the lower-level planning and perception capabilities that are being developed on the ALV program.

One important feature of the mission planning problem is that one cannot decide at system design time which factors are going to be most important when planning a given mission. Minimizing risk will frequently be important, but for some missions it will be more critical to reduce travel time, conserve fuel, plan routes that pass landmarks, or deal with a combination of these factors. Purely algorithmic solutions break down when there are many dimensions to be dealt with (enough so that straightforward optimization is intractable) and one cannot design the system to solve the problem in a few dimensions (determined at system design time) and then extend that solution into the other dimensions. A key aspect of our planner is that we delay until plan generation time the metalevel decisions about which dimensions are going to be most important in solving today's particular mission planning problem.

Examples of Planning Results

The following two example results are selected to show the flexibility of the planner in dealing with a range of planning situations.

The planner generates its plan as a knowledge base object and then prints out a textual summary of the plan object. Figure 2 is a graphic summary of the more significant features of a plan generated when there are four vehicles available for the mission. There are three reconnaissance areas on the right that the vehicles are to observe. Five potential observation points are identified by the solid squares labeled op1-op5. Each of the observation points can be used to observe one or more of the reconnaissance areas. Two reconnaissance areas can be seen from op1, only the nearest reconnaissance area can be seen from each of the other observation points. We assume that likely waypoints can be identified from the map. Waypoints are depicted by open circles in Figures 2–3. Thin lines

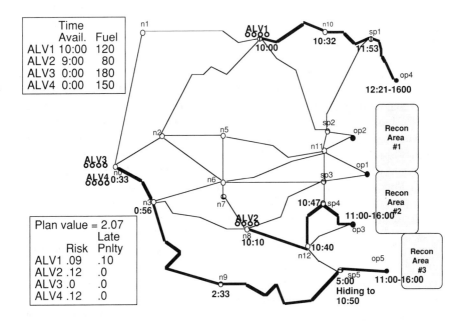

Figure 2. Summary of Plan Generated for 4 Vehicles

in these figures represent routes that have been planned between adjacent waypoints. Our planner currently generates route plans down to the level of choosing waypoints to pass.

The ALV symbols in Figure 2 show the starting locations for the four vehicles, and other properties of the starting state are listed in the box in the upper left. Two of the vehicles will already be in forward positions when they become available for this mission. The heavy lines in the diagram indicate the routes that the vehicles are to travel—the planner has chosen to send ALV1 to op4, ALV2 to op3, and ALV4 to op5.

ALV1 uses the less risky route through a hilly region even though it expects to be a few minutes late in arriving at op4 from which it will observe Recon Area #1. The times indicated near each node give time goals for arriving at that node. In its knowledge base representation, the planner maintains similar intermediate goals for fuel and position error. Missing these goals during execution would trigger replanning. The route for ALV2 involves a deviation from the direct route in order to pass the landmark at sp4. The departure time for ALV2 is chosen based on the tradeoff between the risk involved in arriving too early vs. the danger that unforeseen problems may cause delays. The plan for ALV4, which was available starting at midnight, involves traveling out near Recon Area #3 at night, hiding at a low risk position, then traveling to the observation point. The box at the lower left of Figure 3 shows the key components of the evaluation function that was used in selecting this plan as opposed to the alternative plans that were also generated.

The plan depicted in Figure 3 shows additional capabilities of the planner. This example shows the results of replanning after ALV4 has failed to report back and is believed to be destroyed. In addition, ALV1 has been delayed and will not be available until 10:30. The resulting replan, as shown in Figure 3, now has ALV1 using a different observation point to observe Recon Area #1 because the road leading toward that observation point is much faster, even though it is also riskier. Since the departure time has been delayed, the speed has become more important than the additional risk. ALV2 is now instructed to switch goals and cover Recon Area #3 from op5. ALV3 takes responsibility for covering Recon Area #2. Its plan shows it taking the fastest route and traveling in emergency mode for the first two segments of its trip.

The chief feature of this planner is its flexibility in dealing with different goals and constraints, different numbers of vehicles with differing starting conditions, and different terrain maps and travel restrictions. The control of the planning process adapts to these differences. For example, when landmarks are scarce, transformations that focus on landmark selection are invoked early in the planning process. If there are many landmarks, the planner focuses mostly on reducing risk and other factors. We have run the planner on a variety of other mission

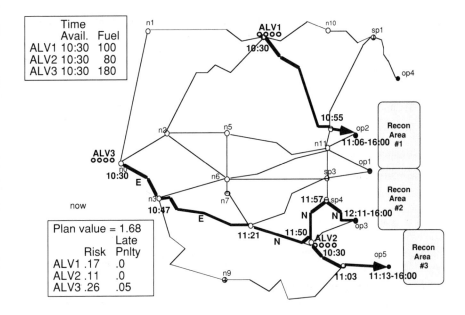

Figure 3. Replan with Three Remaining Vehicles

planning scenarios. The planner is now generating plans that deal appropriately with the constraints and opportunities in a wide range of planning scenarios.

Plan Transformations

This section illustrates the transformational synthesis paradigm by describing the way that specific transformations interact to generate plans.

The mission goals as defined by the mission commander are encoded into a single goal node which becomes the initial state of the plan. The transformations then build alternative plans and evaluate the alternatives. Two transformations do goal elaboration—one identifies all the possible sets of observation points that make sense, and the other chooses which ALV will be used to cover each observation point. Then an abstract plan for each vehicle is constructed by a set of transformations that are applied in a form of backward chaining from the goals. Alternative plans are then evaluated and the more promising ones are refined to a more detailed level using either a route planning algorithm, domain-specific heuristics about landmarks or nighttime travel, or combinations of these. There is also a plan modification transformation that attempts to improve an existing plan by changing part of the travel into emergency mode. Alternative plans are reevaluated as they are refined or modified, and the best one is selected. The other plans are preserved for possible reuse during replanning.

The underlying plan representation that is constructed by these transformations represents:

- goals and alternative or conjunctive decomposition of goals into subgoals,

- plan operations at multiple levels of abstraction,

- subtasking relationships between operations,

- alternative subgoals and subplans, and

- preconditions for operations and sequential relationships between operations.

This plan representation is adequate for current planning functionality, but for other planning functionality it needs to be extended to handle conditional plans, more general representations for concurrent plan operations, and more general temporal and other dependencies among the goals and the operations.

There are two transformations that elaborate a conjunctive goal, and the different approaches used in these transformations illustrate the range of options available to the application designer. In the first transformation, which chooses feasible sets of observation points, the planning decision about which observation points to use is postponed by selecting all of the appropriate and feasible subsets of the observation points and by setting up a search among all the feasible alternative sets. The second transformation, which assigns vehicles to cover the different potential sets of observation points, uses heuristics to make the decision at the time the transformation is invoked. The difference is based on the application designer's decision that adequate heuristic information to make the decision is available in the latter case, but is not available at the time the former transformation executes.

Example Transformation

It is seldom feasible to include actual code in presentations about application software methods, however, with a brief explanation of the syntax involved, the reader will be able to understand the transformation shown in Figure 4 and see how some of the advanced features of the language can be used to specify a large amount of functionality with a very compact notation.

This specification defines a rule or transformation that expands goals for multiple vehicles by expanding the representation to include alternative selections of appropriate observation points that can be used by the vehicles to accomplish their reconnaissance mission. An object of type GOALNODE is a parameter of the rule. The —> notation separates the preconditions of the transformation from the postconditions. The text in single quotes is parsed by a user-defined grammar. The @ and $ inside the quoted text are used by the grammar to introduce variables and set-valued variables, respectively. Thus, the second and third lines of the program assert that the parameter node must be a goalnode with a goal formula that specifies that an observation is to be accomplished. If the parameter node is such a goal, then the variables areas, stime, risk, obs, and etime are bound to the corresponding attributes of formula. The next line causes this transformation to be inapplicable in certain circumstances; for example, this transformation should create children of the plannode only if they do not already exist. The remaining lines of the preconditions use standard set theory notation to bind a variable s to a subset of the set of all possible observation points, to require that the size of s be smaller than the number of available vehicles, and to require that the set s be a minimal covering set when it is mapped by the observes relationship onto the reconnaissance areas that must be observed. For each s for which this is true, the postconditions of the transformation then specify that there shall be an appropriate new goal formula attached to a new goal node, which is a child of node, and that the branching type of the plan tree structure at this point is disjunctive.

```
(defobject ADD-OBSERVATION-POSTS rule (node:GOALNODE)
node = 'the-goal @formula applies-to {$alvs}' &
formula = 'observed {$areas} from-time @stime risk-less-than @risk
  from-observation-posts {$obs} until @etime' &
no-children(node) & undefined?(obs) & ~ empty(areas) &
nobs = {n | (n) landnode(n) & ∃ (a) (a ∈ areas & observes(n,a))} &
s ∈ POWER-SET(nobs) & size(s) ≤ size(alvs) &
® (a) (a ∈ areas => $ (p) (p ∈ s & observes(p,a))) &
® (p,q) (p ∈ s & q ∈ s & p   q =>
    ∃ (a) (a ∈ areas & observes(p,a) & ~observes(q,a)))
—>
nformula = make-structure('observed {$areas} from-time @stime
    risk-to-all-vehicles-lt @risk
    from-observation-posts {$s} until @etime') &
make-structure('the-goal @nformula applies-to {$alvs}
    goal-recon-areas {$areas}')
  ∈ PLANNODE-CHILDREN(node) &
PLANNODE-BRANCHINGTYPE(node) = 'OR)
```

**Figure 4. A Transformation that Extends the Plan
by Choosing Appropriate Sets of Observation Points**

Not all of the transformations written in REFINE are this succinct. Some require one to two pages of text, however, each transformation can usually be understood as an independent entity that depends only on the object-oriented structures in the knowledge base and does not depend on other transformations.

Refinement to Lower Abstraction Levels

While transformations are used by the planner to do goal elaboration, goal reduction, plan evaluation, and plan modification, the planner's most interesting aspects occur as abstract operators are refined to the next lower level of detail. An extended movement operator is an abstract operator for moving a vehicle from one waypoint to any other waypoint. Extended movement operators need to be refined into a plan that is at the next lower level of abstraction and is defined in terms of primitive movements between adjacent waypoints.

When refining an extended movement operator, the planner is trying to find a route which minimizes risk and is satisfactory with respect to elapsed time, fuel, and position error. Handling position error is especially complex because the vehicle's knowledge of its position can be reestablished whenever the route passes a landmark. The opportunity to travel at night when the risk is lower also needs to be handled during plan refinement.

If there were a single algorithm to solve this entire problem, we would implement it in a single transformation that does the refinement, and this aspect of our planner would not be very interesting. Since there is no computationally tractable algorithm that solves the general case, our planner has to put together various partial solutions and know when to use which solution.

There are currently three transformations that are applicable to refining an extended movement operator:

1. One transformation uses a best path algorithm that minimizes some weighting of risk, time, and fuel. It does not know how to deal with replenishable resources like position error. The transformation that uses this algorithm must be given the relative weights for risk, time, and fuel as parameters. Its effect is to generate a complete refinement of the extended move operator. This may or may not be a good refinement depending on the choice of the weightings and the effects of position error.

2. Another transformation looks for landmarks that are near enough to the goal so that a path that passes the landmark results in an acceptable position error when trying to arrive at and find the goal. For each such landmark (up to $n=3$), an alternative plan is generated consisting of an extended move from the start to the landmark followed by an extended move from the landmark

to the goal. This transformation may be applied recursively. When there are more than n landmarks that could be used, then finding landmarks is probably not a problem, and plans generated by other transformations will probably be passing near one of the landmarks.

3. The third transformation is used to generate plans to travel forward at night and then hide near the goal. It looks for extended movement operations where the available start time is before daybreak and the required arrival time is after daybreak. Then it picks a location at or near the goal where the waiting risk is low and generates a plan alternative consisting of an extended move to that hiding point, a hide operation, and a later movement to the goal.

The second and third transformations generate additional extended movement operations that need to be expanded recursively.

The planner chooses which transformations to apply based on metalevel knowledge about which factors are most critical in planning the current mission. By evaluating the abstract plan, the planner can obtain an estimate about the relative importance of position error, risk, time, and fuel. Usually one or two of these factors is not a concern for a particular mission. The planner uses these estimates to choose which transformations and which parameters to use (sometimes it uses one, sometimes several in alternative attempts to find the best plan). Furthermore, the planner reapplies the first transformation with different weightings only when the results of the first application indicate that the initial weightings may have been a poor choice.

Implementation Experience

The plan is represented by structures in the REFINE knowledge base, and our transformations are implemented using the transformation primitive of REFINE. Control is handled largely by REFINE primitives which apply a list of transformations recursively to all of the nodes of a tree structure in the knowledge base; however, subtasks within the transformations are implemented when appropriate by simple function calls. The resulting planner implementation has proven to be easy to understand, modify, and extend.

The REFINE compiler produces efficient implementations of set-theoretic expressions and the high-level control constructs that use pattern matching and transformation rules. A complete plan is generated in anywhere from 15 seconds to about 3 minutes. We have found that so surprisingly good that we have thus far devoted no effort to performance enhancements even though there seem to be many opportunities to elaborate the REFINE specification in ways that would improve the planner's performance.

A large amount of time has been spent in developing the concepts and the design for the planner; however, actual implementation time thus far is only about 4 person months. That included learning REFINE and developing an early version of the planner (also in REFINE) that evolved into the current system. Due to the structure of the planner as a set of independent transformations operating on a common plan representation, the extensions proved to be quite easy. In particular, code written in the REFINE language was readily understood by other project personnel. Ease of understanding was due in part to the clean separation of abstraction levels achievable in REFINE. There are a very large number of other extensions that we would like to make to handle additional mission types and do planning at lower levels of abstraction. Most of these extensions appear to be individually quite easy. The hard extensions are the ones that will force us to expand the plan representation. This is leading us to focus on the plan representation as a key element in achieving generality and flexibility in planning systems.

Conclusions about Flexibility and Extensibility

By using the transformational synthesis paradigm, our current planner has achieved substantially more flexibility than we have been able to test thus far. Over the range of varying mission specifications for which it has been tested, it is generating good plans that make appropriate tradeoffs with respect to the mission constraints and factors involved in evaluation criteria.[2] While the heuristics and algorithms in the current implementation only handle one general kind of reconnaissance mission—and only at the top three levels of abstraction— we have already achieved substantial planning flexibility with relatively little implementation effort.

A goal in developing the current planner is to demonstrate an extensible planning system. While we have already gone through one round of extensions, substantially larger extensions must be completed before that goal is demonstrated. Nevertheless, we believe our current planner can be extended to generate complete plans for a much wider variety of missions. Many of the current transformations are general enough so they will be useful in generating

---

[2]There are many known limitations of the current planner. For example, currently it does not properly evaluate plans that have redundant coverage on a single reconnaissance area, nor does it perform efficiently when it is asked to plan coverage for many independent reconnaissance areas where each area has many potential observation points, but there is no opportunity to cover several areas from any single observation point.

other plans. Thus far, we have found that it is usually easy to extend the planner by adding transformations. The limiting factor in extending the planner is the plan representation; at some point our initial choice of representations for plans will need to be generalized. Our experience thus far indicates that the two elements that are key to achieving extensibility are the generality of the representations and the independence of the transformations.

Since the external dependencies of each of the transformations are focused onto the knowledge base (in the effort to avoid all other hidden dependencies), it is critical that all extensions in the knowledge base be upwardly compatible with earlier representations. It is relatively easy to support multiple views onto the same underlying data, thus syntactic evolution of the representation is not as much of a problem as semantic expressibility. We have found that many extensions of our current planner are quite easy; the hard ones are those that require that more information be kept about intermediate states of the planning. For example, our current plan representation handles subtasks, abstraction levels, and sequential relationships between plan nodes, but doesn't yet represent other dependencies. The expressive generality of the representation is a critical issue that deserves a lot of attention. Fortunately, it appears that the kinds of relationships that are needed in the representation are reasonably independent of the particular application. For example, many planning applications need representations for dependencies, temporal constraints, justifications, and similar relationships. This implies that a lot of leverage can be obtained by developing and demonstrating general representations applicable to a wide class of applications.

There are many subtle ways in which one module can become dependent on other modules. In our experience, a transformational approach, when used together with other good programming techniques, can be used to reduce these dependencies. It is hard to write transformations that avoid making implicit assumptions about what other transformations will have done before this one is invoked, but to the extent that these dependencies are avoided, it becomes relatively safe to modify, extend, or add a transformation and have the rest of the system continue to function correctly.

Transformational synthesis is not the only programming paradigm used in the planning application, nor is it the only paradigm support by the REFINE system. Indeed, as the prototype evolves toward operational use, we expect to see increasing use of direct procedure calling, rather than transformations invoked by pattern matching. This is another natural evolution of an application system as it grows from an early prototyping stage, where flexibility and extensibility are most important, to the operational stage, where the needs of the application are better understood and performance and efficiency are increasingly important.

References

Barstow, D. R. (1985). Domain-specific automatic programming. *IEEE Transactions on Software Engineering, SE-11*, 11.

Barstow, D. R. (1987). Artificial intelligence and software engineering. *Proceedings of the Ninth International Conference of Software Engineering* (pp. 1321–1336). Monterey, CA.

Boehm, B. W. (1981). *Software engineering economics.* Englewood Cliffs, NJ: Prentice-Hall, Inc.

Boehm, B. W. (1988). A spiral model of software development and enhancement. *Computer, 21(5)* 61–72.

Erman, L. D., Hayes-Roth, F., Lesser, V. R., & Reddy, D. R. (1980). The Hearsay-II speech-understanding system: Integrating knowledge to resolve uncertainty. *Computing Surveys, 12(2),* 213–253.

Green, C. C., Luckham, D., Balzer, R., Cheatham, T., & Rich, C. (1983). *Report on a knowledge-based software assistant* (RADC Report RADC–TR–195). Rome, NY: Rome Air Development Center.

Green, C. C., & Westfold, S. J. (1982). Knowledge-based programming self-applied. In J. E. Hayes, D. Michie, & Y-H Pao (Eds.), *Machine Intelligence.* New York: John Wiley & Sons.

Hayes-Roth, B. , Rosenschein, F. S., & Cammarata, S. (1979). Modelling planning as an incremental, opportunistic process. *Proceedings of the Sixth International Joint Conference on Artificial Intelligence* (pp. 375–383). Tokyo, Japan.

Hayes-Roth, B. (1985). A blackboard architecture for control. *Artificial Intelligence, 26(3),* 251–321.

Kotik, G. (1984). *Knowledge-based compilation of high-level data types* (Kestrel Institute Technical Report KES.U.83.5). Palo Alto, CA: Kestrel Institute.

Ladkin, P., Markosian, L. Z., & Sterrett, A. (1988). System development by domain-specific synthesis. *Proceedings of the Third International Conference on Applications of Artificial Intelligence in Engineering.* Southampton, UK.

Linden, T. A. (in press). Planning by Transformational Synthesis. *IEEE Expert.*

Nii, H. P. (1986a). Blackboard systems: The blackboard model of problem solving and the evolution of blackboard architectures. *AI Magazine, 7(2),* 38–53.

Nii, H. P. (1986b). Blackboard systems: Blackboard application systems, Blackboard systems from a knowledge engineering perspective. *AI Magazine, 7(3),* 82–106.

Phillips, J. (1983). *Self-described programming environments.* Unpublished doctoral dissertation, Department of Computer Science, Stanford University.

Reasoning Systems, Inc. (1985). *REFINE user's guide.* Palo Alto, CA: Reasoning Systems, Inc.

Rich, C., & Waters, R. C. (Eds.). (1986). *Artificial intelligence and software engineering.* San Mateo, CA: Morgan Kaufmann.

Swartout, W. R., & Smoliar, S. W. (1989). On making expert systems more like experts. In M. H. Richer (Ed.), *AI tools and techniques.* Norwood, NJ: Ablex Publishing Corp.

Westfold, S. J. (1984). *Logic specifications for compiling.* Unpublished doctoral dissertation, Department of Computer Science, Stanford University.

Part IV

Building Bridges from Knowledge-Based to Conventional Systems

Chapter 11

KEEconnection: A Bridge Between Databases and Knowledge Bases

Robert M. Abarbanel
Apple Computer, Inc.

Frederich N. Tou
Sun Microsystems, Inc.

Victoria P. Gilbert
IntelliCorp, Inc.

Bridging the Gap

Performance vs. Expressiveness

An enduring source of conflict in the evolution of data representation has been the need to choose between performance and expressiveness. In order to support transaction-intensive data processing applications, database technology has made its primary goal performance, which may be described as the ability to store and access ever larger amounts of data with increasing ease and efficiency.[1]

Knowledge base technology, on the other hand, in support of knowledge processing tasks such as diagnosis, configuration, scheduling, and planning, has focused on *expressiveness*, or the ability to represent many different kinds of data and their relationships with increasing depth and precision.

What if it weren't necessary to choose between performance and expressiveness? What if it were possible to have the best of both worlds: to manage data with the efficiency of a high-performance database management system and then analyze that data using advanced knowledge processing techniques?

---

[1]This chapter will refer to basic concepts of relational databases. It is assumed that the reader is familiar with tables and columns, joins, primary and foreign keys, and predicates. For more details, we suggest as reference, *An Introduction to Database Systems* (Date, 1983).

KEEconnection

The KEEconnection™ product from IntelliCorp makes it possible to combine the performance, security, and maintenance of database systems with the expressiveness of knowledge bases by providing a software bridge between relational databases that use SQL® as their query language, and knowledge-based applications developed with the Knowledge Engineering Environment™ (KEE®) system. With KEEconnection, data can be maintained efficiently in one or more databases and accessed as needed by any number of KEE-based applications.

Previously, building a software bridge between a database and a knowledge based application meant months of custom programming by an individual or a team of individuals with expertise not only in database and knowledge base systems, but in data communications as well. And because much of the programming was specific to a particular application and/or database, the same lengthy effort would have to be repeated each time a new database-knowledge base connection was needed. KEEconnection simplifies the implementation and maintenance of database-knowledge base connections.

KEEconnection is not an object-oriented database system, nor is it an enhanced relational system that supports complex datatypes and/or reasoning. It is a technology for linking existing (or newly developed) relational databases to knowledge processing systems built in KEE. These connections form a distributed architecture for knowledge processing that maintains and uses valuable central database resources.

Since SQL has emerged as the industry standard for relational database query and manipulation languages, the connection of KEE to these systems is the obvious choice. Since almost all relational systems are supporting ANSI-Standard SQL, KEEconnection uses this standard for generation of queries; database-specific knowledge bases are provided to allow an application to take advantage of extensions to the standard for a given system.

How KEEconnection Does It

KEEconnection has an architecture that divides the process of building and operating a database–knowledge base connection into two distinct tasks: first, guided by input from the application developer, a mapping knowledge base is built—a description of how the data structures in a particular database should be

---

KEEconnection is a trademark of IntelliCorp, Inc.
SQL is a registered trademark of International Business Machines.
Knowledge Engineering Environment is a trademark of IntelliCorp, Inc.
KEE is a registered trademark of IntelliCorp, Inc.

related to data structures in a particular KEE knowledge base; then, KEEconnection interprets the mapping knowledge base for the purpose of translating queries and transforming data. This system enables developers to connect a knowledge base to more than one database—even to databases running on different machines—by creating a mapping knowledge base for each connection. Once a mapping is specified, KEEconnection dynamically translates the application's requests for data into SQL queries, manages network communications, and transforms downloaded data into the formats specified by the mapping.

The remainder of this chapter and Figures 1–4 provide an overview of the KEEconnection approach to the construction and operation of a database-knowledge base connection.

Mapping

The first step in connecting a database to a knowledge base is to specify exactly which database structures are to provide data to which knowledge-base structures—to build, in effect, a map of the paths connecting the different data structures. KEEconnection expedites this mapping process by automatically creating, within an application knowledge base specified by the developer, a collection of KEE knowledge-base structures, called class units, that correspond on a one-to-one basis to the database tables selected by the developer (Figure 1). For each column in a table, a slot of the same name in the table's corresponding KEE unit is created. These class units will serve as templates for units that KEEconnection will later create to store downloaded data.

In addition to creating classes in the application knowledge base, KEEconnection builds a separate mapping knowledge base. Units in the mapping knowledge base store information about how columns in database tables are mapped to slots in knowledge base units. Each class unit in the application knowledge base has its own mapping unit to keep track of its database connections.

With the aid of a graphic mapping editor, developers can modify the default table-to-class mapping—renaming classes and slots, creating new units and slots, specifying data transformations and computations—until the mapping knowledge base represents the developer's conception or model of the application. This is the knowledge processing model. In Figure 2, the default mapping is modified to introduce a new slot via a database join.

Conditions may also be built into the mapping that can operate when selecting data to be downloaded. These conditions enable KEEconnection to formulate queries that will select only the data relevant to the analyses performed by the application, thereby minimizing downloading and maximizing application performance.

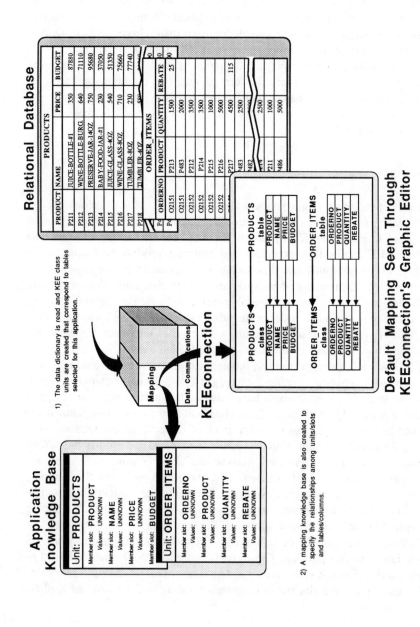

Figure 1. KEEconnection Creates a Default Knowledge Base-Database Connection

292

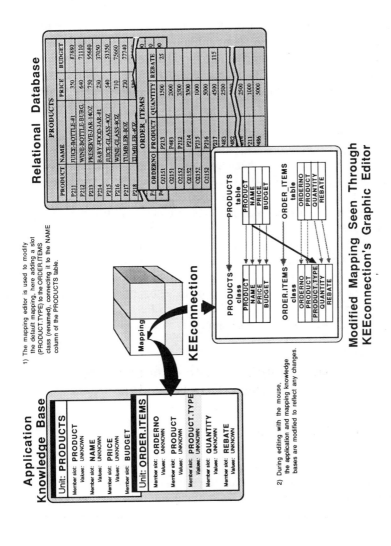

Relational Database

PRODUCTS

PRODUCT	NAME	PRICE	BUDGET
P211	JUICE-BOTTLE-#1	350	87880
P212	WINE-BOTTLE-BURG.	640	71110
P213	PRESERVE-JAR-14OZ	750	95680
P214	BABY-FOOD-JAR-#1	230	37030
P215	JUICE-GLASS-4OZ	540	51350
P216	WINE-GLASS-8OZ	710	75660
P217	TUMBLER-8OZ	250	77740
P218	TUMBLER-4OZ	580	

ORDER ITEMS

ORDERNO	PRODUCT	QUANTITY	REBATE
O2151	P213	1500	25
O2151	P483	2000	
O2152	P212	3500	
O2152	P214	3500	
O2152	P215	1000	
O2152	P216	5000	
	P217	4500	115
	P483	2500	
	P211	2500	
	P486	5000	

Application Knowledge Base

1) The mapping editor is used to modify the default mapping, here adding a slot (PRODUCT.TYPE) to the ORDER.ITEMS class (renamed), connecting it to the NAME column of the PRODUCTS table.

Unit: PRODUCTS

Member slot: **PRODUCT**
Values: UNKNOWN

Member slot: **NAME**
Values: UNKNOWN

Member slot: **PRICE**
Values: UNKNOWN

Member slot: **BUDGET**
Values: UNKNOWN

Unit: ORDER.ITEMS

Member slot: **ORDERNO**
Values: UNKNOWN

Member slot: **PRODUCT**
Values: UNKNOWN

Member slot: **PRODUCT.TYPE**
Values: UNKNOWN

Member slot: **QUANTITY**
Values: UNKNOWN

Member slot: **REBATE**
Values: UNKNOWN

2) During editing with the mouse, the application and mapping knowledge bases are modified to reflect any changes.

Mapping

KEEconnection

PRODUCTS class

PRODUCT
NAME
PRICE
BUDGET

ORDER.ITEMS class

ORDERNO
PRODUCT
PRODUCT.TYPE
QUANTITY
REBATE

PRODUCTS table

PRODUCT
NAME
PRICE
BUDGET

ORDER ITEMS table

ORDERNO
PRODUCT
QUANTITY
REBATE

Modified Mapping Seen Through KEEconnection's Graphic Editor

Figure 2. The Editor is Used to Modify the Default Mapping

293

Translation

Once a mapping has been specified, KEEconnection uses information stored in the mapping knowledge base to generate automatically the SQL commands required to extract the data (Figure 3).

The translator component of the KEEconnection converts data retrieved by the query into KEE formats, performs any conversions specified in the mapping knowledge base, and enters the data into the appropriate application knowledge base structures (Figure 4). KEEconnection also allows the application to upload data so that databases can incorporate the results of a knowledge-based analysis.

What's Ahead

The next section introduces the hypothetical Amber Glass Company and a quality control expert system that accesses the company's database. This example illustrates how a knowledge-based application might interact with a database, and highlights the basic concepts and functionality of the KEEconnection software.

The third section illustrates the process of modifying the mapping knowledge base, followed by an enumeration of a broad range of KEEconnection-supported mappings. In the penultimate section, we discuss how KEEconnection's translation module interacts with mapping knowledge bases to generate SQL queries and transform retrieved data into KEE formats. Finally, we will take a quick look at the architecture of the KEEconnection data communications module.

An Example — The Amber Glass Company Expert System

The Amber Glass Company

The Amber Glass Company manufactures and distributes a variety of glass containers. Their database includes information on customers, sales orders, raw materials purchased from suppliers, and production. The company's KEE-based expert system helps customer service representatives resolve customer problems by interactively accessing and analyzing information stored in the database.

The expert system encapsulates much of the knowledge of the Amber Glass quality assurance engineers and scientists, who have had years of experience diagnosing glassware defects. The system accesses and analyzes data about the plant's production history in order to isolate the probable cause of the defect,

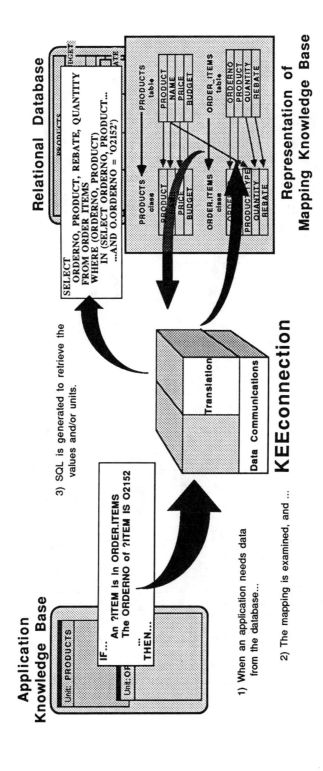

Figure 3. Translation of Requests for Data from the Application into SQL

295

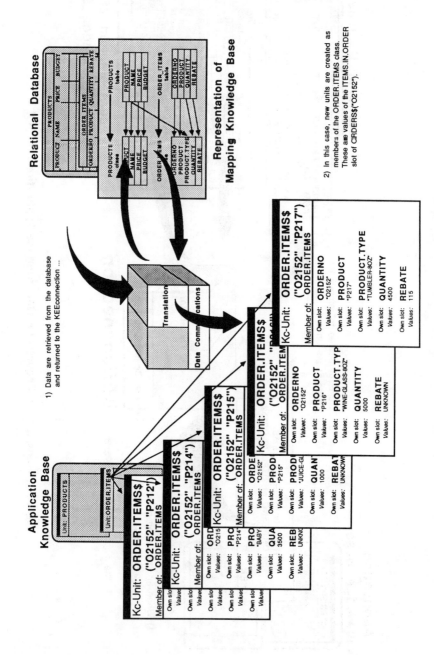

Figure 4. Retrieved Data are Installed in the Application Knowledge Base

296

such as faulty materials, a manufacturing error, or improper packaging. Figure 5 displays the expert system's user interface, a facsimile of a customer complaint form. It is shown as it would appear at the end of the interactive session described below.

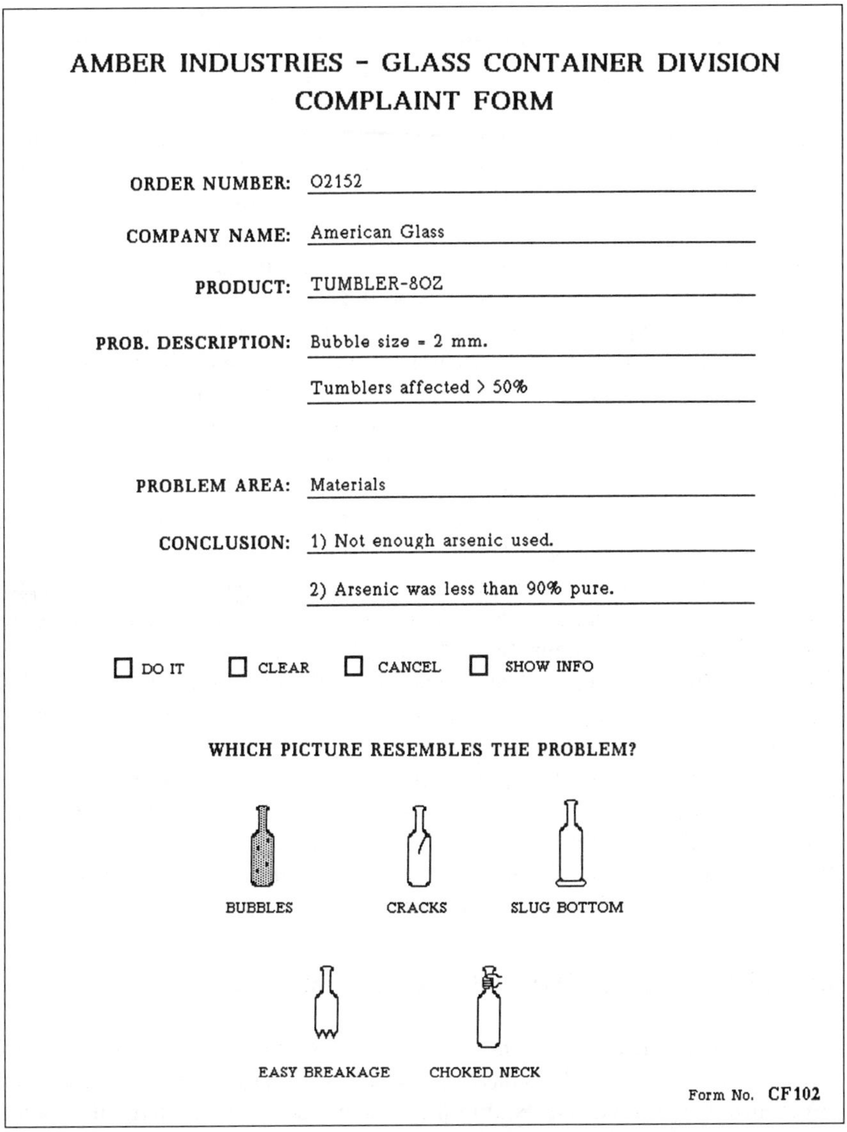

AMBER INDUSTRIES - GLASS CONTAINER DIVISION COMPLAINT FORM

ORDER NUMBER: O2152

COMPANY NAME: American Glass

PRODUCT: TUMBLER-8OZ

PROB. DESCRIPTION: Bubble size = 2 mm.

Tumblers affected > 50%

PROBLEM AREA: Materials

CONCLUSION: 1) Not enough arsenic used.

2) Arsenic was less than 90% pure.

☐ DO IT   ☐ CLEAR   ☐ CANCEL   ☐ SHOW INFO

WHICH PICTURE RESEMBLES THE PROBLEM?

BUBBLES   CRACKS   SLUG BOTTOM

EASY BREAKAGE   CHOKED NECK

Form No. CF102

Figure 5. The Amber Glass Company Expert System's User Interface

A Session With the Amber Glass Expert System

American Glass, an Amber Glass customer, calls to report a defect in the tumblers received in order number O2152. When the Amber Glass service representative types the order number into the complaint form displayed on the computer screen, KEEconnection downloads information about the order from the database, including the company name and address. Upon verification of the address, the KEE-based application enters the company name on the second line of the form.

Next, the application displays a menu listing all the products included in order O2152, from which the service representative selects TUMBLERS-8OZ. After learning that the defect is bubbles in the glass, the customer service representative clicks on the icon on the complaint form that corresponds to the problem.

The expert system begins to determine the cause of the defect by using the information provided by the customer and the data it has already downloaded. As needed, the expert system retrieves additional data from the database or requests information through the customer service representative. In this case, the application prompts the representative to ask the customer how large the bubbles are (2 mm) and what proportion of the batch was affected (> 50%). With this information, the expert system is able to narrow the cause of the defect down to a problem with the materials used to produce the glass, at which point it asks the database to identify the raw materials in the batches of tumblers used to fill the order for American Glass.

The expert system analyzes data from lab tests conducted on the raw materials prior to production. The analysis includes an instruction to the database to perform a statistical examination of tens of thousands of rows of data; this illustrates how the computational capabilities of conventional data processing systems can effectively complement the symbolic reasoning capabilities of knowledge processing systems.

The system concludes that there were two problems: one batch of tumblers was made with impure arsenic; another batch had inadequate arsenic in the mix. The Amber Glass service representative promises to replace the tumblers and forwards the results of the analysis to management for follow-up with the arsenic supplier and factory supervisor.

Behind the Scenes: The Amber Glass Database

In order to understand how KEEconnection enables the expert system to interact with and enhance the Amber Glass database, it is necessary to examine how data is organized in the database. Four of the database tables that contain information used by the expert system are: CUSTOMERS, ORDERS, ORDER_ITEMS, and PRODUCTS. Figure 6 displays a few rows of each of the tables.

ORDERS

CUSTOMER	DATE$ORDERED	DATE$RECEIVED	DATE$SHIPPED	ORDERNO
C206	19-Oct-86	15-Dec-86	12-Nov-86	O2152
C183	18-Oct-86	19-Nov-86	5-Nov-86	O2151

CUSTOMERS

CUSTOMER	NAME	ADDR	CITY	STATE	ZIP	DATE$START
C206	American Glass	1000 Boardwalk	Atlantic City	NJ	O2152	19-Jul-77
C183	Crystal Reflections	1819 N. Boundary	Sunnyvale	CA	94564	17-Jun-81

ORDER ITEMS

ORDERNO	PRODUCT	QUANTITY	REBATE
O2151	P213	1500	25
O2151	P483	2000	
O2152	P212	3500	
O2152	P214	3500	
O2152	P215	1000	
O2152	P216	5545	115
O2152	P217	4500	

PRODUCTS

PRODUCT	NAME	PRICE	BUDGET
P211	Juice-Bottle-#1	350	87880
P212	Wine-Bottle-Burg.	640	71118
P213	Preserve-Jar-14OZ	750	95680
P214	Baby-Food-Jar-#1	230	37050
P215	Juice-Glass-4OZ	540	51350
P216	Juice-Glass-8OZ	710	75668
P217	Tumbler-8OZ	230	77749

Figure 6. Sample Rows from Tables in the Amber Glass Database

The ORDERS table stores each order's unique identifier, the order's shipment date, and the identifier unique to the customer placing the order. The CUSTOMERS table also stores each customer's identification number, plus the company name, address (four columns: street, city, state, and zip), and the date the company became a customer. Note that since the ORDERS and CUSTOMERS tables both have a CUSTOMER column, the information stored in the separate tables may be combined by joining on these columns.

Each row of the ORDER_ITEMS table corresponds to a single line item in a customer order. The rows contain: the quantity of the product ordered, the product's identifier, and the number of the order in which the line item appears. Again, the ORDERNO columns of the ORDER_ITEMS and ORDERS tables may be joined. Likewise, the ORDER_ITEMS and PRODUCTS tables may be joined on their PRODUCT columns. The PRODUCTS table also provides columns for listing each product's name, price, and budget.

This fragmentation of data about orders, customers, and products supports efficient processing in conventional data processing applications, but at the expense of making certain information less accessible. For example, starting with an order number, it would be necessary for a service representative to go through three other tables to determine both the customer name and the names of the items in the order. Standard relational database interfaces help with such retrievals; they do not, however, readily support the interactive, reasoning-directed access often required by knowledge systems. They do not support backchaining for inference, tracing mechanisms, triggers (active values), or graphics. The extensive support for these features in KEE is what makes having KEE and access to databases so valuable.

The Default Mapping

We now look at how KEEconnection initially connected the Amber Glass database to the expert system knowledge base. As was mentioned in the previous section, the default application knowledge base and mapping knowledge base created by KEEconnection simply duplicate the structure and organization of the database.

In the application knowledge base. KEEconnection reads the database's data dictionary and creates a class unit to represent each table selected from the database; each column in the table is represented in its corresponding class by a slot of the same name. The data dictionary tables may be consulted at any time. For example, a developer may want to verify that a knowledge base application still has a valid mapping to the database.

In the mapping knowledge base. For each class, KEEconnection creates a class map unit to store information about how data is mapped from tables and their columns in the database, to descendants of the class and their slots in the application knowledge base; the default mapping stored in a class's class map simply "connects" the class to its like-named table, and each of the class's slots to its corresponding column.

When downloading a row of a table based on this default connection, KEE-connection simply creates a child of the appropriate class unit, and then transfers the row's column values to their analogous slots in this new *member* unit. The default mapping performs no data conversions; that is, string values in the database remain strings in the knowledge base, and numbers remain numbers.

An example of a KEE unit, ORDERS$("O2152"), created from the default mapping is shown in Figure 7a. Note that the customer slot in the figure has a string value C206.

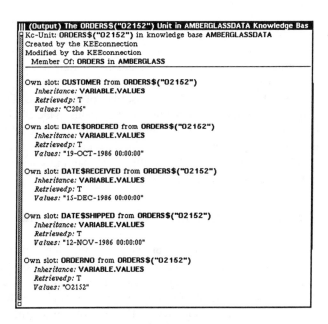

Figure 7a. The ORDERS$("O2152") Unit,
Created with the Default Mapping

Downloading Data

The first step in the Amber Glass session, downloading order O2152, could be performed using the default database-knowledge base mapping. When the Amber Glass service representative typed the order number into the complaint form displayed on the screen, the following KEEconnection function call was triggered:

```
(DOWNLOAD
        '(and  (?ORDER is in ORDERS)
               (the ORDERNO of ?ORDER is "O2152")))
```

(that is, "Download the order whose order number is O2152").

The mapping between the ORDERS table in the database and the ORDERS class in the expert system knowledge base is a simple one-to-one mapping. The SQL automatically generated to perform the retrieval is quite simple:

```
SELECT ORDERNO, DATE$SHIPPED,
       DATE$RECEIVED, DATE$ORDERED,
       CUSTOMER
FROM   AGMKT.ORDERS
WHERE  ORDERNO = 'O2152'
```

The application created ORDERS$("O2152") as a member of the ORDERS class in the knowledge base, and installed values from the table as slot values in the unit. Of course, the triggering of the download function and the SQL generation were transparent to the service representative.

The unit named ORDERS$("O2152") is a member of the class ORDERS. It is named this way, by default, to guarantee that the key fields in the ORDERS table may be derived from the name. The key fields are needed because KEEconnection sometimes needs to find the row or rows in the database that correspond to a given KEE unit. Users are free to supply alternative naming schemes, as long as the key field(s) can be derived from the name.

Modifying the Default Mapping: Creating a Foreign Key

The next step in the expert system session, verifying the name and address of the customer associated with order O2152, used a modification of the default mapping. Since the name and address of the customer is contained in the CUSTOMERS table, and not in the ORDERS table, it is necessary to join the rows of the two tables on their common CUSTOMER column in order to access the name and address data. CUSTOMER serves as a foreign key.

In KEE, such a join may be accomplished by placing a pointer to a CUSTOMERS' member unit in the ORDERS unit's customer slot. In this example, the customer slot of ORDERS$("O2152"), one of the units KEEconnection created when it downloaded the order in the previous step, has as its value another unit, COMPANY-C206. The company unit was created when the order unit was downloaded, though its slots were left empty at that time. This unit is not named in the default way, since both CUSTOMERS' and SUPPLIERS' units will be companies, and some suppliers are also customers.

A difference between a foreign key join in a database and a unit pointer in a knowledge base is that the SQL join must be explicitly stated at the time data is selected; with KEEconnection, the link can be built into the mapping. There is no restriction to foreign keys; a table (and hence, a class) may have an attribute that is self referencing.

In the example above, the developer edited the default mapping between the CUSTOMER column of the ORDERS table and the customer slot of the ORDERS class. It was changed to specify that the string value in the table should be transformed into a KEE unit when downloaded. Moreover, the developer specified that this unit should be a member of at least the CUSTOMERS class.

Consequently, when ORDERS$("O2152") was downloaded, KEEconnection also verified that the COMPANY-C206 unit did not already exist, and then created it as a member of the CUSTOMERS class unit. If COMPANY-C206 had existed, then a new unit would not have been created. Figure 7b shows the downloaded ORDERS$("O2152") unit with its complete mapping done. The value class (KEE's notion of domain) of the customer slot has changed from STRING (Figure 7a) to CUSTOMERS, and the value of the customer slot in the downloaded ORDERS$("O2152") unit has changed from "C206," a string, to the COMPANY-C206 unit.

After the downloading of order O2152 is complete, another instruction tells KEEconnection to install the values from customer C206's row(s) in the CUSTOMERS table into the slots of unit COMPANY-C206, thereby making the customer's name and address available to the expert system. This is accomplished simply by the application requesting the name and address of the customer placing the order.

Another Modification: Mapping to a New Slot

The application needs access to the line items in an order so that a particular product may be identified, and then information about the associated production runs may be determined. To provide this access, the items.in.order slot is defined using the KEEconnection editor (Figure 8). This slot has a value class or domain of ORDER.ITEMS, a class whose members are units representing individual products in an order. The class ORDER.ITEMS has been renamed from the default name of the ORDER_ITEMS table.

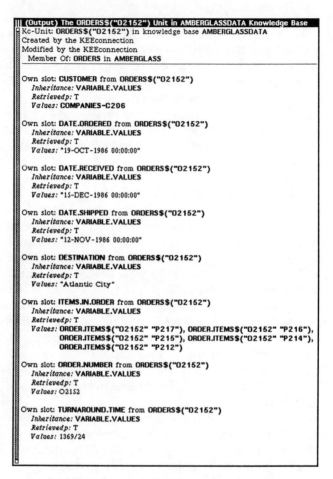

```
(Output) The ORDERS$("02152") Unit in AMBERGLASSDATA Knowledge Base
Kc-Unit: ORDERS$("02152") in knowledge base AMBERGLASSDATA
Created by the KEEconnection
Modified by the KEEconnection
  Member Of: ORDERS in AMBERGLASS

Own slot: CUSTOMER from ORDERS$("02152")
   Inheritance: VARIABLE.VALUES
   Retrievedp: T
   Values: COMPANIES-C206

Own slot: DATE.ORDERED from ORDERS$("02152")
   Inheritance: VARIABLE.VALUES
   Retrievedp: T
   Values: "19-OCT-1986 00:00:00"

Own slot: DATE.RECEIVED from ORDERS$("02152")
   Inheritance: VARIABLE.VALUES
   Retrievedp: T
   Values: "15-DEC-1986 00:00:00"

Own slot: DATE.SHIPPED from ORDERS$("02152")
   Inheritance: VARIABLE.VALUES
   Retrievedp: T
   Values: "12-NOV-1986 00:00:00"

Own slot: DESTINATION from ORDERS$("02152")
   Inheritance: VARIABLE.VALUES
   Retrievedp: T
   Values: "Atlantic City"

Own slot: ITEMS.IN.ORDER from ORDERS$("02152")
   Inheritance: VARIABLE.VALUES
   Retrievedp: T
   Values: ORDER.ITEMS$("02152" "P217"), ORDER.ITEMS$("02152" "P216"),
           ORDER.ITEMS$("02152" "P215"), ORDER.ITEMS$("02152" "P214"),
           ORDER.ITEMS$("02152" "P212")

Own slot: ORDER.NUMBER from ORDERS$("02152")
   Inheritance: VARIABLE.VALUES
   Retrievedp: T
   Values: O2152

Own slot: TURNAROUND.TIME from ORDERS$("02152")
   Inheritance: VARIABLE.VALUES
   Retrievedp: T
   Values: 1369/24
```

Figure 7b. The ORDERS$("02152") Unit,
Created with a Complete Mapping

The use of the mapping of rows from the ORDER_ITEMS table into the items.in.order slot, in units of type ORDERS, involves constructing units in KEE as slot values that are specifically linked to a particular order.

Adding Structure: Mapping One Table to Multiple Classes

Units in KEE knowledge bases are organized into multilevel hierarchies. A class of *objects* (e.g., DEFECTS) may give rise to more specialized subclasses (e.g., SHAPE.DEFECTS, PROCESSING.DEFECTS) which may, in turn, spawn

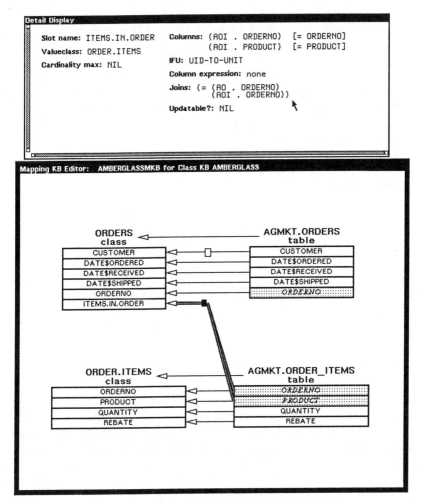

Detail Display

Slot name: ITEMS.IN.ORDER
Valueclass: ORDER.ITEMS
Cardinality max: NIL

Columns: (AOI . ORDERNO)   [= ORDERNO]
         (AOI . PRODUCT)   [= PRODUCT]
IFU: UID-TO-UNIT
Column expression: none
Joins: (= (AO . ORDERNO)
          (AOI . ORDERNO))
Updatable?: NIL

Mapping KB Editor: AMBERGLASSMKB for Class KB AMBERGLASS

ORDERS class — AGMKT.ORDERS table

ORDERS class
CUSTOMER
DATE$ORDERED
DATE$RECEIVED
DATE$SHIPPED
ORDERNO
ITEMS.IN.ORDER

AGMKT.ORDERS table
CUSTOMER
DATE$ORDERED
DATE$RECEIVED
DATE$SHIPPED
ORDERNO

ORDER.ITEMS class — AGMKT.ORDER_ITEMS table

ORDER.ITEMS class
ORDERNO
PRODUCT
QUANTITY
REBATE

AGMKT.ORDER_ITEMS table
ORDERNO
PRODUCT
QUANTITY
REBATE

**Figure 8. Defining the ITEMS.IN.ORDER Slot
with the KEEconnection Editor**

even more specialized subclasses (e.g., BULGED.WARE and SUNKEN.WARE, DIRT.MARKS and FLANGES), ad infinitum, until a sufficiently precise level of detail has been reached.

This structure has several benefits, among them: the ability, via inheritance, to infer information about an object simply by virtue of its membership in a class (e.g., "all jars have wide mouths") and the ability to improve the efficiency of the reasoning component of an expert system application by organizing rules into sets (e.g., JAR.RULES) that apply only to members of a specific class of objects (e.g., JARS).

KEEconnection enables developers to build conditions and constraints into a mapping that will add structure to information as it is downloaded from a database. In the Amber Glass application, for example, PRODUCTS are broken into subclasses—BOTTLES, JARS, and TUMBLERS—as they're downloaded.

This was accomplished by mapping the single PRODUCTS table into the subclasses. Each of the new class maps includes membership conditions, specified via the mapping editor, that classify each downloaded row from the PRODUCTS table on the basis of its name.

The following instruction downloads the products in order O2152:

(DOWNLOAD
```
'(and (?PRODUCT is in PRODUCTS)
      (?ITEM is in ORDER.ITEMS)
      (the ORDERNO of ?ITEM is O2152)
      (the PRODUCT of ?ITEM is ?PRODUCT)))
```

As Figures 9 and 10 indicate, the products became members of the appropriate subclasses when downloaded. For example, product P217, the 8 OZ. TUMBLER, has been downloaded as a member of the TUMBLERS class. Glasses are classified as TUMBLERS according to the Amber Glass mapping.

Links to Reasoning Mechanisms

During the expert system session, information entered by the service representative through the complaint form interface was automatically transferred into slots in a unit, called THE.COMPLAINT, in the application knowledge base. As the expert system began reasoning, it also added information from the database to this unit, at one point determining which production batches (the interesting-batch slot of THE.COMPLAINT) were the sources of the defective tumblers in order O2152.

Finally, the expert system runs rules that result in the impure arsenic diagnosis. These include the following rule:

(IF
```
(an INTERESTING-BATCH of THE.COMPLAINT is ?BATCH)
(LISP (IMPURITY-STAT-TEST 'ARSENIC ?BATCH 0.9 0.1))
```

THEN
```
(a PROBLEM of THE.COMPLAINT is IMPURE.ARSENIC)
(an AGENT of THE.COMPLAINT is ?BATCH)
(the ANSWER of THE.COMPLAINT is "Arsenic was less than 90%
pure"))
```

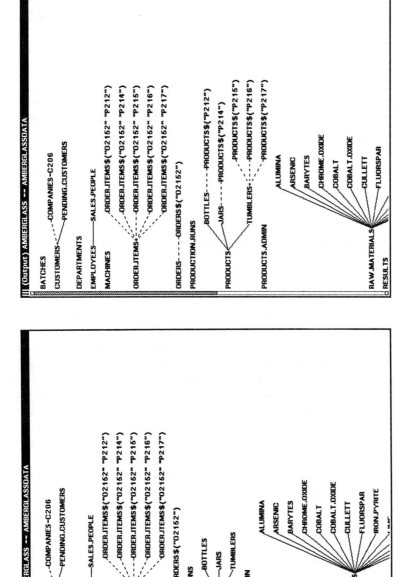

Figure 9. The Amberglass Knowledge Base
After Several Units Have Been Downloaded

Figure 10. The Amberglass Knowledge Base
With Units Classified Under Subclasses

307

Of particular interest is the call to a LISP function (IMPURITY–STAT–TEST) from within the rule. This function causes the database to conduct the statistical analysis of tens of thousands of rows, and returns the results of that query to the knowledge base.

Summary

In this section we've looked at some of the ways in which an expert system might use KEEconnection to interactively retrieve and analyze data. In the Amber Glass application, KEE and KEEconnection enable an end-user to benefit from three sources of information that normally would not be available concurrently: the expertise of specialists, encoded in the application's rules and methods; data on customers and manufacturing history, stored in a database; and dialogue with the customer.

Editing a Mapping Knowledge Base

The KEEconnection Mapping Editor

KEEconnection's graphic mapping editor enables specification of a database-knowledge base mapping by manipulating a graphic representation of the mapping knowledge base. As the developer manipulates objects on the screen, KEEconnection modifies units in the underlying mapping knowledge base and, if necessary, classes in the application knowledge base.

The most important and extensive automation feature in the editor is its ability to read a data dictionary and build the default mapping. This enables the developer to almost immediately download data from the database. The mapping editor is used infrequently: first, when the developer builds the initial mapping, and thereafter only as changes in the database and/or application require.

In this section we will look at how the mapping editor was used to implement some of the mappings used in the Amber Glass quality assurance application.

Using the Mapping Editor to Create a Foreign Key

Figure 11a shows the KEEconnection mapping editor interface soon after the creation of the default Amber Glass database-knowledge base connection. The current task, Edit Slot Maps, has been selected by clicking the mouse on its name in the small Tasks window at the upper left of the screen. The large, central window (labeled *Mapping KB Editor*) is the *canvas* where the mappings between tables and units are represented graphically. On the sides of the canvas are

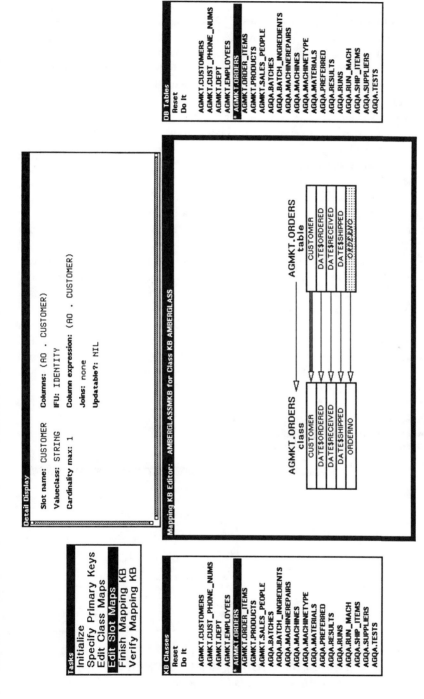

Figure 11a. The KEEconnection Mapping Editor User Interface

309

windows that list the database tables (*DB Tables*, at right) and the classes that
have connections to those tables (*KB Classes*, at left).

In this figure the ORDERS table (called AGMKT.ORDERS in the figures, as
AGMKT is the CREATOR of that table) has already been brought to the canvas
by selecting its name in the DB Tables window with the mouse; KEEconnection
simultaneously brought the ORDERS unit to the canvas. Note that KEEconnection also has drawn arrows to represent the default table-unit and column-slot
mappings. (The grayed-over ORDERNO column in the ORDERS table representation indicates that the developer designated this column the primary key for
the table in an earlier step.)

The bold (double) arrow connecting the CUSTOMER column and slot indicates that this mapping has been selected for editing. The information about the
mapping that appears in the *Detail Display* window running across the top of the
screen is *active*. That is, clicking on the text with the mouse will elicit a response
from the mapping editor. In this case, the developer has clicked on the word
IDENTITY, the name of an *interface function unit* that controls how database
values of the column are converted into slot values (see Figure 11b). (IDENTITY
preserves the format and value used by the database; e.g., string values remain
strings, numbers remain numbers.)

KEEconnection responds to the selection of IDENTITY by displaying a menu
of interface function unit names (seen overlapping the editing canvas and detail
display). Selecting the UID-TO-UNIT option tells KEEconnection that values
from the CUSTOMER column should be transformed into unit structures when
downloaded into customer slots.

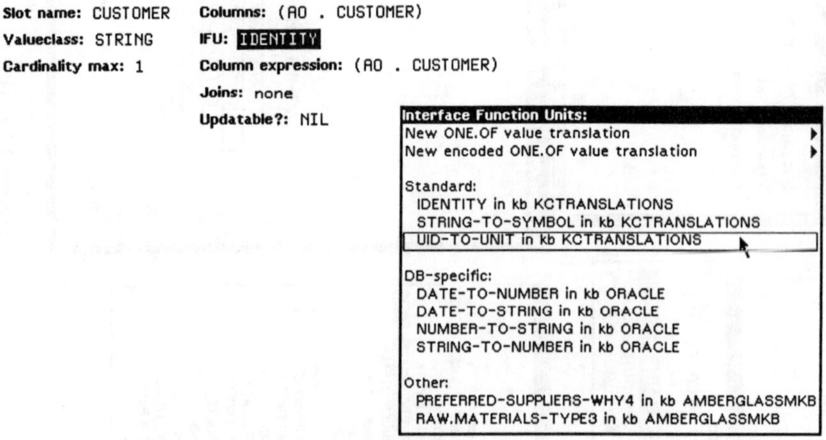

Slot name: CUSTOMER   **Columns:** (AO . CUSTOMER)
Valueclass: STRING   **IFU:** IDENTITY
Cardinality max: 1   **Column expression:** (AO . CUSTOMER)
Joins: none
Updatable?: NIL

Interface Function Units:
New ONE.OF value translation
New encoded ONE.OF value translation

Standard:
IDENTITY in kb KCTRANSLATIONS
STRING-TO-SYMBOL in kb KCTRANSLATIONS
UID-TO-UNIT in kb KCTRANSLATIONS

DB-specific:
DATE-TO-NUMBER in kb ORACLE
DATE-TO-STRING in kb ORACLE
NUMBER-TO-STRING in kb ORACLE
STRING-TO-NUMBER in kb ORACLE

Other:
PREFERRED-SUPPLIERS-WHY4 in kb AMBERGLASSMKB
RAW.MATERIALS-TYPE3 in kb AMBERGLASSMKB

**Figure 11b. Specifying that CUSTOMER Slot
Values are Units (Instead of Strings)**

At this point it is necessary to identify which class unit should act as the parent of the units created and installed in the customer slot. As seen in Figure 11c, KEEconnection helps out by presenting a menu of candidate classes that can potentially be joined to the ORDERS unit. In the current implementation, this list is based on matching number and datatypes of primary key attributes.

When CUSTOMERS is selected from the menu, KEEconnection changes the value class of the customer slot from STRING to the class CUSTOMERS (Figure 11d). Note also that the arrow representing the mapping now has a little box on it to designate that a conversion function is in effect. Now, whenever a row from the ORDERS table is downloaded, KEEconnection will automatically create a unit as a member of the CUSTOMERS class and install that unit in the value of the downloaded order's customer slot.

Slot name: CUSTOMER   **Columns:** (AO . CUSTOMER)

Valueclass: STRING   **IFU:** IDENTITY

Cardinality max: 1   **Column expression:** (AO . CUSTOMER)

  Joins: none

  Updatable?: NIL

```
Classes which could match UIDs
CUSTOMERS of AMBERGLASS
ORDERS of AMBERGLASS
PREFERRED-SUPPLIERS of AMBERGLASS
PRODUCTS of AMBERGLASS
SUPPLIERS of AMBERGLASS
```

Figure 11c. Specifying the Parent Class for the CUSTOMER Slot Values

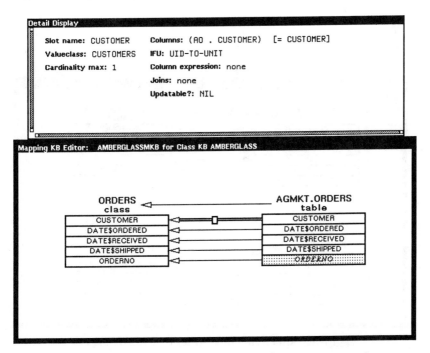

Detail Display

  Slot name: CUSTOMER   **Columns:** (AO . CUSTOMER)   [= CUSTOMER]

  Valueclass: CUSTOMERS   **IFU:** UID-TO-UNIT

  Cardinality max: 1   **Column expression:** none

    Joins: none

    Updatable?: NIL

Mapping KB Editor: AMBERGLASSMKB for Class KB AMBERGLASS

ORDERS class		AGMKT.ORDERS table
CUSTOMER		CUSTOMER
DATE$ORDERED		DATE$ORDERED
DATE$RECEIVED		DATE$RECEIVED
DATE$SHIPPED		DATE$SHIPPED
ORDERNO		ORDERNO

Figure 11d. The Finished Slot Map for the CUSTOMER Slot

Mapping to a New Slot

It is possible to map multiple columns from one or more tables, or even multiples rows (as multiple values), into a single slot. For example, an order typically has several related rows in the ORDER_ITEMS table, joined on their order numbers. The developer might have KEEconnection create units representing each order item in an order (these are created as members of the ORDER.ITEMS class), and install the collection of units in a single slot (items.in.order) in the unit representing the order. Figure 8 showed the result of creating the new items in order slot, and identified the columns which contribute the data to determine ORDER.ITEMS units and the specification of the join conditions. In Figure 12, the developer is specifying the join that defines which ORDER_ITEMS rows are to be used to determine ORDER.ITEMS units as values for the items.in.order slot.

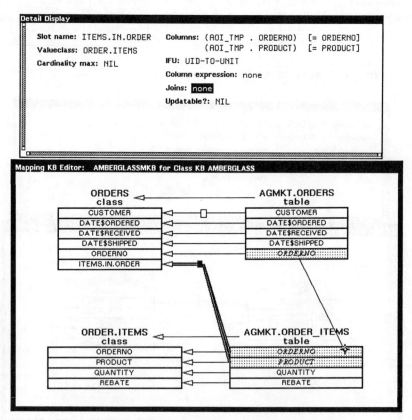

**Figure 12. Specifying how Rows of ORDER_ITEMS
Join to Rows of ORDERS**

A New, Calculated Slot

The turnaround.time slot in ORDERS (Figure 7b) is defined to be the difference between an order date and a date of receipt. This calculation may be done as part of the retrieval in the database, or in KEE using both date columns. The developer of the Amber Glass system calculated the difference in KEE so that special handling of missing values and rounding to weeks could be accomplished.

One.of

It is often desirable to transform the values used by a database into a form that is easier to interpret in the knowledge base. For example, the TYPE column of the MATERIALS table has values of the form MAT22, and so forth. These values can be mapped into units, with names such as SAND or COBALT, by creating a One.Of translation table like the one shown in the Detail Display of Figure 13.

This mapping provides slot values that are themselves units, so that rules and procedures may refer to properties and attributes of structured objects like SAND rather than having to compute a relationship using the strings from the database.

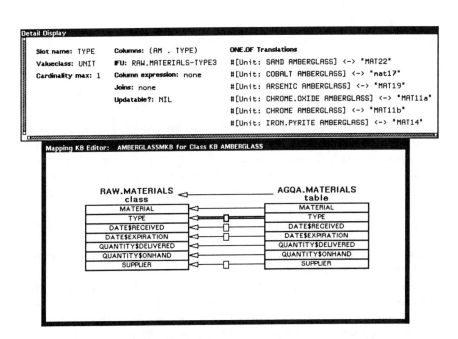

**Figure 13. The TYPE Slot Uses a
Translation Table to Map Strings into Units**

314 Abarbanel, Tou, and Gilbert

Also, rules may refer to SAND and COBALT and other materials by name rather than by their code names from the database.

Mappings Supported

A Broad Range of Mappings

KEEconnection mappings do more than simply connect database and knowledge base structures. Properly used, they enable developers to create a knowledge-based view of data that greatly enriches its value to complex applications. Among the mappings and data transformations supported are:

- the mapping of multiple tables to a single class;
- the mapping of one table to multiple classes;
- the mapping of multiple columns of a table(s) to the value or values of a single slot;
- the mapping of one column of a table to the values of multiple slots;
- the transformation of column values into knowledge base units, numbers, strings, or other types of data structures; and
- the computation of new values, either on the database side (e.g., statistical analyses) or on the knowledge base side (e.g., via reasoning).

Table-to-Class Mappings

Using Membership Conditions to Restrict Downloading. The ORDERS table contains information about all the orders ever placed with the Amber Glass Company. A particular analysis, however, might require only this decade's orders. It is possible to restrict the downloading of data to those rows of the ORDERS table whose DATE$ORDERED column has a date later than January, 1980. This is accomplished by entering the restriction as a *membership condition* for the ORDERS table-class mapping.

Mapping One Table to Multiple Classes. Membership conditions also provide a mechanism for sorting rows of data from a single table into members of different subclasses. For example, the SUPPLIERS table in the Amber Glass database contains a MATERIALTYPE column that describes the material (e.g., SAND, ARSENIC, COBALT) provided by a supplier. It is possible to define subclasses of SUPPLIERS (e.g., ALUMINA.SUPPLIERS, ARSENIC.SUPPLIERS) and specify appropriate membership conditions, for example:

    MATERIALTYPE = ALUMINA.

KEEconnection will then use these conditions to classify the rows of data as they are retrieved from the table and downloaded into KEE units.

An alternate way of dividing a single table into multiple classes is to vertically partition the table, that is, map subsets of the table's columns into different classes. The PRODUCTS table, for example, contains certain columns that describe products as things (e.g., its product number, name, description) and other columns that describe products as departmental entities (e.g., budget). This conceptual distinction can be made explicit by mapping the PRODUCTS table's columns into two separate classes:

PRODUCT–DESCRIPTION and PRODUCT–ADMINISTRATION.

Mapping Multiple Tables to a Single Class. The Amber Glass database includes two tables called SUPPLIERS and PREFERRED. The SUPPLIERS table has information common to all suppliers, while PREFERRED contains special columns that apply only to preferred suppliers. The KEE application developer might define PREFERRED–SUPPLIERS as a new subclass of SUPPLIERS that contains all the slots in the SUPPLIERS class, plus a why slot (mapped from the PREFERRED table's WHY column). The developer can specify that membership in the subclass is conditional on the supplier number appearing in both tables. Figure 14 shows how this mapping is represented in the KEEconnection editor.

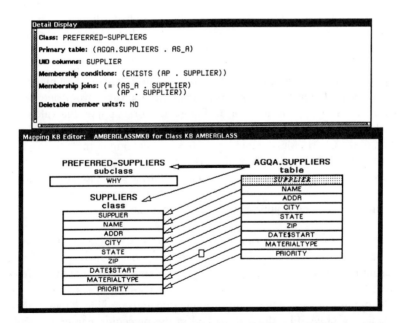

Figure 14. The PREFERRED-SUPPLIERS Subclass is Mapped from the Rows of Two Tables

Column-to-Slot Mappings

One-to-One Value Transformations. This type of mapping was described above for the TYPE column in the MATERIALS table. It is also used to give names to shifts (e.g., day, night, evening) from the productions runs table where they are stored as numbers.

One-to-Many Value Transformations. In good database design, columns, unlike KEE slots, do not contain more than one value. Database developers often circumvent this stricture by assigning codes to values and then stringing a number of coded values together. For example, a value of NI in the WHY column of PREFERRED supplier table might really stand for "Nearby, Inexpensive." Developers may specify an interface function unit containing an Encoded.One.Of translation table that can then be used to transform such encoded multiple values into their individual values. The separator character, if any, may be specified as a value in the interface function unit. Predicates on the KEE side may refer to the slot values, like NEARBY, without users having to construct the proper SQL queries to handle decoding the possible strings in the database values.

Mapping Multiple Columns Or Rows Into a Single Slot. Slots in KEE can have multiple values. It is possible to map multiple columns from one or more tables, or even multiple rows, into a single slot. For example, each ORDER may have several corresponding rows in the ORDER_ITEMS table. The items.in.order slot is such a slot, and in this case, a slot whose values are units.

Computed Data Transformations. The *column expression* of a slot map may be used to tell KEEconnection how to compute a slot value from one or more column values mapped to the slot. In Figure 15, for example, the value of the price slot of an ORDER.ITEMS unit is specified to be the product of the DISCOUNT column of the CUSTOMERS table, the QUANTITY column of the ORDER_ITEMS table, and the PRICE column of the PRODUCTS table. Slots may have their values computed by functions that run in the database or in the knowledge base, or by remote programs called from the workstation. Computations may involve reasoning or statistics if appropriate for the application.

User-Defined Data Transformations. Developers may also create their own functions which KEEconnection will then use when transforming database values into slot values. An example was given above to compute the difference between two dates. The types of transformations available are organized as a hierarchy of units in KEE. These interface function units provide default functions for managing tables like those described in the preceding paragraph, and for calling external routines or sets of rules for deriving the values to be stored in slots in the application knowledge base.

Like relational database views, these transformations may or may not be reversible. If an inverting function is provided, slot values may be converted and written to the database. The system provides several classes of these transformation units; the methods they have can also be used in user-written versions.

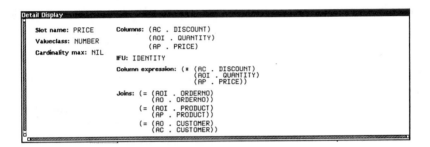

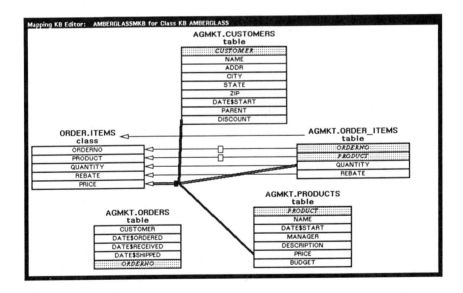

Figure 15. The PRICE Slot Computes its
Value from Columns in Three Tables

How KEEconnection Uses the
Mapping Knowledge Base

Automatic SQL Generation

Once the mapping knowledge base is built, KEEconnection handles most aspects of data retrieval. Requests for data by a KEE application are automatically translated into SQL; the SQL is sent to the database; and the retrieved data are returned and transformed into units and slot values according to the information in the mapping knowledge base.

The SQL generator and data transformer free the developer from the task of writing SQL (which can be quite complex for complicated mappings) and embedding it in the application. They also allow the developer to think and work from a KEE point of view—with objects and concepts—instead of worrying about the relationship between the knowledge base and the database. Moreover, the dynamic generation of SQL, as an application runs, eliminates the burden of having to specify in advance precisely which units should be downloaded; with KEEconnection the reasoning in the application can drive this specification.

Even when database management system vendors adhere to the ANSI standard, minor differences may still arise in the way different products handle SQL code. KEEconnection's SQL translator accommodates these differences by tailoring the SQL code it generates to the particular database system being accessed. This is handled by having knowledge bases in the system which specify the differences among versions of SQL.

Functions are provided for printing the SQL generated, or for saving it to a file, so that the SQL can be used for reports or for other purposes, including database administration.

Controlling the Downloading of Data

The downloading of data is under the control of the developer. Depending on the requirements of the application, downloading may occur in one large step, or in smaller, discrete steps.

In the first scenario, the application may perform an analysis to determine a specified set of units and slots to download into the application. This approach is useful when the application needs to retrieve and reason over a fairly large set of data whose characteristics can be determined in advance.

Alternately, the system may retrieve the slot values for a few units or a single unit, perhaps even one slot at a time, and then after additional processing, retrieve more. This is useful when the application needs a small amount of data at a particular point during reasoning.

Data Retrieval By Rules

The KEE system's TellAndAsk™ query-and-assertion language, which forms the basis for KEE's rule system, has been extended to enable the rule system to download units. The developer can build instructions to download data into rules, which are themselves KEE units. This may occur after the left-hand, IF side of a rule has been matched by putting an instruction in the rule's download-after-premise slot, or after the right-hand, THEN side has been matched by putting an instruction in the rule's download-after-conclusion slot. Bindings of variables in the download instructions derive from the bindings available when the particular rule is evaluated.

For example, the following rule narrows down the cause of a glass defect to a materials problem:

(IF
(the ORDER.ITEM of THE.COMPLAINT is ?ITEM)
(?PRODUCT is in PRODUCTS)
(the PRODUCT of ?ITEM is ?PRODUCT)
(the DESCRIPTION of ?PRODUCT is like "%WINE%")
(the DEFECT of THE.COMPLAINT is BUBBLES)

THEN
(the PROBLEM.AREA of THE.COMPLAINT is MATERIALS))

Since this rule determines a problem area, not a specific error, further analysis must be performed—and additional data downloaded. The following instruction, placed in the rule's download-after-premise slot, tells KEEconnection to generate an SQL query to download data on each of the PRODUCTION.RUNS that contributed product to the defective item in the order. In effect, this makes the rule download production runs data only for wine-glass orders which have material defects:

(and
(?RUN is in PRODUCTION.RUNS)
(the PRODUCTION.RUNS of ?ITEM is ?RUN))

Efficiency

KEEconnection gives the developer other types of control over downloading. The function that triggers downloading can be given an argument to limit the number of units downloaded, and units and slots can be deleted, if desired, as part of the application.

TellAndAsk is a trademark of IntelliCorp, Inc.

Because of the flexibility of the downloading system, the developer can optimize an application's data retrieval. KEEconnection adds to this efficiency via a caching mechanism that checks whether a slot value has already been retrieved before going out to the database.

In addition, in order to accommodate the large amounts of data that KEE applications may download, data are downloaded into a special type of KEE unit called a KC-UNIT. A KC-UNIT requires much less storage than a normal KEE unit. In a KC-UNIT, the only local information about a slot is its value and a flag indicating whether the value was retrieved from the database. Other information, like value class and active values, are stored only in the class units. This other information is used for coercion of values and attachment of methods to slots. By making KC-UNITS as small as possible, KEEconnection is able to download two orders of magnitude more units into the virtual memory of a workstation.

Uploading Data to the Database

KEEconnection supports data transfer from a knowledge base to a database so that the database can reflect the results of a knowledge-based analysis. For example, the customer service representative using the Amber Glass application may need to correct a customer's address or, at the end of the session, enter the expert system's findings into complaint report tables.

Utilities make it possible to update column values, create rows in tables, and delete rows from tables—all from within a knowledge-based application. Uploading is under the programmatic control of the system developer. Transactions are supported so that database and corresponding knowledge-base changes may be committed and/or rolled back.

Changes to a database are subject to several built-in checks, including the database's own access privileges. Upload and commit are independent procedures; no final changes are made to the database until the commit command is issued. Moreover, KEEconnection will not upload data for a slot unless the developer has explicitly set a slot's mapping to indicate that the slot is *updatable*.

Communicating With the Database

The KEEconnection communications software is built upon commercial network communications packages (e.g., DECnet™, TCP/IP, SNA). In a typical

---

DECnet is a trademark of Digital Equipment Corporation.

configuration, KEE and the KEE-based applications will reside on workstations, and databases will reside on separate database servers.

The communications code includes software on the workstation to talk to the network, software on the database server to talk to the network, and software on the server to talk to the database. The database server may, in fact, be the same CPU as the workstation, in which case interprocess communication may be used rather than the network.

In a typical download operation, the KEEconnection sends an SQL select request through the network. The software on the database server receives the request and sends it to the database management system on the server. Finally, the reply travels the reverse path back to the application where further processing of one or more column values may occur. Communications is buffered in both directions. Network code supports error free transmission.

This software also detects such problems as network and mainframe crashes, network unavailability, incorrect passwords, and so forth, and reports them to the user. It will also reopen faulty connections automatically, where possible.

KEEconnection utilizes whatever facilities are provided by the database management system for security, including login/password and time locks. Grants and file access permissions are controlled by the database and operating systems on the database server.

Summary

This chapter has provided an introduction to the KEEconnection, a software bridge between knowledge-base applications and relational databases. This system allows developers of expert systems and other knowledge processing applications to use the valuable data stored in large corporate and special purpose engineering and scientific databases. The mapping facilities of the KEEconnection provide a flexible environment for establishing and maintaining relationships among tables and their columns in a database management system, and KEE classes and slots in knowledge bases.

KEEconnection may be used to download information into a knowledge base and to upload altered or newly computed information into tables in databases. The system takes advantage of database facilities for security and integrity control, rapid search and aggregate computation, and dictionary functions. It also makes available knowledge processing functions of rule-based reasoning and representation. KEE users can work in terms of the natural objects of their applications, and the KEEconnection will manage the translation of their data needs into SQL queries and updates.

References

Abarbanel, R. M., & Williams, M. D. (1987). A relational representation for knowledge bases. In L. Kerschberg (Ed.), *Proceedings from the 1st International Conference on Expert Database Systems* (pp. 191–206). Charleston, SC. Menlo Park, CA: Benjamin/ Cummings Publishing Company.

Brodie, M., & Mylopoulos, J. (Ed.). (1984). *On knowledge base management systems, integrating artificial intelligence and database technologies.* New York: Springer-Verlag.

Date, C. J. (1983). *An introduction to database systems.* Reading, MA: Addison-Wesley.

Fikes, R., & Kehler, T. (1985). The role of frame-based representation in reasoning. *Communications of the ACM, 28 (9),* 904–920.

Jarke, M., & Vassiliou, Y. (1984). Coupling expert systems with database management systems. In W. R. Reitman (Ed.), *Artificial intelligence applications in business* (pp. 65–85). Norwood, NJ: Ablex Publishing Corp.

Newell, A. (1982). The knowledge level. *Artificial Intelligence, 18(1),* 87–127.

Weiderhold G. (1984). Knowledge and database management. *IEEE Software, 1(1),* 63–73.

Chapter 12

ABE: A Cooperative Operating System and Development Environment*

Frederick Hayes-Roth
Lee D. Erman
Scott Fouse
Jay S. Lark
James Davidson

Teknowledge, Inc.

As we have learned more about the usefulness of artificial intelligence (AI) techniques for commercial and military applications, we have discovered the need for a higher degree of integration with conventional computing and a higher degree of modularity in knowledge processing functions. These two needs go hand in hand. Many early AI tools implicitly assumed that the task they addressed was building systems that would stand alone on high-powered and high-priced workstations, usually LISP machines. However, it has become clear

---

*A number of people have contributed substantially to ABE™. Sergio Antoy, Terry Barnes, Stephanie Forrest, Alan Garvey, and Pean Lim have contributed to the design and implementation. Bruce Bullock and Neil Jacobstein have provided significant technical guidance and other support. Michael Fehling was instrumental in the early conception and design of the MOP model of computation. Stephanie Forrest and several anonymous reviewers provided helpful suggestions for this chapter.

This is an early description of in-progress research. The ideas described here require experimental testing and will likely change. This does not constitute a commitment by Teknowledge to any product or service. This research is partially sponsored by the Air Force Systems Command, Rome Air Development Center, Griffiss Air Force Base, NY 13441–5700 and the Defense Advanced Research Projects Agency, 1400 Wilson Blvd., Arlington, VA 22209, under contract F30602–85–C–0135.

Scott Fouse is with Teknowledge Federal Systems, Inc.

ABE is a trademark of Teknowledge, Inc.

that most applications impose many constraints on their delivery environments. These constraints include user interface packages, size and performance requirements, and integration standards ranging from subroutine calling conventions to network communication protocols.

Teknowledge's ABE system addresses the problem of combining conventional computing functions with knowledge processing capabilities. It enables the development of cooperative application systems that can exploit new-generation multiprocessing and distributed hardware. We call these new-generation applications *intelligent systems,* and we believe that ABE embodies excellent methods for engineering these systems.

ABE is intended for system architects and application developers. It supports the exploratory and evolutionary development of applications that must integrate both conventional and knowledge processing capabilities. It provides several high-level graphical design and development environments, which we call *frameworks.* It encourages a high degree of modularity and facilitates radical reorganization of software components and the mapping of those components onto the hardware used to deploy them. ABE, in essence, provides an environment and operating system for intelligent systems.

At present, Teknowledge offers the ABE software system as a prototype to a limited number of advanced users. These users typically face the problem of developing applications that must combine several software subsystems into an effective whole. These subsystems may employ conventional or AI capabilities. Developers typically create a near-solution, then modify it incrementally, extending the system in numerous directions. For one-person programs built on a single workstation, modern programming environments supplied as part of systems such as Smalltalk (Goldberg and Robson, 1983), Symbolics™ Genera (Walker, Moon, Weinreb, and McMahon, 1987), or KEE® (IntelliCorp, 1986) would seem appropriate. We think of that kind of problem as "programming in the small." Evolutionary programming "in the large," on the other hand, requires methods and tools that span multiple system architectures and organizations, machines, languages, and tool packages. ABE provides these methods and tools.

ABE views knowledge processing as merely one facility within a larger computing application. Moreover, ABE projects the benefits of evolutionary programming, which we have so long associated with AI tools, from AI programming in the small to commercial and military programming in the large. We believe that ABE's approach will succeed because it separates the essential benefits of early AI tools from the accidental ones (Brooks, 1987) and repackages those benefits in forms more directly useful for industry.

Symbolics is a trademark of Symbolics, Inc.
KEE is a registered trademark of IntelliCorp, Inc.

This chapter describes the motivations behind ABE, provides an overview of ABE, and relates ABE's characteristics to those motivations. We present an example application to illustrate these points. A more detailed description of ABE's architecture is presented in Erman, Lark, and Hayes-Roth (in press).

Technical Description: A Cooperative Operating System and Environment

Our strategy in designing ABE was to conceive of a next-generation operating system that would provide an excellent environment for building intelligent systems. These systems would combine conventional and knowledge processing functions into cooperative and synergistic applications, all running on a variety of networked and multiprocessing computers. For these reasons, we call ABE a *cooperative operating system* and a *development environment* for intelligent systems.

From our perspective, the principal features of an operating system are its *computational metaphor* and *composition methodology*. Systems such as OS/360® and UNIX® present to the developer a view of system design and computation consisting principally of concepts about program parts, assemblies of composite structures, and interconnections. System developers study and employ operating systems from this perspective. We call ABE's computational metaphor and composition methodology MOP™ (Module-Oriented Programming™).

Composition and Computational Metaphor

Operating systems succeed or fail, in part, based on the usefulness of the tools they provide for assembling applications from parts. We believe that this will become increasingly true as people attempt to build systems that span diverse technologies, languages, machines, multiprocessing architectures, and distribution alternatives.

In the context of these diverse alternatives, ABE provides a common and unifying environment for building application systems. As an operating system, we can usefully compare MOP to UNIX. Where UNIX provides byte streams, pipes, and filters for assembling systems from components, MOP provides *abstract datatypes* (ADTs), *ports,* and *modules.* All modules consume and pro-

---

OS/360 is a registered trademark of International Business Machines, Inc.
UNIX is a registered trademark of AT&T Information Systems.
MOP and Module-Oriented Programming are trademarks of Teknowledge, Inc.

duce instances of ADTs. One module can connect to another module if the first produces through an output port an instance of an ADT that is compatible with the ADT expected by the second module in an input port. In contrast to UNIX's low-level byte-stream datatype, ABE's ADTs are typically high-level structures such as *plans, assumptions,* or *queries.* ABE encourages users to think in terms of meaningful structures, to reuse ADTs from the catalog, and to reuse modules that process the types of ADTs needed. In these ways, ABE follows the successful style of UNIX, but attempts to elevate the connectivity concerns from byte streams to a higher level of abstraction.

MOP's computational model differs substantially from that of UNIX. Instead of a series of filters with relatively straightforward, data-directed control, MOP defines modules as distributed objects that can asynchronously communicate data with each other along flexible communication paths. Modules are persistent (i.e., they retain state between invocations) and can operate concurrently. Modules explicitly supply other modules with the *computational resources* needed to carry out their tasks.

MOP uses *events* as a primitive means for communication between concurrent modules. Events can signal that another module has finished executing, that external data has arrived, or that another module wants to change the computational resources that it has at its disposal. (See Forrest and Lark (1988) for more details on the multiprocessing aspects of the MOP model.)

Frameworks

MOP also introduces a second kind of higher-level concept in lieu of the connectivity model provided by UNIX pipes and shell scripts. In MOP, designers may compose a system from any number of modules according to any arbitrary communication and control topology. MOP provides a computational model for expressing these compositions, which Figure 1 outlines. ABE supplies a virtual machine, called *Kiosk,* for executing MOP-composed systems.

MOP was designed as a general computational model, to allow for a wide variety of structure and behavior descriptions and to support their implementation on a variety of computing systems. That generality makes MOP unsuitable for expressing most applications perspicuously. Therefore, ABE supplies a variety of more conventional and restricted *frameworks* for users to design and develop problem-solving compositions. Each framework supports compositions of a particular sort, such as dataflow (DF), blackboard (BBD), transaction processing (TX), and procedural control (PMC). Figure 2 shows an example of the PMC framework; others are presented later. Within each framework, ABE provides graphically-oriented development tools; the figure also indicates some features of these tools.

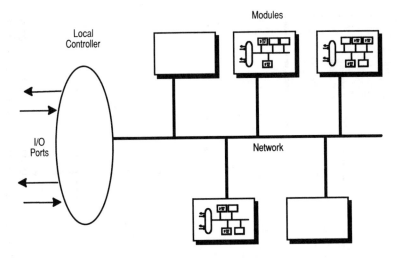

The Module-Oriented Programming (MOP) computational model provides each composite module with a network for connecting a set of interacting component modules. The local controller determines the behavior of the composite system by managing control and communication among the component modules and between the network and the external world. The figure also shows that any module can recursively embed another module. Although not shown in the figure, MOP also supports nonhierarchical composition, called *meshing*, by allowing one module to be included in more than one composite module simultaneously.

Figure 1. MOP: ABE's Underlying Computational Model

ABE enforces an extreme uniformity that enables the radical evolution of application systems: every system composed of ABE modules using any of ABE's frameworks becomes an ABE module, and all ABE modules can be composed with other modules in any of ABE's frameworks. We call this property *uniform composability* of ABE modules, and we refer to modules composed in this way as *composite modules*.

To build systems in ABE, one composes modular subsystems from new or pre-existing modules. Modular composition can embed modules hierarchically, as shown in Figure 1. Modules may also be composed by nonhierarchical *meshing*, permitting the same module instance to participate in—be shared by— more than one composite module. ABE's uniform composability, diversity of composition frameworks, and composition by embedding and meshing provide a solution to the problems of managing complexity.

Modules that are not composed of other modules are called *primitive*. Such primitive modules are considered *black boxes* because ABE has no visibility into

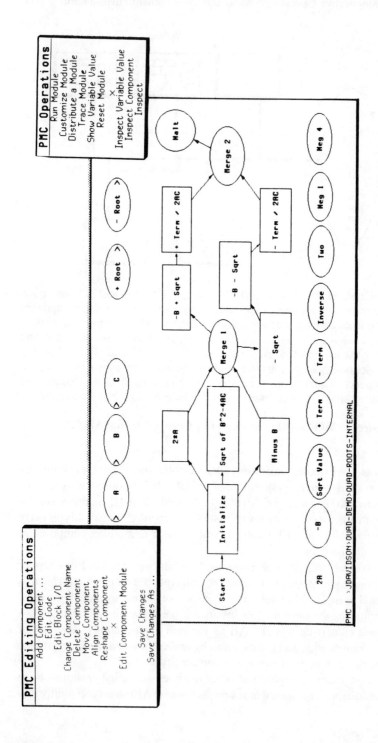

ABE provides a variety of frameworks for constructing composite modules. Each framework embodies its own computational metaphor and provides a language of symbols for expressing programs (i.e., compositions of modules). This figure shows an example of a composite module built in the PMC (Procedural Module Control) framework. PMC allows a system designer to express directly the control flow through a system of modules, much as conventional programming languages express control of subroutines. Within a composite PMC module, component modules can run concurrently.

This PMC program calculates solutions to the quadratic equation, $AX^2+BX+C=0$. The program contains several component modules (Initialize, Minus B, etc.), input variables (A, B, C), output variables (+root, -root), internal variables (2A, -B, +term, etc.), merge nodes (merge 1, merge 2) for synchronizing parallel execution streams, and unique start and halt nodes. The node labeled "Sqrt of B^2-4AC" is itself a composite module, built in the DF (Dataflow) framework; this is an example of one composite module embedded in another.

Each framework provides a graphical interface for viewing and editing the program. Typically, rectangles depict component modules, ovals depict data objects (for PMC, variables), and arrows show movement of control and data appropriate to the framework (for PMC, control flow). The menus in the figure show some of the operations available to the user while developing a PMC module.

ABE's MOP model supports building modules with a wide range of granularities, but it emphasizes large-sized modules. This figure uses a very simple example to convey ABE's constructs clearly. Typically, ABE modules embody more complex functionalities—for example, "replan in the face of the failure of the current plan," rather than "multiply two numbers."

Figure 2. The PMC (Procedural) Framework

329

their internal structure. Developers specify the behavior of such modules by coding them in some convenient programming language. The BBOX framework (see Figure 3) supports the creation of primitive modules. ABE will provide hooks to several programming languages so that developers can create these primitive modules. BBOX ensures that these modules meet the input-output requirements for ABE modules—they consume and produce instances of ADTs and respond to the standard Kiosk control operations.

The developer of a typical application will want to import many modules. That is, the developer will have the desired function in a pre-existing computer program and will want to provide its function through the BBOX "wrapper" that encodes and decodes ADT instances and channels them to the appropriate entry points. Importing an alien capability into the ABE catalog requires a one-time engineering effort to identify the key functionality and code the wrapper; in our

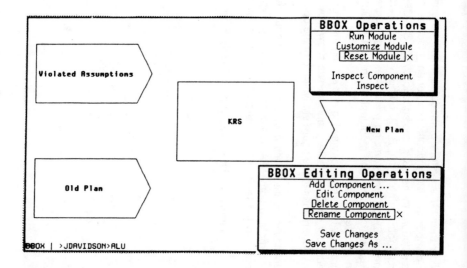

Figure 3. The BBOX (Black Box) Framework

This figure shows an example of a module in the BBOX (Black Box) framework. The application developer uses the BBOX framework to create modules, both from scratch, by programming them in some convenient language, and by importing existing functions. In either case the input and output ports are defined (in this figure: Old Plan, Violated Assumptions, and New Plan) and the basic operation is created (KRS). The basic operation either accesses an existing function (here: the Knobs Replanning System [Dawson, Brown, Kalish, and Goldkind, 1987]), or contains arbitrary code defining a new function.

experience, complex modules require on the order of one person-week to import. Thereafter, the ABE developer views this module no differently than any other primitive module.

If developers want to connect and control modules using some metaphor not provided by one of ABE's supplied frameworks, they can create a customized composite module by creating a custom controller. The code in the custom controller makes direct calls to Kiosk functions to control embedded component modules. Externally, this custom module looks like any other ABE module. ABE's KSK framework, a generalization of BBOX, supports building these custom composite modules.

Distribution

ABE provides a third extension to the computational model of UNIX, namely the notion that modules may run on distributed or multiprocessing computing facilities. When developers originally describe a system, ABE assumes nothing special about the location of the component modules. ABE finds these modules in its catalog and uses its underlying Kiosk operating system to assure that the modules intercommunicate correctly according to the module composition specifications. At the lowest level, this generally means assuring that messages are sent to the right places, received and interpreted correctly, and delivered at an appropriate time or in an appropriate sequential order, and that modules are invoked at the right times. Over time, as the developer wants to change the physical allocation of modules to processors, ABE facilitates this. The developer simply specifies which modules are to run on which machines. Thus, developers can work out problems of architecture, function, and distribution at a logical level, and easily change the mapping to the underlying computing facilities in response to changes in logical structure, physical resources, and experience with system operation.

Reuse

ABE embodies a philosophy of system design and development that emphasizes the reuse of software components. It has always been desirable for developers to reuse code, but this has proved difficult for many reasons. ABE provides tools that address these problems. First, ABE's uniform composability and diversity of frameworks help fabricate new solutions to complex problems by assembling primitive modules into composite modules, modules into subsystems, and subsystems into applications. Second, ABE's *catalog* makes it easy to select, browse, collect, store, organize, and reuse these multilevel modules (see Figure 4).

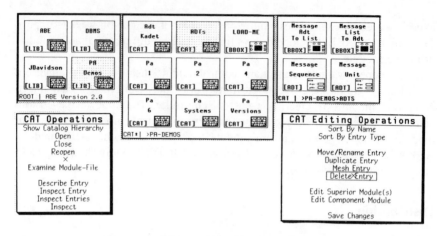

Figure 4. The CAT (Catalog) Framework

The ABE catalog facility is used to select, browse, collect, organize, and document modules. CAT supports a mostly hierarchical structure of subcatalogs, with ABE modules appearing at the leaves of the hierarchy. CAT's structure approximates that of the UNIX file system, and provides these features: hierarchical structure, a single distinguished root, pathnames for referring to catalogs, shared pointers for nonhierarchical structures (i.e., multiple pointers to the same catalog or module from different catalogs, using different names), and separately-mountable libraries (independent subtrees of catalogs). The figure shows a simple example with three catalogs. The root catalog is on the left. PA-DEMOS, in the center, is one of its next-level subcatalogs, and the entry for it is shaded in the root. Similarly, ADTS, on the right, is an entry in PA-DEMOS. The menus in the figure show some of the CAT operations available to the user.

CAT provides facilities for organizing modules according to a particular metaphor. Thus, it is an ABE framework—each catalog is a composite module, with components that are other catalogs, standard ABE modules, and ADTs. Rather than providing for the execution of its component modules, CAT's purpose is to allow for their examination and selection. In addition to unifying the implementation, treating CAT as a framework has been useful for understanding and refining the notions of "module" and "framework."

Third, ABE's emphasis on uniformity and reusability encourages a kind of program structuring that we call *high-dimensional* (HD) modularity. HD modular parts perform functions on ADTs, produce ADT instances, and can be combined freely with other modules that have consistent ADT requirements (see Figure 5). HD modules do not restrict developers to use any particular user interface, language, or framework for developing the rest of their application, or any particular hardware or underlying communication network. In this way HD modules support a high degree of reusability (see Figure 6).

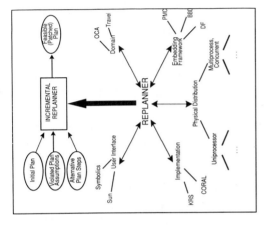

Figure 6. An Example of High-Dimensional Modularity

This figure shows a replanning function as an example of high-dimensional modularity. We have built replanning modules of this functionality with different tool languages (KRS, CORAL), for different machines (Symbolics, Sun®), used within different frameworks (PMC, BBD, DF), distributed to remote machines, and applied to different domains (Offensive Counter Air Mission Planning, Travel Planning).

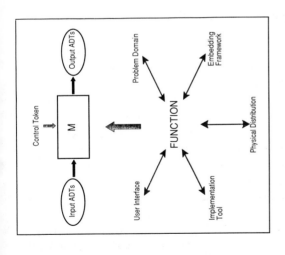

Figure 5. High-Dimensional Modularity in ABE

Sun is a registered trademark of Sun Microsystems, Inc.

333

As previously stated, the ABE catalog contains alien functions that have been imported by wrappers to make them appear as if they had been created in ABE as HD modules. Importing new functions in this way expands the range of capabilities ABE developers can exploit.

We want to make modular functions independent of as many implementation assumptions as possible. ABE currently provides a small collection of HD modules that perform knowledge processing functions, including storage and retrieval of logical formulae, plan analysis, and assumption monitoring. This collection, as it grows with increased ABE use, should allow developers to build new-generation hybrid applications that organize and control pre-existing applications with knowledge-based reasoning.

In sum, ABE provides a common and unifying environment for developing intelligent systems. These systems integrate heterogeneous functions across diverse software and hardware technologies. ABE provides a virtual machine and operating system called MOP/Kiosk for module-oriented programming. Using MOP, developers define intelligent systems as assemblies of modular subsystems. Below the virtual machine layer, ABE keeps separate the details of hardware, processors, resource allocation, and communication. The MOP/Kiosk model provides a portable basis so that applications can move among a variety of platforms. This means that ABE applications can tolerate radical changes in delivery requirements and can exploit revolutionary new ideas in hardware, software, and communications infrastructure. In this way, ABE provides an environment for entering the age of cooperative and intelligent systems.

Example Application

We now describe a representative application development sequence to illustrate the basic capability that ABE provides for developing systems. The particular application used is the Pilot's Associate.

The Pilot's Associate project is a prototype of an expert pilot aid. It has access to a variety of sensors and data channels which allow it to determine a view of the current situation and to make decisions accordingly. Lockheed Aeronautical Systems Co. (LASC) and McDonnell Aircraft are developing separate versions of the Pilot's Associate; the system presented here was influenced by the work of LASC (Smith and Broadwell, 1988).

We present a sequence of stages in the development of our system which serves as a time-lapse record of system evolution. Each stage represents a runnable system. At each stage, problems and issues appear which motivate the transition to the next stage. We show each version using ABE's graphical interface, in which viewers can be opened onto individual modules. Viewers provide a basis for examining, editing, and monitoring modules.

We intend this example to illustrate the basic system development methodology which has motivated the design of ABE. The methodology assumes that designers of intelligent systems cannot specify a complete and correct design on the first iteration. Rather, the system will need to evolve, possibly radically. There are two basic reasons for the need to change designs. The first is the classical need to adapt to changing requirements. This is amplified with intelligent systems, since the requirements themselves are often hard to specify and certainly not commonly understood. The second reason for evolving designs is the fact that the designs for many of the component functions of intelligent systems are not well understood. The conventional approach requires a designer to freeze a general system organization, encapsulating all uncertainty in isolated components. This approach breaks down when the components, as they are elaborated, no longer fit into the original functional organization.

ABE promotes a system development methodology that is based on *experimental design*. There is no set of analysis tools for intelligent systems that will allow us to determine if a design is correct or even adequate, so we must provide an environment that will allow us to discover attributes of an architecture and then easily modify that architecture in response to the lessons learned.

The initial version of our Pilot's Associate system is constructed by lashing together two components, in a simple loop, as shown in Figure 7. The Planner and Simulator are existing components, both written using the KADET planning system (Edwards and Hoffman, 1987), which was developed for the Lockheed Pilot's Associate program. The Simulator models the behavior of friendly and enemy planes, producing as output a situation description. This is fed to the Planner, which plans the activity of the friendly plane. The plan produced is then

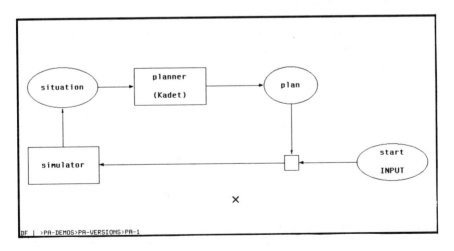

Figure 7. Pilot's Associate, Initial Version

used by the simulator to update its model, and the cycle continues. The Planner and Simulator were developed before ABE was available, and so were not created as ABE modules; the first task for building this initial version was to import them into ABE as modules.

The system is built as a composite module using ABE's DF (Dataflow) framework. The composite module consists of two *nodes* (Planner, Simulator), each of which is a component module, and two *places* (Plans, Situations), which can hold data tokens, represented as instances of ADTs. The nodes and places are connected by *links*. The links define the flow of input data from places to nodes, and the flow of output data from nodes to places. DF also provides constructs for reading and writing exogenous data (in this case, a single input place), and for splitting and joining data streams (in this case, a single join in lower right). The Planner and Simulator are BBOX modules embedded in the composite DF module.

In DF, a node can run whenever it has input data available on each of the input places. Within a composite DF module, nodes can run concurrently, reflecting the natural concurrency of dataflow models.

This system uses ADTs corresponding to the message traffic of the Pilot's Associate system, in particular plans and situations. These ADTs are structured objects, with slots for source, destination, time, type, and body.

This initial system runs, but suffers from performance problems because the planner executes on every cycle, even if the situation has not changed in ways that require replanning. A remedy is to add knowledge in the form of a situation monitor which compares the previous plan to the current situation, checking for potential plan reusability. Such a component has been created as an ABE BBOX module, and is added to the system, in Figure 8.

The revised system is shown in the left of the figure. The Situation Monitor (also shown at upper right) outputs a set of violated constraints, producing an empty set if the previous plan remains valid. Besides the addition of the Situation Monitor, the planner itself has required revision, in order to deal with the additional constraints input. This change has been accomplished by wrapping the original planner inside a layer of functionality that serves to store situations in those cases where replanning is not required and that outputs these buffered situations to the planner when planning is required. The Buffered Planner, built in ABE's KSK framework, is shown in the lower right. KSK provides LISP-level calls to other ABE modules; note that the KADET Planner module itself has not changed. This system executes in the same manner as the previous one, except that in some cycles the call to the KADET planner is bypassed, based on the decision made by the situation monitor.

The performance problem has been addressed, but the system still lacks certain required functionality. Some of this is added in the next version, shown in Figure 9. In this version two components have been added:

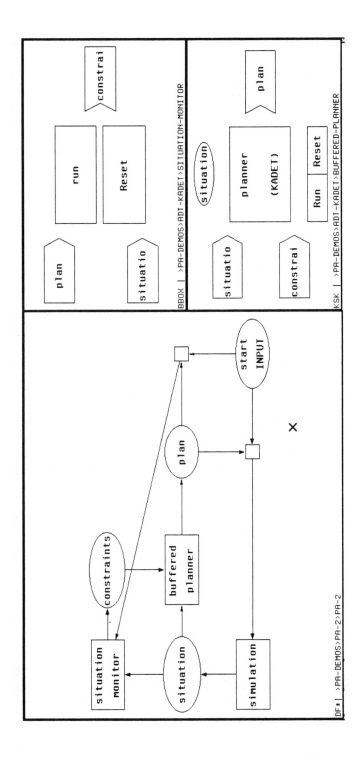

Figure 8. Pilot's Associate, With Situation Monitor

337

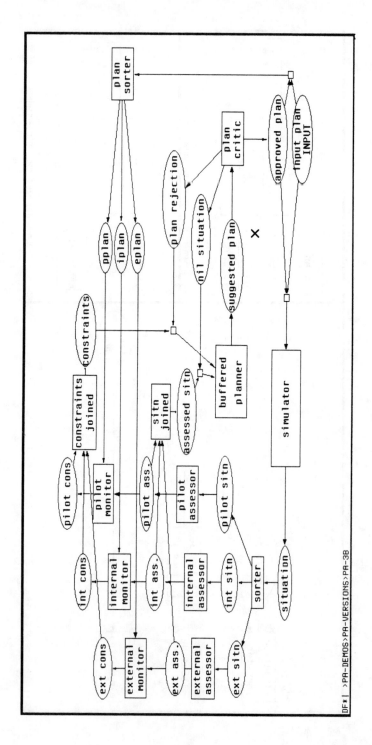

DF#1 >PA-DEMOS>PA-VERSIONS>PA-3B

Figure 9. Pilot's Associate, With Situation Assessor and Plan Critic

- a Situation Assessment capability, to analyze the situation for threat lethality, and to provide a more refined situation description to the situation monitor;

- a Plan Critic, to provide the user (in the role of pilot) with an opportunity to review and reject a given plan, forcing immediate replanning.

Furthermore, the assessment and monitoring capabilities have been split into three separate tracks: External Situation (status of other planes and the environment), Internal Situation (status of this plane), and Pilot Situation (pilot model). This corresponds to the division of knowledge in the Pilot's Associate project.

The system now provides the required functionality, but has become very complex. To facilitate further development, the complexity can be reduced by reorganizing the system, in particular by restructuring the modules and connections and introducing more levels. The result is shown in Figure 10.

The top level (shown at the top of the figure) is once again a simple loop. We have merged the Planner and Plan Critic into a single module. The Assessor and Monitor (with a viewer at lower left) contains three embedded modules, corresponding to the three tracks of domain expertise. A viewer has been opened onto the External Assessor and Monitor, and appears at lower right, showing the separate assessment and monitoring capabilities. Each of these three modules was built using the DF framework.

This system has the same functionality as the previous one, but a simpler organization, reminiscent of the first version. ABE's composition capabilities enable the system developer to deal with complexity by partitioning and hiding it, and by uncovering portions selectively.

The three tracks of the Assessor and Monitor module execute in parallel. To exploit the parallelism, we can use ABE's distribution facilities to move one or more of these modules to remote processors. This is shown in Figure 11.

ABE separates the specification of system functionality from the assignment of modules to individual processors, allowing either to be changed independently. This figure shows how the logical structure of an ABE application can be mapped onto a particular hardware configuration. The hardware configuration has two Symbolics computers and one Sun computer connected by an Ethernet. Symbolics 1 is the machine designated local—it is where the user or developer is working.

The figure shows the mapping of modules to particular machines. The three Assessor and Monitor component modules operate in parallel, so the developer has chosen to distribute two of them to remote machines. Within External Assessment and Monitoring, the External Monitor module has been redistributed back to Symbolics 1. This provides a form of pipelining, in that assessment of a situation could begin before monitoring is completed for the previous situation.

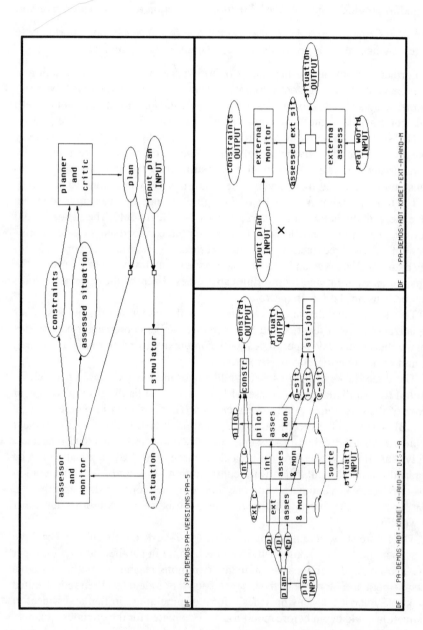

Figure 10. Pilot's Associate, Restructured

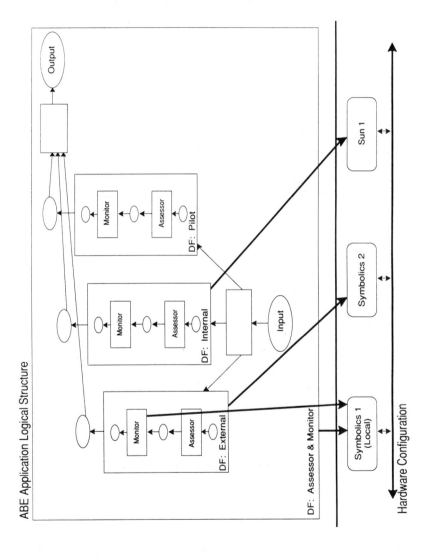

ABE Application Logical Structure

Output

Monitor — Assessor
DF: Pilot

Monitor — Assessor
DF: Internal

Input

Monitor — Assessor
DF: External

DF: Assessor & Monitor

Hardware Configuration

Sun 1

Symbolics 2

Symbolics 1
(Local)

Figure 11. Pilot's Associate, Distributed

341

To this point, the main modules of the system—the Simulator and Planner—have been executing sequentially. In an actual sensor-interpretation application, sensor data (in this case produced by the simulator) will arrive at a rate independent of the system's ability to deal with it. Thus the system must be reconfigured to allow the simulator to execute at its own rate. This change is made in Figure 12.

This version contains three top-level components. The Pilot's Associate module (with a viewer opened in lower left) contains the original Planner and Assessor and Monitor, connected in a new loop. The Simulator is now in its own top-level module (not opened in the figure).

These two subsystems communicate via two global LISP databases—one each for plans and for situations. These databases, shown in the viewer at right, use ABE's TX framework. TX implements a transaction model of processing, providing subroutine-like communications and control between one or more clients and one or more servers. The database module consists of two servers (the actual databases) and four clients. Each of these client modules is also a component module inside either the Pilot's Associate or Simulator module.

In this version, the top level module merely starts the three component subsystems, in parallel. This top-level module is constructed using the PMC (Procedural Module Control) framework.

When this system is run, the Pilot's Associate module retrieves the current situation from the database, performs assessment and planning, and writes the new plan into the plan database. The Simulator executes in a similar fashion, retrieving plans and writing situations. It runs asynchronously at a rate independent of the Pilot's Associate module, which was the objective of this change.

This sequence has shown the use of ABE to evolve a running application and to carry out experimentation at the system level. The changes in the system have been motivated by needs to address performance problems, add functionality, and meet additional requirements. These are typical of the problems that arise in developing large systems. ABE supports experimentation with software architectures, while reusing individual components.

Intelligent Systems Revisited

We began work on ABE as a response to needs evident within DARPA's Strategic Computing applications (Davis, 1985). These applications include the Pilot's Associate project described in the previous section, and Battle Management systems that could automate many functions of situation assessment and planning. We recognized in these applications needs that had also appeared in many of the ambitious plans we had seen for intelligent factory management

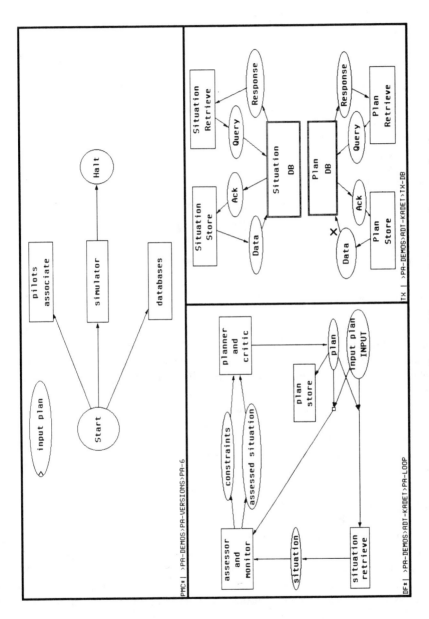

Figure 12. Pilot's Associate, With Asynchronous Communication

343

systems and next-generation professional office-support systems. In all these areas, developers expressed the desire for intelligent systems engineering, with the following primary requirements:

- the combination of knowledge and data processing;

- exploratory development;

- handling complexity;

- high performance;

- reusability;

- heterogeneous software and hardware; and

- next-generation operating environments.

We will elaborate on each of these requirements and describe the tools and techniques that ABE supplies to satisfy them.

Combining Knowledge and Data Processing

While trying to exploit the recent advances in knowledge processing, application developers find that they need to combine symbolic reasoning capabilities with in-place capabilities such as database, display, transaction processing, analysis, and reporting systems. Some knowledge engineering tools are starting to address the problem of integration with conventional capabilities, but the techniques they use are limited in two ways. First, they utilize current conventions for software system integration, namely conventional subroutine calls. This requires some amount of low-level programming to work out interface conventions for each new hybrid application. Second, although there are many paradigms for knowledge processing, any single product provides only a few of these. In the long-run, application developers will need to select and combine specialized knowledge processing functions, preferably from off-the-shelf products. This capability will require more modularity and technological refinement than is available for today's commercial knowledge engineering tools.

In designing ABE, we wanted a flexible way of connecting together software components, and we particularly wanted to accelerate the modularization of functions to perform knowledge processing tasks. We wanted system developers to make use of pre-existing tools and subsystems and to be able to redesign and restructure their systems easily when new and improved components came along. ABE provides such tools for defining interfaces for such capabilities and for cataloging the resulting modules, and we have begun building interfaces to certain standard capabilities, for example, SQL relational databases.

Exploratory Development

Government and commercial application developers have perceived a need for exploratory development "in the large" for the ambitious system they are considering. Although the so-called "waterfall" method of software development (Royce, 1970) has been used for decades, developers have generally found that they cannot get desirable results in new areas when they must specify the systems formally at the outset. Rather, developers have learned to appreciate the higher quality results that are obtained from incremental and evolutionary development. At the same time, major system contractors have begun bidding to build systems like the Pilot's Associate, in which system performance depends critically on uncertain factors such as the amount and quality of know-how extracted from pilots, the amount, quality, and accuracy of data, and the trade-offs between risk aversion and ambitiousness in decision-making. These determinants of system behavior can have a critical impact on the size, complexity, organization, and speed of the overall system. As a result, experimentation and evolutionary development become critical.

In designing ABE, we wanted to support system developers in formulating overall system architectures using very high-level tools so that they could defer low-level implementation concerns until an appropriate time. In addition, we wanted to provide methods and tools for radical restructuring of applications, which inevitably occurs as developers learn more about a problem domain, the computational performance, and the critical trade-offs. The example Pilot's Associate system illustrates many of the changes a complex intelligent system undergoes in its evolution from requirements to fielding and demonstrates some of ABE's capabilities that support those changes.

Handling Complexity

Several kinds of complexities confront those who wish to exploit the power of evolutionary development environments and knowledge processing to help manage the complexity of system development projects. First, they lack good tools for expressing what they want systems to do and how they want them to do it. They have found that implementation languages such as LISP or Ada® are too low-level, and that nonexecutable design languages such as SADT (Ross, 1977) cannot predict performance, assure skeptics that the designed system will actually work, or continue to be used as the implementation evolves. Second, developers want to talk about combining capabilities from existing and proposed new subsystems, but they lack suitable languages or conventions. Com-

---

Ada® is a registered trademark of the U.S. Government (Ada Joint Program Office).

mercial products and standards such as IBM SAA (IBM, 1987) or ISO's OSI (Voelcker, 1986) provide either extremely low-level protocols or vague high-level notions for describing how to interconnect subsystems. They do not help developers formulate and specify how a collection of entities cooperate to solve a problem. Finally, many developers see a need to combat complexity by organizing islands of stability—subsystems that attack parts of the overall problem, and that can ultimately knit together in some effective way. Although some AI paradigms such as the blackboard architecture (Erman, Hayes-Roth, Lesser, and Reddy, 1980) have suggested ways of combining independent specialists into cooperative integrated systems, no general and practical concepts have emerged to help people formulate system architecture strategies for defeating complexity by some divide-and-conquer approach.

In designing ABE, we wanted to meet all three challenges. We wanted to provide executable high-level design languages, abstract high-level tools for describing system interconnections, and practical techniques for easily composing complex systems from subsystems. The ABE features of multiple diverse frameworks, uniform composability of modules, and hierarchical and meshed module organizations all work to control system complexity.

High Performance

Most application developers want systems that can perform quickly, even when dealing with great complexity. In some applications, such as Pilot's Associate, slow performance can prove fatal. AI systems, on the other hand, have generally proven slow relative to conventional systems. Several related requirements emerge from this situation. First, we want modular implementations of knowledge processing functions that will permit the application developer to tune the software, the hardware, and the mapping from software to hardware to achieve a suitable performance level for key functions. Second, these applications should be able to use existing high-performance software and hardware components where appropriate. Third, we would like to exploit the natural concurrency in applications on networked and multiprocessing platforms. Finally, we want special high-level tools for formulating and assuring real-time performance requirements.

ABE supports modularity of knowledge processing functions in ways that do not depend on the underlying implementation machine or language. Second, ABE assumes that most functions will be performed by existing systems and helps system designers use these capabilities and combine them with other native or imported ABE functions. Third, ABE allows application developers to exploit the concurrency in their applications; the MOP computational model supports the natural expression of concurrency in applications, and Kiosk executes modules concurrently on networked workstations. Finally, we are developing a set of high-level tools for defining, designing, and implementing systems that meet stressing time requirements in the face of limited computing resources.

Reusability

Everyone wishes that software could be bought or reused, in contrast to the tendency to build each new system from scratch. This has been a major problem within conventional computing for years, but the situation within AI has been even worse. AI developers face a major roadblock created by the monolithic nature of most knowledge engineering tools. Each such tool provides a complete problem-solving paradigm and an associated programming language and environment intended for all aspects of the application system. The tool and application become combined in a monolithic fashion.

Developers aspire to reuse several different things: data structures for common kinds of tasks, domain-specific knowledge bases, inference engines and other knowledge processing functions, overall architectures for specific kinds of solution systems and, last but not least, conventional application libraries and databases. In ABE, we seek to provide effective support for each of these reusability concerns. We have adopted a methodology to support reuse and have embedded that in the ABE system.

Heterogeneous Software and Hardware

As alluded to several times above, many developers look to AI to add value to existing computing systems. This means they need knowledge processing functions that can work with conventional functions. They increasingly require a way to access and combine functionalities that run on different hardware using different and often immiscible languages, such as Common LISP and COBOL or Ada. They reject the notion of recreating conventional capabilities such as data collection and analysis, simulation, and statistics within the monolithic LISP machine workstation environment.

In designing ABE, we aimed to make it easy for system architects to compose integrated systems from heterogeneous parts using a high-level view of functionalities and their interactive combination. We thought that ABE should simplify the integration task by hiding the details of heterogeneous-systems plumbing from the applications developer.

Next-Generation Operating Environments

The most advanced developers already perceive the outlines of a new generation of information systems. These next-generation systems will combine heterogeneous hardware and software into distributed applications under intelligent control. Functions that were previously centralized will move to workstations. Assumptions of locality will give way to requirements for location-independence. Stable monolithic environments will become highly dynamic, disaggregated, and decentralized. Although end-users will carry some of the burdens for coping with the changes, stresses, and opportunities these new environments provide, application developers will face an increasing demand for systems that effectively coordinate far-flung components. This converts what had been simple applications development tasks into major systems pro-gramming tasks. In this context, application developers will want an environment that simplifies reallocation and redistribution of resources and functionalities.

We have designed ABE to simplify the task of building applications atop distributed and reconfigurable computing infrastructures. We have tried to create a next-generation operating system and system development environment to shield the application developer from what otherwise would become great systems programming requirements.

Relationship to Other Systems

To place ABE in the context of other next-generation system development environments, we first describe a set of abstraction levels for those environments. From lowest to highest these are:

- hardware: memories, processors, and networks;

- virtual machines;

- programming language systems;

- modular functions and abstract datatypes (ADTs);

- system design and development frameworks;

- skeletal systems; and

- applications.

We do not propose this set of levels as a prescription for building systems, but intend it for noting and relating abstractions of particular interest to each of the various development environments, as shown in Figure 13.

The lowest abstraction level deals with the realization and distribution of a system on *hardware*. At this level, a systems programmer must deal with *processors*, *real* and *virtual memory*, and *networks* of distributed hosts.

Several hardware vendors have produced products which focus on the network part of the hardware level, for example, Apollo's NCS (Apollo Computer,

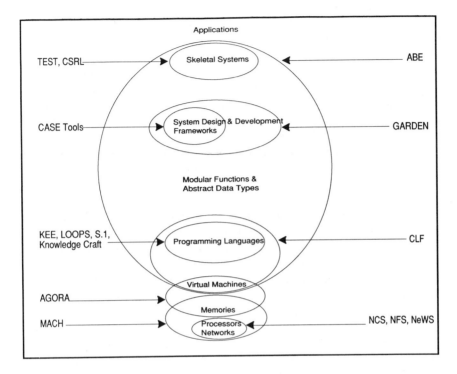

Figure 13. Abstraction Layers for Next-Generation Systems Environments, with Associated Development Efforts

Inc., 1987), Sun's NFS (Sandberg, 1986), and NeWS (Sun Microsystems, Inc. 1986). Carnegie-Mellon University's MACH (Rashid, 1986) also fits into this class. ABE attempts no advance in this area; we are currently using facilities supplied by the Symbolics environment and are also beginning to make use of UNIX and MACH.

At the next level up, the *virtual machine* makes specific commitments on how data and control are passed among computational agents, and provides a buffer between the language developers and the hardware (see, for example, Carnegie-Mellon's Agora system [Bisiani and Forin, 1987]). ABE's MOP virtual machine is loosely-coupled, without either a shared memory model or a shared namespace. ABE's computational model explicitly supports specialization of the local controller for each system. Also, ABE's model allows recursive (and nonhierarchical) embedding of ABE systems. These last two features together support deeply composed and heterogeneous systems.

A *programming language* is implemented on (i.e., its compilers produce code for) a virtual machine. Each language implements a particular programming metaphor, such as procedures, frames, objects, or rules. Most language systems come with tailored development environments.

No single language is best for all programming tasks; the programmer should be able to select a language appropriate for the task at hand. Some systems provide several programming languages integrated at this level. These include, for example, LOOPS (Stefik, Bobrow, Mittal, and Conway, 1983), KEE (IntelliCorp, 1986), Knowledge Craft® (Carnegie Group, 1985), S.1 (Erman, London, and Scott, 1984), and CLF (Balzer, 1986).

ABE allows the development of modules in several existing languages, such as C and Common LISP. ABE also supports modules implemented in various other tools, such as KEE, on the Symbolics computer; with its move to Sun, it will also support S.1, with others, such as FORTRAN, to follow.

Continuing up the abstraction levels, we have a layer of *modular functions and abstract datatypes,* each implemented in some language. FORTRAN statistical packages exemplify this level. ABE supports the accumulation and reuse of modular components via its catalog structure. We are also developing some particular examples of knowledge processing modules, such as a generic database facility.

System developers can use modules and ADTs to build up systems using ad hoc composition and integration techniques. Alternatively, they can use *system design frameworks* (SDFs) to specify how the modules are to be combined. These are special-purpose languages, often expressed graphically, that allow a system designer to express both the decomposition of a complex system into a number of components and the interactions among those components. Dataflow graphs and structure charts are examples of SDF languages, which are exemplified by a number of CASE (Computer-Aided Software Engineering) tools (Suydam, 1987).

In addition to the ability to produce descriptions of a system, some frameworks provide the means to execute that description. We refer to this class of tools as *system design and development frameworks.* ABE's frameworks fall into this class, as do those provided by Garden (Reiss, 1987).

As languages, SDFs are distinguished from those at the *programming languages* level by their design and intent for system composition, as opposed to construction of individual modules. ABE supplies modifiable graphical representations of its frameworks.

ABE supplies several frameworks, including ones built on paradigms of dataflow, procedures, blackboards, and transactions. Although ABE allows access to the framework implementations, it does not currently provide much support for creating or modifying frameworks. ABE does support building arbitrary, ad hoc compositions of modules by direct use of its underlying MOP/ Kiosk virtual machine.

Knowledge Craft is a registered trademark of Carnegie Group Inc.

At the highest level, next-generation systems are built on top of *skeletal systems*. Skeletal systems provide a high level of abstraction to the system developer, reducing the development task to one of "filling in the blanks." Examples of these are TEST (Kahn, Kepner, and Pepper, 1987) and CSRL (Bylander and Mittal, 1986). ABE treats skeletal systems as modules, and thus makes use of the same facilities to support their accumulation and reuse.

Prototype System Status

Teknowledge first made ABE (Version 1) available in February 1987 for a small number of advanced users. Demonstration Version 1 was replaced in early 1988 by Version 2. During 1988, Teknowledge plans to distribute a dozen or so copies of this research product to selected advanced user groups with appropriate requirements and qualifications. These advance licensees will help apply, test, refine, and extend ABE, leading to Version 3, planned for completion in 1989.

Version 2.0 includes the following capabilities:

- the MOP/Kiosk virtual machine, supporting modules, composition techniques, and abstract data types;

- desktop user interface;

- design and development frameworks (including procedural, dataflow, blackboard, transaction, blackbox, native Kiosk, and catalog), each with its specialized graphical development interface;

- a catalog of functionalities, including a selection of ADTs, native modules, imported modules, and skeletal systems;

- interfaces to several commercial tools, such as KEE and the Informix® relational database system;

- support for multiprocessing and distribution;

- operation on Symbolics and Sun computers; and

- several demonstration systems.

Research and Engineering Issues

We believe that ABE represents the first of a new generation of operating systems and development environments that addresses the task of building heterogeneous, cooperative, intelligent systems. Although ABE is already useful

---

Informix is a registered trademark of Informix Software, Inc.

in this arena, we expect to continue its evolution as we learn more about several issues including those described below.

Modular Knowledge Processing Functions

As we gain greater experience with the usefulness of knowledge processing, we will want to precipitate modules to perform the key functions. This work will continue indefinitely.

HD-Modularity and Abstract Data Types

At present we have identified several dimensions of separation (see Figure 5), but we have as yet few modules that possess all these degrees of freedom. Creating more HD-modules will require continued effort. One aspect of HD-modularity derives from the use of high-level abstract data types for inputs and outputs. Although we have collected a few dozen of these, we expect mature application-specific catalogs to contain hundreds of appropriate ADTs that simplify the task of new system development.

Design and Development Frameworks

ABE provides several design and development frameworks based on previous experience. ABE enables us to extend this framework set and to preserve uniform composability. This should make it desirable for tool designers to create new frameworks that effectively address particular kinds of subproblems. Thus, we expect to see a proliferation of frameworks and, ultimately, tools for creating new frameworks.

Importation

To date, we have imported a few dozen modules. However, we anticipate that importation will continue indefinitely. Over time, we expect a great number of capabilities to enter industry-specific ABE catalogs.

Skeletal Systems and Customization

We have demonstrated with ABE the value of storing and reusing nearly complete applications that capture a somewhat general problem-solving structure and that can be easily customized for different application domains. This work is at an early stage, and much remains to be done. The modularization of existing solution systems and the assembly of generic skeletal systems is a challenging task that should attract great interest.

Integrating Interfaces

At present, ABE employs emerging window management standards to enforce a separation of HD-modules from the user interface and to integrate into a single interface the user-oriented communications of multiple cooperating modules. We expect that this metaphor for integrating interfaces will prove limited, and new research will be needed to provide more flexible and customizable tools for merging user-interface communications.

Real-Time Operation

We have an experimental version of a run-time framework for ABE called RT. RT helps system developers create programs that can complete their functions in a timely fashion even when computing resources are limited. We will fully integrate this framework into ABE Version 3.0. This system is being tested by a limited number of users during 1988.

Parallelism and Compilation

During 1988 we will enhance ABE's performance by making better use of parallelism and software compilation. We have designed ABE from the outset for high performance, but Version 2 does not include implementations of our best current ideas. However, we expect to pursue research in this area for several years to exploit the best emerging platforms.

Conclusion: From Knowledge Systems to Intelligent Systems Engineering

Teknowledge focuses on the use of knowledge processing to add value to commercial and governmental operations. Because our first area of business was expert systems, we offered expert system shells on a wide variety of platforms, then reimplemented them in C, and finally consolidated and redesigned them for embedding in mainstream computing applications.

The ABE research product, however, addresses a broader and more ambitious set of objectives that have arisen out of application developers' attempts to envision the next generation of computing applications. These applications will need to combine conventional and knowledge processing functions to achieve higher levels of synergy than previously possible. Although obviously more complex than earlier applications, these systems will need to be assembled primarily from existing parts, at considerably less expense than previously incurred. In addition, these systems will need to withstand frequent and often radical environmental changes that will come with new technology and economies.

In the next generation, the concept "AI tool" will disappear. In its place we anticipate two new kinds of capabilities will appear: specialized knowledge processing functions, implemented either in software or custom hardware, and intelligent integration capabilities to make it easier for system developers to assemble solutions by connecting together parts and customizing them as needed. For such a vision to come true, we require a flexible and powerful environment for evolutionary development. This environment will need to sit atop a new operating system that both isolates application developers from low-level infrastructure details and allows them to exploit some of the revolutionary advances that will occur at that level. We are aiming ABE to fill that role.

References

Apollo Computer, Inc. (1987). *Network computing system: A technical overview.* Chelmsford, MA: Apollo Computer, Inc.

Balzer, R. M. (1986). Living in the next-generation operating system. In H. J. Kugler (Ed.), *Information Processing 86.* Amsterdam: North-Holland. Reprinted in *IEEE Software, 4(6),* 77–85.

Bisiani, R., & Forin, A. (1987). Architectural support for multilanguage parallel programming on heterogeneous systems. *International Conference on Architectural Support for Programming Languages and Operating Systems (ASPLOS-II).*

Brooks, F. P., Jr. (1987). No silver bullet: Essence and accidents of software engineering. *IEEE Computer, 20(4),* 10–19.

Bylander, T., & Mittal, S. (1986). CSRL: A language for classificatory problem solving and uncertainty handling. *AI Magazine, 7(3),* 66–77.

Carnegie Group Inc. (1985). *Knowledge Craft manual guide.* Pittsburgh, PA: Carnegie Group Inc.

Davis, D. B. (1985). Assessing the strategic computing initiative. *High Technology,* 41–49.

Dawson, B. C., Brown, R. H., Kalish, C. E., & Goldkind, S. (1987). *Knowledge-based replanning system* (Tech. Rep. RADC–TR–87–60). Griffiss Air Force Base, NY: Rome Air Development Center.

Edwards, G. R., & Hoffman, M. A. (1987). The KADET planning framework. *DARPA Knowledge-Based Planning Workshop.* Austin, Texas.

Erman, L. D., Hayes-Roth, F., Lesser, V. R., & Reddy, D. R. (1980). The Hearsay-II speech-understanding system: Integrating knowledge to resolve uncertainty. *Computing Surveys, 12(2),* 213–253.

Erman, L. D., Lark, J. S., & Hayes-Roth, F. (in press). ABE: An environment for engineering intelligent systems. *IEEE Transactions on Software Engineering*.

Erman, L. D., London, P. E., & Scott, A. C. (1984). Separating and integrating control in a rule-based tool. *Proceedings IEEE Workshop on Principles of Knowledge-Based Systems* (pp. 37–43). Denver, CO.

Forrest, S., & Lark, J. S. (1988). *Parallel and distributed processing in ABE* (Tech. Rep. TTR–ISE–88–101). Palo Alto, CA: Teknowledge, Inc.

Goldberg, A., & Robson, D. A. (1983). *Smalltalk-80: The language and its implementation*. Reading, MA: Addison-Wesley.

IBM (1987). *SAA: An overview*. IBM order number GC26–4341.

IntelliCorp, Inc. (1986). *KEE software development system user's manual*. Mountain View, CA: IntelliCorp, Inc.

Kahn, G. S., Kepner, A., & Pepper, J. (1987). TEST: A model-driven application shell. *Proceedings National Conference on Artificial Intelligence* (814–818). Seattle, WA.

Rashid, R. F. (1986). Threads of a new system. *UNIX Review, August,* 37–49.

Reiss, S. P. (1987). Working in the garden environment for conceptual programming. *IEEE Software, 4(6)*, 16–27.

Ross, D. (1977). Structured analysis (SA): A language for communicating ideas. *IEEE Transactions on Software Engineering, 3(1)*, 16–34.

Royce, W. W. (1970). Managing the development of large software systems: Concepts and techniques. *Proceedings Wescon*.

Sandberg, R. (1986). *The Sun network file system: Design, implementation and experience* (Technical Report). Mountain View, CA: Sun Microsystems, Inc.

Smith, D., & Broadwell, M. (1988). The Pilot's Associate—an overview. SAE Aerotech Conference, Los Angeles, CA.

Stefik, M., Bobrow, D. G., Mittal, S., & Conway, L. (1983). Knowledge programming in LOOPS. *AI Magazine, 4(3)*, 3–13.

Sun Microsystems, Inc. (1986). *NeWS: A definitive approach to window systems*. Mountain View, CA: Sun Microsystems, Inc.

Suydam, W. (1987). CASE makes strides toward automated software development. *Computer Design, January 1*.

Voelcker, J. (1986). Helping computers communicate. *IEEE Spectrum, 23(3)*, 6–70.

Walker, J. H., Moon, D. A., Weinreb, D. L., & McMahon, M. (1987). The Symbolics Genera programming environment. *IEEE Software, 4(6)*, 36–45.

Author Index

Italics indicate bibliographic citations.

Subject Index

A

ABE, 323–325 (*see also* next-generation
   systems)
   catalog, 331–332, 334
   distributed computing, 331
   example application, 334–342
   frameworks, 326–331, 350, 352
   high-dimensional (HD) modularity,
      332–334
   Kiosk, 326, 330–331, 334, 349
   MOP, 325–326
      abstract data types (ADTs),
         325–326
      compared with Unix, 325–326
      composition and computational
         metaphor, 325
      events, 326
      modules, 325–328
      ports, 325–326
   Pilot's Associate, 334–342
   relationship to other systems, 325–326,
      348–351
Abstraction, 214, 276–277, 282–283, 348
Abstract data types, 325–326
Access-oriented programming (*see also*
      Demons, Elision, Gauges, Indi-
      rection)
   checking data types and constraints,
      58–59
   compared with object-oriented
      programming, 47
   in Loops, 55–62
      Truckin' and the Track Announcer,
         60–62, 228–229, 237
   traps for variables, 56–58
ActiveImages, 85–86, 236
Active values, 47–54, 59, 62, 86, 97, 236
Annotated values, 47–50 (*see also* Active
      Values)
   property annotations, 47, 49, 52–53
   recursive annotations, 53–55

Aquinas, 151–153, 162, 165, 175–177 (*see
      also* Expertise Transfer System)
   analytic hierarchy process, 168
   cluster analysis, 169
   data abstraction, 161
   hierarchies, 156–159
      case hierarchies, 157
      expert hierarchies, 156–157
      solution hierarchies, 156
      trait hierarchies, 156
   knowledge acquisition tasks, 151–153
      combining uncertain information,
         160–161, 168
      decomposing problems, 155–159
      eliciting distinctions, 154–155
      expanding and refining the knowl-
         edge base, 163–164
      integrating diverse data types,
         161–163
      providing process guidance, 164
      testing knowledge, 160–161
      using multiple sources of knowl-
         edge, 164
   rating grids, 154–155, 157–159
   rules, generating, 174–175
   theoretical issues, 177–178
   using Aquinas, 165–175
ART, 78, 95
   active values, 97
   applications in ART, 99
   ART studio, 98
   cost, 100
   debugging and testing, 98–99
   file compiler, 95
   functionality, 99
   knowledge representation
      facts, 95–96
      hypothetical reasoning, 98
      inheritance, 96
      patterns, 96
      propositions, 95–96